GUN COLLECTOR'S DIGEST

3rd Edition

Edited by
Joseph J.
Schroeder

DBI BOOKS, INC., NORTHFIELD, ILLINOIS

GUN COLLECTOR'S DIGEST STAFF

EDITOR
Joseph J. Schroeder

MANAGING EDITOR
Robert S.L. Anderson

GRAPHIC DESIGN
Mary MacDonald

COVER PHOTOGRAPHY
John Hanusin

PUBLISHER
Sheldon L. Factor

ISBN 0-910676-30-5 Library of Congress Catalog Card Number 73-83406

CONTENTS

Gun Collecting in the 80's
by Joseph J. Schroeder 5

An Illustrated Guide to Luger Accessories
by Jon D. Kitts 7

Luger Holster Makers, 1900-65
by John D. Walter 20

The Pinfire Cartridge
by Graham Burnside 26

The Bittner Pistol
by Joseph J. Schroeder 32

400 Years of Airgun Tradition
by Robert Beeman 35

The Wehrmacht's Rifles—Mauser's Karabiner 98k
by Otto H. von Lossnitzer as told to Leslie E. Field 42

Walther & Manurhin—The Story of Postwar PP and PPK Pistols
by James Rankin 49

Collecting the Commemoratives
by Larry S. Sterett 53

The Rare Japanese Hino-Komuro Pistol
by Harry Derby 61

The V-42 Special Service Force Knife
by Steven B. Fox 72

The Spencer Repeater—The First Modern Military Rifle
by Konrad F. Schreier, Jr. 74

Ortgies—An In-depth Look at the German Armsmaker
by Donald W. Koelliker 79

Cutaways . . . Very Special Collectibles
by Joseph J. Schroeder 88

The Search for the Sisters
by Herbert R. Gopstein 95

The Fabulous Auto Mag and its Production Variations
by Wayne Robbins 101

Making the Gun Collector's Grand Tour
by Joseph J. Schroeder 107

A Visit to Enfield Lock
       by W.H.J. Chamberlain. 114

Collecting Modern American Rimfire Rifles
       by Robert S.L. Anderson. 118

Schroeder Finds the Schrader
       by Joseph J. Schroeder. 127

The Audley—A Truly Practical Holster
       by Donald M. Simmons, Jr.. 130

Sixty Years of Rivalry: The Story of British and German Air Pistols 1920-80
       by John D. Walter. 135

The M1 Carbine—G.I.'s Friend and Collector's Prize
       by Gerald R. Reagle, Jr.. 148

William Tranter—Gunmaker to the Trade
       by Douglas A. Nie and De Witt Bailey. 154

Collecting the Sprinfield Model 1903 Rifle
       by Lt. Col. Bill Brophy U.S.A.R. (Ret.). 165

Imperial Japan's Military Revolvers—The Slighted Type 26
       by Harry Derby. 175

Big Guns and Little Bores—U.S. Army Subcaliber Artillery Devices
       by Konrad F. Schreier, Jr.. 186

Your Gun Collection as an Investment/Legacy
       by Rodney Washburn. 194

The Pistols of J.P. Sauer & Sohn
       by Hans Joachim Tillig. 197

Prototype, Pattern and Presentation Daggers of the Third Reich
       by John J. Gabrick. 203

European Revolvers . . . a Fertile Field
       by Joseph J. Schroeder. 208

Software vs Hardware—A Guide to Building a Gun Library
       by Joseph J. Schroeder. 214

Collecting the ABC's . . . The Suicide Special From A to Z (almost)
       by Frank M. Sellers. 218

Mauser Kleinkaliber-Büchsen—A History of Mauser's 22 Rifles
       by Bill Beacom. 226

Periodicals for the Collector
       by Joseph J. Schroeder. 230

Trejo: The World's Smallest Machine Pistol
       by Jack Václav Krčma. 235

Gun Collecting and Gun Law
       by Joseph J. Schroeder. 238

Gun Collecting in the 80's

by Joseph J. Schroeder

THE SERIOUS gun collector will not be able to be too casual toward his hobby during the next decade. Anti-gun sentiment will continue to pressure the collector, along with other law-abiding gun enjoyers, during the next decade, fueled recently by the unsuccessful attempt on President Reagan's life early in 1981. However, the President's continued stand against further gun laws has taken some of the sting away from that unfortunate incident, and the continued hue and cry of the "Guns Must Go!" crowd may even have some positive benefits for legitimate gun owners.

For one thing, the attention anti-gunners have focused on guns has made more people aware of them, and some seem to be reacting in a positive way. While it's true that membership in various anti-gun groups has been growing, it's also true that membership in the National Rifle Association is at an all-time high (about two million, as we go to press) as well. Attendance at gun shows and membership in shooting clubs is also at an all-time peak, so it seems safe to assume that more people than ever are being attracted to collecting and shooting sports, some of them perhaps by the very anti-gun propaganda that's intended to eliminate guns!

The outlook for stringent gun control legislation on the national scene is not favorable. The pro-gun stance of the Reagan administration and the majority of the current Congress bodes badly for the efforts of the dedicated anti-gun legislators. Outlook on the state and local level is less clear, with the on-going pressure to "do something—anything!" about increasing crime rates likely to spawn some additional restrictive gun legislation here and there across the country.

However, no serious threat to continued gun ownership and enjoyment by collectors seems in the cards. At worst we may see some additional obstacles thrown up that will make our collecting activities a little more difficult. On the other hand there are even some efforts to reduce the legal burdens on legitimate gun owners, and the Treasury has even announced that it's considering relaxing its long standing ban on dealers "doing business" at gun shows.

On the economic scene, gun values have increased dramatically in the past few years. There have been several reasons for this, not the least of which is inflation and loss of confidence in the value of money. Tangible goods of all kinds have soared in price, led by collectibles including guns. Articles in prestigious publications such as the *Wall Street Journal* and recommendations by various financial advisors have cited guns as having good investment potential, bringing more well-to-do competition into a field it had not considered before. There are now even some syndicates formed to invest in guns as speculations, buying those guns they believe have the most likelihood of appreciation and putting them away until market indicators say "Sell!"

Though it's nice for the established collector to see his investment climbing in value, higher prices have the negative effect of forcing less affluent collectors out of the market and preventing others who'd like to become collectors from getting started at all. This is not good for the hobby in the long haul, as most collectors began with a few inexpensive guns and were able to establish some sort of a meaningful collection as both knowledge and income grew with time. If gun prices continue to spiral, most of the worthwhile collector guns could go out of reach of the average collector.

This price pressure has spawned some change in direction that is not all bad, however, For one thing, a number of guns which were previously passed over in favor of Single Action Army Colts, Lugers, Civil War carbines and the like are now enjoying collector interest and have become quite respectable. There are several articles in this book on that very type of gun, and they're just as interesting and stimulating as those dedicated to more traditional collecting fare. Another collecting area that's receiving more attention as a result of high gun prices is accessories, again the subject of some attention in this volume. The would-be collector on a shoestring budget can still find areas where he can make a significant contribution, have a lot of fun, and even assemble a potentially valuable collection. It just takes some imagination to find such an area.

Another field that is growing and changing is restoration. Back a number of years the offer of a rare but well-used collector's item would bring snorts of derision and a quick brush-off from any serious collector. No more! Today that same collector carefully examines the deeply pitted areas, non-factory alterations and remaining markings, weighing in his mind how close the ministrations of one of the master restorers will be able to bring it to "factory new"

shape. This change in attitude comes from a basic economic law, that of supply and demand. There are more collectors today than ever before, and (except for new arms, such as commemoratives) a fixed or even shrinking supply of guns for them to collect. Today properly restored guns have taken on an air of respectability that would have been unheard of 20 or even 10 years ago.

Crime will continue to be a concern of the gun collector in the years immediately ahead. As long as violent crime continues to flourish it will fuel the passions of the anti-gun crowd, forcing legitimate gun owners to expend some of their energies and money in support of their rights as gun owners in a free society. It will also have a little-appreciated positive effect on gun owning, as well. As long as the majority of the American people perceive the law enforcement agencies and courts as ineffectual at protecting them against the criminal element, those people will insist on retaining the means for providing their own protection. The gun collector's best friend in the anti-gun fight is the home or store owner who demands the right to protect his own premises.

But, crime must concern the gun collector in even a more direct way. Today burglary is one of the fastest growing types of crime, and little is more desirable to a home invader than a gun collection. A collector who does not protect his guns is a fool, and like the fool and his money, is asking to be "soon parted." Guns should be stored out of sight, locked up, and with at least some minimal form of burglar alarm. Very valuable pieces should be kept out of the home, preferably in a safe deposit box. Fortunately the vast majority of home break-ins today are committed by amateurs, looking for a quick "score" to turn into a drug fix. A little intelligent planning and effort can keep your collection out of the hands of this kind of criminal.

Gun collecting is alive, healthy and growing today, and indications are that it will continue to prosper—literally and figuratively—in the next decade. That it will, depends on us. •

An Illustrated Guide to
LUGER ACCESSORIES

by John D. Kitts

IN THE PAST ten years the collecting of Luger accessories has become increasingly popular. The rising cost of Lugers has put a crunch on anyone trying to build a pistol collection, whereas the price of most accessories is relatively low compared to the cost of a pistol itself.

First produced in 1900, the Luger (Parabellum pistols nicknamed "Luger" after the inventor, Georg Luger) was manufactured by seven different companies during the years it was in production. The early years saw some minor changes in design, but from 1914 until the end of production in 1942, the Parabellum pistol remained virtually unchanged. Deutsche Waffen und Munitionsfabriken (DWM), the original Luger manufacturer, along with several other companies such as Erfurt, Mauser and Vickers, produced or contracted for a variety of accessories. These included cleaning rods, carbine stocks, navy and artillery flat board stocks, drum magazines and drum loading tools.

Holsters were not supplied with the pistols, so the purchasers were forced to supply their own. Probably the most collected of the Luger accessories, Luger holsters have been manufactured in dozens of coun-

Cases like this accompanied presentation Lugers, and were possibly used for salesmen's samples. (Author's collection)

tries in a variety of shapes, sizes and colors—one of the first was the 1900 Swiss commercial and police. A few companies designed and produced their own Luger holster and shoulder stock combinations. Due to their limited commercial success, these items are rare today.

Increased cost of ammunition in the early 1920s made sub-caliber conversion kits so popular that dozens of companies produced them in both 4mm and 22 caliber. A few of these kits are still manufactured today. One of the most popular, used both commercially and by the military, was the Erma 22 caliber kit: It contained a barrel liner, replacement toggle assembly, and magazine. When assembled in the pistol, it was capable of semi-automatic fire.

While Luger accessories are less expensive than the actual pistols, the accessories are often harder to find. Over the years many accessories deteriorated or were simply discarded. Some are still stuffed away in attics. All you have to do is look in the right places.

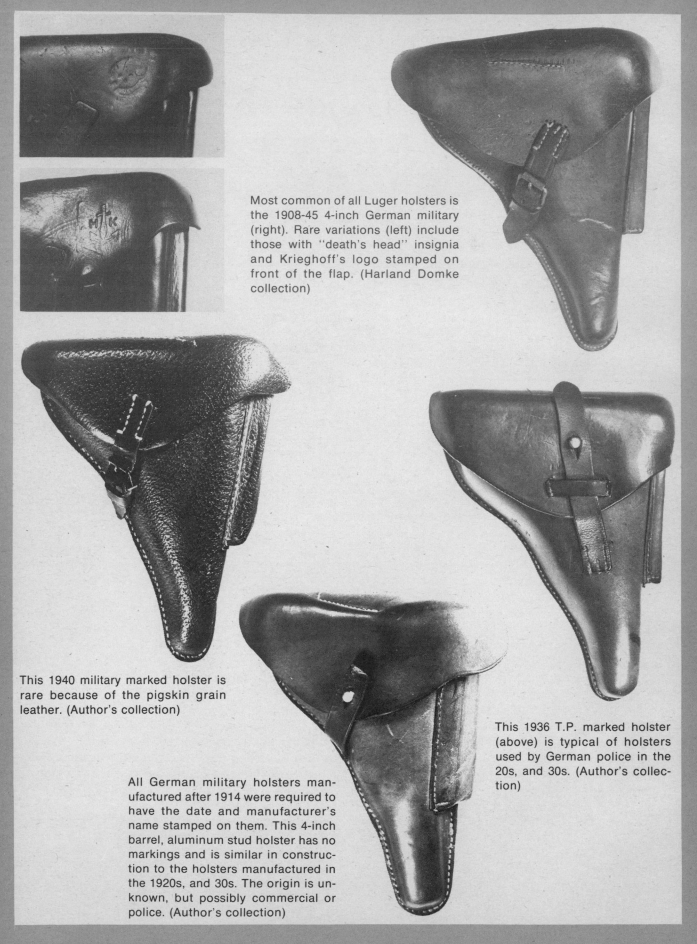

Most common of all Luger holsters is the 1908-45 4-inch German military (right). Rare variations (left) include those with "death's head" insignia and Krieghoff's logo stamped on front of the flap. (Harland Domke collection)

This 1940 military marked holster is rare because of the pigskin grain leather. (Author's collection)

This 1936 T.P. marked holster (above) is typical of holsters used by German police in the 20s, and 30s. (Author's collection)

All German military holsters manufactured after 1914 were required to have the date and manufacturer's name stamped on them. This 4-inch barrel, aluminum stud holster has no markings and is similar in construction to the holsters manufactured in the 1920s, and 30s. The origin is unknown, but possibly commercial or police. (Author's collection)

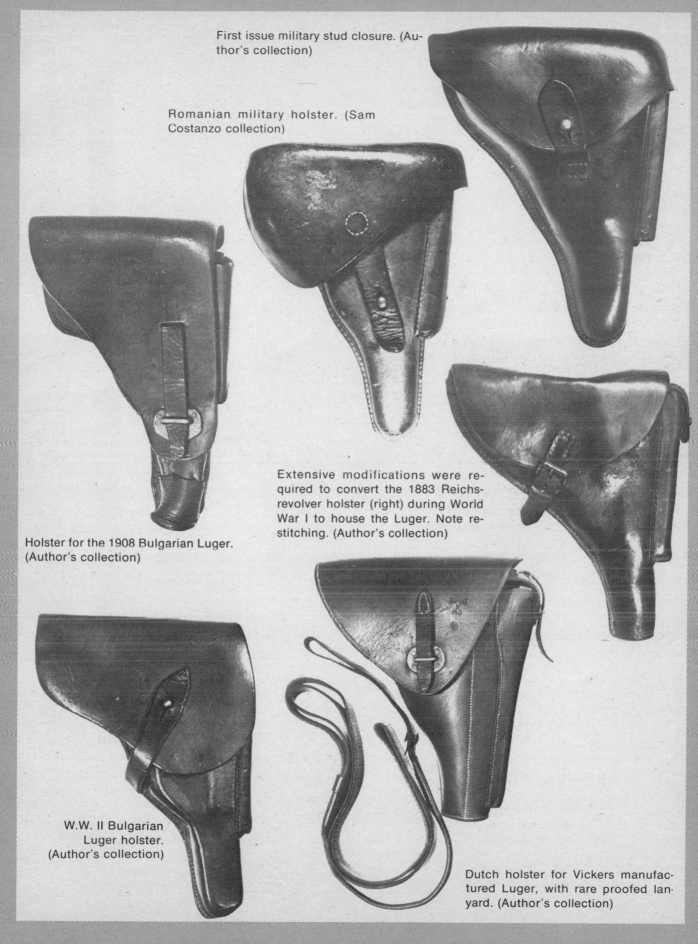

First issue military stud closure. (Author's collection)

Romanian military holster. (Sam Costanzo collection)

Holster for the 1908 Bulgarian Luger. (Author's collection)

Extensive modifications were required to convert the 1883 Reichs-revolver holster (right) during World War I to house the Luger. Note restitching. (Author's collection)

W.W. II Bulgarian Luger holster. (Author's collection)

Dutch holster for Vickers manufactured Luger, with rare proofed lanyard. (Author's collection)

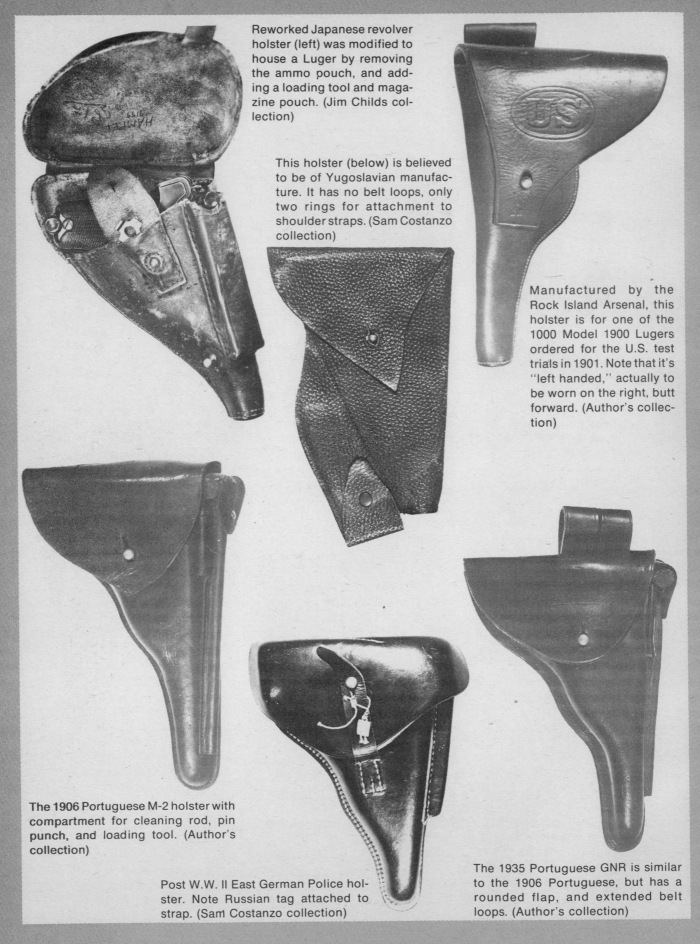

Reworked Japanese revolver holster (left) was modified to house a Luger by removing the ammo pouch, and adding a loading tool and magazine pouch. (Jim Childs collection)

This holster (below) is believed to be of Yugoslavian manufacture. It has no belt loops, only two rings for attachment to shoulder straps. (Sam Costanzo collection)

Manufactured by the Rock Island Arsenal, this holster is for one of the 1000 Model 1900 Lugers ordered for the U.S. test trials in 1901. Note that it's "left handed," actually to be worn on the right, butt forward. (Author's collection)

The 1906 Portuguese M-2 holster with compartment for cleaning rod, pin punch, and loading tool. (Author's collection)

Post W.W. II East German Police holster. Note Russian tag attached to strap. (Sam Costanzo collection)

The 1935 Portuguese GNR is similar to the 1906 Portuguese, but has a rounded flap, and extended belt loops. (Author's collection)

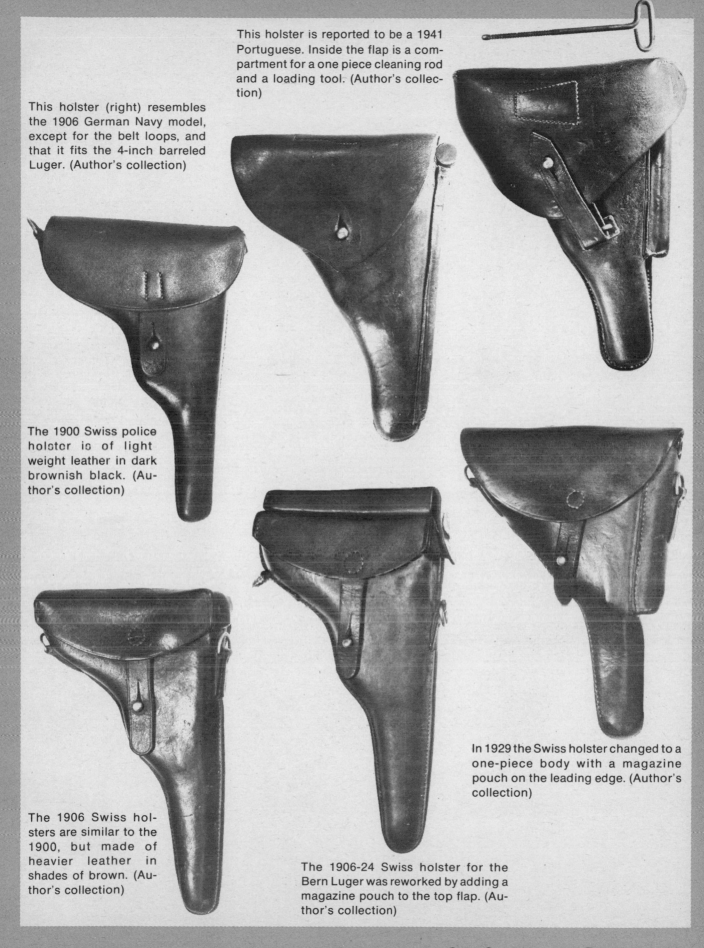

This holster (right) resembles the 1906 German Navy model, except for the belt loops, and that it fits the 4-inch barreled Luger. (Author's collection)

This holster is reported to be a 1941 Portuguese. Inside the flap is a compartment for a one piece cleaning rod and a loading tool. (Author's collection)

The 1900 Swiss police holster is of light weight leather in dark brownish black. (Author's collection)

In 1929 the Swiss holster changed to a one-piece body with a magazine pouch on the leading edge. (Author's collection)

The 1906 Swiss holsters are similar to the 1900, but made of heavier leather in shades of brown. (Author's collection)

The 1906-24 Swiss holster for the Bern Luger was reworked by adding a magazine pouch to the top flap. (Author's collection)

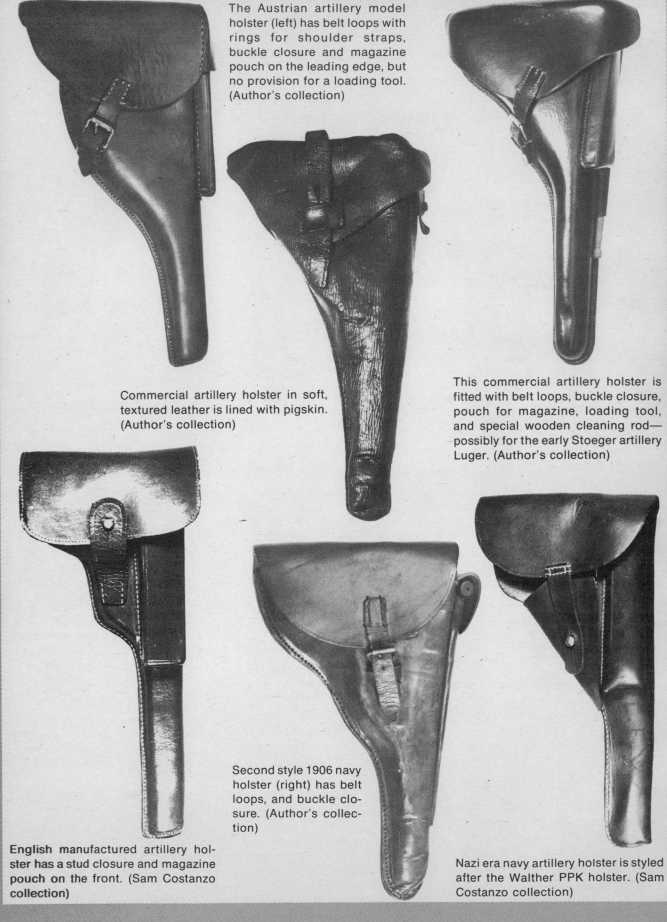

The Austrian artillery model holster (left) has belt loops with rings for shoulder straps, buckle closure and magazine pouch on the leading edge, but no provision for a loading tool. (Author's collection)

Commercial artillery holster in soft, textured leather is lined with pigskin. (Author's collection)

This commercial artillery holster is fitted with belt loops, buckle closure, pouch for magazine, loading tool, and special wooden cleaning rod—possibly for the early Stoeger artillery Luger. (Author's collection)

Second style 1906 navy holster (right) has belt loops, and buckle closure. (Author's collection)

English manufactured artillery holster has a stud closure and magazine pouch on the front. (Sam Costanzo collection)

Nazi era navy artillery holster is styled after the Walther PPK holster. (Sam Costanzo collection)

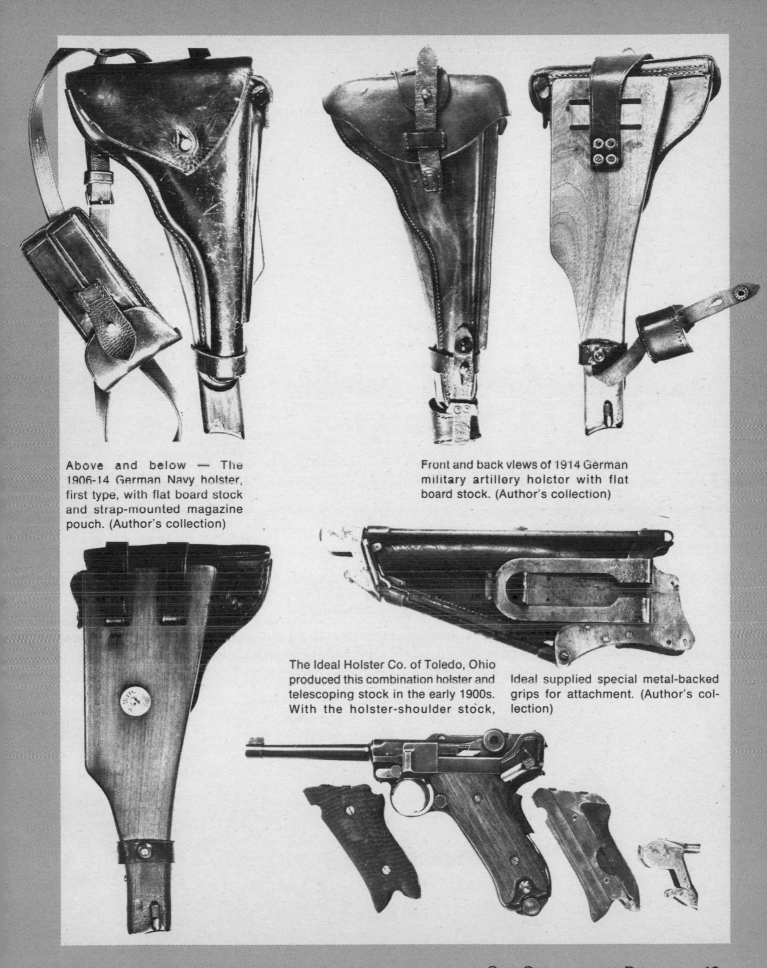

Above and below — The 1906-14 German Navy holster, first type, with flat board stock and strap-mounted magazine pouch. (Author's collection)

Front and back views of 1914 German military artillery holster with flat board stock. (Author's collection)

The Ideal Holster Co. of Toledo, Ohio produced this combination holster and telescoping stock in the early 1900s. With the holster-shoulder stock, Ideal supplied special metal-backed grips for attachment. (Author's collection)

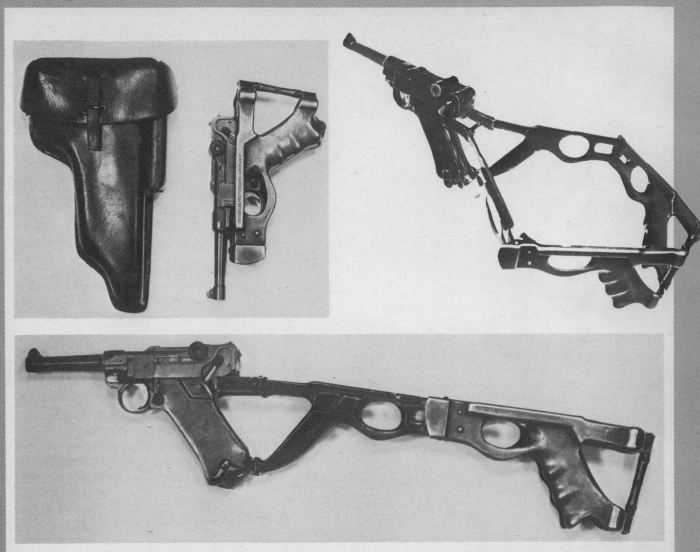

Prototype button-release flat board artillery stock. Close-up shows left side of button release. (Sam Costanzo collection)

In 1926 Benke and Thiemann patented and made a few collapsible shoulder stocks and holsters. The stock remains permanently attached to the pistol, replacing the grips. Its three-piece hinged frame folds out from both sides of the pistol to form the stock. When the stock is collapsed, both pistol and stock fit inside the oversized holster. On the outside of the holster is a pouch for a magazine and a loading tool. (Pat Redmond collection)

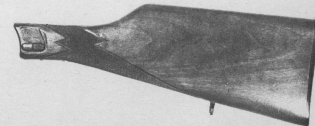

Fully contoured detachable stock for the 1902 commercial carbine. (Author's collection)

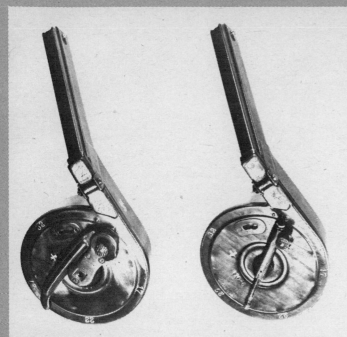

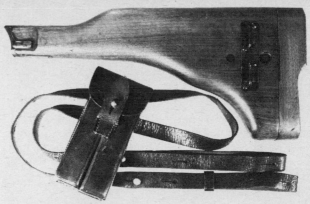

Two rare prototype artillery holster stocks. One has a compartment inside for a cleaning rod and loading tool. The other (lower photo) is similar to the Mauser "Broomhandle" stock. It has no compartment for tools, and does not enclose the whole pistol. These types of stocks were listed in the 1929 Stoeger catalog. Only a few examples are known. (Pat Redmond collection)

Thirty-two round drum magazine used with the 1914 artillery Luger. These magazines made for use with 9mm ammunition only. On right is a first issue drum; on left is the second issue. (Harland Domke collection)

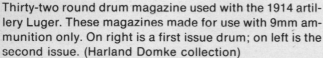

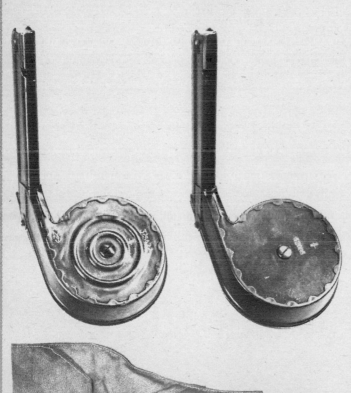

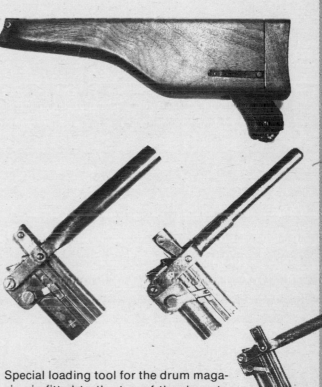

Special loading tool for the drum magazine is fitted to the top of the drum to compress spring during loading (see right). Left tool (above) is believed to be manufactured for DWM and is proofed by that company. Right tool (above) is believed to be manufactured by Krupp for Erfurt and is proofed by Erfurt. (Sam Costanzo collection)

Special canvas carrier for the drum magazine. (Harland Domke collection)

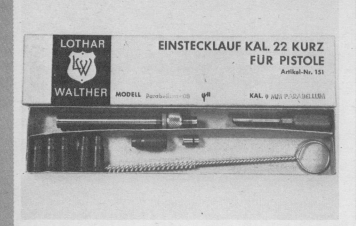

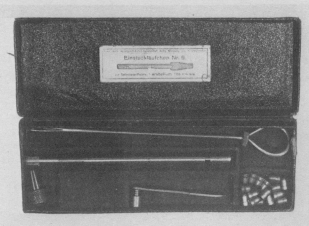

Lothar Walther 22 caliber single shot conversion kit. A **similar kit** was made in 4mm. (Author's collection)

RWS 4mm single shot conversion kit with two-piece barrel insert. (Author's collection)

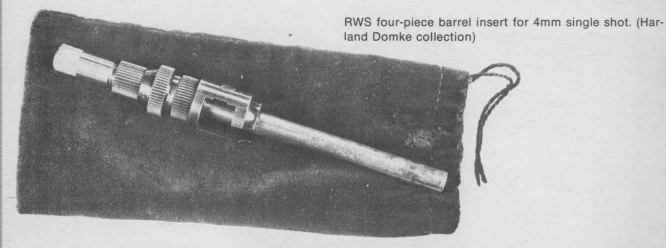

RWS four-piece barrel insert for 4mm single shot. (Harland Domke collection)

Waffen Glaser (Zurich, Switzerland) 4mm single shot conversion kit in **box,** with targets and accessories. (Author's collection)

A

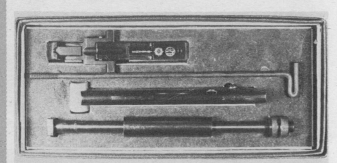

B

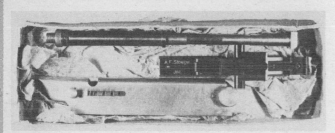

C

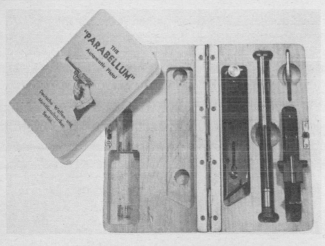

D

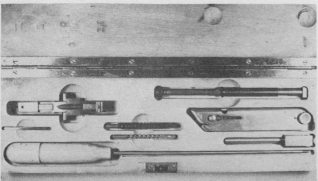

E

Erma auto-loading 22 caliber conversion kits were supplied with a 22 caliber clip and complete breech block assembly for self-loading operation. Variations include (from top):

A. Early commercial. (Sam Costanzo collection)
B. Late commercial. (Author's collection)
C. A.F. Stoeger marked commercial. (Sam Costanzo collection)
D. Military proofed small wooden box. (Author's collection)
E. Military proofed large wooden box. (Sam Costanzo collection)

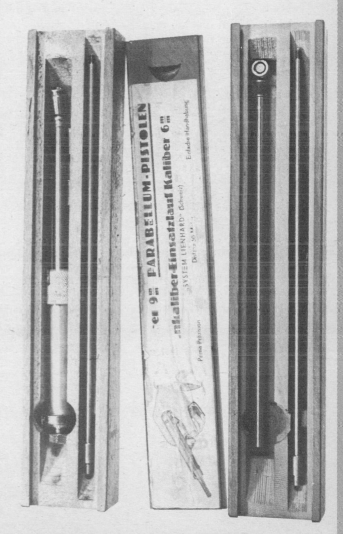

Above—Swiss manufactured 22 caliber single shot barrel insert for the 4¾ inch 7.65mm Luger (left). Note the adjustable sight on the barrel sleeve. A similar kit (right) fits any pistol chambered for 9mm Parabellum. (Author's collection)

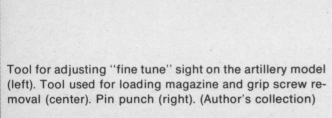

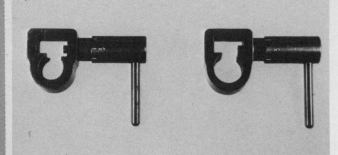

Front sight adjusting tools. Tool on the left is for 7.65mm; on the right is for 9mm. (Harland Domke collection)

Tool for adjusting "fine tune" sight on the artillery model (left). Tool used for loading magazine and grip screw removal (center). Pin punch (right). (Author's collection)

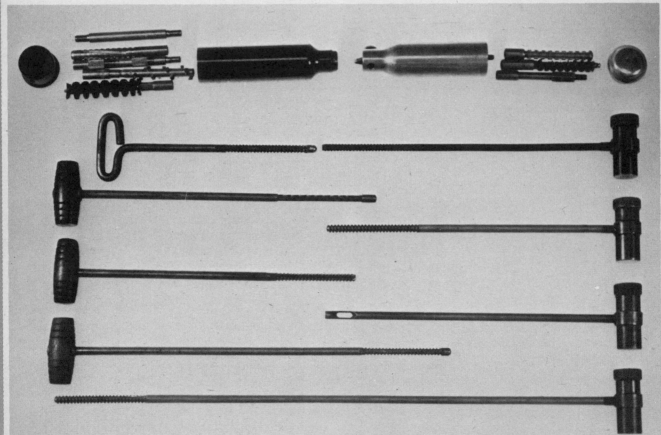

Cleaning rods and components. (Author's collection)
  (Left, top to bottom)
  Late Swiss six-piece cleaning kit.
  Mauser contract cleaning rod.
  Early Navy brass rod.
  Late Navy steel rod.
  1914 Artillery cleaning rod.

(Right, top to bottom)
Early Swiss five-piece cleaning kit
Portuguese steel cleaning rod with oiler.
Commercial cleaning rod similar to Portuguese; has brass rod.
Dutch cleaning rod for Vickers Luger.
Carbine cleaning rod.

Black cardboard box with silver letters used for marketing post-W.W. II commercial Lugers. (Sam Costanzo collection)

Carrying case for 1902 carbine and stock. (Author's collection)

Original German manufactured ammunition. (Author's collection)

(Top left) 1918 military ammunition in boxes of 16 rounds.

(Bottom left) Commercial DWM factory 9mm ammunition.

(Top right) 1943 military ammunition in boxes of 16 rounds.

(Bottom right) Commercial DWM factory 7.65mm carbine ammunition.

Luger Holster Makers, 1900-65

by John D. Walter

THIS LIST CONTAINS fragmentary details of a great number of the companies active in Germany and Switzerland (occasionally elsewhere) known or suspected to have been involved in the manufacture of leatherware for the Parabellum—although many also produced similar articles for the Walther P38 and countless other guns. The list is most probably far from complete, though it contains most of the major leatherware manufacturers; however, further information *is* needed, and additional details will always be welcomed. This includes correction of spelling errors, as there are bound to be a few in the list! It is a pity that such an amazing variety of misspellings and misrepresentations of these company names exist in many books and articles. I have tried to authenticate as many names and locations as possible, but was unable to trace the origin of some of the reports. Entries distinguished by an asterisk (*) in the text indicated doubtful information, or that confirmation is still awaited from other sources.

Editor's Note: John Walter has offered this painstakingly researched compilation of Luger holster makers—without doubt the most comprehensive such listing ever assembled—to complement John Kitts' outstanding presentation of Luger accessories in this Third Edition of GUN COLLECTOR'S DIGEST. With today's ever-increasing interest in accessories, particularly holsters, it is a very welcome addition indeed.

Acknowledgements

This listing of holster makers could not have been compiled without the assistance of many agencies, not least of which are the chambers of commerce, local government bureaus, museums and archives—particularly in Germany—who generously contributed information. I would also like to recognize the contributions of many friends, notably Don Bryans of Salem, Oregon, and Per Jensen in Denmark.

Name, Address*	Working Dates[1]	Letter Code[2]	Production Period[3] FW	WR	TR	PW
1. Karl Ackva Lederwerke AG * Bad Kreuznach, Rüdesheimer Strasse, in 1941	-1923-b60	hjh			•	
2. Reinhold Adam Sattlerwarenfabrik Oberursel/Taunus	-1941-	gxc			•	
3. Albrecht u. Noll Berlin	-1916-18-		•			
4. F. Andrist, Sattlerei Mett-Biel, Switzerland	-1960-65-					•
5. Richard Appel Lederwarenfabrik Frankfurt am Main	-1917-18-		•			
6. Armee- und Marinehaus, Inh. Deutscher Offizier-Verein Berlin-Charlottenburg, Hardenbergstrasse, in 1941	f1911-d45	jme	•	•	•	
7. Julius Arnade Metz, Departement Moselle, France	-1917-		•			
8. Auwärter u. Bubeck KG Stuttgart, Hasenbergstrasse, but in Augsburg (-1935-39/40)	-1935-d68	cdg			•	
9. AWM Sattlergenossenschaft München, Bayern	-1899-1917-		•			
10. Barney u. Companie* Berlin	-1917- (?)		•			
11. Karl Barth oHG Waldbröl/Rheinland, Bahnhofstrasse	f1911-80w			•	•	
12. Wilhelm Friedr. Bauer GmbH Offenbach-Bieber, Bremer Strasse	f1923-80w	gyb			•	
13. H. Becker u. Companie GmbH Berlin-Central, Marsiliusstrasse, in 1941.	-1931-d45?	hft		•	•	
14. Richard Becker, Lesser u. Jobst (Vereinigte Möbelstoff-, Polster-materialen- und Sattlerwaren-Grosshandlungen KG) Berlin-Sudwest, Prinzenstrasse	-1925-d45?	nos			•	
15. Berliner Sattler- u. Polsterer-Werkgenossenschaft Berlin	-1915-18-		•			
16. F(ritz?). Bierenbrier Kehl am Rhein	1913-18-		•			
17. Fritz Bigler der Ältere Bern, Christoffelgasse, Spitalgasse and Schauplatzgasse	-1868-1902/3		•			

NOTES: * Entries distinguished with an asterisk indicate doubtful information, or that confirmation is still awaited from other sources. [1]Working Dates: f=founded; d=dissolved; b=bought out; w=still working. [2]Letter code used by some makers; see accompanying table for cross-referenced list. [3]Production Period: FW=World War I; WR=Weimar Republic; TR=Third Reich; PW=Post-1945; dots indicate production during that period of time.

Name, Address*	Working Dates[1]	Letter Code[2]	FW	WR	TR	PW
18. **Fritz Bigler der Jüngere** Bern, Schauplatzgasse and Munzrain	1902/3-d33		•			
19. **Carl Billess (Biller?), Lederwaren-Fabrik** Spandau	-1915-18-		•			
20. **Chr. Blaser** Zürich (?)	-1910-20-		•			
21. **Karl Böcker, Lederwarenfabrik** Waldbröl/Rheinland and possibly Solingen	-1934-42-	eqf			•	
22. **Böttcher u. Renner** Nürnberg, Rennweg	f1901-80w	bmn			•	
23. **J. Braier, Militäreffekten-Fabrik** Frankfurt am Main	-1944-	nhj			•	
24. **Wilhelm Brand Triebriemenfabrik** Heidelberg, Eppelheimer Strasse (now Wilh. Brand KG, Walldorf, Industriestrasse)	f1900-80w	jvf			•	
25. **Heinz-Dieter Brassard** Jena, Wagnerstrasse (possibly active during the pre-1918 era)	-1940- (?)				?	?
26. **Franz Brehme** Hildesheim (NB; also recorded — wrongly — in Walsrode)	-1915-16-		•			
27. **Breslauer Sattlerei-Genossenschaft** Breslau	-1938-40?				•	
28. **Ing. Karl Brettschneider** Mährisch-Schönberg, Hermann-Göring-Strasse, in 1941	-1940-44-	gcx			•	
29. **Briegl u. Schneider** Ohrdruf in Thüringen	1917?			?		
30. **G. Brönnimann Sattlerei** Zürich	-1942-				•	
31. **Gustav Buchmüller** Karlstrasse and Rosenstrasse, Stuttgart	f1831-d1961	gna			•	
32. **Otto Budischovsky** Wien	-1940-42-				•	
33. **Karl Budischowsky u. Söhne,** Österreichische Lederindustrie AG Wien, Hintere Zollamtstrasse and Industriestrasse	-1935-80w	cey			•	
34. **A.F. Buhler or Bühler** Stuttgart	-1915-16-		•			
35. **N. Burghard** Pasing bei München	-1913-17-		•			
36. **Carl Busse, Fabrik Für Heeresausrüstungen aus Stoff und Leder** Mainz, Kurfürstenstrasse, in 1941	-1940-45-	jkh			•	
37. **Centrale Magazijn** Woerden, Netherlands; succeeded Centrale Werkplatz in 1916	f1916-40-?		•	•	•	
38. **Centrale Werkplaatz** Woerden, Netherlands; succeeded by Centrale Magazijn in 1916	-1892-1916		•			
39. **Hans Clemen, Lederwarenfabrik** Elberfeld	-1916-		•			
40. **J.F. Clude(r)*** Berlin	-1915-16-		•			
41. **Franz Cobau, Fabrik für Militär-Ausrüstungen** Berlin-Reinickendorf-Ost, Rezidenzstrasse, in 1941 and 1942	f1908(?)-d45	hsy kpm			•	
42. **Rudolf Conte, Nachfolger Theodor Seibod, Lederwarenfabrik** Offenbach am Main, Bahnhofstrasse	1934 d55	gjh			•	
43. **Coppenbrügger Sattlerinnung** Coppenbrügge, near Hameln	1914-18?			?		
44. **A. Dahl** Barmen	-1915-18-		•			
45. **F.W. Dammiq*** Riesa, near Leipzig	1914-18?			?		
46. **F.J. Daniel** Bühl in Baden	-1909-18-		•			
47. **Danziger Leder-Industrie AG** Danzig	-1916-17-		•			
48. **Hans Deuter Koffer-, Rucksäcke- u Lederwaren-Fabrik** Augsburg	f1898-1980w		•		•	
49. **Deutsche Lederwerkstätten GmbH** Pirmasens, Margarethenstrasse	f1938-d54	DLWP jln			•	
50. **Deutsche Signalflaggen-Fabrik** Karlsruhe in Baden	f1895?-1915-		•			
51. **Hans Dinkelmeyer, Lederwaren- u. Sportartikel-Fabrik** Nürnberg, Iamnitzerstrasse	-1941-	gyo			•	
52. **Wilhn. Dopheide** Brackwede bei Bielefeld	-1915-b43		•		•	
53. **A. Döppert Triebriemenfabrik** Kitzingen, Mainbernheimer Strasse	f1876-1980w	erg			•	
54. **J.M. Eckart Lederwarenfabrik** Ulm/Donau (often wrongly placed in Köln)	-1913-46-	dyo	•		•	
55. **Eckenhoff u. Companie** Berlin	-1882-1918-		•			
56. **Edelacroix Nachfolger** Berlin	-1916-		•			
57. **Albin Eger** Schmalkalden im Harz	-1932-d37?				•	
58. **H. Eger u. Linde, Lederwarenfabrik** Schmalkalden im Harz until 1938/9, Seligenthal in Thüringen thereafter; possibly a successor to Albin Eger	f1937-45-	nhn			•	
59. **Chr. Ehlers Lederwarenfabrik** Kiel	-1915-		•			

Three-Letter Codes

[2]Three-letter codes ('Kennzeichen') used by some German holster makers after 1941. The numbers are keyed to those on the master list. Letter codes that appear in capital letters, e.g. AKAH, AH, are *commercial* company designations as opposed to the government assigned three-letter codes.

bcb=78
bdq=60
bdr=61
bdw=147
bla=139
bmd=158
bml=183
bmn=22
bmu=120
btt=115

cdo=105
cdg=8
cea=222
cey=33
cfz=129
cga=131
cgn=171
cgu=218
clg=152
cny=172
cvb=210
cvc=249
cww=236
cxb=153
cxm=75

dde=133
dfc=179
dkk=164
dlu=146
dmb=204
dta=232
dtu=63
dtv=73
dvr=70
dyo=54

ekp=79
emj=65
emr=65
eqf=21
eqk=102

eqr=166
erg=53
ett=130
eue=175
evg=165
ewx=228

fsx=203
ftc=71
ttt=97
fuq=229
fys=174
fvz=112

gaq=216
gce=140
gcx=28
gee=84
gfg=88
ggu=184
gjh=42
gmo=174
gna=31
goq=124
gpf=221
grz=116
gtu=127
gut=206
gxc=2
gxq=86
gxy=110
gyb=12
gyd=117
gyo=51

hck=137
hft=13
hrf=190
hjd=89
hjg=106
hjh=1
hlv=148

hmo=202
hsy=41
hud=123

jba=245
jhg=75
jhs=125
jhz=235
jkh=36
jln=49
jme=6
joa=00
jor=159
jsd=176
jsv=151
jtu=128
jvf=24
jwa=213
jxh=108

kot=65
kpm=41
krm=172
ksd=242
kuo=122
kuu=85

lhl=194
lkq=248

ndc=135
nhj=23
nhn=58
nos=14
nyb=132
nzz=165

oaz=165
otg=91

Name, Address*	Working Dates[1]	Letter Code[2]	FW	WR	TR	PW
60. **Ehrhardt u. Kirsten, Koffer- u. Lederwarenfabrik** Tauscha-Leipzig and possibly also Stuttgart (confirmation lacking)	-1934-42-	bdq EKST			●	
61. **Richard Ehrhardt, Lederwarenfabrik** Pössneck in Thuringen	-1937-43-	bdr			●	
62. **Eislebener Sattlerinnung** Eisleben, near Halle	-1915-18-		●			
63. **G.J. Ensink u. Companie, Spezialfabrik für Militärausrüstungen und Stanzwerk** Ohrdruf in Thüringen	-1938-d45?	dtu			●	
64. **L. Estelman(n) u. Companie** Strassburg im Elsass	-1916-17-		●			
65. **Adalbert Fischer, Fabriken für Militärausrüstungen** Berlin-Central, Georgenkirchstrasse, and Guttstadt/Ostpreussen	-1923-d45?	emj emr kot		●	●	
66. **J(ohann?). Fockler or Föckler, Lederwarenfabrik** Berlin	-1916-		●			
67. **A.L. Frank Exportgesellschaft** Hamburg	-1899-1920-	ALFA	●			
68. **Friedrich & Companie*** Eisleben	-1916-		●			
69. **Friedrich, Erben** Berlin-Sudost	-1915-		●			
70. **Johann Fröhlich, Koffer- u. Lederwarenfabrik** Wien, Hütteldorferstrasse	f1940-80w	dvr			●	
71. **Frost u. Jähnel** Breslau, Schlossohle, in 1941	-1940-d45?	ftc			●	
72. **W. Geering*** Switzerland	unknown			?		
73. **C. Otto Gehrckens, Leder- und Riemenwerke** Pinneberg bei Hamburg	-1939-45-	dtv			●	
74. **Fritz Gehri** Bern, Murtenstrasse, Hopfenweg, Steinauweg, Giessereiweg, Schwarzenburgstrasse, Niggelerstrasse and Maulbierstrasse	f1895?-1934d		●	?		
75. **Gustav Genschow u. Companie AG** Berlin-Sudost, Bouchestrasse, and Alstadt-Hachenburg/Westerwald (Abteilung Lederwarenfabrik, f1922)	f1887-b1959	cxm jhg GECO		●	●	
76. **H. Gisler or Gissler*** Switzerland	unknown			?		
77. **Paul Göldner** Halle am Saale	-1933-39-				●	
78. **Otto Graf, Heeresausrüstungen u. Sattlerwarenfabrik** Leipzig-Nord, Planitzstrasse	-1940-d45?	bcb			●	
79. **Fritz Grosse** Dresden-Radebeul and possibly Rabishau/Isergebiet	-1914-44-	ekp*	●		●	
80. **F. Guiremand** Berlin-Sudwest	-1918-		●			
81. **Rich. Haenel or Hänel*** Dresden	-1915-		●			
82. **Lederwarenfabriek J. Haverlach** Amsterdam. The present company of this name was f1964 and could not, as has been claimed, have made holsters	unknown					
83. **Carl Heinichen u. Companie AG, Dresdner Koffer- & Taschenfabrik** Dresden, Dornblüthstrasse, in 1941	-1916-d45?	joa	●	●	●	
84. **Heinrich, Sohn GmbH u. Companie KG Heeresausrüstungen- u. Sportartikel-Fabrik** Neu-Ulm (now Bellenberg/Iller)	f1871-1980w	gee			●	
85. **Carl Henkel GmbH u. Companie KG (Carl Henkel, Uniformen- und Lederwarenfabrik)** Bielefeld, Herforder Strasse	-1870-1980w	kuu			●	
86. **Henseler u. Companie, Militär-Effekten-Fabrik** Ulm/Donau, Zinglerstrasse	-1932-1955d?	gxq			●	
87. **Oscar Hentschell u. Companie** Leusden bei Dresden	-1916-		●			
88. **Carl Hepting u. Companie GmbH Lederwaren- und Gürtelfabrik** Stuttgart-Feuerbach, Burgenlandstrasse	f1922-80w	gtg Hepco			●	
89. **Alexander Hermes** Solingen, Meves-Berns-Strasse	f1909-80w	hjd AH mgm			●	
90. **Franz Herman(n)** Erfurt	-1911-17-		●			
91. **Heinrich Hinkel GmbH u. Companie KG** Mülheim am Main, Borsigstrasse	f1935-d77	otg			?	
92. **E. Hintermann*** Switzerland	unknown				?	
93. **Hein. Hoffman der Jüngere*** Berlin	-1915-		●			
94. **Arn. Hoffmann*** Berlin; see above.	-1915-16-		●			
95. **Hohmann u. Sohn** Kaiserslautern; acquired by Kimnach & Brunn in 1938	f1890?-1938b		●		●	
96. **C. Holste u. Companie*** München	-1917-18-		●			
97. **Eugen Huber, Vereinigte Leder-waren-Fabriken** München, Rosenheimerstrasse	-1915-47-	ftt	●		●	
98. **Joh. Huber** München	-1905-19-		●			
99. **Industrie-Gruppe Stuttgart*** Stuttgart	1914-18?		?			
100. **Julius Jansen** Strassburg in Elsass	-1895-1916-		●			
101. **E.J. Jenni** Bern, Kasernenstrasse, Blumenberg Strasse and Schönburgstrasse (NB: name changed to Jenny in 1912/13)	f1895-d1934?		●	●		
102. **Just u. Companie AG, Koffer-, Taschen- Lederwaren-Fabriken** Geraberg in Thüringen	-1941-d45?	eqk			●	
103. **P.M. Kamerling** Breda, Veemarktstraat, Netherlands	f1840-d1956		●	●	●	
104. **S. Kellendorfer, Lederwaren-fabrik** München	-1913-46d?		●			?
105. **Kern, Kläger u. Companie** Berlin-Nord, Pappelallee, and possibly a branch in Neu-Ulm	f1913?-d1959	cdc	?		●	
106. **Kimnach u. Brunn, Fabrik für Heeresausrüstung u. Lederhand-lung** Kaiserslautern, Industriestrasse	f1938-d1954	hjg			●	
107. **Albrecht Kind AG (now GmbH u. Co.)** Berlin, Nürnberg and elsewhere; now Hunstig bei Dieringhausen	f1853-1980w	AKAH	●	●	●	
108. **F.W. Kinkel** Mainz, Wallstrasse, in 1941	-1911-49?	jxh	●		●	
109. **Kelinheinz Lederwarenfabrik** München	-1916-23?		●			
110. **Gerbrüder Klinge Lederwaren-Fabrik** Dresden-Löbtau. Anton-Weck-Strasse, in 1941	-1937-45?	gxy			●	
111. **Gebrueder van der Kloot Meyburg** Alphen aan de Rijn, Kalkovenweg, Netherlands	f1868-1980w	KMA*	●	●	●	

NOTES: * Entries distinguished with an asterisk indicate doubtful information, or that confirmation is still awaited from other sources. [1]Working Dates: f=founded; d=dissolved; b=bought out; w=still working. [2]Letter code used by some makers; see accompanying table for cross-referenced list. [3]Production Period: FW=World War I; WR=Weimar Republic; TR=Third Reich; PW=Post-1945; dots indicate production during that period of time.

Name, Address*	Working Dates[1]	Letter Code[2]	FW	WR	TR	PW
112. **Paul Klopfer*, Lederwaren-Fabrik** Berlin-Nord, Chausseestrasse, in 1941	-1941-45?	fvx			•	
113. **Ad. Klopfstein** Laupen, Kanton Bern, Switzerland	-1934-				?	•
114. **Otto Köberstein** Landsberg am Warthe	-1940-42-				•	
115. **R. Kreisel*, Gürtler** Gablonz/Sudetengau	-1939-44-	btt			•	
116. **Gebrüder Krüger, Lederwaren-fabrik u. Lederfarberei** Breslau, Freiberger Strasse	1941-44-	grz			•	
117. **Ludwig Krumm AG (Vereinigte Lederwarenfabrik Ludwig Krumm — Gebr. Langhardt)** Offenbach am Main	f1922-80w	gyd			•	
118. **R. Kuhlewein u. Companie** Erfurt	-1916-		•			
119. **Reinhold Kuhn, Sattelfabrik** Location unknown	-1916-		•			
120. **Carl Kuntze Sattlerwarenfabrik** Penig in Sachsen	-1937-43-	bmu			•	
121. **Kunz u. Jakob** Bern	f1899-d1901		•			
122. **Paul Kurtzke Gürtelfabrik** Berlin-Central, Burgstrasse, in 1941	-1942-d45?	kuo			•	
123. **Landeslieferungsgenossenschaft Rheinland für das Sattler- und Tapezierer-Handwerk eGmbH** Aachen, Julicherstrasse ('Lago, Aachen')	1937?-45	hud			•	
124. **Landeslieferungsgenossenschaft des Sattler- und Tapezier-Handwerks Schlesien eGmbH** Breslau, Am Ohlau Ufer ('Lago, Breslau')	1937?-45	goq			•	
125. **Landeslieferungsgenossenschaft des Sattlerhandwerks im Reichsgau Danzig-Westpreussen eGmbH** Danzig, Milchkannengasse ('Lago, Danzig')	1937?-45	jhs			•	
126. **Landeslieferungsgenossenschaft Dresden** ('Lago, Dresden'); possibly the pre-1937 site of the Thüringen (Erfurt) or Niedersachsen (Magdeburg) regional delivery office	1937?				•	
127. **Landeslieferungsgenossenschaft des Sattler-, Tapezierer- und Polsterer-Handwerks Südmark rGmbH** Graz, Josefigasse ('Lago, Graz')	1937?-45	gtu			•	
128. **Landeslieferungsgenossenschaft für das Tapezier- und Sattlerhandwerk Ostpreussen eGmbH** Königsberg in Preussen, Weidendamm	1937?-45	jtu			•	
129. **Landeslieferungsgenossenschaft des Sattlerhandwerkes für Salzburg, Tirol, Vorarlberg, Steiermark und Kärnten GmbH** Salzburg-Parsch, Weiserstrasse ('Lago, Salzburg')	1937?-45	cfz			•	
130. **Landeslieferungsgenossenschaft für das Sattler-, Tapezier- und Polsterer-Handwerk in Württemberg und Hohenzollern eGmbH** Stuttgart-West, Gutenbergstrasse ('Lago, Stuttgart')	1937?-45	ett			•	
131. **Landeslieferungsgenossenschaft des Sattler-, Tapezierer- und Polstererhandwerkes für Wien und Niederdonau GmbH** Wien, Regierungsgasse ('Lago, Wien')	1938-45	cga			•	
132. **Lanio & Companie KG*** Seligenstadt, Jakobstrasse and Steinheimer Strasse	-1933-d54	nyb			•	
133. **Robert Larsen, Fabrik für Leder- und Stoffwaren** Berlin-Sudwest, Wilhelmstrasse	-1927-d45?	dde		•	•	
134. **Carl Lattmann** Arnstadt bei Erfurt	1914-18?		?			
135. **Leder-Schuler-Werke KG*** Hamburg-Altona, Wilhelmine-strasse, in 1944	f1838-1980w	ndc				?
136. **G. Lehmann*** Switzerland	unknown				?	
137. **Georg A. Lerch GmbH** Berlin-Central, Leipzigstrasse	-1939-42-	hck			•	
138. **K. Leuch*** Switzerland	unknown				?	
139. **E.G. Leuner GmbH** Bautzen, Humboldtstrasse, in 1941	-1939-43-	bla			•	
140. **Lieberknecht u. Schurg, Etui- und Holzwarenfabrik** Coburg, Postweg	-1906-80w	gce			•	
141. **Lieferungsgenossenschaft der Sattler** Nürnberg	f1915-d69	LGS	•			
142. **Lieferungs-Verband von Mitglieder der Berliner Sattlerinnung** Berlin, and a branch in München	-1915-18	LVMBS	•			
143. **Ferd. Litzmann** Erzingen/Schwarzwald and later (?) Neu-Ulm	-1915-25-		•	?		
144. **Loh Söhne AG** Berlin	-1915-20-		•	?		
145. **Herm. F, Lohr*** Köln	-1915-		•			
146. **Ewald Lüneschloss, Militär-Effekten-Fabrik** Solingen, Margaretenstrasse	-1914-d48	dlu			?	•
147. **Benno Marstaller, Koffer- und Lederwarenfabrik** München	-1940-42-	bdw			•	
148. **Maury u. Companie** Offenbach am Main, Luisenstrasse	-1915-d60	hlv	•		•	•
149. **R. Max u. Phillip*** Nieder-Schohaus/Erzgebiet (possibly 'R. Max Phillip')	-1915-16-		•			
150. **Meier u. Abitzsch** Berlin, and possibly Leipzig-Gohls	-1914-44-		•		?	
151. **Wilhelm Meissner, Fabrik für Sattlerwaren- und Heeresausrüstungen** Berlin-Nord, Chausseestrasse	-1941-	jsv			•	
152. **Ernst Melzig** Liegnitz, Breslauer Strasse, in 1941	-1941-45?	clg			•	
153. **Josef Moll KG, Moll-Lederwaren-fabrik** Goch/Rheinland, Mittelstrasse	-1915-b78	cxb			?	•
154. **Wilhelm Möller** Hameln, Bäckerstrasse	f1869-1980w		?			•
155. **Claus F. Mordhorst** Kiel, Dänische Strasse	f1860-1980w					•
156. **Muhlenfeld & Companie** Barmen and/or München	-1915-18-		•			
157. **Albert Müller** Düsseldorf	-1917-18-		•			
158. **Max G. Müller, Fabrik für Lederwaren und Heeresbedarf** Nürnberg-Ost, Forsthofstrasse, in 1941	f1887?-d1968	bmd			?	•

NOTES: * Entries distinguished with an asterisk indicate doubtful information, or that confirmation is still awaited from other sources. [1]Working Dates: f=founded; d=dissolved; b=bought out; w=still working. [2]Letter code used by some makers; see accompanying table for cross-referenced list. [3]Production Period: FW=World War I; WR=Weimar Republic; TR=Third Reich; PW=Post-1945; dots indicate production during that period of time.

Name, Address*	Working Dates[1]	Letter Code[2]	Production Period[3] FW	WR	TR	PW
159. **Anton Muzik Sattlerwarenfabrik** Wien, Liniengasse	-1935-d63	jor			•	
160. **R(einhard). Nagel u. Companie*** Bielefeld and later Berlin (?)	-1914-d37		•		•	
161. **Rob. Niederdorfer** Rüti, Kanton-Zürich, Switzerland	-1940-				•	
162. **E. Nussbaumer, Sattler** Mühledorf, Switzerland	unknown				?	
163. **Oberpfälzische Lieferungs-Verband*** Regensburg/Pfalz	unknown					?
164. **Freidrich Offerman & Söhne** Bensberg, near Köln	-1938-44-	dkk			•	
165. **Max Oswald, Lederwaren- und Reiseartikel-Fabrik** Karlsruhe, Schützenstrasse, in 1941-5	f1910?-d47?	evg nzz oaz			•	
166. **G. Passier u. Sohn & Companie GmbH** Hannover, Strasse der Sturm-Abteilung (now Langenhagen, Am Pferdemarkt)	f1867-1980w	eqr			•	
167. **Perina u. Companie, Lederwarenfabrik** Dresden — but often placed in Hannover	-1918-		•			
168. **Peter u. Reiche*** Berlin; interpretation doubtful — see Schäfer u. Reiche	-1917-		•			
169. **C. Pfenninger*** Switzerland	unknown		?			
170. **Platow u. Premer*** Berlin; often interpreted as a brandname, 'Platou Premier'	-1915-		•			
171. **Jos. Poeschl's Söhne, Rohrbacher Lederfabrik** Rohrbach/Oberdonau and later Rennertshofen bei Neuberg an der Donau	-1935-55-	cgn			•	•
172. **C. Pose, Wehrausrüstungen** Berlin-Ost, Boxhagener Strasse, in 1941-2	-1931-d45?	cny krm			?	•
173. **Hugo Pretzel u. Companie, Leder-waren-und Sattlerwarenfabrik** Berlin; often wrongly recorded as 'Pretzlert'	-1916-17-		•			
174. **Rahm u. Kampmann, Raka-Werke** Kaiserslautern and Wuppertal-Elberfeld	f1936?-d78	fys gmo RAKA			•	
175. **Otto Reichel Lederwarenfabrik, Inhaber Rudolf Fischer** Lengefeld/Erzgebiet, Am Markt	-1941-	eue			•	
176. **Gustav Reinhardt** Berlin-Sudwest, Brandenburg-strasse, in 1941	-1913-45?	jsd	•	•	•	
177. **Julius Richter, Militär-Effekten- und Lederwaren-Fabrik** Dresden	-1915-16-		•			
178. **A. Ricke Lederwarenfabrik** Cassel	-1915-d23?		•			
179. **L. Ritgen, Inhaber Dr-Ing. Claus, Fabrik für Wehrmachtausrüstung und Uniformen** Karlsruhe, Vogesenstrasse, in 1941	f1870-d1944?	dfc			•	
180. **Ritter (Kuno Ritter?)** Solingen-Gräfrath?	-1935-				•	
181. **M. Rochat, Sattler** Wald, Switzerland	-1917-		•			
182. **C.A. Roever** Magdeburg	-1915-17-		•			
183. **Hans Römer GmbH u. Companie** Neu-Ulm, Arnulfstrasse	f1871-1980w	bml	•	?	•	
184. **F.W. Rosenbaum, Lederwaren-fabrik** Breslau, Schubrücke, in 1941	-1915-d45?	ggu	•		•	
185. **A(lfred?). Rosenberg** Berlin	-1918-		•			
186. **R. Rothmund u. Companie** Hamburg	-1916-45?		•			
187. **C.E. Rüegsegger** Bern, Marktgasse	-1862-d1927		•			
188. **Carl Ruther*** Berlin	unknown		?			
189. **Ryffel u. Borne KG** Hannover-Kirchrode, Grosser Hillen	f1886-1980w				•	
190. **Sachs u. Deisselberg Leder-warenfabrik** Hamburg, Rödingsmarkt and Steinstrasse	f1919?-80w	hfr			•	
191. **Sattlerei-Lieferungs-Verband*** Submissions-Amt, Leipzig	-1918-		•			
192. **Sattler-Waren-Fabrik GmbH*** Strassburg in Elsass	-1915-d18?	SWF*	•			
193. **Saupe u. Scherf** Chemnitz in Sachsen	unknown				?	
194. **Friedr. Schäfer, Leder- und Lederwaren-Fabrik** Ulm/Donau, Bleichstrasse	-1943-d47?	lhl			•	
195. **Schäfer u. Reiche*** Leipzig? See Peter & Reiche	-1917-		•			
196. **Schambach u. Companie** Berlin	-1926-d45?				•	•
197. **A. Scheidbrandt*** Bensberg, near Köln	unknown		?			
198. **Scherrell u. Companie** Nordhausen, near Halle	-1937-42-				•	
199. **Friedrich Scheuermann** Offenbach am Main, Goethestrasse, but now Frankfurt am Main	-1900-80w		•	?	•	
200. **Friedr. Wilh. Schiemenz** Wuppertal-Elberfeld, Friedrichstrasse, in 1978	-1915-80w				•	
201. **Julius Schloss** Berlin	unknown				?	
202. **Wilhelm Schmidt, Sattler- und Lederwarenfabrik** Berlin-Sudwest, Stallschreiber Strasse, in 1941	-1938-43-	hms			•	
203. **Albin Scholle Lederwarenfabrik** Zeitz. Weissenfelser Strasse	-1937-42-	tsx			•	
204. **Ludwig Schröder KG, Fabrik für Sattlerwaren und Heeresaus-rüstungen** Ansbach/Bayern, Würzburger Strasse	f1891-1980w	amb			•	
205. **L. Schultz GmbH u. Companie** Augsburg. Formerly L. Schultz u. Co.. Lederwarenfabrik	-1918-42-	LSA	•			
206. **Walter Schürmann u. Companie** Bielefeld, Bismarckstrasse	f1934-d53	gut			•	
207. **Fritz Schütz** Offenbach am Main	f1897-d1967				•	?
208. **Schwarzenberger u. Companie** Nürnberg	-1915-17-		•			
209. **Ernst Siegemund(e)*, Leder-warenfabrik** Dresden; spelling open to doubt	-1916-		•			
210. **Otto Sindel, Militäreffekten- und Lederwarenfabrik** Berlin-Ost, Holzmarktstrasse	-1914-45?	cvb	•		•	
211. **J.A. Staniener*** Berlin; possibly 'Stawiener'	-1915-17-		•			
212. **Witwe Stauffer*** Switzerland	unknown				?	
213. **Moritz Stecher, Lederwarenfabrik** Freiberg Bezirks Dresden	-1918-44-	jwa	•		•	
214. **Ernst Steinmetz** Bensberg/Rheinland (sometimes wrongly placed in Breslau)	-1915-16-		•			

NOTES: * Entries distinguished with an asterisk indicate doubtful information, or that confirmation is still awaited from other sources. [1]Working Dates: f=founded; d=dissolved; b=bought out; w=still working. [2]Letter code used by some makers; see accompanying table for cross-referenced list. [3]Production Period: FW=World War I; WR=Weimar Republic; TR=Third Reich; PW=Post-1945; dots indicate production during that period of time.

Name, Address*	Working Dates[1]	Letter Code[2]	FW	WR	TR	PW
215. **Max Steltzer, Lederwaren- und Militäreffekten-Fabrik** Berlin	-1937-45?				•	
216. **Otto Stephan** Mühlhausen in Thüringen	-1920-46?	gaq			•	
217. **Stern & Companie** Offenbach am Main	-1918-		•			
218. **Stolla's Sohne — W.K., K. u. A. Stolla, Wehrmachteffekten** Wien, Floriangasse, in 1941	-1938-45-	cgu			•	
219. **E. Studer*** Switzerland; sometimes listed as 'Jean Studer'	unknown			?		
220. **S. Stuehr*, Braunschweiger Lederindustrie** Braunschweig	unknown			?	?	
221. **Carl Tesch Sattlerwaren-Fabrik** Berlin-Nord, Chausseestrasse	-1941-45?	gpf			•	
222. **Heinrich Thiele AG** Dresden	-1937-43-	cea			•	
223. **F.H. Thieme** Magdeburg	-1913-22?		•			
224. **T. Trautweiler** Suhr, Switzerland	-1913-		•			
225. **Lederwarenfabriek de Valk** Amsterdam, Netherlands	unknown				?	
226. **Vereinigte Fabrikanten für Militär Lederzeuge GmbH** Solingen	-1915-18?	⬧S⬧	•			
227. **Vereinigte Sattelmeister GmbH** Elberfeld	-1914-18?		•			
228. **Franz u. Karl Voegels, Lederwarenfabrik** Köln-Deutz (until 1938) and Köln, An der Wollküche/Cäcilienstrasse	f1922-80w	ewx			?	•
229. **Curt Vogel KG, Cottbusser Lederwarenwerk** Cottbus, Wernerstrasse, in 1941	-1920-45-	fuq			•	
230. **NV Lederwarenfabriek de Volharding** Amsterdam, Admiralengracht	f1935-d70				•	
231. **A. Volken*** Switzerland	unknown			?		
232. **A. Waldhausen GmbH u. Companie KG** Köln, Obermarspforten and Johannisstrasse; now Köln-Nippes	f1834-1980w	dta AWA			•	
233. **L.G. Walther, Sattlerei** Bern, Käfiggässchen, Kesslergasse, Belpstrasse and Seftigenstrasse	f1894-d1922			•		
234. **Robert Weimer u. Companie*** Mülheim/Ruhr, near Essen	-1935-40- (?)				•	
235. **Jean Weipert, Lederwaren- und Reiseartikelfabric GmbH** Offenbach am Main (prior to 1949) and Mülheim am Main	-1935-80w	jhz			•	
236. **Carl Weiss Lederwarenfabrik** Braunschweig	f1837-d1969	cww			•	
237. **Werk-Verband*** Nordhausen	-1917-18?			•		
238. **A. Wertheim*** Location unknown	-1915-		•			
239. **Felix Widmer, Sattler** Gränischen, Switzerland	-1917-		•			
240. **Wilhelm*** Berlin (Ernst Wilhelm, Suhl?)	-1911-		•			
241. **Wimbach & Companie** Berlin	-1935-40-				•	
242. **Walter Winkler, Militäreffekten-Fabrik** Berlin-Spandau, Schönwalderstrasse	-1937-42-	ksd			•	
243. **Hans Wirz** Rothenflüh, Switzerland	-1941-				•	
244. **J.L.L. Woller*** Essen	unknown			?		
245. **A. Wunderlich Nachfolger, Fabrik für Heeres-, Polizei- und Feuerwehr-Ausrüstungen** Berlin and Berlin and Neukölln Finowstrasse	f1892?-d1945?	jba	•	•	•	
246. **Württembergische Waffenfabrik*** Stuttgart and Ulm/Donau?	1940	WWSU			•	
247. **Handswerkskammer Würzburg** Würzburg	-1918?			•		
248. **Werner Zahn, vormals Fürst u. Hoeft, Elwezet-Lederwarenfabrik** Berlin-Sudwest, Oranienstrasse, in 1943	-1920-45?	LVZ* lkq			•	
249. **Gebrüder Zeuschner, L. Zeschke Nachfolger** Müllrose bei Frankfurt an der Oder	-1937-44-	cvc			•	

NOTES: * Entries distinguished with an asterisk indicate doubtful information, or that confirmation is still awaited from other sources. [1]Working Dates: f=founded; d=dissolved; b=bought out; w=still working. [2]Letter code used by some makers; see accompanying table for cross-referenced list. [3]Production Period: FW—World War I; WR—Weimar Republic; TR—Third Reich; PW=Post-1945; dots indicate production during that period of time.

©J.D. Walter, 1980.

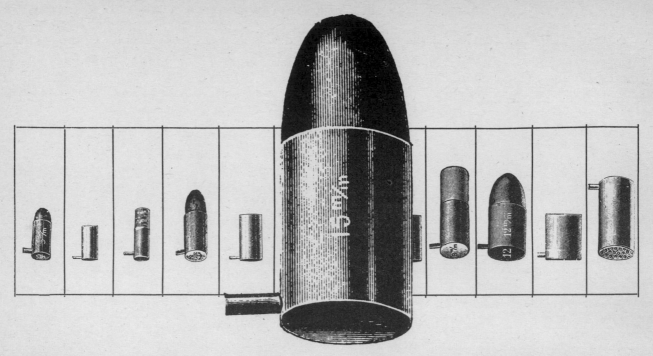

The Pinfire Cartridge

by Graham Burnside

THE PINFIRE cartridge specimen has finally come into its own!

Once-upon-a-not-so-long-time-ago the pinfire cartridge was ignored by many cartridge collectors—even scorned by some. I'm sure the reasons went something like this:

"Pinfire cartridges are so common that you see them all over the place, and they all look alike. They have that silly-looking pin sticking out of the case side, and they may even be dangerous."

"Pinfire cartridges are foreign junk, and real collectors only want American items."

"Pinfire revolvers and shotguns are poorly designed and cheaply manufactured—they have no place in a really good collection."

But things have changed! Over the years collectors have learned a lot, our economy is not the same, and what was once common is becoming hard to find. The profusion of pinfire cartridges is no longer. The box lots of pinfires that once abounded have disappeared. They are now in someone's collection. Let's face it, we have more collectors every day and the collector's items themselves—at least those that are available—are becoming fewer and fewer.

The 12mm long pinfire cartridge as made by Houllier & Blanchard of Paris, France, once was sold by Francis Bannerman Sons for 90¢ a hundred or 9¢ each. This listing was in the Bannerman Military catalogue for many years. I have the catalogues of 1925, 1938 and 1940 and the catalogue cut is identical in all three.

The listing states that the 12mm Long cartridges

A cut from the Bannerman catalogue showing the 12mm long pinfire cartridge. These were offered for many years at this same price. What cost nine cents each in 1940 is now worth a dollar.

200,000 Letaucheaux Pin-Fire 12-mm. Metallic Cartridges. All in first-class condition, in tin-lined cases in paper boxes of 25 each. Made in Paris. Price, 90 cents per 100; $7.50 per 1,000.

are "all in first class condition." I can vouch for that as I have fired at least 100 of them and never experienced even *one* misfire.

Most collectors will recognize the 12mm Long as made by Houllier & Blanchard. They are usually found in very clean condition with the "H.B. PARIS" raised headstamp. (A note of caution: The serious collector will find *two* such headstamps. In one the letters are much larger than the other.)

The "H.B. PARIS" 12mm used to sell for 25¢ or less, but, because of general scarcity, most dealers now want about $1. In other words, a cartridge that cost 9¢ in 1940 is now worth a dollar. And who said that collector's items do not keep pace with inflation?

And while we're talking about money, let's go to the other extreme. More than a few years ago my late friend Col. B.R. Lewis told me that he had sold a 58 caliber Gallager and Gladding inside pinfire for $50 because he couldn't imagine "anyone paying that much money for a single cartridge specimen." If we are to update that somewhat I'll submit that about 3 years ago I sold a like specimen for $500! I would guess that today a fine condition "G & G" would go for about $650 or better.

We could go on and on about values. Suffice it to say that *all* of the rare and good stuff has gone up in value—and it will continue to do so.

Now that we all have gained knowledge and wisdom (you can tell I'm a dreamer), the old charge that pinfires are "foreign junk" is about as groundless as a burned-out, second-story bowling alley! Foreign hell! Just to press the point I will list seven *United States Patent Office* patents. To wit:

AMERICAN PINFIRE PATENTS
NO. 24,730 JULY 12, 1859. M.J. GALLAGER AND W.H. GLADDING, SAVANNAH, GA. "CASE OF PAPER OR WOOD, OR METALLIC SHELL, OR WOOD OR PAPER BANDED WITH METAL, PIN FIRE."

NO. 34,987 APRIL 15, 1862. C. SHARPS, PHILADELPHIA, PA. "DRAWN METAL SHELL, WITH THICK BASE CONTAINING FULMINATE AND PIN."

NO. 58,800 OCT. 16, 1866. G.A. FITCH, KALAMAZOO, MICH. "CARTRIDGES PRIMING—FULMINATE IN FRONT OF PIN EXTENDING FROM BULLET TO BASE OF SHELL." (Etc.)

NO. 74,594 FEB. 18, 1868. S.S. REMBERT, MEMPHIS, TENN. "FIRE-ARM BREECH-LOADING (including a cartridge feature) "NIPPLE OR PIN EXTENDING ACROSS CASE TO EXPLODE CAP ON OPPOSITE SIDE."

NO. 99,721 FEB. 8, 1870. C.E. SNEIDER, BALTIMORE, MD. (a shot cartridge patent using the pinfire system)

NO. 116,640 JULY 4, 1871. C.E. SNEIDER, BALTIMORE, MD. (a patent entitled, "CARTRIDGE FOR BREECH-LOADING FIRE-ARMS, SHOT," utilizing the pinfire system.)

The astute reader will notice that these patents include a name or two of some distinction.

First of all, the M.J. Gallager of "G & G" fame is the same M.J. Gallager of Savannah, Georgia, who was granted a U.S. patent on July 17, 1860 (No. 29,157) for the well-known Gallager carbine that was used by the Union forces in the Civil War. As a matter of note the United States Government purchased approximately 22,728 Gallager carbines for the tidy sum of $508,492.94, and 8,294,023 Gallager cartridges for $211,893.92, or a little better than 2½¢ each. If you find a clean Gallager round today you will probably have to pay about $8.

The second U.S. pinfire cartridge patent as listed here was filed by Christian Sharps, the man who among other things invented one of the most popular single shot rifle systems in the world and who needs no introduction to the firearms fraternity.

The cartridge patent granted to one "G.A. Fitch" makes me wonder. There was a company in New York City that manufactured rimfire cartridges in the 1860's by the name of "Fitch-Van Vechten". I am naturally curious as to whether we have the same man or not. His address of "Kalamazoo, Mich." doesn't help matters either. Well, maybe the "Fitch" name is more common than I first thought—after all, someone had to make that shampoo. (That'll date me!)

As to the idea that pinfires are dangerous, I'll admit that having the firing pin out in plain sight doesn't sound like a good idea, but in all my years of shooting and collecting I've never had an accidental discharge nor have I even heard of one. At the same time one should bear in mind that those pinfires really work. As a high school kid I bought a pinfire 12mm carbine in an antique shop for $14—that was a lot of money, then. The carbine was of the typical Lefaucheux pattern as it came without a top strap to the frame. It had a 19-inch barrel and was of good quality, but nothing fancy. Instead of writing to Bannerman's in New York I bought my ammunition in Chicago. There was an "Army store" that would sell me 12mm long pinfires, boxed, for 10¢ a round (just like the Bannerman stuff) or there was about a bushel basket full of loose rounds that I could have for 6¢ apiece. I never had a misfire. Later I found some short 12mm pinfire cartridges in, of all places, a costume shop. They were headstamped "FUSNOT BRUXELLES." I bought about 90 rounds (all he had) of those Belgian pinfires and would guess that only about 8 or 10 of them simply wouldn't fire.

About a year ago I had a double barreled side-by-

Two high quality pinfire revolvers. They are unusual not only because of their workmanship, but for one reason or another they happen to be "left-handed." Most revolvers have the loading gate and extraction rod on the *right* side of the pistol.

side 12mm pinfire pistol, and I wanted to fire it. I rummaged around and found a single 12mm round, slipped it in and—KER-WHAM! The piece shot a 10-inch flame out of the muzzle and the ball struck 3-inches left of the point of aim at a distance of about 30 feet. Not bad for ammo that was undoubtedly loaded before the turn of the century.

In answer to the charge that pinfire firearms are of poor design and cheap manufacture one must remember that they were designed a long time ago. Sure, many of the pinfire revolvers that were sent to this country were of inferior quality. This country did not offer a good cheap handgun that could compete. At a later date this would change and this land of ours would produce a plethora of the cheapest, most inaccurate revolvers that the world has ever seen.

Pictured with this article our reader will notice two beautiful revolvers of the Lefaucheux pattern. Please take note of the quality workmanship. The little dots in the cross-hatching of the uppermost revolver are silver pins set into the design. With some scrutiny you might see a mark on the base of the barrel of the upper pistol. The mark is an EL under a crown. Since the patentee of the original pinfire revolver was Eugene Gabriel Lefaucheux maybe this is one of his marks.

Although Eugene Gabriel patented the pinfire revolver, he did not patent or invent the pinfire cartridge. In his revolver patent number 10,831 of April 15, 1854, he states that the pinfire cartridge was the idea of his father. The way he makes the statement is rather interesting—in fact what he said is downright astounding! I have a photostatic copy of the original patent papers and although my French is not the best here is how it translates (One must realize that the language is as though he is talking to someone else and that someone else is doing the writing. I don't

know if that is the way that all French patents are written but it is the way this one works out and here is what it says):

HIS FATHER IMAGINED THAT THE WHOLE SYSTEM COULD GO TOGETHER AND WORK, WITHOUT HAVING TO SEPARATE EACH PART SEPARATELY

In other words the elder Lefaucheux, who made no claim to have patented the pinfire cartridge, was described by his son to have "imagined" the whole system! Well, at this point in history we must backtrack and examine what factual material we have at hand.

With this in mind I will list the French patents that cover the principle of the pinfire cartridge.

FRENCH PINFIRE PATENTS

NO. 1,936 1846 HOULLIER
"PINFIRE, CAP IN DISK AT BASE. COPPER BASE CUP COVERED WITH PAPER OR PASTEBOARD."

NO. 3,601 1847 CHAUDUN (Pinfire)
"CUP MADE WATERPROOF BY RESIN"

NO. 4,839 1850 LEFAUCHEUX
"COPPER TUBE WITH COPPER BASE SCREWED IN"

NO. 8,340 1853 DEVOIR & LECLERCQ
"PIN FIRE, METALLIC OR PAPER TUBE WITH METAL BASE" (etc.)

NO. 9,686 1853 BOCHE (Pinfire)
"WOUND PAPER CASE AND WAD, METALLIC BASE."

NO. 11,404 1854 PRELAT
"CASE OF PAPER OR METAL FOIL WITH WAD OR LEATHER AT BASE, CAP NEAR BASE OF BULLET RESTING ON ROD EXTENDING FROM BASE."

NO. 23,200 1859 ROY (Pinfire)
"CAP IN METAL LINED POCKET IN BASE WAD. METALLIC REINFORCE BETWEEN WAD AND PAPER TUBE."
NO. 23,421 1859 CHALEYER
"PIN PASSES ENTIRELY THROUGH BASE AND SERVES TO REMOVE CAP AFTER FIRING."

When one takes the French pinfire patents and puts them in chronological order a rather surprising aspect appears. When Eugene Gabriel Lefaucheux tells about his father "imagining" the system he states that this took place in 1846, and yet the first Lefaucheux patent having to do with the pinfire system was the patent of 1850 (No. 4,839) and this patent is obviously an improvement of that basic principle. Let us also consider that *the* basic pinfire patent *was* in 1846—but it was the patent of Houllier.

In talking back and forth with firearms enthusiasts in France I have formed an opinion.

One, the men Lefaucheux had quite a going operation. Between father and son it is reported that they were granted 177 patents between 1830 and 1875. Their organization was very successful. They held a reputation that was of the finest. They manufactured many products that were the ideas of other men. They fabricated firearms—some of which were not of their design—and put their mark on them and they employed the best workmen available.

I can't prove it—and I probably never will—but I'll bet a Cuban nickel against a standing rib roast that Houllier or Chaudun—or both of them—worked for Lefaucheux! Had there been a controversy or some heavy competition between them, the researcher of today may well have uncovered that information. With all modesty, I have beat the brush concerning this subject for almost 30 years.

The fact that not one or the other Lefaucheux invented the pinfire is something of a bombshell to the collecting world. No big deal, though. The pinfire revolvers are still called "Lefaucheux" and that's as it ought to be. Maybe it's about time that we give credit to someone else.

Pictured with this writing is a box of pinfires that admittedly are for use in a firearm of the Lefaucheux system. They are of the rolled paper case with brass base—a very rare type indeed. This box lot cropped up many years ago in Mexico, and to this day not even one single specimen other than these has ever been found (to my knowledge). The box was broken up, and now there are ten fortunate collectors who have one of these in their display of pinfire cartridges.

The headstamp of these rounds, "CHAUDUN B^{te} 50 PARIS," is something of a quandry. One would assume that the "50" had something to do with caliber, and the label says "CAL. 50 A BROCHES".

An extremely rare box of pinfire cartridges manufactured by M. Chaudun of Paris, France. These pinfire rounds are the earliest type known, and match the basic patent of M. Houllier of 1846.

The problem is that the lead bullets are not 50 caliber—not even the outside diameter of the case itself is caliber 50. Possibly this calibration is based on the idea or circumstance that 50 of these bullets would come to one pound. Could be, but at this late date such a conclusion is hard to confirm.

If one carefully inspects the label of these super-rare cartridges it will be noted that there is no picture of a pinfire revolver. The pistol shown is a single shot with a roll-down barrel, and the shotgun displayed is a simple break-open piece of common design. It is obvious that these cartridges are a product that quite definitely precedes the Lefaucheux revolver.

The odd steel-cased pinfire pictured with the trapdoor in the base is unknown as to maker and nationality, and I cannot connect it with any patent. The late Col. B.R. Lewis told me he thought it was for the French "ROBERT" rifle. The trapdoor in the base is a rather slick idea. You pop open the door, raise the pin and remove the expended cap. Then you reverse the process with a fresh cap and you're back in business. I would have liked to fire this one, but I never saw a "ROBERT" rifle nor anything that would

A steel-case pinfire cartridge, with trap door in base for easy reloading. This round has been described as for the French "Robert" rifle.

chamber the round.

The photograph that displays 37 different pinfires includes some very fine rarities as well as some very ordinary specimens. The top row center shows two sizes of what collectors call horizontal pinfire. The pin comes out the back instead of out the side. Collectors are quick to say that the firearm for these rounds is unknown. I don't think so. In fact, I have chambered these cartridges in several pistols. The fact that there is a pin projecting from the base instead of a primer makes no difference. The bases of these two cases are

Springfield, Massachusetts, and the other was Ethan Allen of Worcester, Massachusetts.

Years ago the 12mm pinfire specimen as made by Ethan Allen was an unknown. We knew it was a 12mm pinfire, but we didn't know who manufactured it. Since the C.D. Leet cartridge was not as long as the French long and was longer than the usual French short, we called it 12mm medium for lack of a better name. The then unknown Ethan Allen was also of this medium length, so I guessed that it was of U.S. origin. To further inform myself I sectioned one of the

Right — A display of pinfire cartridges ranging from the small 5mm to 16 gauge. The collector of some knowledge will recognize pinfires in 7mm, 9mm, 12mm and 15mm as well as specimens in 360, 24 gauge and the very rare 58 caliber Gallager and Gladding.

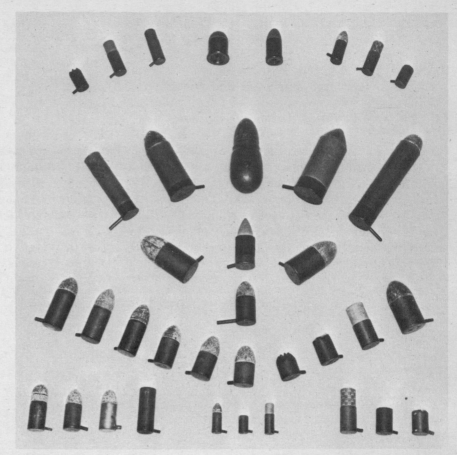

indented and the projecting pins are in effect flush with the base of the cartridge. You put them in a pistol of the right chambering, and the centerfire hammer hits the centrally located pin and there you have it.

Although I know of no pinfire firearms that were made in the United States, pinfire ammunition was manufactured by several concerns. The earliest of American pinfires were made during the Civil War. Not commonly known is the fact that the Union purchased 12,374 Lefaucheux revolvers during the Civil War period. I don't know if the government had trouble shipping in French ammunition for those revolvers or not, but I do know they contracted to have the cartridges manufactured in this country. There were two companies involved. The first was C.D. Leet of

unknown medium cartriges and discovered something of a surprise. Instead of the cartridge having the usual pasteboard wadding to support the percussion cap, there was a lead plug swaged into the base of the cartridge case. The lead plug had a neat little revetment that held the cap, and the pin came through the lead all the way to the far side of the case to where the cap was located. In spite of the fact that many years have passed and I keep grubbing around for more information, I have never found a patent that covered the feature of the lead plug.

The Ethan Allen "medium" pinfire ceased to be an unknown when I found a box of them down in Ohio. It was a black box with gold lettering, and plain as day it said "LEFAUCHEUX CARTRIDGES" and "ETHAN ALLEN WORCESTER, MASS."

I'm fairly sure that the C.D. Leet pinfires were made for the Civil War and I assumed that the Ethan Allen rounds came along at the same time. The Allen company went through several changes of name. Originally it was just "ETHAN ALLEN," then "ALLEN & COMPANY," and later "ALLEN & THURBER." Charles T. Thurber retired in 1857 and again the name was changed, this time to "ALLEN & WHEELOCK." Mr. Wheelock died in 1864 and Allen formed a partnership with two sons-in-law, Sullivan Forehand and H.C. Wadsworth, under the firm name of "ETHAN ALLEN & CO." Since the box of pinfires was marked as it was, it could not have come upon the scene until sometime in 1864.

For the purposes of this article I took one of the 12mm medium pinfires from a labeled C.D. Leet box and sectioned it. As suspected, it contained the lead plug in the base. The only difference between this one and the Allen round is that the percussion cap and the revetment for it are located in the center of the plug, so the pin does not have to reach to the far side of the case.

Because of this additional knowledge another search of the patent papers was made. I even reviewed the English patents, again to no avail. The English patents have not been covered in this article because they are either very minor improvements or merely repetitions of the French patents.

Getting back to the large photograph—the smallest pinfires in the bottom row are a ball load, a blank, and a shot load in 5mm size. The others in that same row are various loads—ball, blank, and shot—in the 9mm size.

The specimen below the Gallager and Gladding is the early Chadun Cartridge, and the one below that was from a box that stated "LONG PIN FOR CARBINES." We would assume from this that this was a somewhat more powerful load, to be used in a carbine with more metal around the chamber, and thus a longer pin was needed to be accessible to the hammer.

On the left of the line next to the bottom, the longer three cartridges are as follows. Far left, the 12mm long "H.B. PARIS." To the right, the 12mm medium by C.D. Leet, and then the 12mm medium by Ethan Allen. The Leet and Allen cartridges can easily be identified. The Leet round has a longer and more pointed bullet and a fairly heavy rolled crimp. I have never seen any of these last two with a headstamp. The odds are they were never made headstamped.

In the second row there are four different specimens that employ paper cases. I have heard people say that some jerk loaded a ball into a shotgun case, just to upset us cartridge collectors. Not true! I have handled three different pinfire rifles. One was a German rifle in 24 gauge, one was a double-barreled English pinfire rifle in 16 gauge, and one was a Belgian proofed double rifle in 360 caliber pinfire. The

Sectioned example of the "unknown" Ethan Allen "12mm Medium" (top), compared to a 12mm C.D. Leet pinfire. Note both have the lead plug in their base, but the cap is positioned differently.

360 pinfire cartridges that I have were manufactured by Ely Brothers, London.

The Union Metallic Cartridge Co. and the later familiar REM-UMC manufactured pinfire cartridges in this country for many years. There were even some to be found on hardware store shelves into the 1930s. Exactly when manufacture was discontinued I don't know. The specimens that I have taken from U.M.C. boxes have all had brass cases. Some were marked with a "U" and some were unmarked.

Every time I get on the subject of pinfires I can't help but get carried away. The more I learn about them, the more I realize that's an awful lot I have yet to learn. As a parting shot—anyone who has waded through this writing must be a kindred soul. •

Bibliography

Burnside, Graham
—"Lefaucheux Brevet" *The Gun Report* Feb. 1960.
—"Rare Box of Pinfires" *Shooting Times* Dec. 1961.
—"Pinfires" *Guns* Sept. 1963.
Gardner, Robert Edward *Five Centuries of Gunsmiths, Swordsmiths and Armourers 1400-1900.* Columbus, Ohio: 1948.
Lewis, Col. B.R. *Small Arms Ammunition in the United States Service.* Smithsonian Institution: 1956.
Thomas, H.H. *The Story of Allen & Wheelock Firearms.* Lexington, Ky.: 1965.
White, H.P. & Munhall, Burton D. *Cartridge Headstamp Guide.* Bel Air, Md.: 1963.
Personal Correspondence
   Robert Barincou, Paris, France.
   J.L. Brown, Liverpool, England.
   J.R. Clergeau, Saint-Palais-Sur-Mer, France.

The Bittner Pistol

by Joseph J. Schroeder

THE BITTNER is an example of a pistol whose time had passed before it arrived. A manually operated repeater, the Bittner is a member of a group of such designs that sprang up in the 1880-1890 period. With a patent date of 1893, however, the Bittner arrived (at best) in the market at the same time that the first successful self-loading pistols from Borchardt, Bergmann and Mauser were being introduced and was thus doomed to failure by their more advanced "automatic" operation.

Late as it was to appear, the Bittner was actually one of the more successful of its breed and is thus well worthy of further study for several reasons. For one thing it apparently worked well—while all too many of the repeaters that preceded it had complex mechanisms that required considerable muscle to operate with one hand, yet jammed frequently anyway. The Bittner's rotating bolt was smooth operating, yet was locked firmly closed at the moment of firing. Magazine and feed were another problem with many of Bittner's competitors, but for reasons that will be explained later the Bittner had a proven, reliable loading system.

Finally, Bittner had an extensive, well-established arms manufactory to make his pistol for him. The result is an arm that is very well made, elegantly finished and apparently achieved some commercial success (Bittners with serials well into the 400s have been observed). However, its popularity must have faded rapidly, as the special 7.7mm cartridge made for it by RWS in Nuremburg does not seem to appear in arms catalogues after the early 1900s.

Although 1893, the year it was patented, is given by most writers as the year the Bittner was introduced, it appears almost certain that the pistol didn't actually come on the market until several years later. Most Bittners bear Austrian proofs of the period, which were serial numbered and dated. The proof itself is on top of the chamber, the proof serial and date are stamped under the barrel, while the gun's serial number is stamped inside the action. The serial number of the gun illustrated in this article is 162; its *proof* serial (number of guns proofed in the Vejprty proof house at that point in the year) is 1688, and the year of proof 1897. The proof number, which appears on this pistol as "1688.97.", has often been mistaken for the *gun* serial, which it definitely is *not*.

Every Bittner that has thus far been examined has borne a Vejprty proof mark dated 1897. If that is indeed the year the Bittner was offered for sale, which seems likely, then it is no wonder that it never caught on. By 1897 not only the elaborate Borchardt but the Mauser 1896 and both 5mm and 6.5mm Bergmann pocket model self-loading pistols were being widely distributed. The Bittner may have been a good idea at its conception, and even when patented

Above — Bittner pistol with its Mannlicher system charger partially inserted into the magazine well. Note that, like some Mannlicher rifles, the charger goes in at an angle rather than vertically. Below — Bittner with the loaded charger completely inserted into the action. The end of the charger protrudes from the magazine well, and the magazine follower can be seen just in front of the charger.

Loaded Bittner charger compared with the charger for the 1895 Austrian army rifle. Other than size the two are very similar, showing their common Mannlicher heritage.

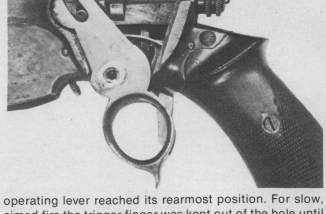

Detail of the Bittner action, open (left) and closed. The operating lever pulls the bolt forward, then cams it into rotation bringing the locking lug into engagement with the recess in the frame at the moment of firing. For rapid fire the shooter inserted his finger in the hole in the operating lever, automatically tripping the trigger when the operating lever reached its rearmost position. For slow, aimed fire the trigger finger was kept out of the hole until ready to fire, and the action was closed by the middle finger working against the stud on the bottom of the operating lever.

in 1893, but by 1897 that idea's time had passed.

Despite its relative lack of commercial success, a number of Bittners have survived and are found in collections today. The Bittner is a well known arm, but not so well known is its background and that of its inventor and maker.

Gustav Bittner was an industrialist residing in the arms making town of Vejprty (Weipert), Bohemia (now part of Czechoslovakia), who along with his brother Raimond founded a firm they named Gebrüder Bittner there in the 1850s. The Bittner family had a long tradition in the Vejprty arms industry. The first iron works in that city was established by Hans Bittner in 1630 to make gun barrels. The Bittners' firm produced parts for sporting arms, prospering and steadily expanding. When Austria adopted the Mannlicher repeating rifle in 1886, Steyr did not have sufficient manufacturing capacity to produce it, so some parts production was subcontracted. In 1887 the Bittners joined with others in Vejprty to form a new and larger company to produce trigger assemblies and other parts for the new arm.

Thus it was that Gustav Bittner had ample backing to support his new project, a repeating pistol. In addition, he also had one major advantage over his competitors in the repeating pistol market, a magazine system that worked. His firm was building components for the rifle that used what was probably the best magazine feed that had been developed up to that time, the Mannlicher clip feed. The feed system was so good that it had been adopted by the Austrian government in 1886!

Study the picture of the Bittner charger, rarer by far than the pistol that uses it, compared with a contemporary Mannlicher rifle charger. The two are essentially identical except for size, with a partially closed off bottom and a stud to retain it in the gun's magazine well on its back. In use, the loaded charger (correct end down!) is inserted into the top of the action and pushed down until it latches. When the action is operated the top cartridge is stripped from the charger, chambered and fired. When the fifth and last cartridge leaves the charger it (the charger) drops from the bottom of the action, making way for another loaded charger to be inserted. An elegant, reliable and efficient system, but one with (at least for Bittner) a fatal defect.

Without its special charger the Bittner cannot be loaded and operated as a repeater! It then becomes a single shot pistol, and not a particularly convenient one to use at that. The necessity for a charger was not much of a problem for the Austrian army's Mannlichers, since their ammunition was supplied in loaded chargers. For the individual who bought a Bittner pistol, which probably came supplied with no more than a handful of chargers, it quickly became a disaster. By the time he'd gone through a box or two of ammunition his chargers would have made a number of trips to the ground, where those that weren't lost were stepped on and put out of action. Unlike the Bergmann and Mauser magazines, which could be loaded with loose cartridges as well as with their chargers, the charger was a necessary part of the Bittner magazine. A Bittner repeater without a charger in it was no repeater at all!

A well-made, beautifully finished, smooth functioning and graceful arm that arrived too late and suffered from a fatal flaw. That is the fate of the Bittner, treasured by collectors today as a prime example of an evolutionary step in the development of repeating arms. ●

400 Years of Airgun Tradition

by Robert Beeman

MANY GUN ENTHUSIASTS are quite unaware that the airgun has a rich and varied history extending back at least 400 years. In the 20th century, since the widespread use of the metallic cartridge, the airgun in America largely has been relegated to its well-known role as a gun for youth. However, the recent trend to the serious use of precision airguns by adults was preceded by centuries of such use in Europe.

European airguns, often made in calibers and power sufficient for large game hunting, were always rather uncommon and generally restricted to the most affluent of sportsmen because of the scarcity of gun makers that could produce suitable valves and air reservoirs. Very few of these truly antique airguns are available today but the modern collector can find delight in the great variety of 20th century airguns. Many of these vintage guns still turn up at gun shows and other places at prices well below what they will probably command as airgun collecting becomes more widespread.

The guns illustrated in this article are from the collection of Robert and Toshiko Beeman. They would be pleased to learn of other vintage airguns which are available for sale or study. They may be contacted in care of Beeman Precision Airguns, 47 Paul Drive, San Rafael, California 94903.

1. KUCHENREUTER DUELING-TYPE AIR PISTOL. Very few experts on antique guns realize that an airgun was made by the famous Kuchenreuter gun-making family. This 30 caliber spring-piston airgun was clearly built to duplicate a dueling pistol in balance and appearance. The external lock and the spring are of flintlock type but instead of flint clamps, the hammer tip is pivoted to a plunger which acts as an air piston when the trigger is released. The compression force comes from a conventional external V-spring. The piston chamber is a brass cylinder fitted into the top of the gun just forward of the lock. One loads the gun by sliding the barrel forward from the air piston chamber. The barrel is marked "J. Adam Kuchenreuter," a maker who was reported to have worked in Regensburg, Germany about 1830.

2. BIG GAME/UPLAND BIRD AIRGUN BY T.M. MORTIMER OF ENGLAND. In the early 1800s, when this unusually handsome gun was made, airguns generally could be afforded only by the rich and landed gentry. Such guns were very difficult to build and required unusual craftsmanship in the valve mechanism. Few antique gun collectors realize that the famous Mortimer gun makers ever made any air rifles, but the engraving on the sideplate and other parts of this specimen makes its origin very clear. This gun has faucet type breech loading and comes with two interchangeable barrels, an octagonal rifle barrel about 40 caliber and a smooth bore barrel about 36 gauge. "Makers to His Majesty" is inlaid with gold on the top of each barrel. Note the ring around the wrist of the pistol grip: the buttstock, beautifully covered in pigskin, is actually a steel air reservoir. This buttstock tank unscrews at this point for attachment to an air pump to take a charge of air which would be good for perhaps 20 shots. Power may equal that of a modern 44 Magnum firearm.

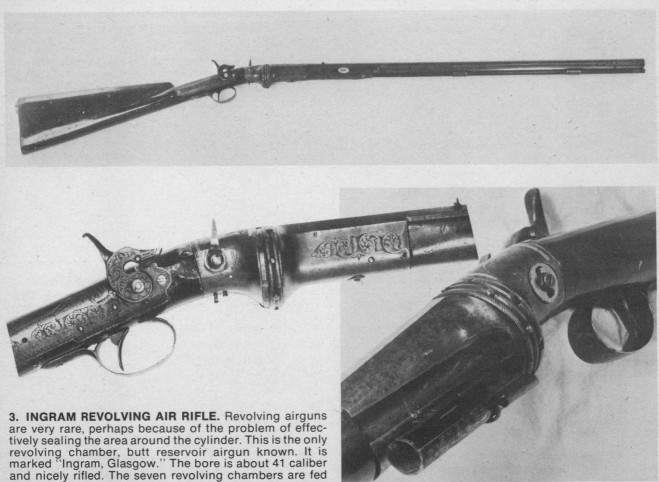

3. INGRAM REVOLVING AIR RIFLE. Revolving airguns are very rare, perhaps because of the problem of effectively sealing the area around the cylinder. This is the only revolving chamber, butt reservoir airgun known. It is marked "Ingram, Glasgow." The bore is about 41 caliber and nicely rifled. The seven revolving chambers are fed from a magazine tube on the left side which can contain another seven balls in reserve. A plug in the buttplate area unscrews to accept an air pump.

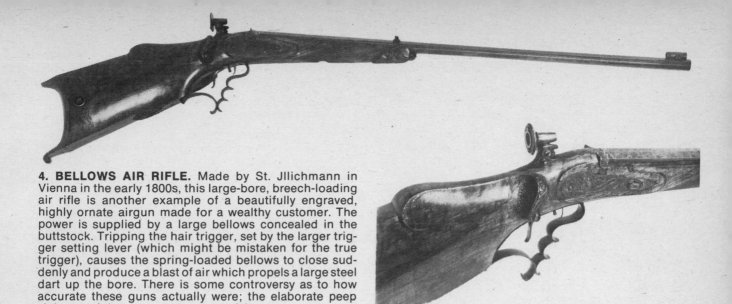

4. BELLOWS AIR RIFLE. Made by St. Jllichmann in Vienna in the early 1800s, this large-bore, breech-loading air rifle is another example of a beautifully engraved, highly ornate airgun made for a wealthy customer. The power is supplied by a large bellows concealed in the buttstock. Tripping the hair trigger, set by the larger trigger setting lever (which might be mistaken for the true trigger), causes the spring-loaded bellows to close suddenly and produce a blast of air which propels a large steel dart up the bore. There is some controversy as to how accurate these guns actually were; the elaborate peep sight certainly suggests great precision.

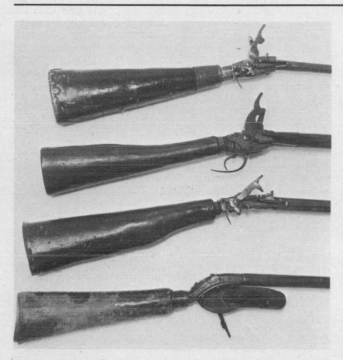

5. EXTERNAL LOCK AIRGUNS is a class of antique airguns that is really rather poorly understood even by specialty collectors. All had butt reservoirs which unscrewed, at the wrist behind the lock mechanism, to accept a separate hand pump. The barrels were quite long, usually over 3 feet. The barrel on the second specimen from the top of this group is made of hardwood! Considering the low pressure and lack of burning powder, a well built, smooth bore, wooden barrel is not at all out of reason.

Most such guns were muzzleloaders but the bottom one has, among its unusual features, a sliding block which can be seen on the curvature of the receiver. The simple block may be pivoted out of the way with the thumb to load this gun from the breech. External lock airguns are extremely rare, but their value is seldom appreciated by the very occasional sellers.

6. THE WONDERFUL GIFFARDS. Paul Giffard was one of the most productive of the late 19th century French inventors. He invented such things as the pneumatic tubes that were used to handle change and messages in department stores, and was an avid hot-air balloonist. He started into air and gas guns with compressed air rifles such as the one shown at the top. He then extended the idea of the removable air cylinder to the use of carbon dioxide (second rifle down). Each cylinder was capable of several hundred shots. The 6mm version of this arm was touted as the weapon which would end all wars. The elegant construction and elaborate engraving stood in considerable contrast to the First Model Daisy that was introduced almost simultaneously across the ocean in the United States.

The bottom gun is a particularly fine specimen of the Giffard pistol, which is a mate to the second rifle. The bottom rifle is what the Giffard gas rifle looked like after it migrated to England, where it was produced in a hammerless underlever version featuring an octagonal barrel and a built-in shot counter. Giffard also produced a pneumatic rifle with a built-in bicycle type air pump. It was that model that was probably the inspiration for the development of the Crosman air rifles in the United States.

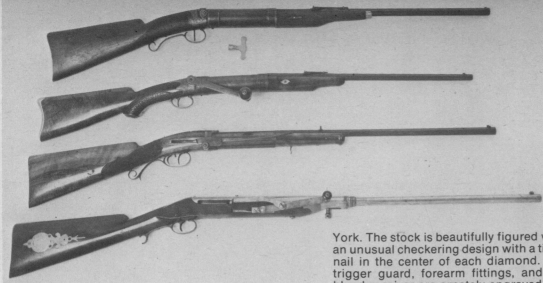

7. GALLERY AIR RIFLES were popular in the United States after the Civil War. These massive, often beautifully built, weapons were usually made in New England, New York, or St. Louis by immigrant European gun makers. All featured a huge double volute spring in a large cylinder in the center of the gun. A variety of ingenious mechanisms provided breech loading. The top rifle, made by Lurch, was cranked by means of the T-shaped key which was used to turn the cocking lug until the sear engaged.

Later versions of the "Primary New York Gallery Gun" used a large crank handle which could be inserted into a ratchet mechanism of the receiver and then removed when the cocking was complete. This system is shown on the second rifle down made by G. Schmaelzlein in New York. The stock is beautifully figured walnut and features an unusual checkering design with a tiny decorative silver nail in the center of each diamond. The German silver trigger guard, forearm fittings, and buttplate and the blued receiver are ornately engraved.

The third rifle is an as yet unclassified gallery gun with no markings to indicate its maker—its construction suggests the New England area. This is obviously from a late stage of the evolution of the gallery guns; a permanent lever on the right side is pulled back to cock the spring. The gun is beautifully made; its stock features an excellent grade of walnut and is finely checkered. The double set triggers attest to precision use.

The bottom rifle is the "New England type Gallery Gun." It too has a permanent cocking lever on the right side, though its design is not as sophisticated as the rifle above it. The barrel twists to open the breech in a most unusual manner. The purpose of the patch box in the buttstock is not clear.

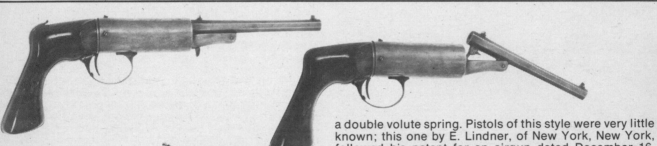

8. GALLERY AIR PISTOL. Heavy, beautifully made air rifles for the popular sport of gallery shooting were made by a number of makers after the American Civil War. A central receiver contains a massive air piston powered by a double volute spring. Pistols of this style were very little known; this one by E. Lindner, of New York, New York, followed his patent for an airgun dated December 16, 1862. It has the usual tip-down barrel of the St. Louis type of gallery airguns. The cocking lever is quite unique in that it wraps all the way around the grip. The first part of this articulated lever is shown in the open position. The rest of the lever is hidden in the front of the grip and is pivoted behind the trigger guard.

9. THE ANCESTOR OF THE GALLERY RIFLES OF AMERICA? This antique spring piston air rifle was made by Rutte in Lieppa of Bohemia about 1830. A 26 caliber rifle, it is powered by a powerful double volute spring and apparently was cocked by a large separate cocking lever which fitted into the hole covered by the circular disc on the right side of the receiver. The metal work is inlaid with silver, and the stock is delicately inlaid in a most unusual manner with contrasting light wood strips in the style of the more easily produced pinned brass scroll inlays popular in furniture of that period. The pistol grip is a carved representation of a bird's head. Silver nailheads serve as the eyes of the bird and also decorate the entire pistol grip area. Much to the delight and surprise of the author, he obtained a matching air pistol years later and thousands of miles from the original purchase of this rifle.

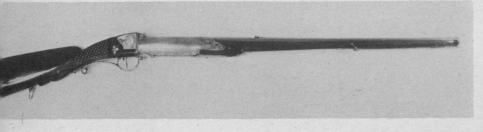

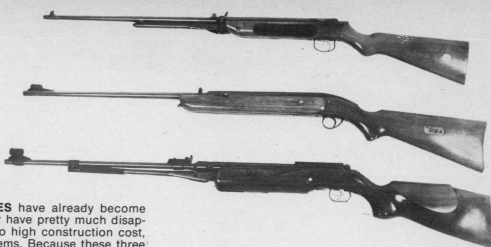

10. UNDERLEVER AIR RIFLES have already become collector's items because they have pretty much disappeared from the market due to high construction cost, performance and repair problems. Because these three models have been off the market for a decade or less, you still have a good chance of locating good specimens.

1) The slimmest and trimmest of all of them is the Webley Mark III (top), which is graced by a lovely tapered barrel.

2) The BSA Airsporter (middle illustration) is intriguing in that pulling down the hidden cocking lever also automatically rotates the loading port into the open position. This, the Mark I version, is the most desirable model and is distinguished by a tapered barrel, a three-piece laminated stock and a plug in the base of the piston grip cap which hides the stock bolt. Later versions, which have many plastic parts, are much less valuable and generally to be avoided.

3) The BSF S54 is probably the sturdiest, most massive underlever rifle ever built and one of the author's favorites. This is the most desirable Match version, with a handsome solid cast aluminum buttplate and beautiful metal checkering on the cocking lever.

11. TWO WEBLEY CLASSICS. Both of these use the classic Webley cocking mechanism as found on their Tempest and Hurricane pistols. The Webley Mark I air rifle (above) was only produced for about 3 years before 1929 and must be considered rare. The Webley Service Mark II air rifle (below) an extremely robust power design, is much sought after. An especially interesting feature is the quick interchangeability of barrels. A cased set containing 177, 22, and 25 caliber barrels is one of the great prizes of the airgun collecting field. There are a number of variations.

12. VINTAGE AIR PISTOLS. The Apache air pistol (top illustration) is even less common than the Apache air rifle. These guns, made in Pasadena, California, appeared and disappeared from the market quite suddenly. They feature a 25 caliber barrel with a 177 caliber insert. The Plainsman pneumatic pistol (middle illustration) and the Plainsman CO_2 pistol are massive, very well built items. Both are uncommon and much to be sought by collectors.

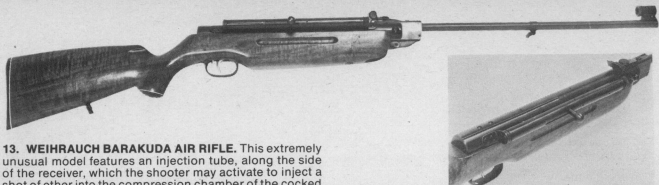

13. WEIHRAUCH BARAKUDA AIR RIFLE. This extremely unusual model features an injection tube, along the side of the receiver, which the shooter may activate to inject a shot of ether into the compression chamber of the cocked gun. Release of the piston then causes a powerful diesel effect which can boost velocities of the extremely heavy 22 caliber pellet (22 grains) to velocities reportedly near 1,000 fps. Ether is not a safe substance to handle and is very hard on seals so the gun was discontinued rather promptly. This specimen was specially assembled at the factory for the author after regular production had ceased and features an unusually select, highly figured French walnut stock.

14. BROWN PNEUMATIC AIR PISTOL. The Brown pneumatic air pistols are among the most beautifully made and most unusual of all American airguns. These single shot pistols were built by an engineer named O.H. Brown of Davenport, Iowa. Their beautiful construction and short commercial life indicates that they were more works of the design engineer and machinist's art than accompanied by a letter from the maker, written during WWII, in which he hopes that $2 is not too great a charge for having repaired the pistol. They were made in 22 caliber only because the maker felt that they were useful for both target and game shooting. Apparently these guns were not marked with the maker's name or with serial numbers, but the shape is unmistakable.

production guns. The pump handle which protrudes from the rear of the receiver activates a unique pump which compresses air on both in and out strokes.

These guns were made in only two versions, this being the short one with a barrel 7½ inches long! The barrel on the long version was 10 inches long for an overall length of 19½ inches. They were listed in the 1939 Stoeger Arms catalog for $12 and $20 respectively. This specimen is

15. PROTOTYPE OF THE DAISY "COLT PEACEMAKER" REVOLVER. This is an extremely rare handmade, heavy brass and walnut prototype specimen. The only mark is #22 on the butt. The factory itself would be fortunate to have such a specimen. It's beautifully made and very heavy.

16. SPECIAL CROSMAN 38T CO$_2$ REVOLVER. This double action copy of the standard police revolver was made by the tens of thousands, but it is reported that only ten factory chrome-plated specimens like this exist. They would well be worth watching for at gun shows, but fakes are entirely possible.

17. MILITARY STYLE CO$_2$ PISTOL. The Crosman 451, a semi-automatic gas pistol, is actually a six-shot revolver with a horizontal cylinder. Built to look and handle exactly like the Colt 45 automatic, this is one of the rarest production airguns. Only 10,000 of them were made between 1969 and 1970. A quarter of a million or more was not an unusual number for other models. A very worthwhile collector's item that may well turn up at gun shows.

18. WEBLEY HAWK AIR RIFLE WITH INTERCHANGE-ABLE 177 AND 22 CALIBER BARRELS. Imported by Beeman Precision Airguns for only a few months, this model was discontinued quickly because of manufacturing expense. Because of the interchangeable barrel feature, it is still much sought after by airgun collectors and those who enjoy using the guns that they gather.

19. ABAS MAJOR AND ACVOKE AIR PISTOLS. These air pistols were produced in England between the World Wars. They are undoubtedly among the heaviest and most beautifully built air pistols ever to come out of England. The barrel serves as an internal guide for a concentric piston which moves to the rear during the compression stroke. This unusual design was the stimulus for the development of the American Hy-Score pistol. In fact, these particular pistols came out of the Hy-Score factory collection. The value of any vintage airgun is increased by the presence of its original container and accessories—such items should be retained and treated with great care. ●

WHILE MANY of the dates and details of the development of the M1898 Rifle by the Mauser Company have been well documented by noted scholars in the field of German Arms, a distinct silence seems to surround the origin of the K98k. One authoritative English language source simply remarks that it was "in use by 1935." If the design of this widely made and used arm, of which millions were manufactured between 1934 and 1945, had been in response to an official German Army requirement, then in spite of the destruction of the end of the war period one could be certain that we would have definite, documented dates of that Army requirement and of official adoption. But like so many other important facts of the early National Socialist regime, we are once again faced by something we know to have occurred, without easily obtainable details as to *how* and *why* it occurred.

rate fire to be brought onto close-order infantry formations at ranges up to 2,000 Meters. The supposition that such sights are impossibly optimistic, designed to hit a single individual at such ranges, merely indicates that the "supposer" does not understand what such sights were intended to do. Secondly, the prewar tactical theorist believed the charge of enemy infantry would be repelled at close quarters, and then the length of the rifle with bayonet attached would be of crucial practical and psychological importance in what would be, in effect, a Twentieth Century duel with spears.

The battles of 1914-1918 rapidly changed such concepts. Any army that charged in neat mass formations left less-neat masses of corpses in profusion, mowed down with mechanical precision by high vol-

The Wehrmacht's Rifles

A German army Kar 98k rifle of very late World War II vintage.

Mauser's Karabiner 98K

by **OTTO H. VON LOSSNITZER**
as told to **LESLIE E. FIELD**

To have any explanation at all, we will have to rely on the recollections of those who were close observers of events at the time, in the right vantage points to make proper observations, and to coordinate their personal testimony with the more general ordnance history of the time.

The first fact to remember is the change in functional importance of rifles in the minds of the German military resulting from the events of the First World War. At the commencement of that war, the infantry regiments of the German Army, and all other armies, primarily relied on rapid mass rifle fire to force their enemies to break out of close, tightly packed formation so that the much-feared Napoleonic rapid charge might be prevented. For this reason, the G98 was provided with a rear sight which would permit accu-

ume machine-gun fire before the defenders were even clearly visible to the attackers, in most cases. The machine gun became the central weapon of infantry combat in the German Army; the infantry squad was organized around it, and all members of that squad not actively engaged in its use were provided only to direct it, to assist it, or to carry ammunition for it.

At the same time, the German sweep across France in 1914, and other circumstances, persuaded the German general staff that the infantryman marching enormous distances to battle, or in battle, was now going to be a less-common occurrence in warfare in central Europe, the German Army's chief concern. The Germans observed that both the United States and Great Britain had adopted so-called "short rifles," equivalent to the German K98—a cavalry carbine with a barrel about 600mm long and a lightened, and thus weakened, receiver—in handling qualities, and with them achieved adequate battle results. Bayonet fighting became of minor importance; by the time one was close enough to use a bayonet the enemy had fled, or one was better advised to employ grenades or pistols, or—in the last days of 1918—the newly-developed machine pistol (submachine gun).

The result was that the soldier needed a shorter, handier rifle, convenient to riding in a truck or railroad car, and its length and fearsomeness for bayonet combat mattered little. In addition, two problems with G98 sights had been revealed in battle, and the German Army worked on both in a new rear sight design. These were, first, the burning heat of the sight parts when rapid fire had put many calories into the chamber area of the barrel where the rear sight was located. The second was that the sight graduations were in too coarse increments at the closer ranges.

Obviously, burned fingers while adjusting sights improve no army's effectiveness or morale, but the second problem is a little less obvious. Trench warfare had created its own unique needs. Often marksmen wanted to accurately hit an aperture in the enemy's trench wall from which a particularly pestiferous and casualty-causing observer was operating. The Germans discovered, to their dismay, that 100-meter sight adjustments did not offer sufficient resolution to permit them to hit such small targets with the older type of G98 sights. Something better was called for, so the new rear sight should have 50-meter adjustments.

However, other than limited production of a rifle known as K98b (a G98 with turned down bolt handle and an improved rear sight), none of the above had resulted in a more modern German army rifle by 1928. The exquisitely skilled "100,000 man army" created by General von Seekt and his associates carried a rifle not substantially different from that carried in August, 1914, by the Kaiser's men invading Belgium. As a matter of fact, it was probably one of the same rifles, except for the sights. The supply of G98s left over from the war was more than adequate for the army Germany was permitted by the Versailles Treaty. As far as most sources can discover, *no* new military rifles were made for army use in the decade after the war. There was not even a require-

Two Bolivian army soldiers on jungle patrol armed with Czech Vz24 short rifles in 7.65mm Mauser caliber, ca. 1935.

ment for one, at least not as a high-priority item. Much more effort was expended to develop a better light machine gun to replace the complex and heavy MG 08/15, which was interdicted by certain provisions of the Versailles Treaty.

The "Machine-Gun Worshippers," as they were known in German military circles, demanded a new, highly maneuverable, belt-fed gun, preferably air-cooled, so as not to contravene the Versailles Treaty. This required the development of quick-change barrel systems, and imposed severe problems for a country in which armaments research was supposed to be largely taboo. But, said General von Seekt, "If we can't have a general staff, no one can prevent us from starting a joint stock company for the same purposes." In the same spirit, covert research on small arms was not abandoned by the Mauser Company, and as is often the case, the research was the efforts of a few men, without much official knowledge or encouragement.

At this time Otto von Lossnitzer was an officer

Standard German army Gew 98 rifle of World War I vintage.

Very late WW I G98 rifle with the improved post-war type rear sight.

Side by side comparison of the improved G98 sight (above) and the original.

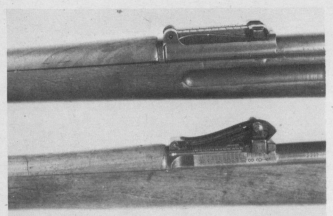

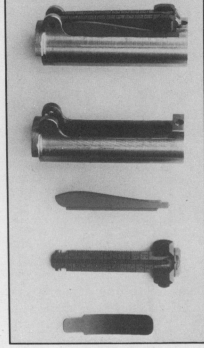

Detail of the improved G98 rear sight and mounting sleeve. The ramp may be changed to allow for cartridges with different trajectories.

attached to the I.W.G., the "Inspection fur Waffen und Gerat," the tactfully named weapons research and development office for the German Army. There he observed the development of the K98 as it progressed at the time, to the extent it was known to the military authorities. Later he learned more details after he joined the Mauser Werke management in 1933.

The Mauser Company had considered various types of improved military rifles as early as 1917. At least two concepts had been realized in prototype form before the end of the war. Nonetheless, no improvement was worth the burden that a major change in the design of service rifles would have imposed on Germany in a period of crisis such as 1914-18, so the G98 and K98 continued to be made much as they had been in 1914. The result was that Mauser never could get permission to retool and commence production of either the simplified 98-type rifle it had designed or the prototype "Trench Rifle."

The ending of the war by the Versailles Treaty put the Mauser Company in the position of being forbidden to produce *any* military rifles, so new designs and retooling were inhibited on that account. At the same time, conditions of the postwar situation caused Mauser to send much of its older production machinery to Czechoslovakia, where an interesting development was about to occur.

The high command of that infant Republic felt it-

self beset on all sides by powerful and implacable enemies, so one of the first national priorities was to adopt and issue a uniform type of service rifle of the best possible design. The outcome, in 1923, was a rifle of 8mm German caliber with a mechanism essentially interchangeable with the G98, a barrel length of about 600mm (24″), and important modifications in the sights, stock and furniture. The design was then slightly changed, resulting in the model of 1924, an immediate success not only in Czechoslovakia, but in a growing export trade to South America and China.

At the close of the war, the Fabrique Nationale in Liege, Belgium, had also embarked on a program of producing Mauser 1898 system rifles for export in competition with the Czechs for the military markets Germany was now forbidden to supply. This commenced with the models of 1922 (generally confused with the Model 1924). After producing the 1922 models for Mexico and others, F.N. announced its own model of 1924, which also boasted the combination of the 98 type action combined with a 600mm barrel and improved sights and fittings.

None of this success was lost on the gentlemen in Oberndorf, who were now back in the military rifle business on a quiet basis. The key to this was a factory making underwear in Kreuzlingen, Switzerland. As Mr. von Lossnitzer recalls, the product line was diverse: "Men's underwear from the first floor; ladies' underwear from the second floor. And Mauser rifles from the basement." By the late 1920s, Chinese warlords were coming to both Kreuzlingen and Oberndorf to buy Mauser military pistols and new rifles. The caliber generally selected by the Chinese was the same as the German service caliber, although some carbines were supplied in 7mm as well.

Undoubtedly, some Chinese customer asked the German factory for a "1924 type" short rifle about this time, but the name of that originator is now lost to us. However, we do know that Mauser had the services of two designers during this period, Engineer Nickl for pistols, and Herr Hauser designing sporting rifles. Mr. von Lossnitzer believes it is almost certain that Mr. Hauser designed the first Mauser export short rifle upon the request of Director Zwillinger, who had the responsibility of keeping Mauser's plant going during this difficult period. At any rate, it was known that Mauser was delivering short rifles to China, both to the National Government and to the independent warlords, by the dawn of the 30s. Powerful inferences as to the form of such rifles can be drawn from the examination of later Chinese specimens and from the rifles supplied to Paraguay as the "Modelo 1932."

In both cases, the rifle has an action dimensionally equivalent to the G98 (and the later K98k) and a 600mm barrel. The stocks are the same in profile as later K98k type rifles, and the sole differences are retention of the G98's straight bolt handle and the cross-pin retained front band. The Chinese rifles are all 8mm caliber, and the Paraguayans are in 7.65mm Mauser caliber, the national caliber in that country, as well as in Argentina, Peru and Bolivia. In 1933, the Oberndorf factory executed a contract for similar rifles in 8mm for Ethiopia, and in 1934, a second. Both were for rifles of the previously established pattern; sometime in this period Mauser also produced 7mm rifles of the same specification for Honduras.

But, meanwhile, there came (at last) some evidence of official German government interest in this pattern of rifle, if from a rather unlikely source. The Reichspost, the German Post Office Department, had

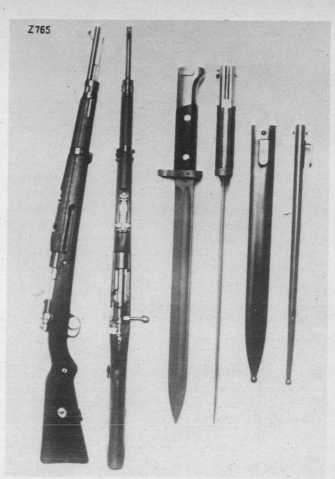

Czech Model Vz24 short rifle, one of the earliest types of short Mauser military rifles with a 600mm barrel. The original factory photo also shows the original bayonet and scabbard.

followed Mauser's Chinese and Paraguayan developments with interest. To help prevent mail robberies, an increasingly popular criminal amusement of that period, in 1933 they accepted delivery of the *Reichspost Rifle*, a close twin of the earlier examples, in the national caliber. When Mauser prepared a briefing memorandum for Otto von Lossnitzer on the

Ethiopian contract rifle of the 1933 series. (Inset) With the elaborate Ethiopian crest on the receiver ring, the Mauser banner has been moved to the rear ring. The three digit serial number begins with "A" and the action bears commercial German proofs.

Ethiopian contract rifle of the 1935 series. (Inset) The Mauser banner is in the normal spot on the receiver ring, while the Ethiopian lion is on the barrel behind the rear sight. Receiver is marked "STANDARD MODELL 1924" on the side, the ring is dated 1934, and the action and barrel are commercially proofed. The five digit serial begins with a "B." The Ethiopian markings on the side of the receiver ring were later additions.

occasion of his first reception in Oberndorf for his old Army I.W.G. friends to see Mauser small arms, the Reichspost Rifle received important mention. After all, it was *the* modern service rifle development that Mauser was immediately prepared to produce. Von Lossnitzer recalls:

At the end of the (Mauser briefing) memo, Mauser standard rifle and the Mauser rifle for the German Post Office are listed. The Mauser Standard Modell rifle was only made for export (mostly China), and looked like the old German M98 rifle but with a shorter barrel. All the countries outside of Germany had only the S-cartridge. Therefore, the sight for this rifle had to be adjusted for this ammunition. The loading handle of the bolt on this rifle stuck out to the side.

The Mauser Rifle for the German Post Office was a K98k. It had a shorter barrel than the G98, its sight was as for the new German sS cartridge which was already standard in the German Army. The loading handle on the bolt was bent down and the rifle sling was that typical for carbines. The German Post Office had organized a security force which had to guard post offices and the postal railroad cars during riots. The armament of this security force was an official act of the German government. The postal service, therefore, preferred a rifle which was identical to what the army would require for future armament. By the way, the Mauser rifle for the German Postal Service was, within the Mauser Works, a camouflage name for all the rifles which were delivered to political formations like SA and SS.

Persuasion for the army to buy this new development did not spring entirely from military considerations, however. Adolf Hitler and his Nazis had come to power, and with them, the legions of the Sturm Abteilung. The S.A. (Storm Troops) were now dominant in the country. The leader of the S.A. was the very able and unconventional Ernst Roehm, who was no admirer of old guard attitudes, especially in the army. Roehm coveted the post of Defense Minis-

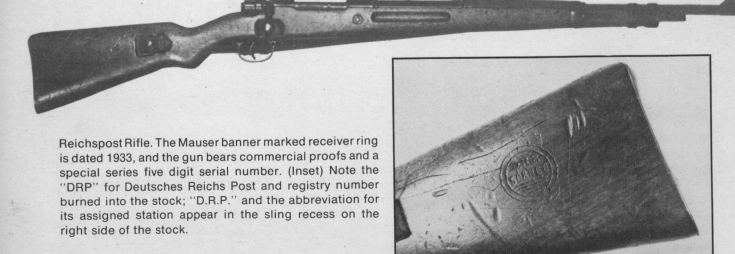

Reichspost Rifle. The Mauser banner marked receiver ring is dated 1933, and the gun bears commercial proofs and a special series five digit serial number. (Inset) Note the "DRP" for Deutsches Reichs Post and registry number burned into the stock; "D.R.P." and the abbreviation for its assigned station appear in the sling recess on the right side of the stock.

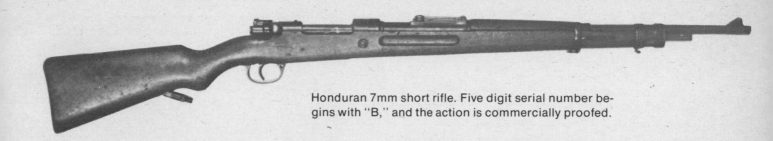

Honduran 7mm short rifle. Five digit serial number begins with "B," and the action is commercially proofed.

ter, with an eventual goal of taking over von Seekt's miniscule but brilliantly-trained 100,000 man army and submerging it in the two millions of his SA men, which by comparison was nothing more than a uniformed mob. Roehm had the ambition of reforming both German society and its army, by ending the aristocratic tradition and creating a vast Militia-Army and the semi-socialist state promised by the designation of the Nazi Party as both "National" and "Socialist."

Roehm's subordinates, either with his knowledge or by his active encouragement, had started to buy military weapons *after* Hitler was already in office and presumably in control of all the levers of power in Germany. This the Army discovered and set out to prevent. Otto von Lossnitzer recollects:

When you resign from a position as I had in the German Army Ordnance, you are entitled to an official farewell party which was usually held during the last days of your service. Due to reasons unknown to me, this was not possible by the end of September, 1933, so my farewell party was held in the big mess hall of the Army Ordnance Directorate shortly after the time I had received the memorandum in question from Mr. Premauer. I attended the party in Berlin and during the festivities General von Bockelberg approached me and asked if I would have one of his favorite drinks, a "Schneegestoeber" (the best translation is "blizzard"). This, by the way, is a terrible drink which went right to your head, but it was considered to be one of the high honors and one had to suffer for it. At this occasion the General talked to me and explained his problems and his objectives, and I think I gave him the simplest answer which he needed to solve the entire affair. I told him that if the Army Ordnance with official orders would simply buy the entire rifle production capacity of Mauser this would be the best solution for both parties. He understood that fully. Of course, such an action, like everything in a government office, required some time to execute, but it finally came about exactly as I had suggested it. Based on that discussion in Berlin, the visit of the Chief of the Army Ordnance Directorate was cancelled.

By mid-1933 therefore, the Mauser Werke had diverted the production of its new military rifle from the S.A. to the Army, leaving none from that source for the S.A. to buy. It is ironic that one of the reports which Heydrich is alleged to have forwarded to Hitler, which was to tip the scales of Hitler's judgment against Roehm in 1934, was that the S.A., under Roehm, was buying military rifles and machine guns

Very late Chinese contract rifle. No commercial proofs or markings other than the Mauser banner. (Inset) The Kuomintang symbol on receiver ring and barrel probably serves as both proof and property marking.

in Belgium for delivery to S.A. formations in Germany; this in direct defiance of Hitler's edict that, "The Army shall be the sole arms-bearer of the German nation." Hitler's decision resulted in the executions carried out in the "Night of Long Knives" of 1934. Those killed included Roehm and all of his handpicked S.A. leaders, including a number of Hitler's party comrades from the earliest days of his political career.

In its early procurement of the new rifle the Waffenamt had prescribed certain minor improvements in Mauser's design. The bolt handle was turned down, and the system of securing the bands was changed. The improved, wider sling band was used, and the sling placed the rifle flat, bolt handle out, against the soldier's back, without any sling swivels on the toe of the stock. But, in basic form the weapon differed only slightly from rifles shipped to Chinese soldiers 5 years earlier. The Second World War emerges as a paradox in that it isn't clear whether the Germans or the Chinese carried more of the K98 rifles into battle. In any event, the story of the K98k has as broad a cast of characters and as colorful a series of incidents as any collector of historical arms could desire.

Comparison of the K98k barrel bands (left) with the transitional type. Note the thin sling ring and pinned in front ring on the earlier rifle.

Bibliography

LA DEFENSA DEL CHACO by Angel F. Rios (1950) published by Editorial Ayacucho - Buenos Aires, Argentina. Approximately 500 pages, in Spanish. See pages 48, 60, 168. A detailed history of armament in the Chaco War. Above references are to 1932 model rifles.

CESKOLOVENSKI RUCNI PALNE ZBRANE A KULOMETY (Czechoslovak Small Arms & Machine Guns) by Col. Dr. Miroslav Sada (1971) published by Nase Vojsko, Prague, Czechoslovakia. Approximately 308 pages, in Czech. See Chapter 4 "Pusky a bodaky" on bolt-action rifles, detailing development from the founding of the Republic to the present. Shows predecessors and development of Vz24.

GESCHICHTE der MAUSER WERKE by Dr.-Ing. E.h.C. Matschoss, et al (1938). VDI-Verlag G.M.B.H., Berlin, Germany, 230 pages in German. Many good large photographs of the manufacture of K98k type rifles in the period before World War II commenced.

EL FUSIL UNIFORME SYSTEMA STEYR-SOLOTHURN M.31. (Anonymous—in Spanish and German. Date unknown but believed to be late 1931.) 9 pages of text and appendices, 4 plates, including those of the M.31a, which has unique features like Manchukuo Mauser. Believed to be a company sales brochure for the Steyr-Solothurn rifles of the period, published in very limited quantities. Discusses rear sight problem and its solution.

Unpublished letters and book manuscript of Otto H. von Lossnitzer (1974 to present). In English, about 500 pages. A detailed history of the Mauser Werke in the period 1933-45, with special depth in the areas of aircraft armament and machine guns developed by Mauser during this period. Details visit of Mme. Chiang to Oberndorf and 1933 conference in which the army order to exclude purchases by the S.A. was set up, as well as colorful detail on Ethiopian contract, and Iranian rifle contract lost by Mauser through activities of a Nazi party zealot.

NIGHT OF THE LONG KNIVES by Nikolai Tolstoy (1972) published by Ballantine Books, Inc., New York, N.Y. in English. Heavily illustrated paperback detailing rivalry between the S.A. and the Army. Strong portrayal of events and personalities. No direct material, except for S.A. in training, using transitional rifles, at page 56.

THE NIGHT OF LONG KNIVES by Max Gallo (1972) published by Harper & Row, New York, N.Y., etc. 310 pages, translated into English from the French original edition. Attempt to form an hour-by-hour synopsis of the events leading to, and following, June 30, 1934 in which Roehm and his subordinates were killed on Hitler's order. Little direct material, but has discussion of alleged arms deliveries to the S.A. from Belgium at pages 102 and 103.

WALTHER & MANURHIN

The Story of the Postwar PP and PPK Pistols

by JAMES RANKIN

AFTER World War II ended in Europe in 1945, the town of Zella-Mehlis, Germany—where the great arms firm of Carl Walther was located—was in the hands of the American forces. Fritz Walther remained in Zella-Mehlis during the American occupation, but when Germany was divided between the occupying forces giving Zella-Mehlis and Waffenfabrik Walther facilities to the Russians, Fritz Walther moved into the American Zone. Upon taking over Zella-Mehlis the Russians moved into the Walther plant, dismantled it, and sent most of the equipment to East Germany and the Soviet Union. Thus Fritz Walther's world-renowned arms business was completely wiped out.

But the 57-year-old Walther still retained patent rights to his arms and, by adroitly using these rights, was soon back in the arms business with two respected arms companies in two other countries. One of these companies was the French firm, Manufacture De Machines du Haut-Rhin, known as Manurhin, and the other, Hammerli in Switzerland, which still makes target 22 pistols based on Walther patents.

The Manurhin Company is located at Mulhouse-Bourtzwiller in Haut-Rhin Province, France. For nearly 10 years the Manurhin Company manufactured Walther Models PP and PPK, and a 22 caliber target and sporter version of the Model PP, under Walther's license.

The Manurhin firm and Fritz Walther began their mutually profitable relationship in 1950 when Fritz Walther contracted with Manurhin to use his patent rights to manufacture the Models PP and PPK. These Manurhin pistols were like the pre-war Walther pistols in almost every way, except for minor mechanical changes in the 380 caliber models and, of course, external markings on the pistols and their grips. There were really no differences from the original Models PP and PPK in 22 and 32 caliber manufactured at Zella-Mehlis and the new ones manufactured at Mulhouse in France except for markings.

The Manurhin Walthers in 380 caliber had the identical external markings as the other Manurhins, but now incorporated the same push-button magazine release behind the triggerguard that was used for the 22 and 32 pistols. The original Walther-made Models PP and PPK in 380 had the magazine release catch placed at the rear bottom of the butt, but when Manurhin began to manufacture the Models PP and PPK they produced all calibers with the same button magazine release so as to use a common frame. Manurhin did not produce a 25 caliber Model PP or PPK as had the Walther Company in the early 1930s. They did manufacture some Model PPK pistols in 22

Manurhin Model PP, Caliber 22.

Manurhin Model PPK, Caliber 9mm kurz.

Manurhin Model PP Sport, Caliber 22 LR, 6-inch barrel. Reversed eagle beak grips and knurled locking nut at the muzzle.

and 32 caliber with duraluminum frames, however.

The external markings on the Manurhin pistols showed the full name of the company, **Manufacture De Machines du Haut-Rhin,** on the left side of the slide. This is followed by the Manurhin trademark, a wheel with the Manurhin name across the center of the wheel, with **Made in France** beneath it. Following the trademark is the legend, **Lic. Excl. Walther** with the model designation and the caliber.

On the right side of the Manurhin pistols the serial numbers were placed on the slide to the front of the ejection port and on the frame directly to the rear of the trigger. The French nitro test proof, a crown over a shield, was generally placed on the chamber inside the ejection port and on the slide to the front of the ejection port. There were some early Manurhins produced in 1951 and 1952 that had the serial number only on the right side of the slide forward of the ejection port, while a nitro test proof only appeared on the right side of the frame behind the trigger.

The grip plates for the Manurhin Models PP and PPK were of the same design and material as the original Walthers, but differently marked. The Model PP grip plates were two-piece checkered plastic in black, white or a mottled red color. The Manurhin trademark is centered at the top of each grip within a diamond design. Along the bottom of each grip is the inscription, **Lic. Walther PP.** The Model PPK grips are one-piece wraparound checkered plastic in the same colors as the Model PP, and the Manurhin trademark and inscription are on the same locations as on the PP. Also, along the bottom sides of the grip is **Lic. Walther PPK.**

The finish found on the Manurhin Models PP and PPK are like the Walthers of the 1930s. It is generally a high-gloss blue, but guns could be obtained finished in gold, silver or nickel. The PP and PPK were also available with engraving, and these showed excellent craftsmanship.

In addition to the PP and PPK, a new model that had never been made by Walther in Germany was introduced by Manurhin. The Manurhin 22 target pistol, the Model PP Sport, was manufactured in two barrel lengths, 6 and 7⅝ inches. This pistol fired the 22 Short and 22 LR, and had a magazine capacity of 10 rounds. The PP Sport was identical to the Model PP except for the length of the barrel, special front and rear sights, grip plates and barrel weights for target shooting.

The PP Sport's front sights are adjustable with variations in both sight blades and sighting ramp. Rear sights are adjustable for both windage and elevation. The front sight assembly is completely removable by means of a knurled barrel locking nut. The removable front sight attachment was necessitated by the PP Sport's takedown design, which required the slide of the pistol to be removed over the end of the muzzle the same as with the Model PP.

The grip plates for the PP Sport were generally made of checkered plastic and resembled a reversed bird's head, with the beak upside down facing toward the muzzle. The magazine has a special plastic extension which when seated within the grips leaves the extension barely visible. The base of the grips is rounded and there is a thumbrest on the left side. The PP Sport grips were usually produced in a reddish mottled color and were marked in the same way as the Models PP and PPK, with the Manurhin trademark centered on each side of the grip plate, and **Lic. Walther** at the bottom of each grip. The PP Sport bore no special model designation on its slide.

There is one special variation of the PP Sport model, the Model PP Sport C, Competition. This model had a single action lock and a 7⅝-inch barrel. It could be ordered with a duraluminum frame, and was equipped with more precise micrometer sights for precision shooting.

The PP Sport pistols were also manufactured with detachable muzzle brake, checkered wood target stocks and barrel weights. There were two types of barrel weights. One type was a flat rectangular shaped weight, attached to the barrel by sliding it over the muzzle, replacing the front sight, and setting both firmly in place by tightening the barrel locking nut. The other type of weight had the front sight attached to it, and was to be placed over the muzzle

Manurhin Walther Mark II, Model PP, Caliber 7.65. Walther banner grips.

Manurhin Walther Mark II, Model PPK, Caliber 7.65. Checkered wood grips.

Manurhin Walther Mark II, Model PP Sport, Caliber 22, 7⅝-inch barrel. Spur hammer, micrometer rear sights, knurled locking nut at muzzle and plain unmarked grips with boxed extension.

and held in place by the barrel locking nut. This weight was rounded and looked like a fat barrel.

When the first Manurhin PP Sports were produced the hammer was rounded in the same style as the Model PP. Later, the hammer was given a spur which made it much easier to cock when target shooting. The finish on the PP Sport models was a high gloss blue, though there were a few pistols produced with a nickel finish and white grips. In the United States the Thalson Company of San Francisco imported the first Walther Manurhins in the summer of 1953. These Manurhin models began with the serial number 100001 for the Model PP and 500001 for the Model PPK.

In 1956, Interarms, the International Armament Corporation of Alexandria, Virginia, began to import the Models PP, PPK and PP Sport produced by Manurhin. These were the same Manurhin-licensed Walthers but now had new markings, which designated them the "Mark II." The slide legend no longer had the Manurhin trademark and inscription, and in its place appeared **Mark II** along with the traditional Walther Banner. The Mark IIs were marked on the left side as follows:

Walther Banner Mark II	Mod. PP Cal. 5.6mm 22 L R Automatic Made in France
Walther Banner Mark II	Mod. PPK Cal. 7.65mm 32 Automatic Made in France

Walther Banner Mark II
Mod. Sport Cal. 5.6mm 22 L R Automatic Made in France

The right side of the Mark II has the serial number on the frame behind the trigger. The nitro test proofs are on the side of the chamber in the ejection port, and usually on the right side of the frame near the serial number as well. They are also found on the right side of the slide.

Some very early Mark II pistols were marked somewhat differently, with both the Walther and Manurhin name being placed together in a banner on the side of the slide:

Manufacture De Machines Du Haut-Rhin Made in France	Walther Manurhin Mark II	Lic Excl. Mod. Sport-Competition Cal. 5.6mm 22 LR Automatic

After Interarms took over the importation of the Model PP Sport the grips were changed to more closely resemble the standard Model PP grip plates, though with the left grip having a thumbrest and both grips unmarked. Also, the new plastic magazine extension was attached to the bottom of the magazine. This extension was the same style as an optional magazine extension offered by Walther in the 1930s. This plastic extension had the same cross section as the butt of the PP Sport model, and thus created a longer, more supportive, grip. The extension material was the same color as the grip plates, and was checkered in the rear. The grips and the extension were offered in white, black or a reddish mottled color. In a few examples the grips and matching extensions were made of wood.

The Mark II Models PP and PPK imported by Interarms were mechanically identical to the earlier Manurhins, with the only real differences being the markings on the pistols. On both models the grip plates had either the Manurhin trademark or the original Walther Banner. Generally, on the Mark II Model PPK the grips were the one-piece wraparound

Manurhin-marked PPK grip. The Mark II Model PP in 22 caliber in some cases had a left grip plate with a thumbrest. On these grip plates there was no name identification of any kind. Also, for both the Model PP and PPK Mark II the box extension magazine was offered as an option. Grips were black, white or a reddish mottled color.

The Mark IIs were produced in a deep blue Walther finish. They could also be obtained finished in silver, gold or chrome. Engraving could be special-ordered in the basic oak leaf and acorn styles.

Eventually Walther reestablished its own manufacturing facilities in Ulm, West Germany, only about 50 miles from the Manurhin plant. There Walther began manufacturing its own PP and PPK pistols, though they continued to subcontract a number of components to Manurhin. With the resumption of Walther production of these two popular pistols, an interesting chapter in the Walther story ended and gave collectors still another sideline for study.

Editor's Note: While Mr. Rankin's excellent article covers the various early post World War II Walthers made by Manurhin for the commercial market, there is another Manurhin-made Walther that also deserves mention. There has long been a rumor of a Manurhin P.38, but until quite recently no firm evidence to either confirm or deny that rumor was forthcoming. Then, during a visit to Switzerland several years ago, the editor found a Manurhin-made P.38 slide (only) in a Swiss gun dealer's parts box.

The markings on the left side of this unusual find identify it as being from a **PISTOLET P1 9mm x 19** and significantly omit the **Lic. Excl. Walther** that is found on every commercial Manurhin-made Walther, while the right side is stamped **Bund** and bears a crossed cannon proofmark. "P1" is the German government's designation for the P.38.

Subsequent investigation turned up some additional stripped slides and a few complete slide assemblies, but no complete guns. As pieced together, their story appears to be this: These pistols were originally built by Manurhin for the German Army, probably in the mid '50s, hence the "Bund" marking. For some reason the Germans did not accept the guns. The entire lot, apparently 5,000 (serials observed run from the low three digits to high 4000s), then went to Portugal where they've been in service ever since.

As no complete guns and only a relatively small number of slides have turned up thus far, it appears that the thrifty Portuguese have broken up some unserviceable pistols to sell for parts, while retaining the bulk of their supply as service weapons. ●

Manurhin Walther P1 (P.38) slide, from the group sold to Portugal in the 1950s.

The information for this article on Manurhin-made Walther pistols comes from Jim Rankin's new book *Walther—Volume III— 1908-1980*, published by the author.

Collecting the Commemoratives

by Larry S. Sterett

INFLATION getting ahead of you? Like to invest your money in some item that will increase in value over the years, based on past experience, and at the same time provide the satisfaction of ownership? Why not consider collecting commemorative arms?

You can specialize in one brand of commemoratives, such as Colt handguns, or Winchester rifles, or one type of commemorative, such as handguns only, or rifles only. There are a few commemorative shotguns, but such a collection would be relatively small. You might even decide to collect by caliber, such as those models chambered for the 22 Long Rifle rimfire cartridge, or the 45 Colt. Or, you might even decide to collect those arms commemorating a special event, such as the centennial of a city, or town, or similar event. (The commemorative field as we know it today started back in 1961, when a gentleman by the name of Robert Cherry had the Colt Firearms Co. stamp a limited number of the single shot 22 Short derringer [Fourth Model] they were then producing with **1836 Geneseo Anniversary 1961** to commemorate the 125th Anniversary of the founding of his hometown, Geneseo, Illinois. This first of the modern commemoratives came in a walnut case, and carried a retail price of $27.50. Today, the asking price is over 16 times that amount, if you can find someone willing to sell. That's not a bad return on an investment.)

It started slow, but it did start, and a few years later commemorative issues were being introduced with some degree of regularity. Colt issued a special grade Single Action Army Model to commemorate the firm's 125th Anniversary, and Marlin issued a 90th Anniversary Model 39A rifle and carbine set, and then some of the states climbed on the bandwagon. Not all such commemoratives have increased tremendously in value, but many of them have shown a substantial value increase.

The Colt firm has produced the largest number of commemorative arms, and the year 1964 saw 26 different Colt handgun models being introduced. Winchester has introduced more such rifles than any other firm. Many collectors of commemoratives at-

The Colt Heritage Walker Commemorative was limited to 1847 sets, the same as the year in which the original model was issued to Captain Sam Walker of the U. S. Mounted Riflemen. Etched on the left barrel lug in gold plate is the legend "The Colt Heritage Commemorative;" on the right barrel lug in gold plate are portrait busts of Captain Walker and Colonel Colt. Other features include a special serial number range—C Co 1 through C Co 1847—a cylinder roll marked with the W. L. Ormsby "Ranger and Indian" scene, solid brass trigger guard, and a one-piece oil-finished walnut grip with inspector and military markings. A deluxe custom signed and numbered edition of *"The Colt Heritage"* book accompanies each gun. A French-fitted, green velvet lined, mahogany presentation case with book lectern and brass hinge lock, holds the gun and book.

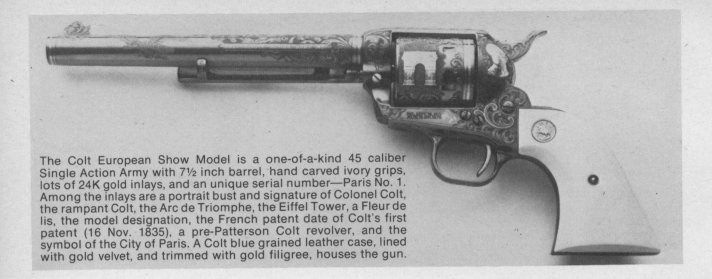

The Colt European Show Model is a one-of-a-kind 45 caliber Single Action Army with 7½ inch barrel, hand carved ivory grips, lots of 24K gold inlays, and an unique serial number—Paris No. 1. Among the inlays are a portrait bust and signature of Colonel Colt, the rampant Colt, the Arc de Triomphe, the Eiffel Tower, a Fleur de lis, the model designation, the French patent date of Colt's first patent (16 Nov. 1835), a pre-Patterson Colt revolver, and the symbol of the City of Paris. A Colt blue grained leather case, lined with gold velvet, and trimmed with gold filigree, houses the gun.

tempt to obtain the same serial number on all their commemoratives. The Colt firm has a Reserved Serial Number Program under which a collector may reserve a special serial number—if it has not already been reserved by another collector. There is an extra charge per gun for this service, and the order must be placed through a bona-fide Colt dealer. In addition, the program requires the customer to accept one of each Commemorative model produced by Colt, and each time he or she will receive the same serial number; the gun will automatically be shipped to the dealer through whom the original order was placed.

As mentioned, 1964 was the big year (numberwise) for commemorative issues. However, the Bicentennial year of 1976 saw several arms being introduced with 1776-1976 stamped, etched, or engraved thereon. Such simple stamping alone does not make such guns commemoratives in the sense of the term as used here. A true *commemorative* gun, regardless of whether it is a handgun, rifle, or shotgun, is gen-

erally considered to be one especially pre-planned to commemorate a particular historical event, place, or a person. Simply stamping some dates and adding a bit of etching or engraving to an otherwise standard production arm does not necessarily make it a commemorative. Said gun should have better than standard wood on it, select quality with figure would be better if it is a rifle or shotgun, and even the stocks on a handgun should be of extra high quality with a different checkering pattern. The finish on the metal should be the best possible, and the etching or engraving, if there is any, should be in keeping with the theme of the commemoration.

In 1981, for example, the Justin Boot Company introduced Italian-manufactured reproductions of the Model 1866 Winchester rifle and the Model 1873 Colt Single Action Army revolver, as a set, to commemorate the firm's 100th Anniversary. Both arms were manufactured by the firm of Aldo Uberti, and each is chambered for the 44-40 Winchester car-

The Winchester Limited Edition Model 94 was introduced with a fitted wooden case which included a leatherette-bound booklet featuring the histories of the engravings of the late John Ulrich and the Model 94 carbine. Also included were an instruction manual, plus a certificate of authentication listing the carbine's serial number and the date of production.

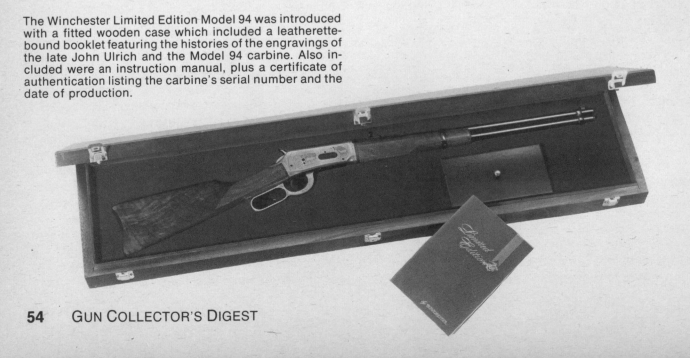

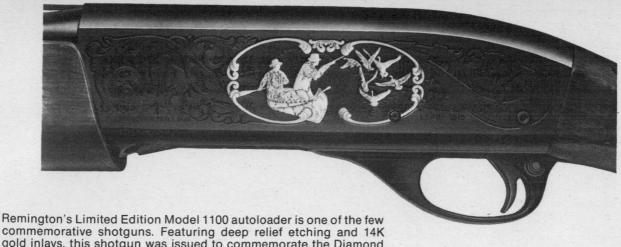

Remington's Limited Edition Model 1100 autoloader is one of the few commemorative shotguns. Featuring deep relief etching and 14K gold inlays, this shotgun was issued to commemorate the Diamond Anniversary of Remington's production of autoloading shotguns.

tridge. Only 1500 sets were to have been manufactured, and each set had a suggested price of $1500. The rifle has the standard brass frame, engraved on the left side with a scene of the Justin Company as it appeared in 1879, with the right side of the frame engraved with a western scene; the revolver is engraved in gold. The rifle and revolver carry the same serial number in each set, and a solid brass "Justin 100" belt buckle with the same serial number accompanies each set. In addition, the Justin Commemoratives are housed in a choice of natural finished oak wall case with glass door and inset lock, or an oak carrying case with two keyed locks and a cartridge block with space for 50 rounds of 44-40 ammunition. Both the wall case and the carrying case are lined with red suede, and the rifle and revolver have polished brass commemorative plates on the right side of the stocks.

An interesting commemorative to watch will be the Limited Edition M1 Carbine introduced by Universal Firearms to commemorate the 40th Anniversary (1941-1981) of the introduction of this design. Each carbine comes in a fitted carrying case, with bayonet and sheath, special inlaid brass medallion, a belt buckle, scope and mount, sling and oiler, and 15-round and 30-round magazines. The carbine has a specially selected walnut stock with hand-rubbed finish, and the metal finish is supposed to be extra special. There are a lot of original users of the M1 still around, but whether they are collectors remains to be seen.

As mentioned, commemorative shotguns are not issued as often as are rifles and handguns. However, in 1980, the Remington Arms Company introduced the Model 1100 Limited Edition to commemorate the firm's 75th Anniversary of autoloading shotgun manufacture, starting with the famous Model 11 in 1905. Only 3000 of the 12 gauge Limited Edition 1100 guns were to be manufactured, and each was to have

a 28-inch modified choke, ventilated rib barrel, with serial numbers running from LE-80-0001 to LE-80-3000. The matched stocks and forearms are of specially selected, highly figured American walnut, with a hand-applied satin finish, while the metal parts were given a highly polished deep blue finish. Finally, the receiver sides are deep-etched with a Diamond Anniversary motif and 14K gold inlays. The original price was $1125 each, complete with factory registered certificate of authenticity.

Ithacagun celebrated its Centennial in 1980, and to commemorate the occasion, they introduced three Presentation Series versions of the 12 gauge Model 37 pump and Model 51 autoloading shotguns, and the 10 gauge Mag-10 autoloader. Only 200 of each model were produced, and each featured a Supreme grade finish, with extra fancy grade walnut stock and forearm, and gold-mounted receiver, plus a leather-covered compartmentalized take-down case. In addition, Ithacagun introduced 2500 of the 12 gauge Model 37 pump in a special 2500 Series. This commemorative featured the Super Deluxe grade finish, with semi-fancy grade walnut stock, and silver-plated antique-finish receiver with an etched portrait of Lou Smith—Mr. Ithacagun for many, many years. The 2500 Series commemoratives included a full-length hard leather case. Original suggested prices on the Ithacagun commemoratives ranged from $795 to $1495 depending on the series and model, and the Presentation Series could be obtained as a 3-gun matched set, if desired, all with the same serial number.

Since Colt started the modern commemorative series, and is the largest producer of commemorative arms, it is not surprising to find an organization was formed for members dedicated to collecting the Colt issues. Originally formed in 1966, and expanded in 1967 as the Colt's Commemorative Committee, the result was the incorporation in California on January

27, 1969, of the Colt's Commemorative Gun Collectors Association of America. Bob Cherry was President of the Board of Directors. Yearly dues were set, and an illustrated newsletter—*The Commemorative Collector*—was mailed quarterly to collectors, with news of new issues, future gun shows, and other items of interest to collectors. In addition, a book—*Colt Commemorative Firearms*—by R. L. Wilson, was published in 1969. A second edition in 1974, updating the commemoratives, was published by Cherry's—the World's Largest commemorative dealer—in Geneseo, Illinois. (Hopefully, a third edition will be forthcoming in the near future.)

Up until 1981, the *Arms Gazette* magazine devoted a page per issue to CCGCAA, but this publication has been taken over by *Man At Arms* magazine, and whether the previous policy is to be continued remains to be seen. Another source of information on Colt Commemoratives is the *Colt American Handgunning Annual,* which usually has an article or two on this branch of collecting. Finally, Cherry's "Sporting Goods News," $2 per year, carries lots of commemorative information.

Earlier, value increase was mentioned. Exactly how much of an increase can be expected? Nothing is worth any more than someone else is willing to pay for it. Thus, the fewer there are of a particular model, and the more people there are wanting it, the greater will be the expected increase in value. However, scarcity does not always increase value, unless it is coupled with interest for that particular model. As an example, in 1964, Colt introduced the Nevada "Battle Born" 22/45 Combo at $265. Only 20 of these Combos were produced, and the 1980 value was listed at $1950, or an increase of slightly over seven times the original investment. Yet, only 3 years before, Colt introduced the Sheriff's Model with a nickel finish at $139.95. Only 25 of these were manufactured, and the 1980 value was listed at $3250, or over 22 times the original price. In 1967, the Colt World War I Series—Chateau Thierry Special Deluxe 45 auto—was introduced at $1000. Only 25 were produced, and the 1980 price is $2250, or slightly more than twice the original value. But the same year, 500 of the Bat Masterson SAA 45 revolvers were brought out at $180 each, and this model today is worth $750 each, or over four times the original asking price. There has to be interest, and the Bat Masterson name is better known than Chateau Thierry, at least in many circles.

Sometimes a rifle or handgun becomes more valuable due to the demise of the company manufacturing it. Such might be the case with some of the Wickliffe '76 rifles, as produced by the Triple-S Development Co. of Wickliffe, Ohio. A one-of-a-kind Presentation Grade, 1000th Production Rifle was produced in 1979, for sale to the highest bidder over $2500. The

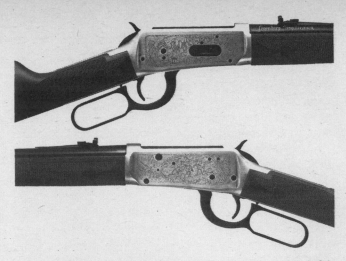

The Winchester "Legendary Frontiersman Model 94 Rifle" commemorated America's early pioneers with scenes of the old frontier etched on the antique silver-plated receiver. Chambered for the 38-55 Winchester cartridge, this commemorative carried an original suggested price of $425.

rifle features the Wickliffe '76 action with a Merkle acid gray finish, special American walnut stock and forearm with crotch figure, a nickel silver grip cap with inlaid gold "W," and 24K gold full-relief inlays on the receiver sides—a dall ram on the left side and a plains antelope on the right side.

Triple-S also produced a Limited Edition Series of rifles commemorating America's big game animals, with the first of the series being the Kodiak bear. Only 200 of this particular design, in 338 Winchester Magnum caliber, were to have been manufactured, and each rifle was to have a pile-lined, wood-grained case embossed on the cover with "Wickliffe '76 Limited Edition," gold-filled receiver etching, and hand-cut checkering on the special section American walnut stock and forearm. The rifle carried an original suggested retail price of $525, but how many rifles were actually built before the company folded is not known.

Another Wickliffe Limited Edition was the '76 American Bicentennial Commemorative, which featured fancy grade figured American walnut forearm and buttstock with a genuine 1876 U.S. silver dollar inlaid into the right side, a 26-inch sporter weight barrel in a choice of six chamberings, and a leather grained wooden presentation case lined with golden pile. Only 100 of this commemorative were to have been built, serial numbered 0001 through 0100 inclusive.

Getting started in collecting commemoratives is relatively easy, since at least one or two new models will generally be introduced each year. Models by such firms as Colt, Remington, and Winchester are generally well researched before being introduced, and being new, they are in perfect condition, plus they are reasonably priced, especially when you consider the extra or select quality of such arms when compared to standard production arms. From time to time, models of a past issue become available on the market, and by careful selection, a collector can upgrade or add to the models he or she already has. The prices on older issues will almost always be higher than on a recent issue.

Since 1968, all out-of-state purchases must be made through a dealer, unless you have a collector's license. Check around, ask questions of other collectors, and once you find a reliable dealer, stick with him. It's to your advantage, since he can help you in making selections, be on the lookout for a model you want, or obtain scarce commemoratives other dealers might have available.

It is almost a physical (not to mention financial) impossibility for any collector—beginner or old-timer—to put together a complete collection of every commemorative ever issued. It's tough to even obtain one of every revolver or pistol issued with the same serial number. However, it is possible to build a small commemorative collection of a particular type of arm, such as commemorative shotguns, which are relatively few in number, without expending gigantic sums of money. It may take time, particularly on a budget, but it can be done with any type of commemorative . . . providing the collector is selective. This means planning ahead. Decide how much you can afford to spend and exactly what you are going to spend it on, rather than purchasing commemoratives in a haphazard fashion.

To assist the beginning collector in getting started, commemorative guns have been categorized in five basic ways, with some variations, as follows:

1. Statehood or Territorial Anniversary (Ruger Colorado Centennial Single Six, etc.)
2. Historical Personality Commemorative:
   a. Military Figures (Colt 1851 Navy U.S. Grant, Robert E. Lee, etc.)
   b. Lawmen (Winchester Legendary Lawmen, Colt Pat Garrett Scout, etc.)
   c. Other Historical Figures (Winchester "Oliver Winchester," Jonathan Browning Mountain Rifle, etc.)
3. Historical Location Commemorative (Colt Appomattox Centennial Scout, etc.)
4. Historical Organization Commemorative (Winchester Wells Fargo, Colt Abercrombie & Fitch "Trailblazer" - Chicago, etc.)
5. Historical Event Commemorative (NRA Centennial Winchester Musket, Browning Centennial Hi-Power 9mm, etc.)

There are no doubt some commemoratives which do not fit neatly into one of the above listed five categories, so possibly a sixth (miscellaneous) listing should be provided. However, with a bit of imagination, most commemoratives will fit one of the original five categories.

Although all modern commemoratives are fully functional, they were intended for collecting. As such, they should not be fired, or otherwise used. They may be admired extensively, but if you want to fire or otherwise use a commemorative, save your money and purchase a standard issue. Anyone desiring to purchase a commemorative arm from your collection expects to find it in new condition. Keep it that way, and keep with each commemorative the packing box, box cover or sleeve, warranty, instruction manual, and so on. All of these add to the overall value of the commemorative, should you decide to sell it later.

Collecting commemoratives can be educational, financially rewarding, and just plain fun. The benefits include: education, in learning more about the person, place, or event the arm was issued to commemorate; reward, in realizing a profit from the value increase in the commemorative over the years; and fun, in looking forward to each new purchase, whether a new issue or the tracking down of a desired model. Remember, some issues increase in value more rapidly than others, so think first, and make your purchases wisely. However, as stated, financial gain should not be the sole reason for becoming a commemorative—or any other kind—of collector.

As Omar Ibn stated, "Four things come not back: The spoken word; The sped arrow; Time past; The neglected opportunity." The time is now; the opportunity is yours.

●

Only 1500 of the Winchester Limited Edition II Model 94 carbines were produced. The receiver has a satin gold-plated finish with triple-etched relief productions of the classic Winchester Style No. 1 engraving by the late John Ulrich.

COMMEMORATIVE GUN LISTING*

Above—This nickel-silver medallion in the shape of a lawman's badge is inlaid into the right side of the semi-fancy American walnut buttstock on the Winchester Legendary Lawman Model 94 Carbine. Below—Right and left side receiver views of the Legendary Lawman Carbine.

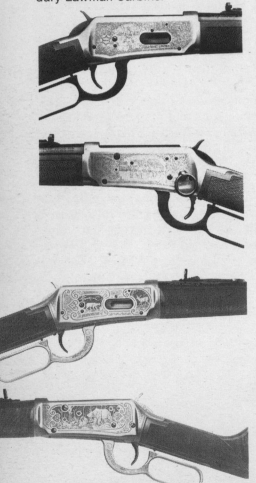

The Winchester Limited Edition Model 94 featured a satin gold-plated receiver with triple-etched reproductions of the late John Ulrich's classic Winchester Style No. 1 engravings, in addition to fancy scrollwork.

CHERRY'S No.	Total Production	Original Price	Current Price
1961 ISSUES			
C 1 Colt Geneseo, Illinois 125th Anniversary Derringer	104	27.50	**450.00**
C 2 Colt Sheriff's Model — Blue & Case-hard	478	129.95	**1450.00**
C 3 Colt Sheriff's Model — Nickel	25	139.95	**3250.00**
C 4 Colt 125th Anniversary Model SAA	7390	150.00	**595.00**
C 5 Colt Kansas Statehood Scout	6201	75.00	**250.00**
C 6 Colt Pony Express Centennial Scout	1007	80.00	**425.00**
C 7 Colt Civil War Centennial Pistol	24114	32.50	**75.00**
C 8 Marlin 90th Anniversary 39-A Rifle & Carbine	1000	100.00	**495.00**
1962 ISSUES			
C 9 Colt Rock Island Arsenal Centennial Pistol	550	38.95	**175.00**
C 10 Colt Columbus, Ohio Sesquicentennial Scout	200	100.00	**525.00**
C 11 Colt Fort Findlay, Ohio Sesquicentennial Scout	110	89.50	**525.00**
C 12 Colt Fort Findlay Cased Pair — 22 LR - 22 Magnum	20	185.00	**2500.00**
C 13 Colt New Mexico Golden Anniversary Scout	1000	79.95	**295.00**
C 14 Colt Ft. McPherson, Nebraska Centennial Derringer	300	28.95	**295.00**
C 15 Colt West Virginia Statehood Centennial Scout	3452	75.00	**250.00**
1963 ISSUES			
C 16 Colt West Virginia Statehood Centennial SAA .45	600	150.00	**595.00**
C 17 Colt Arizona Territorial Centennial Scout	5355	75.00	**250.00**
C 18 Colt Arizona Territorial Centennial SAA .45	1280	150.00	**585.00**
C 19 Colt Carolina Charter Tercentenary Scout	300	75.00	**395.00**
C 20 Colt Carolina Charter Tercentenary 22/45 Combo	251	240.00	**895.00**
C 21 Colt H. Cook "1 to 100" 22/45 Combo	100	275.00	**1050.00**
C 22 Colt Ft. Stephenson, Ohio Sesquicentennial Scout	200	75.00	**525.00**
C 23 Colt Battle of Gettysburg Centennial Scout	1019	89.95	**250.00**
C 24 Colt Idaho Territorial Centennial Scout	902	75.00	**325.00**
C 25 Colt Gen. John Hunt Morgan Indiana Raid Scout	100	74.50	**650.00**
1964 ISSUES			
C 26 Colt Cherry's Sporting Goods 35th Anniversary 22/45 Combo	100	275.00	**1150.00**
C 27 Colt Nevada Statehood Centennial Scout	3984	75.00	**250.00**
C 28 Colt Nevada Statehood Centennial SAA .45	1688	150.00	**595.00**
C 29 Colt Nevada Statehood Centennial 22/45 Combo	189	240.00	**850.00**
C 30 Colt Nevada St. Cent. 22/45 Combo W/Extra Engr. Cyls.	577	350.00	**995.00**
C 31 Colt Nevada "Battle Born" Scout	981	85.00	**250.00**
C 32 Colt Nevada "Battle Born" SAA .45	80	175.00	**1095.00**
C 33 Colt Nevada "Battle Born" 22/45 Combo	20	265.00	**1950.00**
C 34 Colt Montana Territorial Centennial Scout	2300	75.00	**250.00**
C 35 Colt Montana Territorial Centennial SAA .45	851	150.00	**750.00**
C 36 Colt Wyoming Diamond Jubilee Scout	2357	75.00	**250.00**
C 37 Winchester Wyoming Diamond Jubilee 94 Carbine	1501	99.95	**1450.00**
C 38 Remington Montana Territorial Centennial 600 Rifle	1005	124.95	**295.00**
C 39 Colt General Hood Centennial Scout	1503	75.00	**250.00**
C 40 Colt New Jersey Tercentenary Scout	1001	75.00	**250.00**
C 41 Colt New Jersey Tercentenary SAA .45	250	150.00	**795.00**
C 42 Colt St. Louis Bicentennial Scout	802	75.00	**250.00**
C 43 Colt St. Louis Bicentennial SAA .45	200	150.00	**650.00**
C 44 Colt St. Louis Bicentennial 22/45 Combo	250	240.00	**895.00**
C 45 Ithaca St. Louis Bicentennial Mod. 49 22 Rifle	200	34.95	**150.00**
C 46 Colt California Gold Rush Scout	500	79.50	**295.00**
C 47 Colt Pony Express Presentation SAA .45	1004	250.00	**950.00**
C 48 Colt Chamizal Treaty Scout	450	85.00	**275.00**
C 49 Colt Chamizal Treaty SAA .45	50	170.00	**1095.00**
C 50 Colt Chamizal Treaty 22/45 Combo	50	280.00	**1850.00**
C 51 Col. Sam Colt Sesquicentennial Presentation SAA .45	4750	225.00	**795.00**
C 52 Col. Sam Colt Sesquicentennial Deluxe Pres. SAA .45	200	500.00	**1950.00**
C 53 Col. Sam Colt Sesquicentennial Spec. Deluxe Pres. SAA .45	50	1000.00	**2950.00**
C 54 Colt Wyatt Earp Buntline SAA .45	150	250.00	**1650.00**
1965 ISSUES			
C 55 Colt Oregon Trail Scout	1995	75.00	**250.00**
C 56 Colt Joaquin Murietta 22/45 Combo	100	350.00	**1450.00**
C 57 Colt Forty-Niner Miner Scout	500	85.00	**250.00**
C 58 Colt Old Ft. Des Moines Reconstruction Scout	700	89.95	**295.00**
C 59 Colt Old Ft. Des Moines Reconstruction SAA .45	100	169.95	**750.00**
C 80 Colt Old Ft. Des Moines Reconstruction 22/45 Combo	100	289.95	**1095.00**
C 61 Colt Appomattox Centennial Scout	1001	75.00	**250.00**
C 62 Colt Appomattox Centennial SAA .45	250	150.00	**850.00**
C 63 Colt Appomattox Centennial 22/45 Combo	250	240.00	**895.00**
C 64 Colt General Meade Campaign Scout	1197	75.00	**250.00**
C 65 Colt St. Augustine Quadricentennial Scout	500	85.00	**295.00**
C 66 Colt Kansas Cowtown Series — Wichita Scout	500	85.00	**295.00**

*This listing of commemoratives has been arranged with data provided by Cherry's Sporting Goods, Geneseo, Illinois. Some of the one-of-a-kind commemoratives have not been listed, nor have all of the regular commemoratives been included. It should be used for comparison purposes only, and not necessarily as the final word. The prices listed were current as of mid-1980.

1966 ISSUES

	Total Production	Original Price	Current Price
C 67 Colt Kansas Cowtown Series — Dodge City Scout	500	85.00	295.00
C 68 Colt Colorado Gold Rush Scout	1350	85.00	250.00
C 69 Colt Oklahoma Territory Scout	1343	85.00	250.00
C 70 Colt Dakota Territory Scout	1000	85.00	250.00
C 71 Winchester Centennial '66 Rifle —		125.00	350.00
C 72 Winchester Centennial '66 Carbine	102039	125.00	350.00
C 73 Colt General Meade SAA .45	200	165.00	795.00
C 74 Colt Abercrombie & Fitch "Trailblazer" — New York	200	275.00	1750.00
C 75 Colt Kansas Cowtown Series — Abilene Scout	500	95.00	250.00
C 76 Colt Indiana Sesquicentennial Scout	1500	85.00	250.00
C 77 Winchester Nebraska Centennial 94 Rifle	2500	125.00	1250.00
C 78 Colt Pony Express .45 SAA 4-Square Set (4 Guns)		1400.00	3850.00
C 79 Colt California Gold Rush SAA .45	130	175.00	1095.00
C 80 Colt Abercrombie & Fitch "Trailblazer" — Chicago	100	275.00	1750.00
C 81 Colt Abercrombie & Fitch "Trailblazer" — San Francisco	100	275.00	1750.00

1967 ISSUES

	Total Production	Original Price	Current Price
C 82 Remington Canadian Centennial 742 Rifle	1000	199.95	299.95
C 83 Ruger Canadian Centennial 10/22 Rifle	2000	99.95	125.00
C 84 Canadian Centennial Matched No. 3 Rifle Sets	1900	319.00	425.00
C 85 Canadian Centennial Matched No. 2 Rifle Sets	70	450.00	575.00
C 86 Canadian Centennial Matched No. 1 Rifle Sets Special Deluxe	30	600.00	895.00
C 87 Colt Lawman Series — Bat Masterson Scout	3000	90.00	295.00
C 88 Colt Lawman Series — Bat Masterson SAA .45	500	180.00	750.00
C 89 Colt Alamo Scout	4250	85.00	250.00
C 90 Colt Alamo SAA .45	750	165.00	750.00
C 91 Colt Alamo 22/45 Combo	250	265.00	1050.00
C 92 Colt Kansas Cowtown Series — Coffeyville Scout	500	95.00	250.00
C 93 Winchester Canadian '67 Centennial Rifle		125.00	295.00
C 94 Winchester Canadian '67 Centennial Carbine	90301	125.00	295.00
C 95 Winchester Alaskan Purchase Centennial Carbine	1501	125.00	1500.00
C 96 Colt Kansas Trial Series — Chisholm Trail Scout	500	100.00	250.00
C 97 Colt World War I Series — Chateau Thierry .45 Auto	7400	200.00	425.00
C 98 Colt World War I Series — Chateau Thierry Deluxe	75	500.00	1350.00
C 99 Colt World War I Series — Chateau Thierry Spec. Deluxe	25	1000.00	2250.00
C100 H & R "Abilene Anniversary" .22 Revolver	300	83.50	125.00

1968 ISSUES

	Total Production	Original Price	Current Price
C101 Colt Nebraska Centennial Scout	7001	100.00	250.00
C102 Colt Kansas Trail Series — Pawnee Trail Scout	501	110.00	250.00
C103 Winchester Illinois Sesquicentennial 94 Carbine	37468	110.00	295.00
C104A Winchester Buffalo Bill Rifle "1 of 300"	300	1000.00	1500.00
C104 Winchester Buffalo Bill Rifle		129.95	295.00
C105 Winchester Buffalo Bill Carbine	112923	129.95	295.00
C106 Colt World War I Series — Belleau Wood	7400	200.00	425.00
C107 Colt WW I Series — Belleau Wood Deluxe	75	500.00	1350.00
C108 Colt WW I Series — Belleau Wood Special Deluxe	25	1000.00	2250.00
C109 Colt Lawman Series — Pat Garrett Scout	3000	110.00	295.00
C110 Colt Lawman Series — Pat Garrett .45 SAA	500	220.00	750.00

1969 ISSUES

	Total Production	Original Price	Current Price
C111 Colt Gen. Nathan Bedford Forrest Scout	3000	110.00	250.00
C112 Colt Kansas Trail Series — Santa Fe Trail Scout	501	120.00	250.00
C113 Colt WW I Series — Battle of 2nd Marne .45 Auto	7400	220.00	425.00
C114 Colt WW I Series — Battle of 2nd Marne Deluxe	75	500.00	1350.00
C115 Colt WW I Series — Battle of 2nd Marne Spec. Deluxe	25	1000.00	2250.00
C116 Colt Alabama Sesquicentennial Scout	3001	110.00	275.00
C116A Colt Alabama Sesquicentennial .45 SAA	1	————	15000.00
C117 Winchester Golden Spike Carbine	69996	119.95	350.00
C118 Winchester Theo. Roosevelt Carbine		134.95	350.00
C119 Winchester Theo. Roosevelt Rifle	52296	134.95	350.00
C120 Colt Golden Spike Scout	11000	135.00	250.00
C121 Colt Kansas Trail Series & Shawnee Trail Scout	501	120.00	250.00
C122 Colt WW I Series — Meuse-Argonne .45 Auto	7400	220.00	425.00
C123 Colt WW I Series — Meuse-Argonne .45 Deluxe	75	500.00	1350.00
C124 Colt WW I Series — Meuse-Argonne Spec. Deluxe	25	1000.00	2250.00
C125 Colt Arkansas Territory Sesquicentennial Scout	3500	110.00	195.00
C126 Colt Lawman Series .45 SAA Wild Bill Hickock	500	220.00	750.00
C127 Colt Lawman Series Wild Bill Hickock Scout	3000	116.60	295.00
C128 Colt California Bicentennial Scout	5000	135.00	250.00

1970 ISSUES

	Total Production	Original Price	Current Price
C129 Colt Kansas Fort Series — Ft. Learned Scout	500	120.00	250.00
C130 Colt WW II Series — European Theater	11500	250.00	425.00
C131 Colt WW II Series — Pacific Theater	11500	250.00	425.00
C132 Winchester Cowboy Commemorative Carbine	27549	125.00	425.00
C132A Winchester Cowboy Carbine "1 of 300"	300	1000.00	1500.00
C133 Winchester Lone Star Carbine		140.00	375.00
C134 Winchester Lone Star Rifle	38385	140.00	375.00
C135 Colt Texas Ranger SAA .45	1000	650.00	1450.00
C136 Savage 75th Anniversary Mod. 99 Rifle	9999	195.00	250.00
C137 Colt Kansas Forts — Ft. Hays Scout	500	130.00	250.00

The Wickliffe '76 Limited Edition Kodiak Series rifles featured gold-filled receiver etching, and only 200 of this commemorative were to have been manufactured.

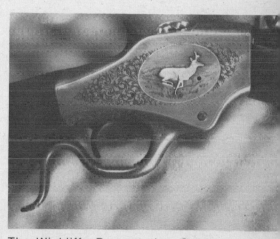

The Wickliffe Presentation Grade 1000th Production Rifle receiver featured 24K gold full relief inlays—a Dall ram on the left side and a plains antelope on the right.

COMMEMORATIVE GUN LISTING

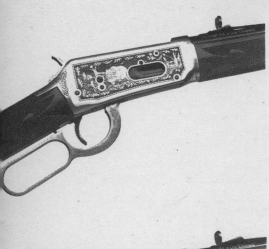

	Total Production	Original Price	Current Price
C138 Colt Maine Sesquicentennial Scout	3000	120.00	**250.00**
C139 Colt Missouri Sesquicentennial Scout	3000	125.00	**250.00**
C140 Colt Missouri Sesquicentennial .45 SAA	900	220.00	**595.00**
C141 Colt Kansas Forts — Ft. Riley Scout	500	130.00	**250.00**
C142 Colt Lawman Series — Wyatt Earp Scout	3000	125.00	**350.00**
C143 Colt Lawman Series — Wyatt Earp .45 SAA	500	395.00	**1250.00**

1971 ISSUES

	Total Production	Original Price	Current Price
C144 Winchester NRA Centennial Musket	23400	149.95	**295.00**
C145 Winchester NRA Centennial Rifle	21000	149.95	**295.00**
C146 Colt NRA Centennial .45 SAA	5000	250.00	**595.00**
C147 Colt NRA Centennial .357 SAA	5000	250.00	**595.00**
C148 Colt NRA Centennial Gold Cup .45	2500	250.00	**425.00**
C149 Colt 1851 Navy — U.S. Grant	4750	250.00	**425.00**
C150 Colt 1851 Navy — Robert E. Lee	4750	250.00	**425.00**
C151 Colt 1851 Navy — Lee-Grant Set	250	500.00	**1250.00**
C152 Colt Kansas Series — Ft. Scott Scout	500	130.00	**250.00**
C153 Harrington & Richardson Officer's Mod. 45-70	10000	250.00	**295.00**
C154 Marlin Zane Grey 30-30 Carbine		150.00	**195.00**
C155 Stevens Favorite '71 .22 Single Shot	10000	75.00	**195.00**
C158 Marlin 336-39A Engraved Cased Pair	1000	750.00	**1050.00**

1972 ISSUES

	Total Production	Original Price	Current Price
C157 Harrington & Richardson Little Big Horn 45-70		200.00	**295.00**
C158 Colt Florida Territory Sesquicentennial Scout	2001	125.00	**250.00**
C159 Colt Arizona Ranger Scout	3001	135.00	**275.00**
C160 High Standard Olympic .22 Auto		550.00	**850.00**

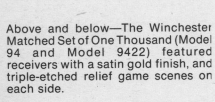

1973 ISSUES

	Total Production	Original Price	Current Price
C161 Harrington & Richardson 1873 Springfield		250.00	**295.00**
C162 Smith & Wesson Texas Ranger w/Knife	10000	250.00	**495.00**
C163 Harrington & Richardson Custer Memorial — Officer's Model	25	3000.00	**3750.00**
C164 Harrington & Richardson Custer Memorial Enlisted Men's Model	243	2000.00	**2000.00**

1974 ISSUES

	Total Production	Original Price	Current Price
C165 High Standard Griswold & Gunnison	500	175.00	**195.00**
C166 High Standard Presidential Derringer		150.00	**250.00**
C167 High Standard Leech & Rigdon	500	175.00	**195.00**
C168 Winchester Texas Ranger Carbine	5000	129.95	**595.00**

Above and below—The Winchester Matched Set of One Thousand (Model 94 and Model 9422) featured receivers with a satin gold finish, and triple-etched relief game scenes on each side.

1975 ISSUES

	Total Production	Original Price	Current Price
C169 Colt Peacemaker Centennial .45	1500	300.00	**595.00**
C170 Colt Peacemaker Centennial 44-40	1500	300.00	**595.00**
C171 Colt Peacemaker Cent. Cased Pair	500	625.00	**1350.00**
C172 High Standard Schneider & Glassick	1000	325.00	**325.00**

1976 ISSUES

	Total Production	Original Price	Current Price
C173 Ruger Colorado Centennial Single Six		250.00	**250.00**
C174 Colt U.S. Bicentennial Set	1776	1695.00	**2250.00**
C175 Winchester U.S. Bicentennial Carbine	20000	325.00	**695.00**
C175A High Standard Bicentennial Revolver		250.00	**250.00**
C175B Browning Bicentennial '78 45-70 Rifle	1000	1500.00	**1850.00**

1977 ISSUES

	Total Production	Original Price	Current Price
C176 Colt 2nd Amendment .22	3020	194.95	**295.00**
C177 Winchester Wells Fargo	19999	350.00	**495.00**
C178 Smith & Wesson 125th Anniversary Model 125	10000	350.00	**495.00**
C179 Colt U.S. Cavalry 200th Anniversary Set	3000	995.00	**995.00**
C180 Winchester "Limited Edition"	1500	1500.00	**1750.00**
C181 Winchester Legendary Lawmen	19999	375.00	**425.00**

1978 ISSUES

	Total Production	Original Price	Current Price
C182 Browning Centennial Superposed Rifle-Shotgun	500	7000.00	**7000.00**
C183 Browning Centennial M92-44 Mag.	6000	219.95	**395.00**
C184 Browning Centennial Hi-Power 9mm	3500	495.00	**650.00**
C185 Jonathan Browning Mountain rifle	1000	650.00	**750.00**
C186 Winchester Antlered Game Carbine	19999	375.00	**425.00**
C187 Colt Statehood 3rd Model Dragoon	52	12500.00	**12500.00**

1979 ISSUES

	Total Production	Original Price	Current Price
C188 Winchester Legendary Frontiersman Rifle	19999	425.00	**425.00**
C189 Winchester Limited Edition II	1500	1750.00	**1750.00**
C190 Colt Ned Buntline .45 SAA	3000	895.00	**895.00**

1980 ISSUES

	Total Production	Original Price	Current Price
C191 Colt Heritage-Walker .44 Percussion	1847	1475.00	**1475.00**
C192 Winchester Matched Set of 1,000	1000	3000.00	**3000.00**
C193 Winchester "Oliver Winchester"	19999	519.60	**519.60**

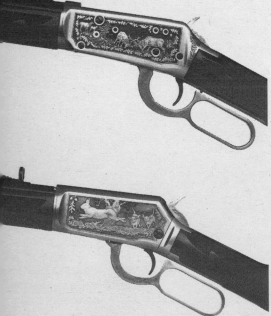

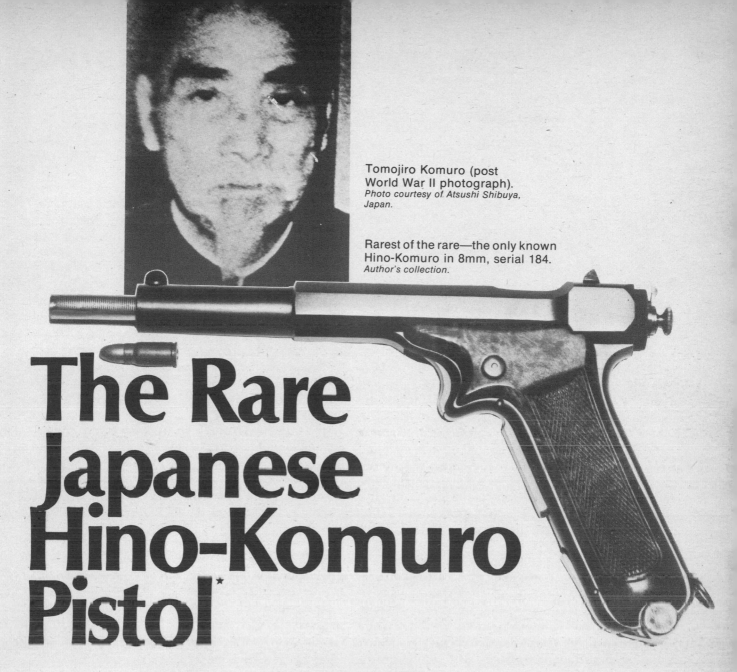

Tomojiro Komuro (post World War II photograph). *Photo courtesy of Atsushi Shibuya, Japan.*

Rarest of the rare—the only known Hino-Komuro in 8mm, serial 184. *Author's collection.*

The Rare Japanese Hino-Komuro Pistol*

by HARRY DERBY

HISTORICALLY, and from a design standpoint, the 1904 Hino-Komuro pistol is without doubt the most unusual and interesting of all cartridge handguns native to Japan. On December 7, 1903, Imperial Army Lieutenant Kumazo Hino and civilian Tomojiro Komuro applied for a Japanese patent covering a 7.65mm blow-forward pistol designed by Lieutenant

---

*Editor's Note: The information in this article and in Harry Derby's article on the Type 26 revolver came from his forthcoming book, *The Hand Cannons of Imperial Japan*, which is scheduled for publication by the author later this year.

Hino. Subsequently, on March 5, 1904 (Meiji 37), patent number 7165 was obtained. Unlike any other pistol known today having its design origin in Japan, applications for patents were also made in England on March 5, 1907, with acceptance granted on May 30 of the same year, and in the United States. The U.S. Patent—No. 886,211—was first filed on September 23, 1904, five and one-half months after the Japanese patent had been awarded. It was renewed on February 7, 1908, and ultimately issued on April 28, 1908. In it Komuro's surname was, interestingly, misspelled "Tomijiro."

Because the English patent application listed Komuro as "manufacturer," over the years, within

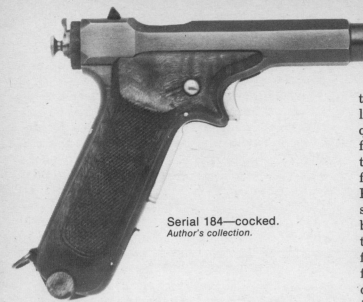

Serial 184—cocked.
Author's collection.

the firearms fraternities of most countries, this rare pistol has acquired the label of "Komuro," rather than "Hino" or "Hino-Komuro." Today in Japan among interested and knowledgeable students of the history of Kumazo Hino and his handgun, this is a somewhat sensitive subject. Later we shall examine in detail the historical background of both men and the Komuro Gun Factory, which supports proper identification of this unique pistol more correctly as the "Hino-Handgun" if one wishes to shorten the full and accurate name of the Hino-Komuro. In our discussion, consistent with the Japanese preference, we shall refer to this "ghost pistol" as it is known today in Japan, simply as the "Hino" or "Hino-Handgun."

Initial introduction of the "Hino's" vital statistics for the interested reader is a complex challenge, because each pistol was individually crafted, offered to the potential purchaser in many calibers, and experienced several significant design changes during its evolution from patent to final basic configuration. The author has chosen to present the 8mm caliber first for several reasons. Although larger in size than the more frequently encountered 7.65mm model, the 8mm exhibits the final design characteristics which are found in examples of both known calibers. As a rarity, the sole example stands today as the only "Hino" in other than 7.65mm caliber known to exist. Found in early 1946 by a member of the 81st U.S. Infantry Division in an abandoned Japanese Army barracks, near the city of Aomori on the northern tip of Honshu Island, serial number 184 in the Japanese 8mm caliber perhaps best exemplifies the Hino handgun.

The "Hino" action, although certainly of questionable practicality as a military or self-defense weapon, is ingenious considering that in 1897, before young Kumazo Hino was 20, he recorded his pistol design. The simple unique action is first cocked by gripping the serrated barrel and pulling it forward until latched. In addition, the pistol can also be cocked quickly by a strong snapping motion while held firmly in one hand, as explained in the original factory sales catalog. This cocking movement activates a feeder which strips a cartridge from the magazine. Pressure on the trigger and the front-strap grip safety releases the barrel latch. This allows the barrel, which is under tension from the main spring, to drive rearward against the standing breech with fixed firing pin, taking the feeder and cartridge to be fired with it. The discharge of the cartridge again drives the barrel and feeder assembly forward, ejecting the spent case and positioning the next cartridge for the next pull of the trigger. In this cocked position, the breech is open, and the barrel has been extended 38mm. This is truly a blow-forward *action,* unlike that of the 1908 Schwarzlose or other similar blow-forward designs.

Its major weaknesses of an open breech, and an elongated and moving barrel, are as apparent as its appearance is peculiar. But one must admit that there is a certain graceful oriental beauty in the long, slim receiver and barrel, undisturbed by trigger guard, and further enhanced by the long grip frame appointed with select grained and finished wood found in the final design configuration.

Since each pistol was individually hand made, great attention was given to the complicated machining processes necessitated by the basic design, as well as to the final finish. Receiver, sights, lanyard loop and breech block are rust blued, while the barrel, feeder, grip safety and magazine release latch are brightly polished tempered steel. Typical of the finish techniques used during this period, trigger, firing pin and grip panel retainer have been heat treated to a straw color. The magazine body has been tinned rather than nickeled. Grip panels and magazine base are of wood: Juglandaceae, of the walnut family.

As with other known 7.65mm "Hino" examples, serial 184 exhibits all three digits of the assigned serial number on all major parts and several minor ones. In addition, 184's rear grip strap was stamped —sometime after the pistol received its final finish —with the Japanese patent number **7165** and two unidentified Japanese characters. The patent number was probably added for some protection as the 8mm model was not covered by the original 7.65mm patent. No model or type, caliber, inspection, or other markings have been noted.

The Hino-Komuro is a rare and desirable collector's item today, with only the single 8mm and ten

7.65mm examples known to exist. Serials 31, 32 (a "Chicom-rework") and 372 are maintained in the firearms reference library of the National Research Institute of Police Science, National Police Agency, Tokyo, while serials 36, 56, 69, 371 and 434 are held in private U.S. collections. Two other incomplete "Hinos"—serial numbers 21 and 245—were discovered recently in Japan.

Until 1976, when serial 184 in 8mm came to light, it was generally accepted that all "Hinos" were produced in 7.65mm caliber only. Then in 1979 the dedicated efforts of Atsushi Shibuya, author of *The Life of Kumazo Hino,* produced another major discovery. Following up on a request made by this author concerning the personal history of Tomojiro Komuro, a historian in Saitama Prefecture contacted by Shibuya located a former home owned by Komuro. In the "godown" (basement) of this old house, not only were desired early photographs of Tomojiro Komuro uncovered, but also an original factory catalog. The cover and last page of the eight-page brochure have been reproduced here.

Prior to this discovery, it appeared that all pertinent records, and perhaps most other examples of the pistols themselves, had been lost during and following World War II. On April 15, 1945, the Hino home in Tokyo, along with his last pistol and remaining files, was completely destroyed by fire as a result of an American air raid. Another example of the pistol had been listed in the old Yushukan inventory for the Yasukuni Shrine in Tokyo, but it, too, disappeared during the postwar period. As a result of such losses, the "Hino-Handgun" is now considered as one of the "ghost" guns of Japan.

The original factory catalog is a significant find, for it now offers supportable documentation that, not only were 7.65mm and 8mm "Hinos" produced, but that the Komuro Gun Factory, at least initially, offered the pistol for sale in all calibers from 5mm to 8mm.

Several interesting details about the various pistols described in the original catalog are highlighted for the reader's benefit. Variation in data is, of course, relative to the pertinent caliber pistol. In Meiji 36, 1903, $1 equalled 2 yen.

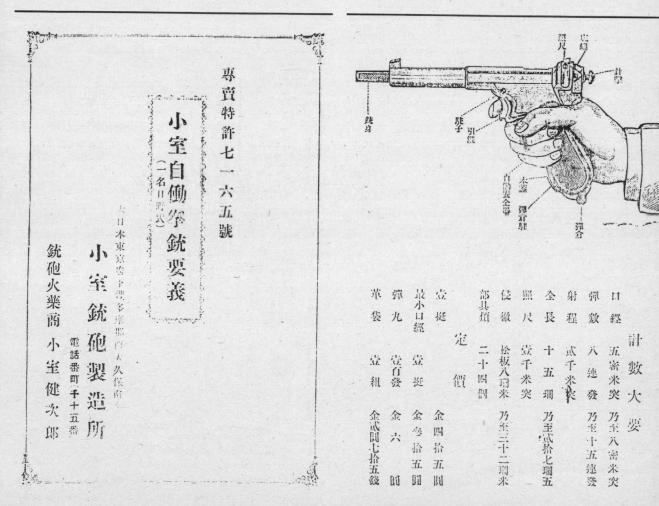

Front and back pages of original Komuro catalog.

No. 886,211.

PATENTED APR. 28, 1908.

K. HINO & T. KOMURO.
PISTOL.
APPLICATION FILED SEPT. 23, 1904. RENEWED FEB. 7, 1908.

3 SHEETS—SHEET 1.

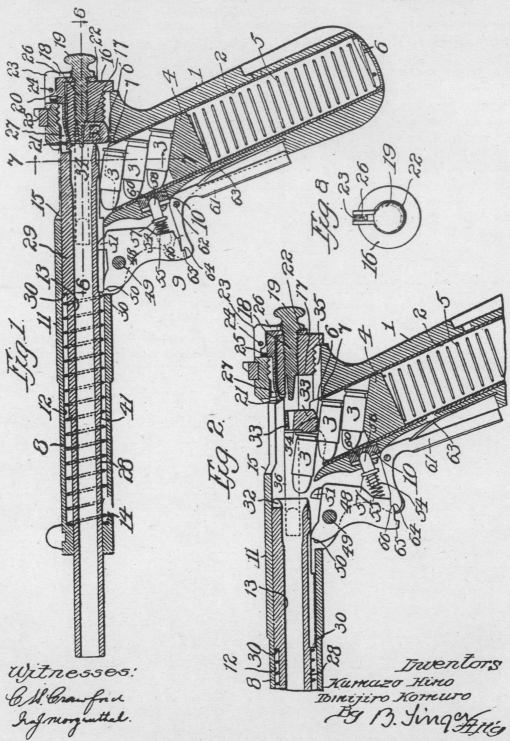

Witnesses:
C. A. Crawford
Ing Morgenthal.

Inventors
Kumazo Hino
Tomijiro Komuro
By B. Singer
Atty.

No. 886,211.

PATENTED APR. 28, 1908.

K. HINO & T. KOMURO.
PISTOL.
APPLICATION FILED SEPT. 23, 1904. RENEWED FEB. 7, 1908.

3 SHEETS—SHEET 2.

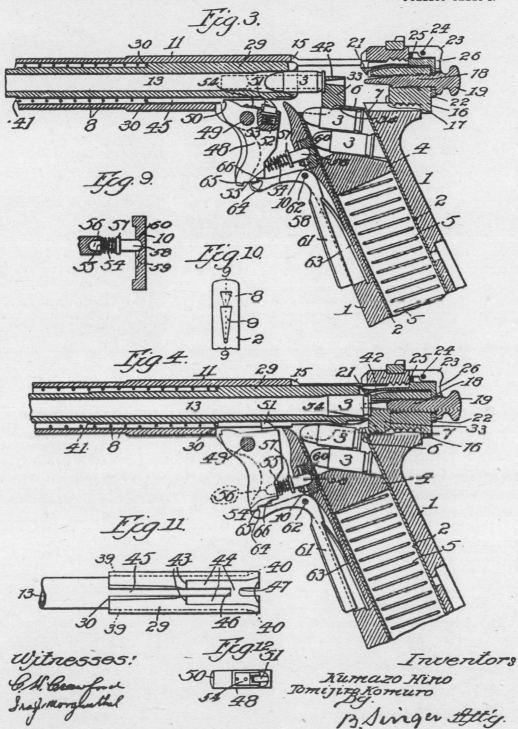

Fig. 3.

Fig. 9.

Fig. 10.

Fig. 4.

Fig. 11.

Fig. 12.

Witnesses:
C. M. Crawford
Graf Morgenthal

Inventors
Kumazo Hino
Tomijiro Komuro
By
B. Singer Att'y.

No. 886,211.

PATENTED APR. 28, 1908.

K. HINO & T. KOMURO.
PISTOL.
APPLICATION FILED SEPT. 23, 1904. RENEWED FEB. 7, 1908.

3 SHEETS—SHEET 3.

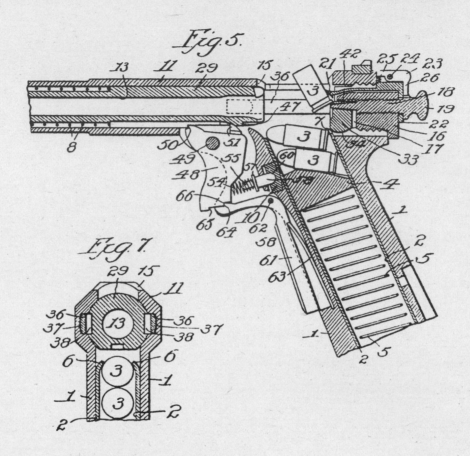

Fig. 5.

Fig. 7.

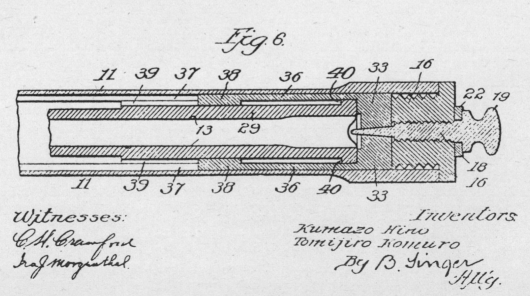

Fig. 6.

Witnesses:
C. M. Crawford
Ira J. Morgenthal.

Inventors
Kumazo Hino
Tomijiro Komuro
By B. Singer
Att'y.

- Calibers: 5mm-8mm.
- Magazine capacities: 8-15 cartridges.
- Range: 2,000 meters.
- Overall pistol lengths: 15cm-27.5cm.
- Rear sight setting: 100 meters.
- Pine board penetration: 8cm-32cm.
- Number of parts: 24.
- Price of pistols: 35 yen-45 yen.
- Price of 100 cartridges: 6 yen.
- Price of one leather bag: 2.75 yen.

Because very small caliber weapons were apparently not accepted or widely used in Japan prior to the early 1900s, it is somewhat unlikely that many—if any, other than prototype—5mm caliber pistols were produced. It is, however, possible that a limited number of 6.35mm (25 ACP) and 7.65mm Luger pistols were manufactured, for examples of foreign pistols in these calibers had found their way into Japan during and prior to the 1904-1912 Komuro factory production period. In any case, the collector and firearms student are alerted to new possibilities.

In early 1903, prior to the patent application, Hino maintained a small shop in his home, located at 9 Yamazato, Yarai-cho, Ushigome-ku, Tokyo. Later that year he turned to Tomojiro Komuro for financial assistance. Komuro readily assisted because he and his wealthy brother Kenjiro Komuro were actively supporting the revolutionary endeavors of Sun Wen (also known as Sun Yat-Sen and Chung Shan)

against China's Manchu Dynasty. Sun Wen, along with his comrade Ko-Ko, were in exile in Japan at the time. It was Komuro's plan to not only make money from the sale of the "Hino" pistols, but also to mass produce them for export to China to assist in arming the revolutionaries. As is apparent, the plan failed after only a few years.

With the Hino-Komuro relationship now established, and the patent application filed, the new Komuro Gun Factory was constructed in Nishi-Ohkubo, Toyotama-gun, Tokyo, in 1904. Kumazo Hino was in charge of design and production, Tomojiro Komuro headed sales, with Kenjiro Komuro as financial supporter. The "Komuro Automatic Pistol," as it was called, could now be offered for sale. It was at this time that the less accurate or desirable label of "Komuro" was applied to the "Hino" design.

As a result of limited initial acceptance and poor sales, Hino, with the assistance of only two employees, made each pistol himself. For this reason (although pure speculation), it is very doubtful that a separate serial series was established for each caliber of pistol produced or offered for sale. Only time and the discovery of either additional data or two pistols of different calibers with the same serial number can support or disprove this conjecture.

The "Hino" pistol underwent several notable modifications from the original design until the final basic configuration was established—as shown by

Design Evolution of the Hino-Komuro

Components and Features	Source					
	Japanese Patent	U.S. Patent	Serial # 31	Serial # 56	Serial # 69	Serial # 372
Barrel Length	203mm	203mm	203mm	194mm	194mm	194mm
Firing Pin and Breech Block	Original	1st Variation	1st Variation	1st Variation	1st Variation	1st Variation
Sights: Front	Original	1st Variation	1st Variation	1st Variation	1st Variation	1st Variation
Rear	Original	Original	Original	1st Variation	1st Variation	1st Variation
Receiver Contour	Original		1st Variation	2nd Variation	2nd Variation	2nd Variation
Grip Frame and Safety	Original	1st Variation	1st Variation	2nd Variation	2nd Variation	2nd Variation
Grip Panels: Checkering	Unknown	Unknown	1st Pattern	2nd Pattern	3rd Pattern	4th Pattern
Retainer	Original	Original	Original	1st Variation	2nd Variation	2nd Variation
Magazine: Body	Original	Original	Original	1st Variation	1st Variation	1st Variation
Latch	Original	1st Variation	1st Variation	2nd Variation	2nd Variation	2nd Variation
Base	Original	Original	Original	1st Variation	Non-original	2nd Variation

both 8mm serial number 184 and 7.65mm serial number 372. Fortunately, this evolution can be traced through the newly discovered catalog, original patents and known examples of the 7.65mm model. The most noticeable changes are found in the areas of:

- Barrel length.
- Firing pin and breech block.
- Sight design.
- Receiver contour.
- Grip frame and safety shape.
- Grip panel checkering pattern.
- Grip panel retainer.
- Magazine body design.
- Magazine latch design.
- Magazine base configuration.

To assist the reader in identifying and understanding these modifications, photographs with accompanying data have been provided for several 7.65mm caliber examples—serials 31, 69 and 372. In addition, reference should be made to the original catalog, the Japanese, English and U.S. patents, and to the reproduction of serial 56 appearing in *Japanese Hand Guns*, by Federick E. Leithe, a Borden Publishing Co. publication, now in its second printing. A tracing of the modifications made during production, from the original Japanese patent to final design variations is also presented in chart form.

7.65mm Hino-Komuro
Serial no.: 31.
Overall Length: 256mm (10.08 in.).
Height: 144mm (5.67 in.)
Weight: 0.820 kg.
Barrel Length: 204mm (8.03 in.).
Rifling: 5 lands and grooves—right-hand direction of twist.
Magazine Capacity: 8 cartridges.

Serial no.: 69.
Overall Length: 237mm (9.33 in.).
Height: 149mm (5.87 in.).
Weight: 0.818 kg.
Barrel Length: 194mm (7.64 in.).
Rifling: 5 lands and grooves—right-hand direction of twist.
Magazine Capacity: 8 cartridges.

Serial no.: 372.
Overall Length: 237mm (9.33 in.).
Height: 145mm (5.71 in.).
Weight: 0.815 kg.
Barrel Length: 194mm (7.64 in.).
Rifling: 5 lands and grooves—right-hand direction of twist.
Magazine Capacity: 8 cartridges.

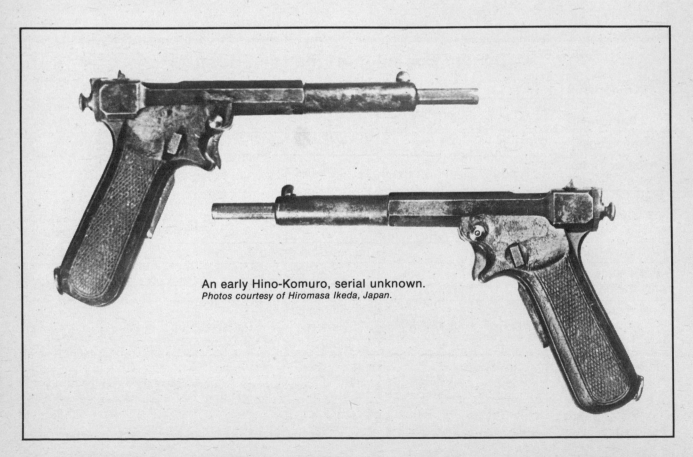

An early Hino-Komuro, serial unknown.
Photos courtesy of Hiromasa Ikeda, Japan.

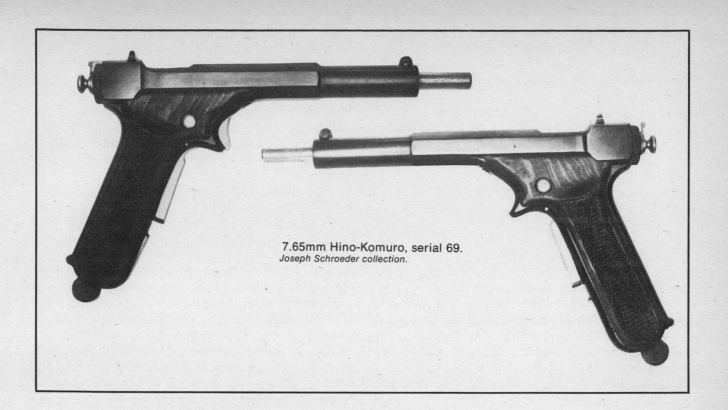

7.65mm Hino-Komuro, serial 69.
Joseph Schroeder collection.

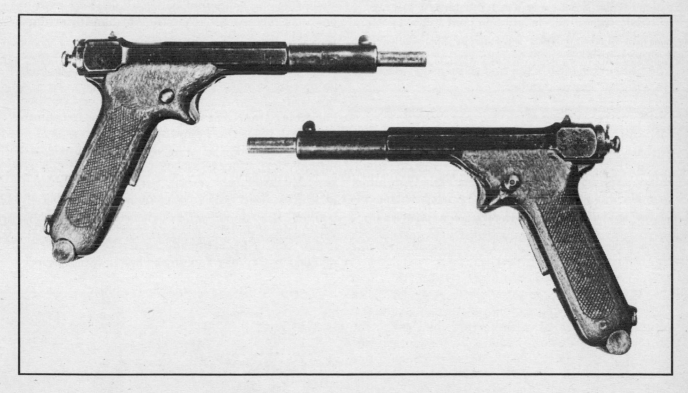

The most significant improvements were those made to the magazine and its latching assembly; these greatly facilitated its removal from the pistol. The change in grip frame shape undoubtedly resulted in a far more comfortable feeling pistol with perhaps better pointing qualities. The shorter barrel length was an improvement, although not significant when the basic weakness of the open breech-forward barrel extension design is considered. A single centimeter difference in length would have little positive effect on the weapon's accuracy or carrying convenience. To the student of design evolution, the other modifications are interesting, of course, but of little real consequence.

8mm Hino-Komuro
(Serial No. 184)

Designation: 1904 Hino-Komuro.
Caliber: 8mm.
Action: Blow-forward—fixed firing pin.
Overall Length: 265mm (10.43 in.) uncocked; 303mm (11.93 in.) cocked.
Height: 150mm (5.91 in.).
Weight: 2 pounds, 0 ounces.
Barrel Length: 217mm (8.54 in.).
Rifling: 5 lands, 5 grooves—right-hand direction of twist.
Magazine Capacity: 8 cartridges.
Distribution: Private purchases.
Manufacturer: Komuro Gun Factory, Nishi-Ohkubo, Toyotama-gun, Tokyo.
Production Period: 1904-1912.
Quantity Produced: 8mm, one known—possibility less than 500 in all calibers.
General Serial Range: 1-500, inclusive of all calibers.
Known Serial Range: 8mm, one known, no. 184—all calibers, 31-434.
Markings: Serial and Japanese patent number.
Finish: Rust blue—bright and heat treated parts.
Grip Panels: Wood—checked Juglandaceae, walnut family.
Serialization: All major and some minor parts—assigned serial number.

Kumazo Hino

The "Hino-Handgun" is an interesting ingredient in the study of Japanese firearms, but is of minor importance compared to the other accomplishments of its inventor. Army Lieutenant Colonel Hino gained national acclaim and fame as a successful aircraft designer and Japan's premier aviator during the first two decades of this century.

Kumazo Hino was born June 9, 1878 (11th year of the Meiji Era, Japanese calendar year 2538), in Hitoyoshi City, Kumamoto Prefecture, Kyushu. Cut off from the neighboring prefectures by the Kyushu Mountains, and dominated by the isolationist policies of its *daimyo* (feudal lord of the Sagara line —which ruled the district for 670 years), the area today is blessed with the beauty and culture of its historical past.

Hino was graduated from the Army Military Academy, (10th Class) as an infantry lieutenant. But he did not remain in the infantry. His inventive genius was recognized through his research and design development in such varied fields as automotive engineering, hand grenades, rifles and pistols. In May 1903, just before reaching his 25th birthday,

young Hino was appointed staff engineer in the army technical inspection department upon the recommendation of Lieutenant General K. Nakamura, chief aide-de-camp to the Emperor. This department was responsible for the review and development of all army weapons. During his first year as a military engineer, Hino developed several rifle modifications, significant enough in design to be honored by a request from the Meiji Emperor for a personal demonstration.

In December of 1903, he finalized his "Hino-Handgun" design, and applied for the Japanese patent along with his backer, Tomojiro Komuro. Interestingly, the military was so impressed by Lieutenant Hino's design that War Minister Masaki Terauchi personally endorsed the application for a "world" patent (i.e., English and U.S. applications).

While finalizing the design and firing a prototype, Hino shot himself in the thumb of his left hand—a crooked thumb remained as a lifetime reminder. Sometime later, Hino was more seriously wounded when an employee working on a pistol accidentally fired it. The bullet pierced Hino from back to stomach. The silk *haori* which he was wearing at the time, showing the bullet hole and blood stains, was one of the mementoes lost in the April, 1945, bombing raid that destroyed Hino's house.

Although the weapon designs for the army were noteworthy, it was in the air that Kumazo Hino gained his greatest recognition. In 1909, he was nominated to the newly formed Provisional Military Dirigible Research Society, and promoted to captain. On April 11 of the following year, he was sent to Germany to study flying techniques and to select an airplane for purchase by the Japanese military. He returned six months later, on October 25, after completing his study, and recommended the purchase of a German Hans-Grade which was powered by a two-cycle, four-cylinder air-cooled engine of 24 hp. His choice, and a French-made Henri Farman, recommended by Captain Yoshitoshi Tokugawa (a descen-

Kumazo Hino—age 60—February 11, 1938.
Photo courtesy of Atsushi Shibuya, Japan.

Kumazo Hino piloting the German-made Hans-Grade on the first successful airplane flight from Japanese soil, December 14, 1910.
Photo courtesy of Atsushi Shibuya, Japan.

Tomojiro Komuro (seated on the right in Western clothes), 1905. "The pride of victory over a world power (Russia) is evidenced in the face of young Komuro."
Photo courtesy of Atsushi Shibuya, Japan.

dent of the famous Tokugawa *shogun),* were the first two airplanes imported to Japan.

Captain Hino (along with Captain Tokugawa) was selected by the Dirigible Society to conduct the first test flights, which were held at the Yoyogi Army Training Field.

On December 14, 1910 (Meiji 43) Hino flew the German-made Hans-Grade on two limited flights—the first was only 30 meters in length, and attained an altitude of just one meter. His second flight of the day covered 100 meters at an altitude of two meters. The next day he again flew the "Grade," this time to an altitude of 30 meters, covering a distance of 250 meters. Unfortunately, none of these three flights was officially recorded.

Four days later, on December 19, after correcting difficulties with the engine of the French Farman, Captain Yoshitoshi Tokugawa succeeded in flying 3,000 meters, attaining an altitude of 70 meters. This flight was officially recorded for history, and thus somewhat incorrectly established Captain Tokugawa as Japan's first airplane pilot.

Captain Hino's mechanical genius prevailed, however, for he later designed, built, and flew his own airplane—the Hino Model No. 1, soon followed by the

The Hino Model No. 2 with the designer at the controls, May 1911.
Photo courtesy of Atsushi Shibuya, Japan.

Hino Model No. 2, which employed an engine of his own design. Fortunately, he has been recognized for these accomplishments, and also credited for his participation in the design of the Kayaba Type HK-1 tailless glider and Japan's first rocket, the *Shusui.* The Kayaba company was also a manufacturer of two- and three-barrel signal pistols for the Imperial Navy.

Outspoken and lacking the necessary finesse for dealing with the military hierarchy of the time, Hino was transferred to the Fukuoka Infantry Regiment in 1911, and there continued his research activities until his retirement from the army with the rank of lieutenant-colonel. He died on January 15, 1946 (Showa 21) at age 68—sadly in poverty, of malnutrition.

In addition to the "Hino-Handgun," he will long be remembered for his significant contributions to Japan's aviation history. In 1978, a monument in recognition of his 100th anniversary was erected in Hitoyoshi, the city of his birth.

Tomojiro Komuro

By comparison, the background of Tomojiro Komuro holds little significance in the history of Japan. He is perhaps important only for his belief in the excellence of the "Hino" design and for his support of its patent and manufacture. Without this belief and his financial assistance, the "Hino-Handgun" could well have been nothing more than an idea.

He was born on September 21, 1873 (Meiji 6), in Kawakado-mura, Iruma-gun, Saitama Prefecture, and died November 2, 1951 (Showa 26) at age 78.

Like the Hino-Komuro handguns themselves, the memories of the men responsible for them can also be preserved with relatively little effort, where otherwise they might be forgotten and lost through the passing of time. It has been the intent of this article to preserve the total story of both man and gun. •

The V-42 Special Service Force Knife

by Steven B. Fox

THE V-42 First Special Service Force Knife is one of the most desirable and sought-after knives of World War II. It was manufactured by W.R. Case and Sons in 1943, so is often also referred to as the "Case V-42" as well as simply the "V-42." Case made over 3000 of these knives for the First Special Service Force, a highly trained, select commando unit consisting of both United States and Canadian soldiers.

There were, in actuality, four variations of this commando stiletto, but only three were produced in quantity and issued. Because of the rarity of the V-42, confusion often exists about which variation a particular example is.

The First Variation is the prototype (not shown). It has a bright blade and is very similar to the second variation, except that the prototype has no thumb print on the ricasso (the flat area of the blade just below the crossguard), smoother leather washers on the handle, and a blade that is almost 2 inches longer than any of the later versions. It is believed that only one or two of the prototypes were made; the V-42 was never issued in its prototype form.

The Second Variation has a serrated thumbprint on one side of the ricasso, a rounded and flared pommel, as on the prototype, and a handle with shallow serrations. The 7⁵/₁₆-inch blade was polished bright, as was the crossguard. It is not known exactly how many of the Second Variation were made, but the number seems to have been very, very few.

The Third Variation is exactly the same as the second except that it has a blued blade and a pommel ending in a sharp point instead of being round. The serrations in the grip were also slightly more pronounced.

The Fourth Variation very closely resembles the third except that it had a shorter ricasso and consequently a shorter thumbprint.

The ricassos on the Second and Third Variations are 1⁹/₁₆ inches long and the thumbprints consist of 21 grooves. On the Fourth Variation the ricasso is 1⅜

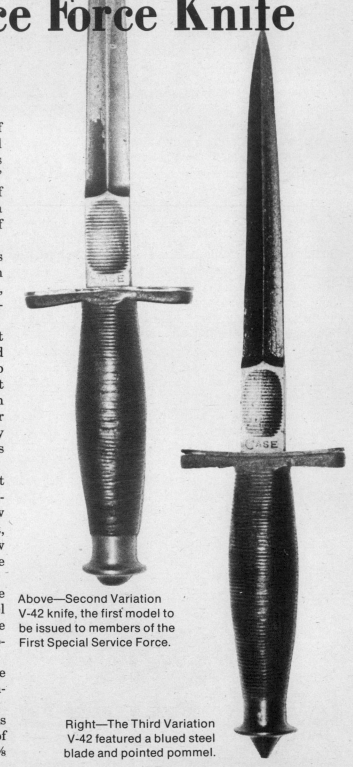

Above—Second Variation V-42 knife, the first model to be issued to members of the First Special Service Force.

Right—The Third Variation V-42 featured a blued steel blade and pointed pommel.

inches long and the thumbprint consists of 18 grooves.

Just about all of the V-42s that were issued to the First Special Forces are Third Variations with the long ricasso and long thumbprint and Fourth Variation with the short ricasso and short thumbprint.

On all the V-42s the crossguard was bright metal although many will be found with the crossguard painted black.

All V-42s were issued with a rather crude long brown leather scabbard (as shown in the group picture) which is 20 inches long.

To sum up, the major differences between the variations are:

Prototype (First Variation)
- no thumbprint
- round pommel
- bright blade
- smooth handle

Second Variation
- thumbprint
- round pommel
- bright blade
- long ricasso and thumbprint

Third Variation
- thumbprint
- pointed pommel
- blued blade
- long ricasso and thumbprint

Fourth Variation
- thumbprint
- pointed pommel
- blued blade
- short ricasso and thumbprint

The First Special Service Force was a select fighting group with an exciting combat record in World War II. Any of the special tools created for this elite unit is an exciting find for the military collector, and the graceful and deadly V-42 knife is certainly the prime collectors' item from this unique unit. Fortunate indeed is the collector who has even one V-42 knife in his collection, let alone several variations! ●

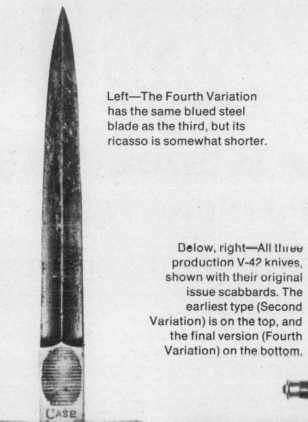

Left—The Fourth Variation has the same blued steel blade as the third, but its ricasso is somewhat shorter.

Below, right—All three production V-42 knives, shown with their original issue scabbards. The earliest type (Second Variation) is on the top, and the final version (Fourth Variation) on the bottom.

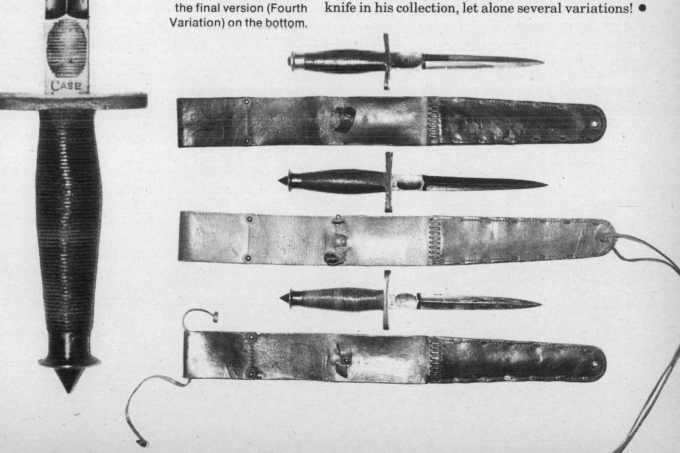

The Spencer Repeater
the first modern military rifle

by Konrad F. Schreier, Jr.

THE Civil War was a transition time in military weapons, equipment and logistics. Much of its tactics and many of its weapons came from earlier days of warfare, but a multitude of new things ranging from rifled field artillery to iron-clad armored warships received their baptism of fire in the conflict. Of the new weapons used in the Civil War the importance of one—the Spencer repeating rifle and carbine—is often neglected among the mass of novel weapons involved in that conflict.

As a matter of historic fact the Spencer had a much more important influence on the outcome of the war than it is usually credited with. It was undoubtedly one of the most important new military weapons ever introduced. It was the first repeating military rifle that fired metallic cartridges to be used in combat. It was the first *modern* military rifle.

Of course the Spencer was not the first breech-loading military rifle to see service. However it was the first breech-loading, metallic cartridge firing rifle designed specifically for military use. It was not the first magazine loading repeater, but it was the first specifically designed for military service. The only rifle contemporary with the Spencer which was a metallic cartridge, magazine-loading repeater was the Henry rifle, and it was not designed to be a military weapon. Though Henry rifles saw use in the Civil War before the Spencer did, the delicate Henry

mechanism could not stand the rigors of military service unless special care was given it. That often proved impossible in the field, severely limiting the Henry's combat value, but the rugged Spencer could stand the roughest of service.

The 44 Henry rimfire cartridge fired a 200-grain bullet with 26 grains of black powder, making it comparable to contemporary pistol loadings, while the Spencer rimfire load pushed a 52 caliber bullet weighing 362 grains backed by a powder charge of some 42 grains. The Spencer's load was something like 75 percent of that of the Civil War 58 caliber muzzle-loading rifled musket, and thus was several times as powerful as any contemporary pistol. Under the combat conditions of the Civil War the Spencer's ammunition proved more than adequate, and most records show it was pretty accurate, reliable and effective by any standard.

When 25-year-old Christopher Miner Spencer set out to invent his rifle in 1859, there wasn't suitable ammunition around. The first rimfire cartridge had only been in use for a couple of years, the first being the Smith & Wesson No. 1 or 22 Short. The new 44 Henry rimfire rifle was just beginning to meta-

Above—A Union calvalryman with a Spencer carbine holds off a group of the enemy, as portrayed in an illustration from Spencer's 1866 catalog.

The Spencer carbine, about 50,000 of which were made and issued to Union soldiers between 1863 and 1865.

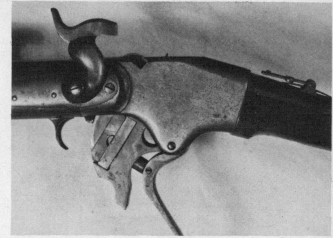

A Spencer carbine with the action open, shown from both the side (above) and top (below). Note the saddle ring visible in the top view.

morphose out of the primitive Volcanic repeating rifle. In fact, Henry's repeating rifle patent is dated October 1860, while Spencer received his first repeating rifle patent in March of 1860—some seven months before Henry's. Spencer was in the mechanical manufacturing business in the same part of New England as Henry, and the two men knew each other. It is believed that Spencer's first prototype rifles were chambered for Henry's rimfire cartridges.

Henry had the advantage, however, since he was remodeling an existing mechanism while Spencer had to develop his from scratch. The Spencer patent first showing the design actually used in Civil War production arms wasn't issued until July of 1862. The Civil War had begun in April of 1861, at the time Spencer's rifle was still in the development stage, and there was still the major problem of getting it into production.

In the mid-19th century getting any complicated piece of precision machinery like the Spencer into production was a monumentally difficult and time consuming task. You couldn't run out to the local tool sales store and buy equipment, and due to wartime demands local machine shops were already loaded with more work than they could handle. It took months of advance planning and ordering to get equipment and tools made, with almost everybody in the arms-making centers of New England trying to do the same thing.

Spencer got his first rifle contract from the U.S. Navy on 22 June, 1861—just a couple of months after the war had begun. It was for 700 rifles and 70,000 cartridges—a hundred rounds for each. More small Navy orders followed, all based on the demonstration of a single handmade prototype rifle which fired practically handmade ammunition. Twenty-eight-year-old Spencer was a mechanical genius, and he had to have been to have gotten as far as he had with his new rifle. It still took him another year, however, before he could make his first shipments to the Navy in 1862. That was remarkably good time considering the obstacles he faced, but Spencer was well known and respected in New England manufacturing circles—he got considerable help and cooperation from his friends. And he got the Navy orders which

put his rifle in production. Total Navy procurement totaled only about 1000 pieces, however.

He still had to sell the U.S. Army, and its most difficult Chief of Ordnance, Brig. Gen. James W. Ripley. Spencer went on a campaign: He got officers, politicians, and even President Lincoln to try his rifle. Spencers were privately and publicly purchased for several state volunteer units, and many individual soldiers also bought them! One of the first Spencers fired in combat was used in the Antietam Campaign of October, 1862. It was the personal property of Sgt. Francis O. Lombard of the 1st Massachusetts Cavalry, a very nice touch since the Spencer was made in Boston, Massachusetts (there are no other reports of other Spencers at Antietam). U.S. Army records state the first combat use of Army issue Spencers was "late in June, 1863."

Of course the first official use of the Spencer was in the Gettysburg Campaign—during the last days of June and the first week of July, 1863. Buford's

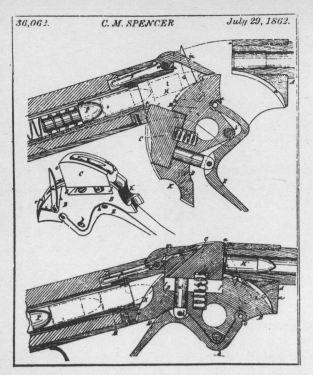

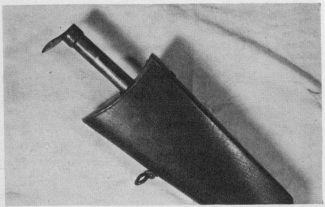

Spencer's 1862 patent drawing, showing details of the improved action used in his Civil War and subsequent arms. Below is Spencer's patent model.

Closeup of the butt of a Spencer, showing the loading tube partially withdrawn.

Cavalry used Spencers in the first fire fight of the Battle of Gettysburg on July 1, 1863, and the Spencers halted the Confederate advance. Among the other units using Spencers were some of the Michigan Volunteer Cavalry commanded by George Armstrong Custer, and they helped knock Stuart's Confederate Cavalry—"Lee's eyes and ears"—out of the campaign. Reports indicate that there were some 3,500 Spencer-armed Union troops in the Battle of Gettysburg, and that their firepower made an important contribution to the Union success. To understand just what affect the Spencers had in combat it is necessary to understand what they could do compared to the other arms in use at the time.

The vast majority of troops on both sides in the Gettysburg Campaign—and the entire Civil War for that matter—were armed with muzzle-loading rifles firing paper cartridges. Even in the hands of the calmest veteran troops the maximum rate of fire of these arms was two or three shots a minute, according to contemporary publications such as the Civil War *Scott's Military Dictionary*. In the heat and excitement of battle it was common for a soldier to load his muzzleloader improperly—usually putting the bullet instead of the powder in first—and thus rendering it inoperative. After Gettysburg there were estimates that as many as 30 percent of the soldiers on both sides were unable to fire in action because they had misloaded their arms.

A few Colt revolving rifles and carbines were used at Gettysburg, and they were afflicted with some firing problems all their own. Six shots from a cylinder, and then the man had to find a safe place to reload. Using the self-contained cartridges issued it still took about a half-minute or more to reload and re-cap the Colt. Their rate of fire was reckoned at about six to nine aimed shots per minute; and, while this was three times the firepower of a rifled muzzleloader, it took perfect discipline to maintain fire at a steady rate so the enemy couldn't overrun Colt armed troops while they were reloading.

A large number of single-shot breech-loading rifles and carbines were used by Union troops at Gettysburg, and they did well. They were difficult to load improperly, and easier and faster to load than a muzzleloader or Colt revolving rifle. Of them the Sharps was the most important, and what it could do was typical of all of them whether they fired externally primed combustible cartridges as the Sharps did, or self-contained metallic cartridges as others did. A good soldier could fire a breech-loading single-shot long gun at a rate of ten or twelve aimed shots a minute, or about four times the rate of a man armed with a muzzle-loading rifle.

But, when it came to the magazine loading Spencer, this was a rifle of a new dimension. The seven cartridges it carried in its magazine could be delivered as

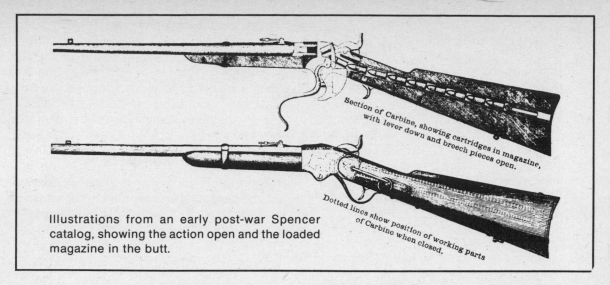

Illustrations from an early post-war Spencer catalog, showing the action open and the loaded magazine in the butt.

Section of Carbine, showing cartridges in magazine, with lever down and breech pieces open.

Dotted lines show position of working parts of Carbine when closed.

aimed fire in something around 15 seconds. Reloading the Spencer's buttstock magazine was, at best, a clumsy operation, but a well-trained soldier could get the job done in some 15 seconds. The Spencer's rate of fire was calculated at a rate of some 14 aimed shots a minute, about six times as fast as the muzzle-loading rifle could do. An additional benefit often overlooked is that the Spencer could also be loaded and fired as a single shot when combat conditions didn't allow time to reload its magazine. After the Civil War ended many Spencers were fitted with the Stabler Magazine Cut-Off, so they could be fired as single shots with the seven cartridges in the magazine held in reserve in case a burst of rapid fire should be required.

One drawback of the Spencer's magazine system was that it was possible to load cartridges into it backwards, and this could jam its action. A cartridge so loaded might even explode outside the chamber if the action lever was worked energetically enough. However there are no contemporary mentions of this potential problem afflicting the Spencer in Civil War battles, so it is to be assumed that the troops using Spencers seldom, if ever, loaded them improperly.

Another way of looking at the Spencer's potent firepower is that a soldier armed with one could put out the same number of shots per minute as seven men armed with muzzle-loading rifles! Civil War veterans were quoted as saying: "A company with Spencers was worth a regiment with muzzleloaders," and that was about right.

Another advantage of the Spencer which was also shared by breech-loading single shots and the Colts, was that they could be loaded while in the prone position. It is difficult, but not impossible, to load a muzzle-loading rifle in any position other than standing up. This gave the Spencers, breech-loading single shots, and Colts another big advantage over muzzle-loading rifles.

There were, unfortunately, Spencer ammunition supply problems, and there were occasions when much needed Spencer armed Union troops had to be withdrawn or withheld due to lack of ammunition. On the other side the Confederates did not have facilities to manufacture the Spencer cartridge, so they could only use the arms when, and if, they captured them with an ammunition supply—this hardly ever happened. The rapid and concentrated fire from Spencers was extremely demoralizing, according to Confederates who recalled facing it, and this alone made it difficult for the Confederates to capture any Spencer arms or ammunition. Official records show that the Confederates practically never defeated Spencer armed Union Troops, even in cases where they outnumbered them as much as ten to one!

It was reported by practically all the important and responsible officers of the Union Army that the Spencer was, without doubt or reservation, the best military rifle produced to that time, and that the short cavalry carbine version of the rifle was superior to any cavalry arm of the period. During the Civil War the Union Cavalry fought dismounted, as infantry, most of the time, since the tradition of the U.S. Mounted Service was to use the horse for mobility, and not to fight on horseback unless it became absolutely necessary. The Spencer cavalry carbine was, to all intents and purposes, as effective as the rifle, but it unfortunately could not mount the bayonet that infantrymen believed to be an essential part of their weaponry.

A total of about 12,000 Spencer rifles and 50,000 Spencer carbines were delivered to the Union Forces in time to see action in the Civil War. Their illustrious combat record proved that these first military repeating magazine loading arms were superior—far superior—to any other issue military rifle or carbine in the world at that time. In the light of this universally held opinion, the subsequent record of the Spencer is difficult to understand.

The Spencer rifle was *never* made a *standard* U.S.

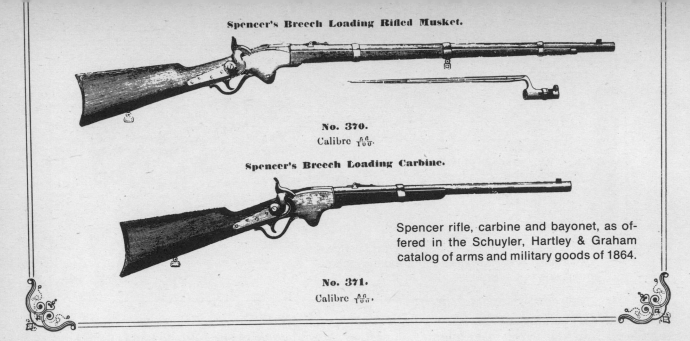

Spencer's Breech Loading Rifled Musket.

No. 370.
Calibre $\frac{AA}{100}$.

Spencer's Breech Loading Carbine.

Spencer rifle, carbine and bayonet, as offered in the Schuyler, Hartley & Graham catalog of arms and military goods of 1864.

No. 371.
Calibre $\frac{AA}{100}$.

Army weapon, and it was not used by the regular U.S. Army after the trap-door, single-shot Springfield was adopted in 1866. It has been suggested that the Army didn't want the Spencer rifle because the movements required to load its buttstock magazine were clumsy and un-military—what ever that might mean—and there might be a bit of truth in this. In 1870-1871 about a thousand Spencer carbines were rebuilt into infantry rifles for repeating rifle field trials being held at the time, but these could not have had much affect on U.S. Army rifle history since the trap-door Springfield single shot was retained until the 1890s.

It has also been suggested that the Spencer was discarded due to problems of power and reliability of its rimfire ammunition, and there is a little truth in this. Early rimfire large caliber ammunition was not as reliable or as accurate as centerfire, but it would have been a relatively simple matter to convert the Spencer to fire centerfire ammunition. While this change was made experimentally, the Spencer rifle was nevertheless discarded and speculation on what might have happened if it hadn't been is useless.

The Spencer carbine, on the other hand, was retained as the U.S. Army's co-standard cavalry arm until the introduction of the improved 1873 model of the trap-door Springfield single shot. The Spencer was co-standard with the old Civil War single shot Sharps carbine modified to fire centerfire metallic cartridges. The arms and equipment issued a cavalry regiment at that time was pretty much up to its commanding officer, subject to what was on hand in stores available for issue. In any case when, in 1873, it came time to turn in the Spencers for the trap-door Springfield single shots, some cavalry officers and men objected loudly, and asked to be allowed to retain their repeaters—they were not.

In any case the Spencer Rifle Company had gone bankrupt in 1869, and its assets were bought up by Winchester and the manufacture of Spencers was discontinued. The manufacture of Spencer rimfire ammunition was continued until about World War I, and new and reconditioned Spencers were still offered in arms catalogs as late as 1900—more than 30 years after the last of them had been manufactured.

After his Civil War rifle company folded Christopher M. Spencer joined Charles Ethan Billing, a Winchester-trained man, to form the firm of Billing & Spencer Co. This company was a very successful maker of small drop forgings for all kinds of things including guns. Spencer was also involved in the development of machine tools of a number of types including the automatic screw machine—an automatic lathe—which he invented in 1873.

Spencer never lost his interest in guns and shooting, and, under his instigation, the firm of Billing & Spencer produced the Roper repeating rifles and shotguns from about 1869 to 1876. He also involved the firm in the manufacture of his Spencer repeating shotgun from 1882 until 1889, and this would appear to have been Spencer's last venture into the manufacture of arms. In any case the arms business was nothing but a small sideline in Spencer's business life by then, and his Civil War repeating rifle and carbine was ancient history.

Spencer died in 1922 at the age of 89. He marveled at the new weapons introduced for World War I, and maintained an active interest in them and their manufacture up until his death. After all, Billing & Spencer was a key producer of gun parts, and there wasn't a gun plant in America that didn't use machine tools Spencer had invented. But the Civil War Spencers were all but forgotten, even by Spencer who doesn't seem to have even reminisced about them even though he had invented what may well be the world's first modern military rifle.   •

A well-known but little studied German armsmaker of the early post-war years

ORTGIES

by DONALD W. KOELLIKER

Very early Ortgies 7.65m. (32 ACP) pistol, serial 282. Note the first style slide marking.

THIS IS a story of Ortgies produced pistols, first made by Heinrich Ortgies himself and later by Deutsche Werke, Aktiengesellschaft, which also produced rifles and shotguns under Ortgies' name.

First let us consider only Ortgies pistols in 7.65mm and 9mm. Both caliber pistols were manufactured simultaneously and serialed in the same consecutive serial range. The only difference between the two is the barrels. Ortgies pistols of 6.35mm were not manufactured until approximately 2 years after production of the larger calibers began, and these are serialed in their own separate serial range.

The Ortgies pistols were designed and patented by Heinrich Ortgies during World War I. Heinrich Ortgies started manufacturing his pistols in his own plant in 1919 after World War I had ended. A resident of Erfurt, Germany, Ortgies located his gun manufacturing business there under the name Ortgies & Co. The pistols have several slide address markings, which vary as production continued. The first guns were marked:

Ortgies & Co. - Erfurt
Ortgies' Patent

found on the left side of the slide. On the right side of the slide there are no markings other than the Crown "N" German nitro proof mark. We will call this the first-style slide address.

Pistols bearing the first-style slide address are found in two variations: The first variation marking is all capital letters of a vertical style of lettering

while the second has upper and lower case letters which are italicized.

The lowest serial number pistol observed with the first-style address, first variation, is number 282, a 7.65mm pistol with Portuguese army proof marks (a circle with a triangle inside it). The wood grips of these early pistols have a ½-inch diameter brass medallion with the Ortgies trademark or *schutzmarke*. This mark is an intertwined **HO** (Heinrich Ortgies) in a circle.

The magazines for these early pistols have a rust blue finish and are marked with the "HO" Ortgies trademark on both sides. The left side is marked **9mm**, with a row of six vertical holes to indicate the number of 9mm cartridges, while the right side is marked **7.65mm,** and has a row of seven vertical holes. An unusual feature of the early Ortgies magazines is their capability to be used for both the 7.65mm and 9mm cartridges. All early magazines are so marked and may be used in either caliber pistol.

The lowest serial number pistol observed with the first-style address, second variation, is number 4430, a commercial model in 7.65mm. The magazine is the same as described above.

Shortly after production of Ortgies pistols started in 1919, Heinrich Ortgies passed away. Soon after his death, manufacture of his pistols was resumed by the Deutsche Werke Aktiengesellschaft, with a Berlin address. Whether this Berlin address is that of the home office or a manufacturing plant has not been determined. Only a few thousand pistols will be found with the Berlin slide address, however. This transition occurred between pistol serial number 13830, which has the **Ortgies & Co.** address, and pistol serial number 15894, which bears the address:

Ortgies - Patent
Deutsche Werke Aktiengesellschaft Berlin

or simply **D.W.A. Berlin** for short. This address is the second-style slide address found on Ortgies pistols.

Serial number 15894, a 7.65mm pistol, is a cutaway: This is serialed in the consecutive series but is not proofed or otherwise marked on the frame. On the right side of the slide is engraved **O.P. Hbg.** The significance of this marking is not known except for the "Hbg.," which is the abbreviation for the city of Hamburg, Germany. This cutaway pistol could possibly have been a sample sent to the Hamburg police department for a training aid or as an armorer's instructional weapon.

A number consisting of one to three digits may have once been engraved after the O.P.Hbg. marking. Pistol serial number 13830 also has this identically engraved marking, O.P.Hbg., on the right side of its slide with the addition of the number 931,

A slightly later 7.65mm pistol, serial 4430. (Inset) "HO" (Heinrich Ortgies) logo inset in grip.

reading **O.P. Hbg. 931.** On the cutaway this section has been removed to expose the action, so, if there ever was a number, it shall remain lost forever. No other markings are on the right side of this pistol other than the Crown "N" nitro proof mark.

It appears that "Ortgies & Co." manufactured only 7.65mm pistols—there may be other calibers but I have not seen any to date. The original Ortgies instruction booklet, however, lists all three calibers, 6.35mm, 7.65mm and 9mm.

How long the Deutsche Werke Aktiengesellschaft manufactured pistols with the Berlin address is unknown, but it must have been a short time only. Whether a pistol of 6.35mm was manufactured there is not known; I have in my collection Berlin marked pistols only in 7.65mm and 9mm and I have serious doubts as to whether any 6.35mm pistols were manufactured with the Berlin address. A 6.35mm pistol serial number 282 in my collection bears D.W.A. markings with an Erfurt address (yes, I have both 7.65mm and 6.35mm pistols with the same serial number, 282).

The earliest Berlin addressed pistol I have is the cutaway. The second Berlin addressed pistol I have is serial number 20515, which is a 9mm commercial. This is the lowest 9mm serial number I have observed to date. This pistol is unusual as it is the first Ortgies to use a screw to fasten the grips to the frame. Also, it does not have a button safety, nor did it ever have one. This is one of two pistols known with the grip screw and may be a prototype. Button safety pistols came later in the late 28,000 serial range.

A sectioned 7.65mm pistol, serial 15894. It bears the marking "O.P. Hbg" on the left side of the slide, indicating probable police or other official ownership.

Right side view of a 7.65mm pistol, serial 13830, which also bears an "O.P. Hbg. 931" issue marking.

The third Berlin addressed pistol I have is serial number 23865, a 7.65mm Czechoslovakian contract gun with Czech proofs. These proofs are stamped into the slide on the left side in front of the serrations, and consist of the number 3344, a standing lion and the number 38. No other markings are found on this pistol.

The fourth Berlin addressed pistol I have is serial number 28902, a 9mm contract with Czechoslovakian proofs. These proof marks differ from the above contract as follows: The left side of the slide is marked behind the serrations with the numeral 8, followed by a standing lion and lastly by the numeral 4. The right side of the frame trigger guard is marked with the numerals 22, and near the front of the trigger guard appear the intertwined letters CRS. This pistol has a button safety and is the lowest serial number pistol observed with this feature. The finish on this gun is rust blue, as are all of the others, but the metal parts were not highly polished before bluing as the other pistols were. It is more or less a military finish, and this is the only pistol observed with this military finish on it.

The fifth Berlin addressed pistol in my collection is serial number 30537, in 7.65mm caliber. On the left side of the slide is the date 1920 followed by the letter S within a circle. This date and letter combination is also found on Luger pistols: Some Luger collectors believe these marks were put on by Simson Factory, and the date represents the year the pistol was repaired or reworked by Simson. However, it may also stand for Spandau Arsenal. Close examination reveals nothing—all of the forged and machined parts are properly marked and appear to be original. This does not prove it was not repaired, however. Another theory is the date may have been put on by plant security identifying it as one of theirs. Take your pick as to which theory you wish to believe at this time—possibly at a future date we will find the true meaning of it.

Another interesting feature of this pistol is the heat temper blue trigger. This pistol is one of two examples I have observed with the offcolor trigger. Both of them appear factory original.

The sixth Berlin addressed pistol I have is serial number 30872, a 9mm contract. This pistol is a Czechoslovakian contract gun with proof marks again different than the two Czech pistols described previously. The slide on this pistol has no Czech proof marks at all—they are all on the frame. On the right side of the frame, on the trigger guard, the number 22 and intertwined initials CRS are found. On the left side of the frame the trigger guard is marked with the numeral 1. The rear of the frame above the squeeze safety has a two-line marking: The upper line is marked 46 P; the lower line is the number 108. There are no other Czechoslovakian proof marks on this pistol. All of the Czechoslovakian pistols have rust blue magazines with them, while all commercial pistols (after, approximately, serial number 12,000) have nickel plated magazines.

Somewhere between serial numbers 30872 and 37373 Ortgies pistols appeared with the Erfurt slide address of Deutsche Werke, Aktiengesellschaft. This new slide legend reads:

Ortgies' Patent.
Deutsche Werke Aktiengesellschaft
Werk Erfurt.

This new address is a three-line address which we will refer to as the third-style address. No markings are found on the right side of the slide except the Crown '"N" nitro proof mark. I have observed a pistol

An early example bearing the Berlin address, serial 20515, in 9mm. Note the grip retaining screw.

Czech contract 9mm, serial 28902. (Insets) Detail of the Czech proofs and (right) those found on an earlier Czech 7.65mm pistol, serial 23865.

(serial number 29078) with an Erfurt third-style address. You will note an overlap in serial numbers with the Berlin second-style address on pistol serial number 30872. It is possible the new slide address was in use before the Berlin marked slides were used up. Another possibility is that Berlin pistols were manufactured in Berlin at a plant which was later moved to Erfurt. The Erfurt addressed pistol serial number 29078 is a 7.65mm with a button safety; the left side of the slide is marked 1920 S.

Deutsche Werke Aktiengesellschaft in Erfurt was the last place of manufacture, and Ortgies pistols were produced there until 1924. Pistols were manufactured in all three calibers, 6.35mm, 7.65mm and 9mm Kurz, with third-style slide addresses on them. Also manufactured were pistols with button safeties on them in 7.65mm and 9mm. I do not know if a button safety pistol was ever manufactured in 6.35mm—I doubt it. Pistols equipped with button safeties are very rare.

Somewhere between serial number 48317 and serial number 59147 a fourth slide address appeared. It read:

DEUTSCHE WERKE AKTIENGESELLSCHAFT* WERK ERFURT
ORTGIES PATENT

We shall refer to this marking as the fourth-style slide address. The right side of the slide is unmarked except for the Crown "N" nitro proof mark. Pistol serial number 59147 is a 9mm button safety model, while pistol serial number 61765 has a button safety also, but is in 7.65mm.

Somewhere between serial number 66384 and serial number 70949 the fourth-style slide address transition pistol appeared. It is similar to the earlier fourth-style slide address pistols with only two minor differences: The wooden grips now bear the new medallion of the couchant cat with its tail curving

upwards over its head, while the nitro proof mark on the slide has been moved upwards to above the extractor, near the ejection port. Everything else is identical to the fourth-style address pistols. I have observed no button safety pistols with a number four transition address, and I doubt if any exist.

Somewhere between serial number 71173 and serial number 74865, the fifth-style slide address appeared. This is the last and final slide address found on Ortgies pistols, and it was used until production ceased in 1924. The last style of stamping features a one-line address with the new Ortgies emblem of a couchant cat with its tail curved upwards over its head. Some observers mistake this emblem for a written letter "D." This slide address reads:

DEUTSCHE WERKE WERKE ERFURT

on the left side of the slide. The right side of the slide is marked:

ORTGIES' PATENT

This address, like the fourth-style address is marked in small type but in all capital letters. The crown "N" nitro proof mark on the slide has been moved upwards to above the extractor, near the ejection port. This final slide address is the type most frequently encountered—pistols were manufactured in all three calibers, 6.35mm, 7.65mm and 9mm. However, no button safety pistols were manufactured with the fifth-style address. All factory nickel plated Ortgies pistols were manufactured with the fifth-style address, in both bright and matte nickel. There are also some minor variations to be found in this group, which will be described later.

Ortgies serial numbers are now no longer a mystery. Pistols of 7.65mm and 9mm are numbered together in a consecutive serial range. Pistols of 6.35mm are numbered consecutively in their own serial range. All pistols noted to date bear this out.

Ortgies production figures are no longer a mystery either. No original factory production figures are available, but a safe guess would be approximately 250,000 pistols of 7.65mm and 9mm combined, plus approximately 185,000 pistols of 6.35mm, for a total production of approximately 435,000 pistols manufactured in all calibers at all plants. Though this is a guess, serial numbers thus observed bear this out. The highest 7.65 mm serial number observed is 248498, a blue finish commercial pistol. Highest 6.35mm serial number observed is 182625, a matte nickel finish commercial pistol.

A note of interest: Pistol serial number 241309, a blue 7.65mm commercial for export, has the full serial number stamped into the magazine floor plate. This had to be stamped before the magazine was assembled and plated, so it is factory marked. The question is why? No other Ortgies pistols observed have the magazine serialed to the gun.

The following serial number ranges listed are only assumptions by the author, but should provide a reasonable indication of the number of 7.65mm and 9mm pistols bearing the various addresses:

A very early 7.65mm pistol to have a button safety, serial 30537. Note unusual "1920" date on slide.

A 7.65mm pistol with the third-style slide address, serial 48317. Note "Made in Germany" stamped into the grip, indicating it was destined for export.

A button safety 9mm pistol with the fourth-style slide address, serial 59147.

Approximate Serial Ranges 7.65mm and 9mm

	Approximate quantities
First-style address, first variation up to serial no. 4,000	= 4,000
First-style address, second variation serial no. 4,000 to serial no. 15,000	= 11,000
Second-style address serial no. 15,000 to serial no. 30,000 with overlaps	= 15,000
Third-style address serial no. 30,000 to serial no. 55,000	= 25,000
Fourth-style address serial no. 55,000 to serial no. 70,000	= 15,000
Fourth-style address (transition) serial no. 70,000 to serial no. 74,000	= 4,000
Fifth-style address serial no. 74,000 to serial no. 249,000	= 175,000

The 6.35mm Ortgies

To date I have never seen or heard of a 6.35mm pistol with a first- or a second-style slide address. The earliest 6.35mm pistol I have is serial number 282, which bears the third-style address.

Somewhere between serial number 754 and serial number 9776 the fourth-style slide address appeared. You will note the large gap between these two pistols. It is my belief that few pistols of this caliber were imported into this country and probably few were exported by Germany to any country outside the central European area. As a result, this little pistol is scarce. Very few are found exhibited or for sale at gun shows, and they are rarely offered for sale in trade publications. Attrition should account for a few pistols, however they seem to be missing in quantity.

I have not seen or heard of any pistols of 6.35mm with the fourth-style transition markings on them. I doubt if any were made. Somewhere between serial number 26460 and serial number 29448 the fifth-style slide address came into use. It is the same as described in the 7.65mm and 9mm section.

Approximate Serial Ranges 6.35mm

	Approximate quantities
Third-style address up to serial no. 8,000	= 8,000
Fourth-style address serial no. 8,000 to serial no. 27,000	= 19,000
Fifth-style address serial no. 27,000 to serial no. 183,000	= 156,000

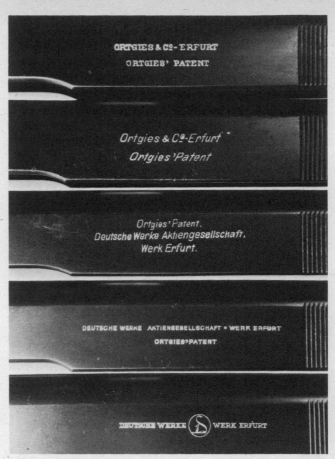

Detail of slide markings on Erfurt-made 7.65mm and 9mm Ortgies pistols. Earliest is at the top.

Third- and fourth-style slide address pistol quantities are just guesses by the author, and numbers may vary by a few thousand pistols. So far, too few have been examined by me to narrow the gap.

A note of interest: The crown "N" nitro proof mark on the slide of 6.35mm pistol serial number 11933 is located on the lower right rear corner of the slide behind the serrations and not in the usual place. This is one of two 6.35mm pistols I have examined marked with the crown "N" on the lower corner of the slide. All other 6.35mm pistols observed have the crown "N" nitro proof mark in the usual location as described in the 7.65mm and 9mm section.

Another note of interest: 6.35mm pistol serial number 21075 has a lower case letter **a** underneath the serial number, the significance of which is unknown at this time. I have not observed any other Ortgies pistol with a lower case letter underneath the serial number. This pistol has a fourth-style slide address with the "HO" marked grips and is definitely an early gun. Some European manufacturers add a letter to a serial number to denote a modification or a production change. I have examined this pistol closely and cannot find any change or modification. This does not mean a change or modification does not exist, however.

Button Safety Pistols

Button safety Ortgies pistols are very rare, and few are ever found for sale. You will find them in 7.65mm and 9mm only and only with second-, third- and fourth-style slide addresses. The button safety's function is unique. It does not block the sear, or the striker from hitting the primer. It merely blocks the squeeze safety from being pressed forward, while the squeeze safety blocks the sear bar. Since all Ortgies pistols are equipped with a squeeze safety, this additonal button safety must have resulted from a request from customers or prospective customers for a more secure loaded pistol. The button safety was a made-to-order feature, hence its rarity.

The wooden grips of a button safety pistol are fastened with a screw through the frame rather than the clamp used on most Ortgies pistols. The wooden grips are inletted to accept the button safety which slides up and down, and the frame is machined to accept it. The frame is marked with the letter **F** indicating "feuer" or fire and the button safety itself has the letter **S,** marked below the button, exposed when the pistol is on safe. To make the pistol ready to fire the button safety is slid downward, whereby the letter "S" is now covered by the wooden grip. The letter "S" stands for "sicherung" or safety. The slide itself has a notch milled into it above the button safety to accept the safety when it is slid upwards to block the squeeze safety. The notch on early production button safety pistols is about 2.5mm deep. As production continued, the notch became shallower, until late production where the depth of the notch will be about 1.5mm. The button safety is a ball of about .233 inches or 5.9mm serrated horizontally. The serrations are all hand cut and will vary from seven lines to 11 lines.

Listed below are some button safety pistols in my collection.

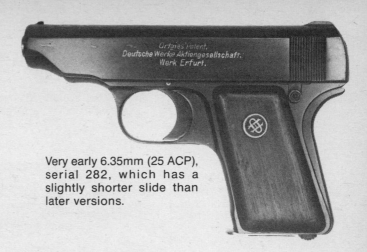

Very early 6.35mm (25 ACP), serial 282, which has a slightly shorter slide than later versions.

Button Safety Pistols

Second-style address

Czechoslovakia contract. 9mm military finish. Lowest serial number button safety observed.	serial no. 28902
Slide marked 1920 S. 7.65 mm commercial. Heat temper blue trigger.	serial no. 30537

Fourth-style address

.380 (9mm) commercial for export.	serial no. 59147
7.65mm commercial for export.	serial no. 61765
7.65mm commercial for export. (Highest known serial number button safety to date.)	serial no. 66384

Finishes

Ortgies pistols and long runs, regardless of caliber, were all European rust blued, the exceptions being the nickel plated pistols. Two pistols I have in my collection have a heat temper blue trigger—the balance of these two pistols are rust blue. These two are the only Ortgies observed with the off-color trigger. Pistol serial number 30537 is a second-style address, button safety, 7.65mm with the slide marked **1920 S.** Pistol serial number 48317 is a third-style address 7.65mm commercial model for export.

Some Ortgies pistols were nickel plated, some in bright nickel and some in matte nickel. Bright nickel plated pistols were the first produced: They were made in both 6.35mm and 7.65mm for the commercial market. All nickel plated pistols were manufactured at Erfurt and all bear the fifth-style slide address. The earliest 6.35mm bright nickel plated pistol observed is serial number 46531, and the latest 6.35mm observed is serial number 180699. Why the large gap in serial numbers is a mystery. A possibility could be nickel plating was done to order, hence its rarity. I have seen only three bright nickel

plated pistols of 6.35mm to date; and the 7.65mm bright nickel plated pistol is even rarer—I've seen only one that is factory original. I have never seen or heard of one in 9mm—they could exist, however. Bright nickel plated pistols are found with heat temper blue trigger, extractor, takedown button and grip retainer. Barrels and sears were left in the white.

Matte nickel plated pistols were manufactured near the end of production in 1924. All matte nickel plated pistols bear the fifth-style slide address and are found in both 6.35mm and 7.65mm—I have never seen or heard of one in 9mm. Matte nickel plated pistols are found with heat temper straw colored trigger, extractor, takedown button and magazine catch. Barrels and sears were left in the white.

A word of warning to the collector. Many of the Ortgies pistols examined by the author that were plated were not factory work but rather backyard and gunsmith reworks. Beware the phony—no *chrome* plated pistols were ever produced at the factory.

Engraving

I have in my collection a salesman's sample Ortgies pistol engraved on one side of the slide only. The engraving is not of first quality. This is the only factory engraved Ortgies known to date. The serial number is 12907 and the slide address is first-style, second variation. I doubt the existence of any other factory engraved Ortgies pistols—I have heard of them, but to date I have never examined one. You must remember Ortgies pistols were produced after World War One when the economies of Germany and much of the rest of the world were near chaos. Thus very few frills were offered or asked for as German arms manufacturers pushed sales of standard guns to relieve unemployment and bring needed cash into their country. However, pistols already purchased by new owners could be sent to custom engravers to be engraved to individual taste. To date I have not been able to examine any such pistol. Proceeding further along this line of thinking, presentation Ortgies pis-

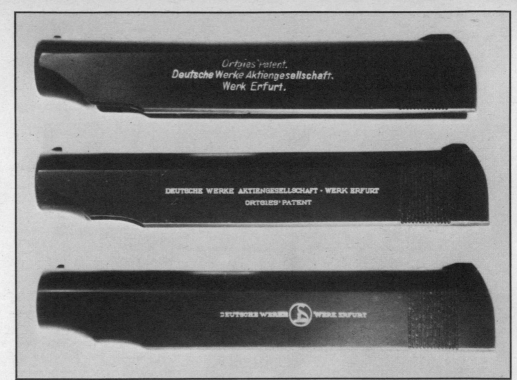

Slides of three 6.35mm Ortgies, showing the variations in slide markings. Note the top (early) is slightly shorter.

tols, cased or otherwise, were probably not offered for sale or presented as gifts. If so, no such pistol has yet surfaced.

Prototypes do exist, however: I have a 6.35mm prototype in my collection serial number 754. I may also have another in 9mm—so far I have not been able to authenticate it. Serial number is 20515, a commercial model.

Ortgies Rifles

Ortgies rifles are found in caliber 5.4mm or, as we call it, 22 Short and 22 Long Rifle. So far I have seen only two models of this rifle: The first is a plain, standard, rifle with a flat board type stock with no

Very late grip medallion, clearly showing the highly stylized cat that was the late Ortgies trademark.

butt plate. The rear sight is formed by bending the forward part of the breechblock housing upward. Serial numbers are stamped into the wood on the front of the forestock. The Ortgies emblem of the couchant cat is stamped into the top of the receiver, and also on the left side of the stock.

The second version is a deluxe model with a longer barrel, sling swivels, a dovetailed rear sight milled into the receiver and a full contoured stock with a steel butt plate. The pistol grip is checkered. Serial number locations vary: Early models have the serial number stamped into the stock under the butt plate. Later models have the serial number stamped on the bottom of the breechblock, the bottom of the barrel extension, and the inletted part of the stock. Also, the last two digits of the serial number are stamped on *some* parts. There is also stamped on the stock under the butt plate a stock number with a corresponding number stamped on the reverse of the butt plate. The Ortgies emblem of the couchant cat is stamped on top of the receiver and also the butt plate. The stock has the cat emblem made of wood inlaid into the left side. All rifles examined by the author are stamped on top of the receiver **Model I.** If there was to be a "Model II" it apparently never was manufactured. None have surfaced to date.

Ortgies Shotguns

A very unusual shotgun bears the Ortgies emblem of the couchant cat. It is a 12 gauge automatic and was manufactured at the Deutsche Werke at Erfurt,

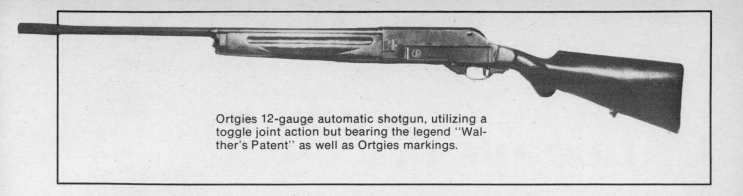

Ortgies 12-gauge automatic shotgun, utilizing a toggle joint action but bearing the legend "Walther's Patent" as well as Ortgies markings.

Germany. The address is on the left side of the receiver and reads:

DEUTSCHE WERKE ERFURT WALTHERS PATENT

A two-line address of very small type but all capital letters. Preceding the address is the Ortgies emblem of the cat. The butt plate also has the emblem of the Ortgies cat molded into it.

The gun itself is a gunsmith's nightmare. It uses a toggle action system much like the famous Luger pistol, but the joint breaks downward rather than upward as in the Luger. The toggle system is totally enclosed, including the breechblock, which is shrouded by a metal cover which retracts with the breech block on recoil to expose the ejection port. The action is worked by a crank on the right side of the receiver. The recoil springs and the toggle springs extend into the butt stock. The magazine is in the fore-end.

This unusual gun is of top quality, with parts forged and machined. Over 60 parts comprise its action. By pressing a release on the front of the receiver the magazine assembly extends downward by spring action, to allow charging. Simply pressing upwards on the magazine returns it to place. It was apparently manufactured in the early 1920s and uses the old standard 2½-inch shells (12 gauge x 65mm). I do not know if it was manufactured in any other gauges. This shotgun is certainly very rare and this is the only example yet encountered.

Another, much cheaper, shotgun also bears the Ortgies emblem. It is a 9mm rimfire model looking like the plain 22 rifle with the flat board stock. In fact it is identical to the 22 except for the barrel and extractor, and is a single-shot Flobert action. Very few are known to exist.

In Conclusion

The Ortgies pistol was an advanced design in its day. It featured smooth outlines, no projecting corners, no openings through which dirt could enter, and excellent balance; few and extremely solid parts (all forged), and (with exceptions) no screws.

Ortgies pistols have a grip or squeeze safety of unusual design. With the pistol cocked the safety button can be depressed allowing the grip safety to be forced rearward by the firing pin spring. This rearward movement blocked the sear while relieving some of the tension on the firing pin spring. The action has no hammer so it uses the spring-loaded striker or firing pin to discharge the cartridge.

Another function of the striker is to act as the ejector after the pistol has fired, pushing the spent casing away from the breech block and ejecting it as the slide traveled rearward. (This method was also used in the early Colt and Browning pocket pistols.) The grips are fastened by a unique spring loaded clamp which presses into a recess on the inner rearward edge of the grips, holding them firmly in place. This method of fastening eliminates the need for grip screws. However, some models of Ortgies pistols do have a grip screw fastening the grips to the frame.

This pistol, although simple and inexpensive, was highly efficient. This point was proven adequately during all principal shooting competitions in 1921. The caliber 7.65mm pistol won more than 70 percent of all prizes, and at the championship shooting competition at Halensee, Germany, on September 26, 1921, the Champion, Mr. Janich, used an Ortgies pistol.

Collectors of Ortgies pistols have found data and information very hard to obtain on calibers, manufacturers, dates, production figures, etc. Almost all of the information in this work has evolved from examination of pistols collected and seen by the author and scraps of information obtained by other collectors and passed on to me.

This work is by no means complete, though I believe it to be the most comprehensive look at Ortgies pistols to date. I also believe new information will turn up in the future, especially since readers can now examine pistols in their collections, find a category to put them into and discover new variations.

Pistol collecting can be fun and rewarding. Pocket pistols, though as yet not too expensive, can still offer a challenge to finding rare and unusual variations from which to build a meaningful collection. The art of locating a new variation is true gun collecting at its best.

●

Cutaways . . .
Very special collectibles

by Joseph J. Schroeder

YOU'RE WALKING DOWN the aisle at a gun show, glancing at the tables, when an incomplete gun catches your eye. It's a model you've been looking for parts for, so you pick it up and look at the price tag. Good grief! The owner has it priced at twice what you'd ask for your incomplete gun, once you had it together and working!

"How come?" you ask him, indicating the price tag. "It's a cutaway," he responds in a somewhat superior voice, "How many of those have you seen at the show?" Then you take a better look at it and realize it is really all there . . . It's just that the action, barrel and wood are all neatly sectioned, exposing much of the usually concealed mechanism from view. It's different all right, and fascinating. You'd always wondered just how that particular action functioned, and there it was, right before your eyes.

Cutaways, also known as "skeleton" arms (at Colt's) or *Schnittmodells* (by the Germans) have been around for some time. Sutherland illustrates a Colt Model 1849 cutaway, and mentions a second model Dragoon cutaway that Colt demonstrated at a London lecture in *The Book of Colt Firearms*. He then goes on to include a number of other Colt factory cutaways, from that period up through the latest models, in his book. Cutaways from even earlier in the 19th century are on display at the Musee d'Armes in Liège. It's very likely the practice of sectioning the mechanism of an arm for study or instruction began as soon as gun mechanics got complicated enough to justify the effort and "destruction" of an otherwise functional arm.

Cutaway arms are made principally as instructional devices or sales tools. Far and away the largest number seem to have been made for and/or by the military, for the instruction of both the armorers who'll be maintaining and adjusting arms and the soldiers who'll be using them. A picture may be worth a thousand words, but when it comes to understanding how a complex automatic mechanism works, a cutaway whose internal operation you can watch in action can well be worth a thousand pictures!

Factory cutaways are often made of reject parts, by apprentices who learn both about the guns and the machinery they'll later be using for their manufacture in the process. Military cutaways may be every bit as well done as their complete, front-line-issue equivalents, or crudely hewn from an assemblage of battle-weary and discarded parts. When a small group of Persian army factory cutaway Lugers came into the country a few years ago, I was fortunate enough to acquire the one gun of the group that was not factory. Its Farsi serial numbers indicate its parts came from a number of different Persian Lugers, including an artillery model toggle (the gun has a 4-inch barrel). The cuts, though in the right places, are crude, but if that gun could talk I'm sure it would have a much more interesting tale to tell than its more pristine brethren!

Factory instructional cutaways for internal plant use may be rather crude indeed, as their purpose was to demonstrate a point or points in the function or fit and such niceties as finish were of no great im-

Above—Not all cutaways are functional. This Czech Model CZ 24 is nearly sectioned in half, with so much material removed around the barrel that it can actually come out if the action is manipulated. Extreme cutaways such as this one are more likely to have been intended for a display board than for active instructional use.

Above—Cutaway British Short Model Lee Enfield (SMLE) rifle. Note the cut in the stock to show the brass cleaning kit in its storage space, and the sectioned barrel near the muzzle. Complete cutaway rifles are scarce; more often only the action of a rifle is sectioned and the barrel and stock removed or cut off to make a more convenient training tool. Right—Cutaway Iver Johnson revolver. It bears 12 cuts, all but one on its left side, and is apparently factory as the cut surfaces are nickel plated along with the outside.

Right and left side views of an Astra Model 900 cutaway that was apparently used as a factory instructional piece. It is unfinished, in the white and without any markings, but the internal lockwork is all exposed for study.

Champion noted thus far for number of cuts, this French army Model 1935S pistol has 22 cuts on both sides and top.

Cutaway Mosin-Nagant rifle action bears no marks indicating manufacturer, but finish is that of a World War I vintage Remington.

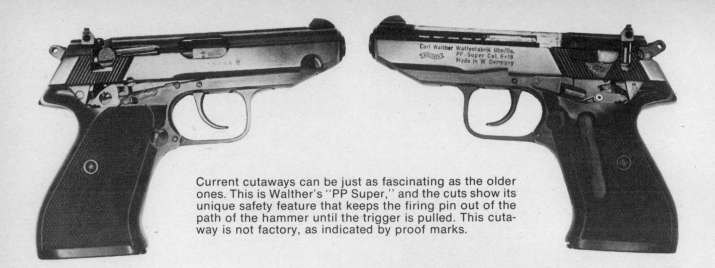

Current cutaways can be just as fascinating as the older ones. This is Walther's "PP Super," and the cuts show its unique safety feature that keeps the firing pin out of the path of the hammer until the trigger is pulled. This cutaway is not factory, as indicated by proof marks.

portance. One of my most interesting cutaways is an Astra Modelo 900, still in the white with machining marks and scribe lines to indicate where in the production process it was sidetracked for use as a teaching tool. The internal lockwork and breech locking mechanisms are entirely exposed by judicious cuts in the frame and barrel extension. The internal parts, though not finely finished to Astra's commercial standards, are all there and functional. What's also obvious, upon careful examination, is that at least some of the major parts are rejects. On the barrel extension, for example, one of the rear sight elevating ramps is neatly cut partly away by an improper pass of a milling cutter.

Sales samples are another story. With these arms a salesman hoped to convince a prospective buyer—police, military or even a large commercial outlet—that this was the gun for them to adopt/use/purchase. As a result, fit and finish, both inside and outside, are usually of the finest. In addition, such sales samples will often bear special markings or low or unusual serial numbers: A Heckler & Koch P9S I have is numbered **Sch 2,** the "Sch" meaning either *Schule* (school) or *Schnitt* (cut); but my Colt 1903 pocket 32 auto cutaway is numbered in the normal commercial series. A Colt factory letter established, however, that it was carried on Colt's books as a "skeleton" pistol. A beautifully finished 32 caliber French Mab Modele D cutaway bears the number 13, while a much earliér Mab 25 cutaway is not serialed at all. Variety in serials, as in the sectioning itself, is the rule.

My interest in cutaways is the offspring of my interest in self-loading pistols, whose ingenious mechanisms determined the direction of my collecting effort many years ago. The operation of certain guns in my collection seemed to be inadequately or improperly explained in the literature, and it wasn't until I had a chance to manipulate the action of a cutaway that some of the interrelationships normally

Cutaway Sauer Model 1930 Behorden Model auto pistol. There are 17 cuts on this pistol, all of them on the left side. Every internal function, including the unique "grip safety" built into the trigger, is exposed. The lack of proof marks confirms this as a factory cutaway.

Three Russian Baikal shotgun cutaways, purchased recently from an importer who was distributing them for a short time. Surprisingly, the single barrel model has the most cuts. Note the details of the distinctly different actions—the over/under is on top, single barrel in the middle, and side-by-side below.

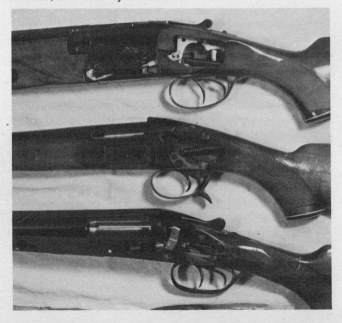

A recent cutaway is this P.08 model Mauser Parabellum, one of a very small group of "Schnittmodells" made by Mauser for Interarms.

Exotic cartridges and bullets make good cutaways, too. The cutaway Danish Schouboe bullet clearly shows its unique aluminum jacketed wooden cored bullet. To left of it is a 50 caliber armor piercing machine gun bullet, showing the tungsten carbide hardened steel inner projectile, open at the base for tracer material.

Heavier ordnance makes interesting cutaways, too. On left is a fuse for an 81mm mortar, on the right a standard U.S. Army issue Mills grenade.

buried inside the frame became clear. As my interest in cutaway automatics deepened, I found myself becoming interested in cutaway mechanisms of all kinds. Soon I'd added not only cutaway rifles, shotguns and revolvers to my collection, but even a sectioned hand grenade (very simple), mortar fuse (ingenious) and several unusual cartridges.

Cutaways are rare guns. Of the Colt Model 1903 hammerless 32, Sutherland says Colt made about 10 as skeleton pistols . . . out of over half a million of that model that were produced! A recent government contract issued to a major European auto pistol manufacturer for many thousands of their latest model pistol specified just 40 *Schnittmodells* for instructional use. The Persian army purchased at least 4,000 Lugers in the 1930s, and for that contract no more than 50 cutaways were supplied. Some cutaways do seem to turn up with surprising regularity, of course. Hundreds or perhaps thousands of Webley revolver and Enfield rifle action cutaways were sold as surplus in the United States a few years ago, and though those quantities were relatively large (and both cutaways are still turning up regularly) their number is miniscule compared to the number of operational examples of those two arms that were made for service in two World Wars.

Of course, a cutaway is a prime candidate for "faking." It is generally, after all, simply a garden variety example that has had certain areas trimmed away to expose the mechanism. Presumably, a hundred dollar gun and a few hours with a milling machine, and you now have a rare and valuable cutaway. In practice, however, it's rarely that simple. In the first place, any well done cutaway tells a story and is an attention getter, so it has an intrinsic value. To make a *good* cutaway requires a considerable investment in sophisticated machinery, the skill to use it, a study of the mechanism so the attempt is successful (one bad cut and that hundred dollar gun is just a bag of

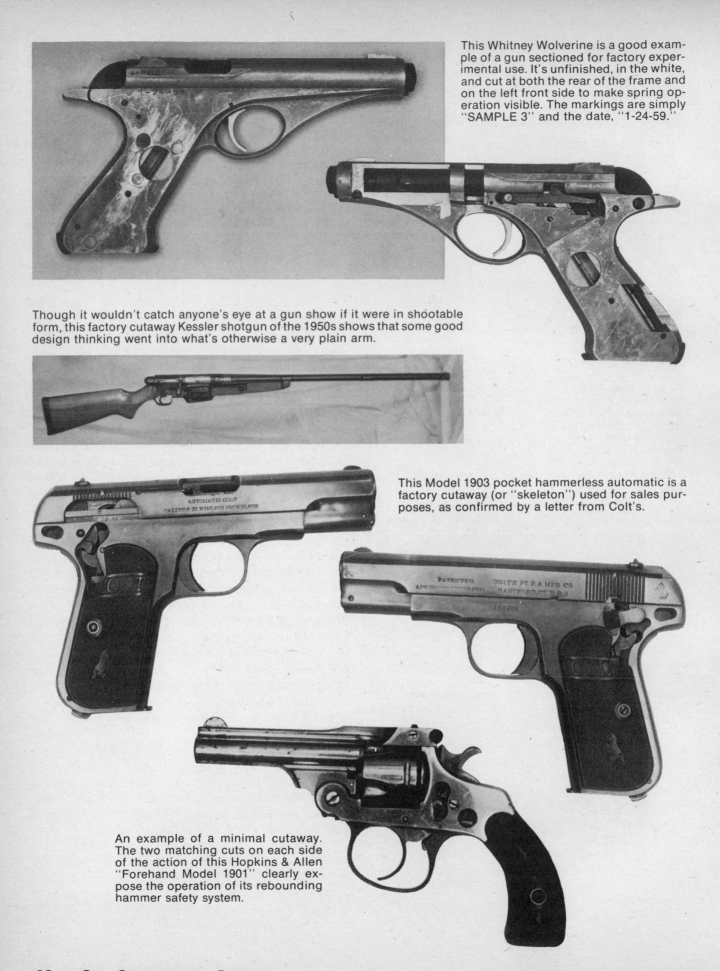

This Whitney Wolverine is a good example of a gun sectioned for factory experimental use. It's unfinished, in the white, and cut at both the rear of the frame and on the left front side to make spring operation visible. The markings are simply "SAMPLE 3" and the date, "1-24-59."

Though it wouldn't catch anyone's eye at a gun show if it were in shootable form, this factory cutaway Kessler shotgun of the 1950s shows that some good design thinking went into what's otherwise a very plain arm.

This Model 1903 pocket hammerless automatic is a factory cutaway (or "skeleton") used for sales purposes, as confirmed by a letter from Colt's.

An example of a minimal cutaway. The two matching cuts on each side of the action of this Hopkins & Allen "Forehand Model 1901" clearly expose the operation of its rebounding hammer safety system.

parts), and a good deal of time. Figure 10 to 20 hours minimum machine shop time at $20 an hour (cheap!) plus the price of the gun—thus a recently made cutaway could well cost more than an original.

There are no hard and fast rules about what determines "factory" from "post-factory" when it comes to cutaways. A lack of proofmarks is a very positive indication of authenticity, as are special or unusually placed markings. Very low or peculiar serial numbers, or no serialing at all, are favorable indicators. Though in many cases a bright polished surface, with or without paint, has been used to set off the cut surfaces, a factory finish that includes the cuts can place it in the factory category. My Beretta 951 is blued in the cuts, while an inexpensive Spanish cutaway shotgun boasts very colorful case hardening in the cuts in its frame. Any or all of these factors are positive but not absolute indicators. A cutaway made by one of the top gun restorers (see *Gun Collector's Digest, Volume I*) could satisfy most if not all of those criteria.

A factory letter is the best kind of proof of authenticity, of course. Source is another supporting element; my Springfield Armory 1911 Colt came from Rock Island Arsenal many years ago, and its mate is still on exhibit there in the Browning Museum. However, if a cutaway's pedigree is suspect or even if you know for a fact that a given cutaway was "made" recently, it is still a fascinating and desirable addition for a collection. The contractor who does the cutaways for one of Germany's leading handgun manufacturers has also made a number of cutaways of interesting European military auto pistols. "Factory" they are not, but they're certainly as exciting to

Russian Tokarev pistol recently sectioned by a German gunsmith who specializes in such work. Despite its lack of "pedigree," the design features in this arm make it a fascinating subject for study.

Japanese Model 1925 Nambu pistol cutaway. Its two digit serial and lack of the usual other markings indicate this to be original

The crudeness of some of the cuts in this Persian Luger "ordnance cutaway" can be seen from the photos, but it served its purpose just as well as the working pistols made in the plant in Oberndorf.

look at and as instructive to manipulate as if they'd always been cutaways!

One final criteria, cutaway "quality" needs to be considered. Factory or recent, just how good a cutaway is it? Two factors usually determine cutaway quality. First is the number of cuts . . . the more the better; and second, how well do they do the job? That is, how well is the mechanism exposed for all phases of operation, and do some cuts cause problems with functioning? My all-time champion for number of cuts is a French MAC Model 1935S pistol, with 22! My Enfield rifle has 17, while a single barrel Russian Baikal shotgun boasts 10. A Forehand & Wadsworth revolver has only four, two on each side to show the action of the sear and rebounding hammer.

Cutaways as collectibles have never been very widely appreciated, though those of the more important makers command good prices from collectors of that company's arms. My Nambu cutaway came from a friend who'd retrieved it from a gunsmith who was using it for parts! I had to replace many of the small parts, but it's one of only a handful known and I'm not at all interested in letting go of it.

Whether you collect cutaways as a part of a larger collection, e.g., Colts, Lugers, Enfield rifles or some other group, or as an end in themselves, as a specialty they provide a fascinating study. They've got a history, they're rare, but they are still turning up. The next time you spot an "incomplete junker" on a gun show table or in a gunsmith's parts box take a second look. It might just be a cutaway, and your collecting interests may just take a new direction! •

Mayor William G. Gaynor of New York City moments after he was shot by James Gallagher, a disgruntled city employee, on the deck of the liner "Wilhelm der Grosse" as it was about to embark from Hoboken harbor. One of the great news photos of the early 20th century, it was taken by William Warnecke of the *Evening World*. It was a clipping of this photo, along with a crumpled business card and a nickel plated H & R revolver, that launched "the Search for the Sisters."
From the book "Great News Photos and the Stories Behind Them" by John Faber.

The Search for the Sisters

A collector's detective work turns a "Saturday Night Special" into a valuable piece of history.

by HERBERT R. GOPSTEIN

EVERY COLLECTOR anticipates the phone call offering him a rare and valuable Colt-Paterson revolver or mint Henry rifle. If it is inscribed, so much the better, because then some research can be done to identify the owner, adding to its value . . . and perhaps affording enough material with which to write an article for a collector's publication.

A nickel plated, two dollar, turn-of-the-century revolver with a couple of letters scratched into the frame hardly seems a likely prospect to have much potential value . . . or to provide the basis for historical research. Nevertheless, I did acquire such a revolver, and this is the story of the search it led to.

There was not a great deal to start with . . . a gun, a photo clipped from a 1951 issue of *Life Magazine*, a business card . . . and a story.

The gun was a Harrington and Richardson Model

1904 revolver, with a five-chambered cylinder and short barrel, chambered for the 38 S & W cartridge. Its original nickel-plated finish was unmarred except for an encircled letter "B" scratched on the left side and a similarly scratched circled letter "K" on the right. The somewhat rumpled *Life Magazine* photo was of a man, blood-spattered and close to collapse, being supported by two others.

The business card, slightly browned and showing an old fold, was engraved in a fine, flowing style: "Pierre P. Garven, Counselor at Law, Prosecutor of the Pleas, Hudson County, 586 Newark Ave., Jersey City, N.J." On the reverse side of the card was the handwritten notation: "Revolver used by James J. Gallagher when he shot Mayor Gaynor of New York. Aug 9/1910."

The story was told to me by the lady from whom I

Detail of the revolver's right side, showing the other clue initial, the letter "K".

The gun that shot Mayor Gaynor, a 38 caliber H & R Model 1904 revolver. Note the initial "B" scratched into the left side of the frame, one of the key clues in the identification of the gun.

bought the gun, the wife of a minister. She had acquired the gun 30 years previously, and here's what she remembered about it. She had been a graduate student at Rutgers University in New Brunswick, New Jersey. It was about 1950 and she lived in a nearby rooming house with several other Rutgers students. One of them, an undergraduate, was always short of money and was having a tough time making ends meet. He came to her one day with the gun and asked if she would buy it for $10. He explained he was the gardener for two old spinster ladies who lived in a house in New Brunswick. They were the sisters of a former prosecutor to whom the gun had earlier belonged. They no longer wanted it around the house, and they either gave or sold it to him for very little.

I began to research the apparently related events as well as the authenticity of the business card and the gun. The research took many avenues before it was completed.

The events proved to be real enough. On August 9, 1910, New York City Mayor William G. Gaynor had been aboard an ocean liner about to depart for Europe from a pier in Hoboken, New Jersey. James Gallagher, a disgruntled New York City civil servant, shot the Mayor in the neck from a distance of one or two feet. Gallagher was seized and arrested. Pierre Garven prosecuted the case and the gun was identified for trial purposes with the letters B&K . . . for Bell and Kiley, the witnesses to Gallagher's booking at the Hoboken police station. Gaynor later recovered and Gallagher was sent off to the New Jersey Institute for the Insane.

The research involved in tracing the possession of the gun from the time of the shooting until the time that I acquired it developed into a fascinating (and often confusing) chase.

It was easy enough to accept that Prosecutor Garven retained the gun as a souvenir after Gallagher's trial. Gaynor did not die and there was no legal requirement to keep evidence or records after nonhomicide cases. The handwriting on the back of the business card could be verified as belonging to Garven. I had the gun now, and I knew it was in the minister's wife possession since 1950 (verified through New Jersey State Police gun registration records in 1967). All I needed, therefore, was to verify the "existence" of Garven's sisters in the right place at the right time and this piece of the research would fall into place along with the tracing of the events and the identification of the gun.

I had several pieces of information. The ladies were the *sisters* of the prosecutor (probably spinsters). They lived in *New Brunswick*. They sold (or gave) the gun to their *gardener*, and it was done in *1950* . . . four pieces of basic information . . . and each one just a little bit wrong! This, then, is the story of the search for the sisters . . . a small part of the overall research . . . but fascinating in terms of the intricate puzzle-solving directions that such a search can take.

The first step was uncomplicated. I called local telephone information in New Brunswick and asked for a listing of any Garvens at all. If I would be able to locate a Garven, I could discuss Pierre Garven with them and see if they were relatives or if they knew anything about sons, daughters, cousins, etc. This

Pierre P. Garven
Counsellor at Law.

Prosecutor of the Pleas   *586 Newark Ave.*
Hudson County   *Jersey City N. J.*

Revolver used by James J. Gallagher when he shot Mayor Gaynor of New York. Aug 9/1910

Front and back sides of the card that accompanied the attack weapon. Garven, who prosecuted the would-be assassin and was later mayor of Bayonne, New Jersey, kept the revolver as a souvenir after the case was closed.

first step resulted in no information at all. There were no Garvens listed in the New Brunswick directory. So, this approach proved nonproductive.

Concurrently with the search for the sisters, I was still researching the shooting and still looking for verification information about the gun. I called my lawyer and explained what I was trying to find. He suggested I contact the present Prosecutor of the Pleas in Hudson County and he gave me the phone number. I called and was referred to the Assistant Prosecutor, John A. McLaughlin. When I explained what I was looking for he told he he would not have any direct information, but he suggested I call the County Clerk's office and to see if they had the records from 1910. He also suggested I contact the official Jersey City Historian, J. Owen Grundy.

At the County Clerk's office, I spoke to Katherine Sherrock, the Trial Records Office clerk. She did some preliminary checking and could not locate the index of trial records for the year 1910. She explained that the records were incomplete because of earlier fire and water damage. J. Owen Grundy at the Jersey City Public Library, where he maintains his office, however, did remember the case and was fascinated by the fact that I had the gun. We talked quite a while and he told me that Prosecutor Garven's son, also Pierre P. Garven, had been the Chief Justice of the New Jersey Supreme Court, and had died in recent years. He believed that Garven, Jr., had lived in Glen Ridge, New Jersey, and suggested I try directories for that area. Further, he offered to contact both the Mayor and the Police Chief of Hoboken (with whom he was on good terms) and see if either one could give me additional information about the gun or the event. He also suggested I check over the microfilm files of two newspapers, the *Jersey Observer* and the *Jersey Journal,* at the Jersey City Public Library.

I tried Glen Ridge, New Jersey, telephone information for any Garvens and, in fact, found there was an A. Garven listed. I called, with some excitement, and

explained the reason for my call. He was sympathetic, but explained he was black and most likely I wanted a white Garven. He didn't know any. Dead end again.

Still following the New Brunswick trail, I tried their library for a local telephone directory covering the year 1950. They did not have one, but they did have a City Directory for the years 1949 and 1950. There were no Garvens listed at all. So again, this lead fell through.

Since Garven, Jr., had been a New Jersey Supreme Court Justice, I tried calling the court in Trenton for any information on the Garven family. There was no information. They suggested that I try the Trenton Libraries, both state and city. I was still searching for a 1950 New Brunswick telephone directory, trying to find any Garvens. Neither library had such a directory.

About this time I had visited James T. O'Halloran, the present prosecutor of Hudson County, New Jersey, for more information on the event and the trial. It developed that he was researching former prosecutors and was doing a brief biography on each of them. Garven's biography included the date of his death, which opened a new possibility for me. A check of the March 3, 1938, obituaries might show survivors and give me a clue to his sisters. This lead was to prove productive.

At my next stop, in the New Jersey History Room of the Jersey City main library, I found a volume entitled *Bayonne Biographies,* that identified Garven's children as Margaret, Elsie and Pierre, Jr. This was my first clue that the two "sisters" were really two "daughters." The *Jersey Journal* microfilm provided a great deal of information about Pierre Garven. Toward the end of the obituary there was a small item: ". . . besides his wife and son there survived two daughters, Elinor and Margaret of Jersey City, (my second reference to these sisters), a sister, Mrs. Arthur Orme of Roselle, three brothers, James F. of

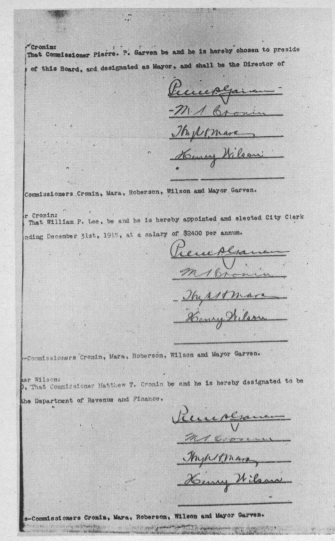

A page of the city records of Bayonne, showing Garven's signature.

Closeup of the letter "G" in Garven's signature in the Bayonne city records, (above), showing its similarity to the letter "G" in Gallagher's name written on the back of Garvin's card (below).

Bayonne, Eugene E. of Detroit, and Allan G. Winchell of Westfield." It went on to say that he was a member of the various lodges, including the Masons. (This indication that he was not Roman Catholic turned out to have value later.)

The thing that was the most interesting (or distressing), depending on the point of view, was that there did not seem to be two unmarried sisters of Pierre Garven, Sr., and so I continued searching. Obituaries seemed promising. My next approach, therefore, was to seek out the obituary of Pierre Garven, Jr. At the Princeton Library I searched the *New York Times* index. Mr. Grundy had indicated that Pierre Garven, Jr., had died only a few years ago. The search of the *New York Times* index under the heading of "deaths" from 1978 backwards through 1974 produced no Garvens. 1973 did! Pierre Garven had died on October 19, of that year. The *Times* microfilm obituary was not lengthy, but it did include a reference to his having

lived in Ridgewood, New Jersey, and that he was survived by his wife . . . so this was some headway. The Princeton Library had the 1979 telephone directory for Ridgewood, and checking under Garven I found Mrs. Katherine Y. Garven.

I assumed that Mrs. Katherine Garven was Pierre Garven, Jr.'s wife, so it looked like the chase for information was still alive. I tried phoning Katherine Garven, however there was no answer. I followed up instead with a call to the Ridgewood Public Library. The *Ridgewood Sunday News* obituary on Pierre Garven, Jr., referred to his leaving a wife, Sandra. This confused me since I was on Katherine's track and the current directory showed no Sandra in Ridgewood, although as mentioned, it did show a Katherine. I called the postmaster to see if I could find a local or a forwarding address for Sandra. The postmaster indicated he had a forwarding address but that he would supply it only on a written request.

Photocopy of the Hoboken, New Jersey daily police blotter of August 9, 1910, recording the attack on Mayor Gaynor and the booking of his assailant.

Obituaries still seemed a promising source of information and I called the *Newark Star Ledger*. The newspaper librarian did not have obituaries available but she did have a file on Garven and was able to tell me that the Garven family had attended a Supreme Court ceremony in 1975, after Pierre, Jr., died. At this function was his *mother, Katherine, his wife, Sandra,* and their five children, Susan, Gail, Barbie, Karen, and Steven. This put a new light on the situation because now I knew that Katherine was not Pierre, Jr.'s *wife* but rather his *mother*. It also somewhat puzzled me since there was quite a discrepancy in ages. Garven, Sr., had had a responsible position in the year 1910 and would not have been a youngster. Yet, here was his probable wife still alive 70 years later.

I called Katherine Garven again and this time she was at home. I explained that I was trying to find two sisters of Pierre Garven, Sr. who lived in New Brunswick in 1950. Katherine Garven said that there were no such people. No Garvens that she knew of ever lived in New Brunswick. Mrs. Katherine Garven explained she was the second wife of Pierre, Sr. Pierre, Sr., had fathered two daughters in his first marriage, Margaret and Elsie (a correction from the Elinor listed in the obituary), and that in his second marriage to Katherine he had fathered Pierre Gar-

ven, Jr., who later became the Justice of the Supreme Court. The two ladies Margaret and Elsie, then, would be the half-sisters of Pierre Garven, Jr., and the gardener (or handyman) could easily have mixed up the two Garvens when he referred to these ladies as Pierre Garven's sisters. Mrs. Katherine Garven did confirm that Margaret and Elsie were spinsters, which matched the original information. However, they lived in the Jersey City area all their lives and were never near New Brunswick. She thought that Elsie had died before 1950 but that Margaret had lived past 1960. Pierre Garven, Sr., had only one sister by the name of Anna Orme (which matched the earlier obituary information) and who was probably alive in 1950. She lived near Newark.

It was beginning to look as though Margaret and Elsie were the probable ladies from whom this gun was purchased. Katherine Garven had also mentioned that Sandra, her daughter-in-law, had moved to Houston, Texas, had remarried and taken the five children with them. She didn't think that Sandra would have much information about these two ladies so I did not pursue that route any further.

Makes a Formal Confession.

In this statement, Gallagher says:

I am James G. Gallagher of 410 Third Avenue, New York City, 58 years old, was born in Ireland, and was employed as a watchman in the Docks and Ferry Department of New York.

I came to Hoboken at 9:20 o'clock this morning and went to the steamship piers and boarded the Wilhelm der Grosse. I met a clergyman and I asked him to point out Mayor Gaynor. He did so and shortly afterward I shot at the Mayor. I do not know whether I fired more than one shot or not.

Knowing that the Mayor was going to Europe this morning after depriving me of my bread and butter—not porterhouse steaks—I was irritated to the point of committing this act.

The revolver you show me is the one that I did the shooting with. I don't know how many shots were in the revolver when I used it. I had the revolver in my possession a long time. I carried it when I was in the employ of the city.

JAMES G. GALLAGHER.

Witnesses:
ROBERT H. BELL, Acting Chief of Police.
DANIEL J. KILBY, Detective Sergeant.

N.Y. TIMES
AUG. 10, 1910

Gallagher's confession as it appeared in the *New York Times* the day after the attack. Note that names of the witnesses to the confession, a vital link in the identification of the pistol.

Gallagher had sold in cash, four pawn
tickets, and a wallet of papers. The revolver with which the shooting was done
was also taken by the police. It was
of 38 calibre Harrington & Richardson
make, short barreled, five chambered.
Three chambers had been fired. There
was one shell which had the mark of the
firing pin, showing that Gallagher had
tried to fire once more, and one other
loaded shell. Gallagher had a little bag
in his pocket with the additional cartridges in it. He wore a rather old blue
suit, but it was in fairly good condition.

N.Y. TIMES
AUG. 10, 1910

Description of Gallagher's revolver as it appeared in the
August 10, 1910 *New York Times*.

At this point I felt a call back to the minister's wife was in order. I explained the information that I had so far. She was sure that the "gardener" had said two spinster-ladies but that she was not entirely sure about the time and certainly had only guessed about where they lived. From our conversation she felt sure that "Margaret and Elsie" were the ladies from whom the gun was bought.

The search for the sisters thus moved to Jersey City. A call to the main library produced a 1949 phone book with a listing for M.B. Garven at 2600 Boulevard. There was no listing for Elsie. At this point I discussed my information with J. Owen Grundy. He thought it all fit. First, this was an expensive apartment house in a good neighborhood that would be right for these ladies. Initially, I had visualized a private house since a gardener was mentioned. Mr. Grundy pointed out that after many years recollections are not apt to be perfect. The gardener could have easily been a handyman for the ladies.

My next area of investigation centered on dates. I wanted to know if the sisters had been alive in 1950. Mr. Grundy suggested that since Garven was Protestant, I try calling John Murphy, the Superintendent at the New York Bayview Cemetery in Jersey City, to see if they have any Garvens buried there. A call to John Murphy produced the information that several Garvens were indeed buried there and he finally did find Elsie (this time with a middle initial M.), who had been interred on May 3, 1947. Margaret (Y.) was interred July 27, 1968.

Though not off by much, the timing did puzzle me. I was wondering, did the gardener or handyman at this point buy the gun somewhat before the 1950 date and keep it for a couple of years before reselling it. Or, was

the minister's wife perhaps mistaken by a few years. In any event, the time seemed close enough so that it no longer was to be a problem in terms of confirming ownership and transfer information.

The pieces of the puzzle now seemed to be pretty well pulled together. Gaynor was shot by Gallagher. Garven became the prosecutor. The trial was not a homicide, and therefore the records and evidence were not kept. Garven retained the revolver as a souvenir, wrote the business card notation and put it in a box for safe-keeping. The gun was given to or left with his daughters when he moved out of the state in later years. Interestingly enough, in Garven's obituary, mention is made that he died in Margaret and Elsie's home of a heart attack. The gun remained there until the late 1940s. Then the gardener, or handyman, bought it sometime between 1947 and 1950. He resold it to the minister's wife between 1947 and 1950. She, in turn, sold it to me 30 years later, in 1980.

At this point one could reasonably accept Margaret and Elsie as the two sisters in question, and the "Search for the Sisters" can be considered brought to a successful conclusion.

Postscript: *The effects of Gallagher's assault on Mayor Gaynor were to be more far-reaching than any of those concerned could have foreseen. The day after the shooting the* New York Times *ran an article urging that revolvers be banned, and within a few months a New York state senator, Timothy D. "Big Tim" Sullivan, introduced a gun control bill in the New York state legislature. That bill eventually became New York's infamous "Sullivan Law."*

For further details on this aspect of the story of Gaynor's shooting, see "The Gun That Triggered the Law" in Guns Illustrated 1982. •

Acknowledgments

The author is grateful for the valuable assistance in this research
   rendered by the following:
J. Owen Grundy, City Historian, Jersey City
Frank Percoskie, Detective, N.J. State Police, Firearms Investiga-
   tion Unit
James T. O'Halloran, Prosecutor, Hudson County
James F. Quinn, County Clerk, Jersey City
Robert F. Sloan, City Clerk, Bayonne
John T. Murphy, Superintendent, Bayview, N.Y.—Bay Cemetery
George W. Crimmins, Chief of Police, Hoboken
Horace K. Roberson, Attorney, Historian, Bayonne
Roland Barth, Director, New York Assembly Research Service
Paul A. Senecal, H&R, Manager of Customer Services
Jersey City Library Staff, particularly Joan Doherty
Princeton Borough Library Staff
Laverne, my wife and best critic.

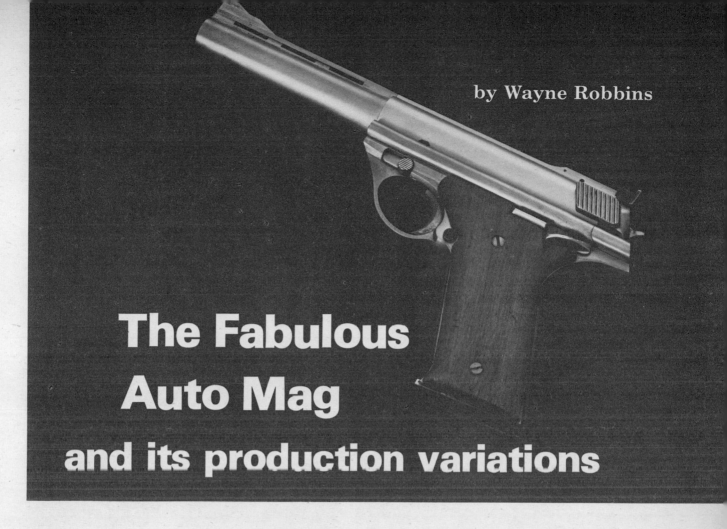

by Wayne Robbins

The Fabulous Auto Mag
and its production variations

THE AUTO MAG is the most powerful auto pistol that has ever been commercially manufactured. A specialized auto-loading design, the Auto Mag gives ballistic performance comparable to the most powerful revolvers and single shot pistols. Originally designed for the 44 AMP (Auto Mag Pistol) cartridge, the Auto Mag was offered in 357 as well.

Today Auto Mag pistols are getting harder and harder to find. Occasionally they can be found for sale at gun shows, but a number of handgun shooters are using them because of the AMP cartridge's performance and the gun's production class in IHMSA (International Handgun Metallic Silhouette Association) competition. Collectors have also taken an interest in the Auto Mag. Its low total production, short production period and the many variations present a challenge to the collector.

Constructed of stainless steel, the Auto Mag weighs 57 ounces with a 6½-inch barrel and an empty magazine—with the 6½-inch barrel it has a 10½-inch sight radius. Each pistol came in a black plastic case with foam lining, stainless Allen wrenches, special lubricant and instruction manual.

Ammo has been produced by C.D.M. (a Remington affiliate located in Mexico), Super Vel, Lee Jurras, Norma and some custom reloaders. Cases for handloading can be fabricated from 308 Winchester brass. Information on handloading the AMP cartridge is found in *Handloaders Digest Seventh Edition*—"Handloading the Auto Mag" by Kent Lomont.

During the brief history of the Auto Mag its markings have changed to meet the requirements of various companies and promoters. The markings are located on the barrel extension and are etched into the stainless steel. Serial numbers are stamped into the bottom rear of the grip frame.

Auto Mags produced by the original Auto Mag Corporation are marked with the **AM** logo; these pistols are generally referred to as the Pasadena Auto Mag. The Pasadena guns were made in 44 AMP, with a 6½-inch barrel. It was designated as the **Model 180,** and **Patent Pending** also appears. The right side of the barrel extension is marked **Made in USA.** Serial numbers are prefixed with the letter **A.** The 357 AMP was in the development stage during the Pasadena period. Several barrel extensions were assembled for testing and promotion, but no complete 357 AMP Pasadena Auto Mags were marketed.

Above—Handmade prototype Auto Mag. This photograph accompanied a factory news release on the new gun in late 1969 or early 1970.

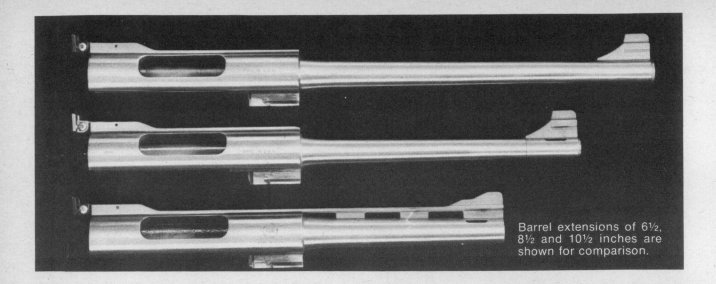

Barrel extensions of 6½, 8½ and 10½ inches are shown for comparison.

Rear sight variations from left to right: Pasadena, TDE, TDE/OMC and AMT.

Rib tops: milled, etched and plain. Note how front sight styles varied between Pasadena, TDE and AMT.

The original Auto Mag Corporation went bankrupt in 1972, about one year after Auto Mag was introduced to the public. At public auction most tooling and parts were purchased by a newly formed company, TDE. The **TDE North Hollywood** marking was the first for TDE. There are two North Hollywood markings of interest. The standard North Hollywood carries the TDE logo and other regular markings. **Model 180** indicates 44 AMP and **Model 160** indicates 357 AMP. Barrel lengths of 6½, 8½, and 10½ inches are found.

A few of the first barrel extensions manufactured by TDE did not bear the name **Auto Mag** or **Patent Pending** marking. These "two-line" North Hollywood models are very rare. Less than 100 were marked in this manner and most were 357 AMP.

TDE soon changed the marking of the Auto Mag to show their actual location, El Monte. The standard El Monte Auto Mag is marked in the same manner as the North Hollywood except for the address differ-

ence. Model designations and barrel length remained the same. The **Patent Pending** marking, however, was changed to **Patented** while at El Monte. As a result, barrel extensions can be found marked either way.

An El Monte Auto Mag of special interest bears the Jurras "Lion Head" logo. Auto Mags with this marking were distributed by Lee Jurras and Associates, when Jurras was exclusive worldwide distributor. Other markings and specifications remained the same. As an early promoter of the Auto Mag, Lee Jurras formed the Club de Auto Mag International and also commissioned TDE to produce 100 limited editions, special feature, L. E. Jurras Custom Model 100, 357 AMP Auto Mags. These guns were serialed LEJ 001 to LEJ 100. Serial numbers LEJ 080 through LEJ 090 have 8½-inch barrels, while the remaining guns had 6½-inch barrels. Special features included Mag-Na-Port barrels, custom laminated grips and a presentation case.

Jurras Custom Model 100, here in 44 AMP, featured custom laminated grips.

Auto Mag with action open, showing the open style bolt.

The "B" and "C" series Auto Mags are equipped with solid bolts.

With the success of the custom Model 100 in 357 AMP, Jurras commissioned TDE to build 100 custom Auto Mags in 44 AMP. These guns carried matching serial numbers, followed by the letter **X** and the same special features. The last edition of the custom Model 100 Auto Mags was offered chambered for a new cartridge—the 41 JMP (Jurras Magnum Pistol), a new cartridge developed by Lee Jurras. These guns were serial numbered in the TDE prefix sequence. However, the frames were marked **100-3** under the grip panel. Only a small number of complete guns for this cartridge were ever assembled, though a number of 41 JMP barrel extensions were sold separately.

Also, in the early TDE promotional period the High Standard Firearms Company took an interest in the Auto Mag. TDE produced several hundred Auto Mags for High Standard which bore TDE's name and logo on the right side of the barrel extension. Of the number produced, just over 100 pistols have an **H** serial number prefix. The remainder are serialed in

the **A** prefix sequence. High Standard Auto Mags were offered in 357 AMP and 44 AMP with 6½-, 8½- and 10½-inch barrel lengths.

The next variation is the TDE/OMC. This is referred to as the B series. The serial number was changed to the **B** prefix to signify the first major design change since the pistol was introduced. Model numbers were changed from 160 to 260 for the 357 AMP and 180 to 280 for the 44 AMP. The design change replaced the open style bolt with a solid bolt, with modification to the bolt rotation pin. The solid bolt offered increased weight which improved functioning. Less than 100 B series Auto Mags were made.

The AMT Auto Mag was the last produced. This C series offered the new Behlert rear sight as well as the solid bolt—less than 100 C series Auto Mags were produced.

Other Auto Mag variations were made by TDE and custom Auto Mags were also offered by Lee Jurras—

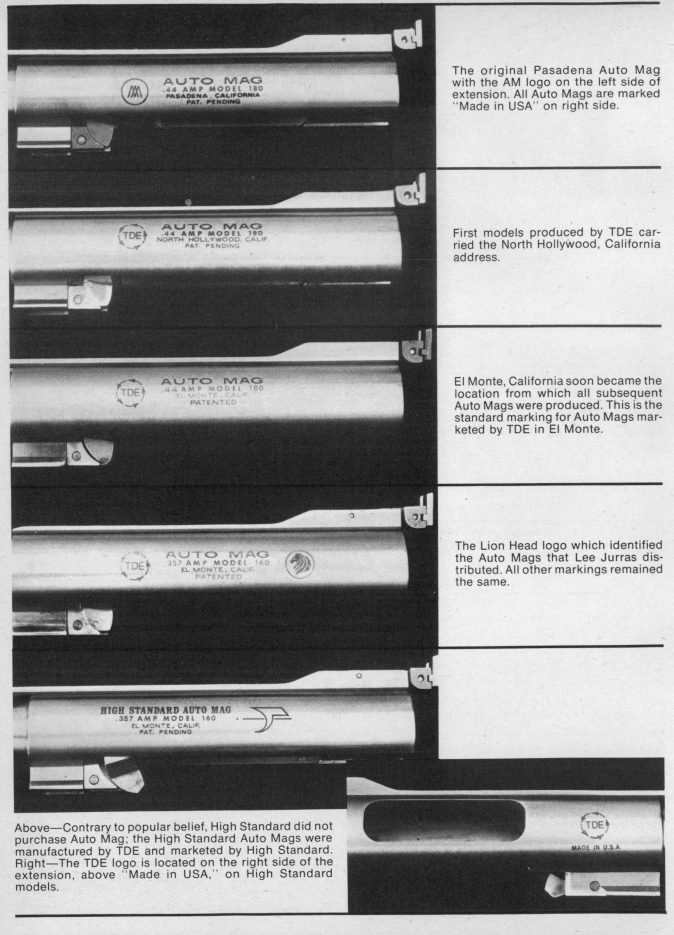

The original Pasadena Auto Mag with the AM logo on the left side of extension. All Auto Mags are marked "Made in USA" on right side.

First models produced by TDE carried the North Hollywood, California address.

El Monte, California soon became the location from which all subsequent Auto Mags were produced. This is the standard marking for Auto Mags marketed by TDE in El Monte.

The Lion Head logo which identified the Auto Mags that Lee Jurras distributed. All other markings remained the same.

Above—Contrary to popular belief, High Standard did not purchase Auto Mag; the High Standard Auto Mags were manufactured by TDE and marketed by High Standard. Right—The TDE logo is located on the right side of the extension, above "Made in USA," on High Standard models.

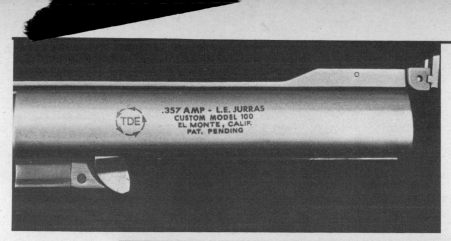

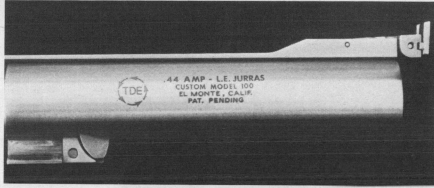

The L.E. Jurras Custom Model 100 in 357 and 44 AMP and 41 JMP was manufactured for Jurras by TDE, prior to Lee Jurras becoming distributor.

The TDE/OMC Auto Mag showed model number changes and the "B" serial prefix.

AMT Auto Mags have a new rear sight and the "C" serial prefix.

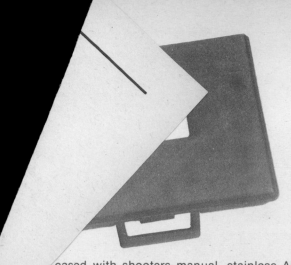

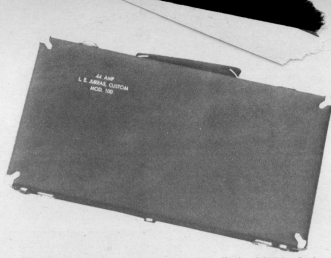

...cased with shooters manual, stainless Allen ...s in pouch, and the special Auto Mag gun oil. ...of the first guns from Pasadena were also supplied ...extra magazine.

The carrying case L.E. Jurras supplied with his Custom Model 100 is a deluxe version, much better than the factory style.

these were: the "Bicentennial," "International," "Backpacker," "Alaskan," "Condor," "Grizzly" and "Silhouette." Others were also in this individually hand-crafted group of pistols, however, the quantities of these variations are not sufficient to consider them as standard production guns.

There are standard design features and minor design changes that the collector should note. Standard 6½-inch barrels are full vent ribbed, while 8½- and 10½-inch barrels are ribbed on the extension. Grips supplied on Pasadena models are full checkered black plastic, but TDE manufactured grips are checkered in the grip section only. The top of the barrel ribs have milled grooves on Pasadena, North Hollywood and some guns produced in El Monte. Later rib tops were etched to cut manufacturing costs. (This is the same process used for barrel extension markings.) The last guns produced came with plain sandblasted ribs.

Rear sights on Pasadena guns are stainless, with a groove for white outline and lower cross lines. TDE rear sights are blued with lower cross lines. B series sights are blued-plain. C series guns have Behlert rear sights, blued with white outline. Front sights on Pasadenas have a milled recess on the rear for colored tape inserts, while other guns have a plain ramp.

Those interested in shooting a superb big bore auto-loading pistol will enjoy the Auto Mag. However, special attention must be given to proper lubrication and obtaining ammunition of quality, to provide the necessary recoil impulse to function the action. When encountering exotic variations, the novice collector should be aware of the ease with which parts and especially barrel extensions can be interchanged. •

Switzerland is a beautiful country with a real sense of history, as this view in Lucerne attests.

Making the Gun Collector's Grand Tour

by JOSEPH J. SCHROEDER

A gunshop is a gunshop wherever you go. Here's Chris Reinhart behind the counter at Hofmann & Reinhart, in Zurich.

BACK IN THOSE good old days before World War II, it was the fashion of the well-to-do to take the "Grand Tour"—a two or three month odyssey to the capitals and culture centers of Europe. For the dedicated gun collector—at least one whose interests don't lie wholly on this side of the ocean—a similar journey can be most rewarding in both knowledge and (with luck) a choice addition for the collection.

However, the days are gone when the shrewd collector paid his travel expenses by buying cheap over there and selling at an outrageous profit over here. In 1960 my wife and I returned from Europe with five Swiss Lugers, all different models, for which I'd paid (with holsters and extra magazines) $50-75 each. At that time they were bringing $250-350 in the U.S. Today a Swiss Luger is bringing at least as much in Switzerland as it is here, if you can find one! That doesn't mean you shouldn't be looking around, though. I've been fortunate enough to make my own Grand Tour three times in the last 3 years, and each time I—and those with me—have come home with something worthwhile for our collections.

The basic question about an arms Grand Tour is, of course, where and when. My first one came about in 1978, when Fred Datig invited me to exhibit my Bergmann pistol collection at his annual International Arms Exhibition in Lucerne, Switzerland. It's traditionally held on the next-to-last weekend in April, making it ideal for those who wish to go from Lucerne to London where the spring London Arms Fair is held the end of April. (There's also a fall London Arms Fair, in September.)

My first personal Arms Grand Tour was so successful that several friends asked me to take it again, with them along. This worked out very well, using Lucerne and London as bases but with suitable side trips in between. Scheduling your Grand Tour around a gun show or shows gives it a concentration and a focus, as well as providing an opportunity to meet fellow collectors and dealers from all parts of the continent. Major European gun shows are held in Germany and France as well as Switzerland and England . . . all are advertised in the European arms journals.

Of course, there are other considerations that can influence both the timing and itinerary of your Grand Tour. Alternate interests such as skiing, music festivals, even hunting seasons or shooting competitions can help determine what's best for you. However, since the basic goal of this trip is gun collecting, and based on personal experience, here is my recommendation for that first Arms Grand Tour.

Where to Start

Barring family or business obligations which might demand another initial destination, I'd recommend starting your Grand Tour in Switzerland. In the first place, it probably has the most relaxed attitude towards guns of any nation in the world. It's very refreshing for an American, coming from the incessant barrage of anti-gun media propaganda, to see a man (sometimes a woman) climb on a streetcar with a rifle slung over his(her) shoulder and find a little old lady with a shopping bag edging over with a smile to give him room to sit down. The Swiss are a nation of shooters, with a big-bore shooting range near practically every town; so, a rifle attracts no more notice in public than a golf bag or tennis racquet does over here.

The Kolping is a typical businessman's hotel, located on a side street in Lucerne but spotlessly clean, with excellent food and drink at reasonable prices.

Swiss gun laws, though strictly enforced, also seem to have been written more by and for the gun enthusiast than ours do. Thus a gun chambered for an unavailable cartridge—for example an 8mm Japanese Nambu pistol—is treated as an antique with practically no bars to purchase. Modern guns are more strictly controlled, of course, by laws that vary from canton (Swiss state) to canton and city to city. However, the Swiss citizen of good repute has

European gun shows generally are set up with walk-in stands, much more formal than the "flea market" table arrangement of most U.S. shows.

Collectors speak the same language wherever they are. Two Italian gun buffs discuss one of his miniatures with American Joe Kramer.

The Festhalle, Allmend, home of the Lucerne International Arms Festival, even includes a full service restaurant, serving hot meals and beer and wine to wash them down, to serve show goers.

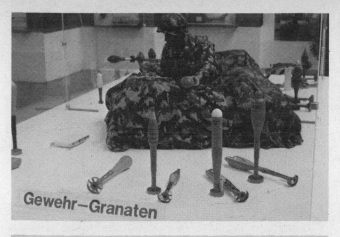

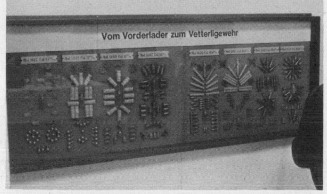

The Swiss government arsenal at Thun participated in the 1980 Lucerne show with an exhibit of Swiss ammunition manufacture, both antique and modern.

little problem in buying and owning rifles or pistols—though for some reason semi-auto rifles, even 22s, are treated like machine guns.

Even you as a visitor to Switzerland will have little problem buying a gun there, and, if it's an antique by their standards, taking it along with you . . . if you wish. It's almost always better not to, as will be explained later. Gun shops are to be found everywhere in Switzerland, though relatively few carry much in the way of used guns or collector's items. Some notable exceptions include Hofmann & Reinhart and Glaser of Zurich, Mayer in Basel, and Poyet and Schwartz in Bern; each generally has interesting used items in stock. Most prices will be high to very high by U.S. standards, but if you look carefully enough there are always some goodies at prices you'll be willing to pay and sometimes even a real bargain or two.

Finally, Switzerland is one of the world's most beautiful countries at any time of the year, and you really weren't going to go all that way just to look at guns, were you? The mountain scenery is simply breathtaking, and the narrow streets of the older sections of cities that haven't changed much since centuries before North America was even discovered are always fascinating to prowl. Language will be something of a problem, of course, though most shops and the larger restaurants and hotels will have English speaking people to help you when needed. If you don't speak some German or French (for northern Switzerland—the south speaks Italian instead of German) take a German or French phrase book with you and spend some time learning to use it before you leave. You will survive, though not without some anxious (and sometimes hilarious) moments!

The official languages of Switzerland are German, French and Italian, but the Swiss know good gun books in any language.

Swiss gun maker Leon Crottet displays two of his fully operable half-size miniature arms, a Thompson submachine gun in his left hand and a 1911 Colt in his right.

Solothurn, a beautiful walled city, is just a few hours from Lucerne or Zurich. The Altes Zeughaus arms museum there is worth the trip for its full floor of armor, not to mention the other floors full of small arms, cannon and uniforms.

Crossing the channel by ferry boat provides the traveler with an inspiring view of the white cliffs of Dover. Here Bob Simpson checks out the author's camera technique as the boat train pulls out for London.

Train travel between cities in Europe is fast and frequent, and generally much less expensive than air.

The Second Stop

England is the second stop on our recommended Grand Tour. First, if this is to be a "tour" it should include more than one country, and I have put England second on the itinerary because I find it easier to cope with language problems early on a trip when I'm still fresh. It's a real relief, after a week or two on the road, to find yourself in a place where communication is no longer a problem! Second, despite the braying of the anti-gun U.S. editorialists there is still a significant and active gun-owning fraternity in the United Kingdom, and if you've set your schedule properly you'll meet a lot of it at the London Arms Fair or one of the other English gun shows.

London, Birmingham and a number of other cities

The Musée d'Armes in Liège is small and unobtrusive, but it contains an outstanding collection of arms of all vintages displayed in roomy, well lit cabinets.

Every collector who has handled a Belgian made firearm has seen this, symbol of the proof house in Liège.

The Royal Lancaster is the home of the London Arms Fair. Be prepared to pay "oil sheik" prices if you stay here while in London.

The twice annual London Arms Fair packs the exhibit room at the Royal Lancaster. At peak times the aisles are almost impassable.

boast a substantial number of gun shops. Though most are hunting and shooting oriented, a number such as Kempster in London and Outwoods specialize in collectors arms and accouterments. In London, Christies, Sotheby's, Wallis & Wallis, and Weller & Dufty always seem to have worthwhile firearms coming up for auction and are thus worth a visit. And don't miss Ken Trotman Arms Books, where visitors will almost always find worthwhile out-of-print or obscure current arms literature that's simply not available in the U.S. marketplace.

A current copy of *Guns Review* or *Antique Arms & Militaria* is your best guide to the worthwhile gunshops in the British Isles. They'll also provide schedules for the various gun shows. And when in London,

Everything from ancient broadswords and armor to modern Colts, Lugers and Webleys is displayed for sale at the Arms Fair.

The English obviously have good taste in gun books, too. The author shakes hands with an English counterpart with *Gun Collectors' Digest*, Volume II in the background.

London hotels like the Park Court offer first class accommodations at a much more reasonable price than a deluxe hotel like the Royal Lancaster, just a few blocks walk away.

No visit to London would be complete without a visit to Holland & Holland, still offering the finest in sporting arms.

don't pass up the Imperial War Museum, whose scope is breathtaking. The Museum features outstanding special displays that are changed frequently. Though the IWM has an excellent arms reference collection, only a small part of it is ever on display. By prior arrangement, it is possible to examine specific items for research purposes. The Tower of London is also a must for the London visitor, both for the incredible sense of history that permeates it and for an outstanding arms collection—much of it on display.

The Pattern Room at Enfield Lock is the arms collector's Mecca, of course, but as Jake Chamberlain carefully points out in his accompanying article, it is not a museum and it is not open to the general public. It is a working portion of the British government's small arms development facility. If you are ever fortunate enough to be able to arrange a visit there, plan to make good use of it!

Additional stops on our arms collector's Grand Tour will certainly be influenced by individual tastes and by the season for best sightseeing conditions. Sweden's gun laws are much less restrictive than those of its neighbors, and, like Switzerland, it was a non-combatant in World War II. The Swedish gun shops frequently turn up some interesting pre-World War II rifles and pistols in like-new condition. Despite strong gun laws, Germany is still full of gun collectors and shooters. Most German cities have a number of gun shops, some of them collector oriented (see *Deutsches Waffen Journal* for their ads). Private gun ownership is severely limited in the Netherlands and

Denmark. France, Belgium, Austria and Norway all permit some degree of private gun ownership and use.

Europe abounds in excellent museums, many of them with outstanding arms collections. A sampling of some of these is included at the end of this article. Whenever possible, a sidetrip to one or more of these should be part of your Grand Tour.

So far we've talked a lot about the trip but not about what it costs, yet economics has to play a major role in establishing the itinerary for your Grand Tour. The newspaper travel sections and cocktail party circuits are full of horror stories of costs in Europe, but the smart traveler is not going to sleep in a $150-a-day hotel room or eat $45 lunches. Even with today's daily markups in air fares there are opportunities for special discounts, and once in Europe train or bus transportation often provides real savings compared to continental air travel.

Find, if you can, a travel agent who knows what he's doing in Europe and with whom you're comfortable, tell him what you'd like to do and where you can be flexible, and you shouldn't come out too badly. There are businessmen's hotels in every European city with bright, clean rooms for $30-40 or even less, providing you don't mind having the bathroom facilities down the hall. The shop clerks and bank tellers in Lucerne and London eat lunch every day for under $5, and so will you if you eat where they do. You can spend a lot of money in Europe if you insist on going first class, but you don't have to and it can be a lot more fun and educational if you "go native."

If you decide to buy any guns on your Grand Tour, there are a few cautions you should keep in mind. Under the 1968 gun law you cannot bring a modern (post-1898) gun back into the U.S. with you. It must be shipped into the U.S. to someone who holds a Federal Firearms License. If it is military, such as a

After a hard day at the show, there's nothing like a pint of 'alf and 'alf to ease the aches.

You can't appreciate just how big a 15-inch gun really is until you've stood behind the breech of the pair mounted in front of the Imperial War Museum. The author's gun tour poses for a group picture.

Kar 98k Mauser rifle or an S/42 Luger, it is simply not importable. If it's a small pistol that doesn't meet BATF's point criteria, for example the Walther PPK, you won't be able to bring it in. If it's an "antique" by U.S. standards, that is made in or before 1898, there's no problem with either size or origin and you should even be able to bring it back with you, if you choose.

European gun laws vary widely, and even a muzzleloader may be a "gun" to a customs guard. Unless you thoroughly know the customs regulations of every country you plan to visit, it doesn't pay to take a chance and carry a gun of *any* vintage in your luggage. Almost any dealer will agree to ship it for you. Just be sure that (if it's "modern" and needs an import license) he understands that it's not to be shipped until you can get home and make the proper arrangements.

There's so much to see and do on a Grand Tour, and even though yours has a theme—guns—that will only be a part of a wonderful overall experience. Take your Grand Tour, and then let me know where you went and what you saw. You're bound to find some things I'll want to incorporate into my next Grand Tour!

●

SOME EUROPEAN MILITARY MUSEUMS
WITH WORTHWHILE ARMS COLLECTIONS

Austria, Vienna—*Heeresgeschichtliches Museum:* through 1918, with 2,200 small arms.

Belgium, Brussels—*Musée Royal l'Armee et d'Histoire Militaire:* very large, all inclusive, with over 500 small arms.

Belgium, Liège—*Musée d'Armes:* excellent, well laid out comprehensive small arms displays; arms not on display may sometimes be available for researchers by prior arrangement.

Denmark, Copenhagen——*Tøjhusmuseet:* military arms from pistols through cannon, with over 4,300 small arms.

England, London—*Imperial War Museum:* war in all its phases, including aircraft, tanks and small ships. Limited small arms displays, but extensive research collection can be made available by prior arrangement. Very worthwhile special exhibits, changed frequently.

England, London—*Royal United Service Museum:* limited weapons displays, but worthwhile for accouterments.

England, London—*Tower of London:* excellent small arms displays, and full of history. A must!

France, Paris—*Musee de l'Armee:* 2,000 small arms.

France, Paris—*Musee de la Marine:* less than 300 small arms, but widely considered the finest naval museum in Europe.

Norway, Oslo—*Haermuseet:* Over 2,000 pistols and revolvers, 750 rifles.

Portugal, Lisbon—*Museu Militar:* more than 5,000 small arms.

Netherlands, Leiden—*Leger en Wapenmuseum* (General Hoefer): more than 3,300 small arms.

Spain, Madrid—*Museo de Ejercito:* about 1,000 small arms.

Sweden, Stockholm—*Armemuseum:* 4,500 small arms.

Switzerland, Solothurn—*Altes Zeughaus:* very comprehensive Swiss collection, from crossbow through submachine gun and cannon. More than 400 stands of armor.

Note: Few if any museums will ever have their entire small arms collections on display, and in many only a small fraction of the collection will ever be seen in the public areas. Some include swords in "small arms," so actual firearms collections may be much smaller than the number shown. Some permit photographs, some only with prior permission. Still others strictly prohibit cameras. Almost all will, with adequate notice, make reference collection items available for study by qualified researchers.

A Visit to ENFIELD LOCK

The original sign, on the left-flanking wall of the Factory entrance, just over the bridge across the canalized River Lea.

The Twentieth Century entrance symbol, on the right-flanking wall of the main entrance.

Credit: Malcolm Pendrill, Ltd. Both photographs.

by W.H.J. CHAMBERLAIN

To A RESEARCHER of British service firearms and edged weapons, the Pattern Room at the Royal Small Arms Factory, Enfield Lock is a gold mine and, like most gold mines, it attracts tourists but is not prepared to entertain them. I've happily and profitably mined its ore three times now; perhaps my experiences might help researchers and spare tourists a rejection.

The Pattern Room began in the 1830s as a repository for specimens of small arms and their "implements" which had been "sealed" by authority to govern manufacture and supply, and to serve as inspectors' references. The official collection has grown and evolved, acquiring specimens of weapons which competed for adoption but were not "sealed," arms used in experiments, speculative embodiments of de-signs, and, lately, small arms of many nations acquired, it seems, to provide information and inspiration. The range is from flintlock to full-automatic, pocket knife to pike, grass-common to unique, and arms fired from the hand, the shoulder, or the tripod.

The reference collection is supported by such internal working documents as the *List of Sealed Patterns*, and by external documentation, including a complete set of the *List of Changes*.

The Pattern Room's mission controls access to these nuggets. It is a reference store for information required in support of decisions and activities of the British Government. In the early days, it was solely a part of the Royal Small Arms Factory, within the boundaries of which it lies. Now, it is a part of the Quality Assurance Directorate (Weapons), Ministry

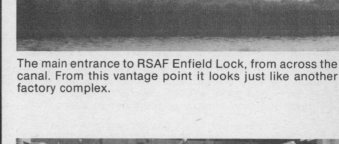

The main entrance to RSAF Enfield Lock, from across the canal. From this vantage point it looks just like another factory complex.

The Royal Seals on the butt of this musket, displayed by Herb Woodend of the Pattern Room staff, show it to be the "Sealed Pattern" for this model.

The scope of the Pattern Room's collection is simply overwhelming, as can be seen from the machine gun section of the second floor. Note the racks of rifles to the left.

of Defense, sited at the RSAF. It is budgeted only to perform QAD(W) tasks; non-government researchers and unofficial questions are catered to only by securing QAD(W) permission and consuming the spare time and good-will of the Pattern Room's staff of three. A private researcher must write well in advance of his intended arrival date, state his purpose, and negotiate a date and time. He should not hope for three days of access, and should be grateful for two.

The RSAF is an active Ministry of Defense site and the researcher must comply with security rules. Cameras are forbidden; those brought will be "detained" at the gatehouse. Packages and briefcases will be searched; one's person may be searched. An approved researcher will wait at the gatehouse, reading posters instructing RSAF employees how to de-

tect surprises the IRA might rig to their cars, until one of the Pattern Room staff comes to collect him and his pass. One of the three staff members will remain with the researcher during his visit, keeping the pass, and will return him to the gatehouse.

Photographs of specimens held in the Pattern Room are obtainable, provided the subject, the camera, and the photographer are made part of the planning and receive prior approval. Ministry of Works photography was once arranged for me, and I once contracted with a commercial photographer who then followed his own path to entry. However, in August, 1979, the Ministry of Defense established a fee of £10 for each photograph. The amount of the fee has been deservedly complained of—its purpose seems worthy—but it remains at £10 per photograph.

Two American researchers examine German MP-44 equipped with a "Krummlauf," a curved barrel that enables the gun to shoot around a corner without exposing the user. One rack of rifles appears behind them.

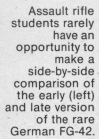

Assault rifle students rarely have an opportunity to make a side-by-side comparison of the early (left) and late version of the rare German FG-42.

The Pattern Room rifle collection spans arms history, from flintlock through the latest in automatic weaponry.

Now, if you are a researcher who just cannot survive without an intimate experience with a British piece at the Pattern Room, and you have made a rendezvous by mail, then here are some hints for your day.

First, go to Enfield Lock, not Enfield. The two points are on different rail lines leaving from the same depot. Enfield Lock lies on the Cambridge line of British Rail, leaving from the Liverpool Street Station. If one stays in London, Liverpool Street Station can be reached handily by the Central, Circle, or Metropolitan subway lines. A same-day round-trip fare between Liverpool Street and Enfield Lock costs £1.24 as I write, and puts one on trains with posted running times of 29 minutes, departing at half-hour intervals. One may also beat the costs of living in

London by staying up the line in Bishop's Stortford, which is the main hotel point for charter aircraft crews flying into Stanstead airport.

From the rail platform at Enfield Lock (minimal shelter from the weather while awaiting the return train; dress for the field and try to stay dry), the main gate at RSAF is less than 1½ miles eastwards. It's a refreshing walk, which can be completed long before a bus will appear.

As for the noon meal, pack your own rations and take another walk. The Pattern Room's hours are from 0730-1230, 1330-1630. It is *cleared* during lunch, and it is really unkind to ask whichever staff member escorting you within the RSAF to come along to the RSAF Canteen. I'll say naught about the pubs between the rail platform and the RSAF, except

Just one row of the World War I vintage heavy machine guns on display in the Pattern Room. Note the crossed lances on the wall.

A sampling of the heavy machine guns displayed on the Pattern Room's ground floor.

A group of recently acquired submachine guns waits final cataloging.

that in 1976 I noticed, too late, that most of the RSAF employees who were eating in one of them had brought their own sandwiches. At the other, one can buy a pint and take one's sandwiches on to the canal banks and possibly even watch a commercial narrow-boat lock through—given the weather and season.

I was lucky enough to hear of The Plough, a pub in Sewardstone. This is reached by being escorted to the Cattle Gate on the east side of the RSAF, marching briskly along an access road for not more than 10 minutes, then turning smartly left for another 100 yards. Prices were low, the grub good, the service efficient. Make a point of returning to the Cattle Gate to meet the escort at the agreed time. Also, if ordering beer at lunch, remember that there are no latrines in the Pattern Room's old, cold brick building, a situation which can generate another escorted brisk walk.

There are two points to make about the Pattern Room at the Royal Small Arms Factory. First, entry into it provides a rare opportunity to examine, understand, and record specimens from a nearly complete set of British small arms. Second, each time I have complied with regulations and gained entry, the staff assisted me in a manner I consider personally kind and operationally superb. ●

COLLECTING MODERN AMERICAN

This Remington Model 37 "Sporter" is, perhaps, the only sporter version ever made of the now-famous Remington rimfire match rifle. Its location is unknown to the collecting fraternity. This photo is probably the only picture ever taken of the rifle.

RIMFIRE RIFLES

by **ROBERT S.L. ANDERSON**

Made from 1969 through 1978, the Remington 40-XB Sporter is one of the rarest U.S. production rimfires ever produced. Approximately 700 were made, according to the Remington Museum in Ilion, New York.

IT WAS A lazy August afternoon in 1969 when I wandered into Shelly's Sporting Goods store in the suburbs of Harrisburg, PA. There, sitting uneventfully in a rack of rimfires, was a Savage autoloading rimfire of odd description and proportion. "It came in yesterday," Shelly said as he handed the rifle across the counter. We both scratched our heads as we went over the unusual features: a full length military oil-finished stock; no front sight (or dovetail for one); hand guard; a receiver drilled and tapped in an unusual fashion; military-style steel buttplate; a larger-than-normal trigger guard and military-type sling swivels.

I surmised that the "little" man-sized Savage might have been set up as some sort of military trainer. Shelly agreed, but cautioned that in his eyes he could only see a Savage auto rimfire, hence the reasonable selling price of $45.

As I handed him the money, Shelly admitted that he too felt it was an unusual rimfire but was hesitant to sell it on those merits since he had never seen anything in print on anything like it. As I departed, Shelly intoned, "Why don't you contact Savage?"

I did.

That call to Savage was interesting. The fellow in Customer Service at first advised that he had never heard of such a gun. I persisted saying that gun, from my limited perspective, was factory-original. The man at the other end of the phone paused and said, "If you'll wait a minute, I'll pose your question to one of the guys here who's ready to retire. He was here during World War II."

A few minutes later a smoke-mellowed voice came through the receiver. "Mr. Anderson, I always wondered what happened to those guns. You're the first

Remington's 521T Bolt action rimfire was made in good quantity (66,338) between 1947 and 1968. The 521T's popularity is such that it seldom surfaces in gunshops.

Only 26,947 Remington Nylon 76 rimfires were made between 1962 and 1965. Seldom seen, they should be given more than a casual glance by the rimfire collector.

person who ever asked about them." As it turned out, the fellow at Savage advised that they got a rush order for a "few hundred" rimfire autoloaders made to the unusual specifications I outlined.

The soon-to-be retired Savage employee further advised that he remembered this odd rimfire because, during "The War," they were so busy with Enfield and Tommy Gun production that anything else produced was, indeed, unusual.

As you can see, all of the above took place over a decade ago; and, at that time, my rare little find didn't gather much attention in the collectors' market. In fact, when I foolishly sold it some months later I only managed to make $10 on my original investment.

Hindsight tells me that I let a superb, very collectible rimfire slip through my fingers. In this "loss" lies a motto that should read, *Para Buckus Unum Minisculum Currenti,* or, "Who says there ain't money in modern rimfires!"

Admittedly, the above rimfire is unusual; however,

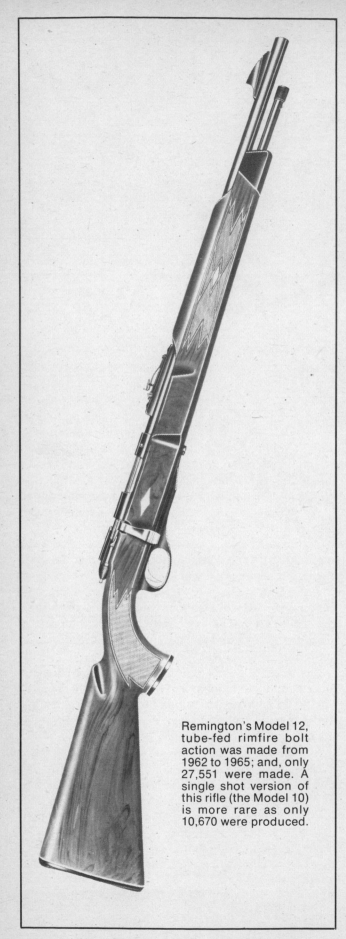

Remington's Model 12, tube-fed rimfire bolt action was made from 1962 to 1965; and, only 27,551 were made. A single shot version of this rifle (the Model 10) is more rare as only 10,670 were produced.

over the past 10 years, 22s have carved out a very real economic niche for themselves. No, we're not talking about ultra-rare, pre-1900 Winchesters, Colts, Smiths, and others. We're talking about more modern guns, most of them made well after 1920—a market that has, until recently, been left alone by serious collectors.

To me, it seems, modern rimfires have received their greatest collector attention during the past 5 to 7 years. Why? Just check the price tag on collectible centerfire, percussion or flintlock firearms. Some of these prices would make for a substantial down-stroke on a new Mercedes. Fortunately, rimfires (most of them) are still economically approachable. More importantly, many "collectible" 22 rifles are still very "findable." And at prices that have been described by my wife as "grand-theft-gun."

An example would be the Model 59 Winchester; no, not the autoloading shotgun, but the 22-caliber single shot made only in 1930. Less than 10,000 of these guns were made and it's not impossible to find one. Why? Even though the survival rate on low-cost single-shot rimfires is less than spectacular, many of these same guns will often get passed from generation to generation by caring owners who recognize the value of their "first firearm." When the last kid in line graduates to something larger, the single-shot rimfire gets traded. Yes, it may take a couple of generations (or more) of kids to get to this point, however, it *will* happen. When that single shot gets in the hands of the *average* dealer it goes out on the rack—it's just another single shot 22.

I know of two guys who have wandered into gun shops and bought Winchester 59s right off the rack for less than $50. The value? Depending upon condition, a 59 Winchester can bring anywhere from $100 to $300 from a knowledgeable buyer who needs to fill out his collection.

In a recent conversation with author George Madis (*The Winchester Book,* Taylor Publishing, Dallas, TX) we ran through Model 52 production figures starting with 1934 and ending in 1943. Through deduction, based on styles of barrels sold, George came to the conclusion that somewhere in the neighborhood of 10,000 (or less) 52 Sporters were made. While it should be noted that this is an educated guess at best, Mr. Madis' estimates cannot be taken lightly.

The 52 Sporter was never a cheap rifle. Back before the war it sold for a hefty $94.60 ($79.45 without sights). When discontinued in 1958, the same sporter sold for $197.25. Since its discontinuance, no other production rimfire collectible has gained in value like the 52 Sporter. As little as 6 or 7 years ago, you could pick one of these rifles up for around $400, depending upon geographic locale and who was doing the buying or selling.

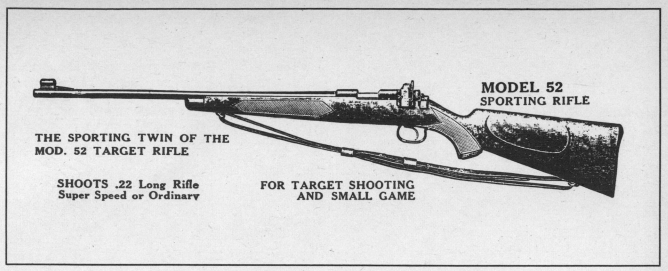

MODEL 52
SPORTING RIFLE

THE SPORTING TWIN OF THE
MOD. 52 TARGET RIFLE

SHOOTS .22 Long Rifle
Super Speed or Ordinary

FOR TARGET SHOOTING
AND SMALL GAME

Prior to WW II, Winchester's Model 52 Sporting Rifle sold for $94.60 complete with sights. Today, the same gun sells for over $1000.

Today that same gun is selling for a dead low of $750 on up to (believe it or not) $1500, again depending upon the circumstances listed above. To add a little fuel to the collectors' fire, the Q-D swivels that originally came with many sporters are currently selling for around $100 a set, if you can find 'em!

Early 52 Sporters had a cheekpiece that was more European in styling than later versions which carried a Monte Carlo comb. Also, earlier guns carried their safeties (the winged version) on the left, rear side of the action, while later guns had their rocker-type safeties located on the right, mid-rear of the action just in front of the bolt.

Fully adjustable Lyman peep sights were normal factory equipment, but you could also order the gun set up complete with Unertl, Fecker or Lyman-type scope blocks. The front sight was forged to the 24-inch barrel and was (from the factory) furnished with a hood.

During the mid-'30s certain improvements were made on the 52. The relocation of the safety from the left, rear to the right, mid-rear of the receiver was part of one of those improvements. At the time the change was made, Winchester had on hand a good supply of stocks that had been relieved to accommodate the older safety. These stocks were not scrapped, they were recut to suit the new safety lever's location and used until the supply dried up.

As a result, you will, on occasion, find what I call "interim 52s" that have their stocks cut for *both* styles of safety. Lastly, the 52 Sporter is chambered for the Long Rifle cartridge and the extended

The early 52 Sporter above has the European cheekpiece and the winged safety at the left rear of the bolt. The 52 Sporter below is a later version with Monte Carlo comb and a safety positioned just ahead of the bolt handle on the right rear side of the receiver. From a collector's standpoint, both guns are equally desirable.

This 52 Sporter has the safety (not seen) on the right-hand side of the receiver; however, note that the stock is also relieved for the winged (earlier) safety.

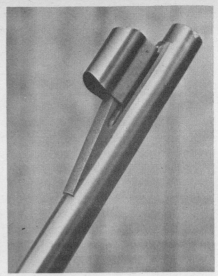

Front sights on 52 Sporters were forged and came complete with hood. Note that the ramp is stippled, not grooved.

Original Q.D. Winchester swivels for a 52 Sporter are getting scarce—they sell for as much as $100 a pair.

stamped steel trigger guard is marked **SPORTING** —all in capital letters. Like many Winchester products, the wood on this gun is checkered fore and aft in a traditional pattern with two diamond-shaped blocks of checkering found on the belly of the forend.

Another bolt-action Winchester rimfire that has recently gained ground in the collector's arena is the Model 75 Sporter—a true sporting version of the 75 Target rifle. A scant 6 years ago I paid $125 for mine; they now sell for around $275 to $500 depending upon condition and geographic location of sale.

Slightly under 90,000 Model 75s were produced; but, just how many of these rimfires were sporters is difficult to say. All sporters feature a forged ramp front sight on a 24-inch barrel. Sighting options were numerous; however, the Lyman quick-detachable Model 57E receiver sight seems to be frequently found. Just ahead of the extended stamped steel trigger guard you will find the **SPORTING**—all in capital letters.

One quick (at-a-glance) way to determine production period on Model 75s (Sporters as well as Target rifles) is to look at the bolt handle. Early bolts have their handles bent straight down, while later handles are gracefully swept down and to the rear in a Model 70-ish fashion. When you get close to a 75 Sporter, check the serial number on the bottom of the bolt and the right, front side of the receiver—they must match. Again, low-numbered 75s have straight-down bolt handles while high-numbered guns have their bolt handles swept rearward.

The time to buy a 75 Sporter is *now,* not next year. Prices are rising proportionate to, or better than, 52 Sporters. I anticipate a time not too far down the line when a minty 75 Sporter will *easily* command a

The Winchester 75 Sporter (top) and the 52 Sporter (bottom) are both marked "SPORTING" on the trigger guards.

$600-plus price. The Model 75 was introduced in the late '30s and dropped in 1958 according to George Watrous' book, *The History of Winchester Firearms 1866-1975*.

At this point it should be said that Winchester's Models 56 and 57 bolt action rimfires are equally sought after by collectors; they can be snatched up, quite often, for less than $100. However, to a collector who needs one, a minty 57 will sell for as much as $300 or more. The 56 is even rarer as fewer—around 8,000—were produced. Together, these rifles paved the way for the Model 69 series bolt action rifle that was so popular in the '40s and '50s.

Certainly, you cannot mention Winchester rimfires without discussing the Model 63 autoloader, the 62 and 61 pumps, even the Model 69 bolt action repeater. All of these guns are currently caught between two gun-fraternity factions—the men who shoot them, and the men who collect them. Like everything else, these guns, too, will probably end up in the collectors' arena with the passage of time.

Before moving on to other guns, it must be men-

tioned that a collector of Winchesters should have two books at hand: *The History of Winchester Firearms*, by Geo. Watrous; and, *The Winchester Book*, by Geo. Madis. Both are available from Ray Riling Arms Books Company, 6844 Gorsten St., Philadelphia, PA 19119.

Modern Remington rimfires have never had a collectors following—it's that simple. In the past 2 years, however, shooters and collectors alike have come to recognize the Remington 40-XB or 700 Custom rimfire sporter as one of the finest 22s ever produced.

Between 1969 and 1978, orders for these superbly made rimfires were accepted by Remington, and, according to Larry Goodstal, the Curator of the Remington Museum, approximately 700 of these guns were made in Remington's Custom Shop in Ilion, New York. Even rarer are the 40-XB Sporters that were made in D & F grades—about 12, again according to Remington.

Basically the "40-X Sporter" was nothing more (or less!) than a taper-barreled 40-XB rimfire action that

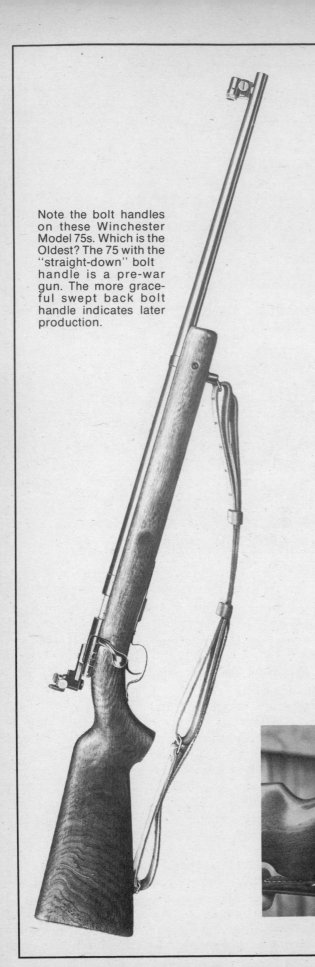

Note the bolt handles on these Winchester Model 75s. Which is the Oldest? The 75 with the "straight-down" bolt handle is a pre-war gun. The more graceful swept back bolt handle indicates later production.

was opened up to accept a 5-shot magazine. While this sounds simple, it wasn't. The 5-shot magazine used in the 40-X Sporter was, in fact, made by a competitor of Remington. And it had to be modified before it could be used in the 40-X. In my opinion, the cost of this one part alone was, at best, prohibitive. The cost of milling out the bottom of the receiver and fitting the attendant parts proved to be quite a time-consuming drain on the Custom Shop personnel. In short, the 40-X Sporter got damned expensive and was dropped when the retail price started to nudge the $750 mark.

Again, none of those rifles were made on a production-line basis—they were all built one-at-a-time in the Custom Shop.

If you can find one, the price will be right around a thousand dollars. Given the extremely small run of guns over a 9-year period, it's safe to say that the 40-X Sporter has the potential to eclipse the Model 52 Winchester Sporter as America's most sought-after rimfire rifle.

Because these guns were made so slowly, Remington was (finally) able to meet its committed orders for the 40-X Sporter in February of 1980—2 full years after it was dropped from the line!

Your author considers himself lucky that he owns the last 40-X Sporter made by Remington. At the time my gun was ordered, Remington's P.R. man Dick Dietz indicated that he might not be able to fill this writer's order as he had been at the Custom Shop just one day earlier and learned that the 40-X Sporter had been dropped. I got lucky, *very* lucky. The Custom Shop extended the list of Sporters to be produced by one—serial number 52505B.

Perhaps the rarest of the full-size rimfire sporters ever made is the Remington Model 37 Sporter. To my knowledge, the title page photo is the only one ever taken of this ultra-rare rimfire. How many were made? In a fortunate phone call to the Ilion plant, I was able to talk with both Mike Walker and Larry

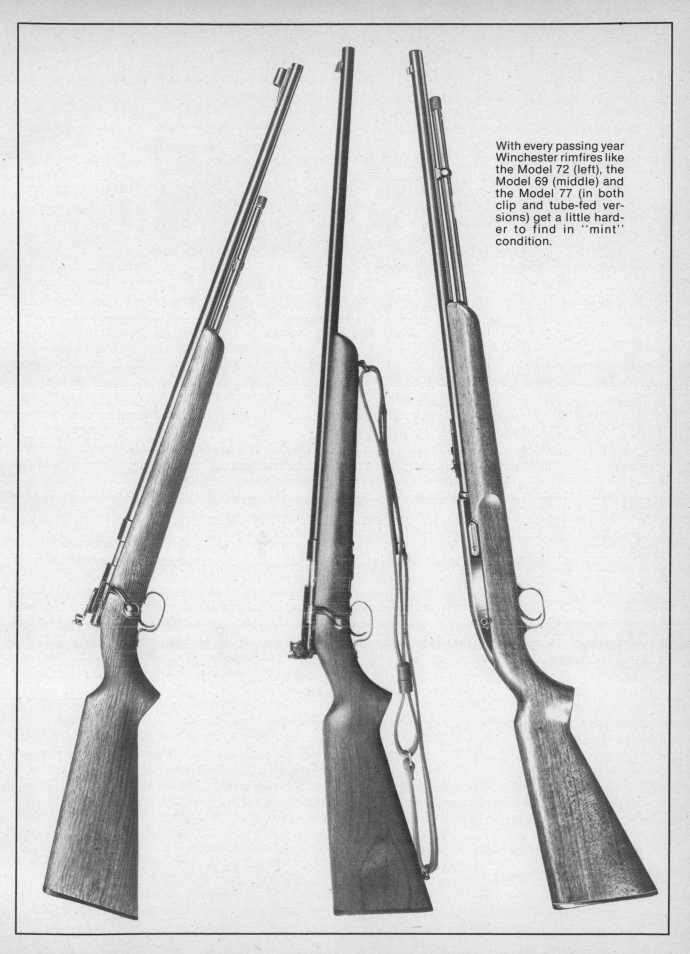

With every passing year Winchester rimfires like the Model 72 (left), the Model 69 (middle) and the Model 77 (in both clip and tube-fed versions) get a little harder to find in "mint" condition.

This Model 75 Sporter has a serial number in the 62,000 (late) range —note the bolt handle.

Goodstal. Mike worked for Remington during the mid-'40s and could recall the sporter. Larry backed Mike's comments with his own knowledge of this unusual 22.

The Model 37 Target rifle is well known to target shooters of the '30s, '40s and early '50s; however, the 37 Sporter is something of a mystery to most. In the opinions of Mike Walker and Larry Goodstal, the first Model 37 ever made was the sporter, *not* the target version.

Best estimates indicate that, in 1934, a single Model 37 Sporter was made, followed by the production of another Model 37 (*possibly* another sporter) in 1935. In 1936 the target version was produced in good quantity prior to its major debut the following year. The sporter was never put into production, hence Remington never went for a 1-2-punch approach in an attempt to lessen Winchester's iron grip on the target 22 market. While one, possibly two 37 Sporters were made, the disposition of a surviving specimen (or specimens) is unknown by Ilion. Larry Goodstal personally feels the only examples of the 37 Sporter were scrapped, possibly just prior to or during World War II.

If a surviving specimen should ever surface, you can be assured that it would stand as the unchallenged king of rare prototype rimfires. Certainly, it must be noted that only 12,198 Model 37 "Target" rifles were ever made; you can also count on these guns to increase in value.

While we're on the subject of prototypes, it must be mentioned that Winchester disposed of many prototype rimfire (and centerfire) guns prior to moving the Winchester Museum to its current home in Cody, Wyoming. Antique dealer Norm Flayderman bought most, if not all of those guns and sold them through his catalog and to selected dealers around the country.

Every gun came with Museum hanging tags (metal tabs on circular, spring-steel rings) and letters of authentication from retired Winchester Museum Curator Tom Hall.

How many were there? According to Norm Flayderman, there were about 20-25 rimfire prototypes. As to their value I can only answer that question in this way: When was the last time you bought a *fully authenticated* Winchester Museum firearm? The point is that those guns *do* exist, and they *are* valuable. *Very* valuable. In short, that small 20-25 gun lot of rimfire prototypes stands out as one of the most rare and unusual stands of Winchester firearms ever sold to the public.

As time passes, mint specimens of such rifles as Winchester's more common Models 69 and 72 bolt action repeaters will climb higher on the collectible list of rimfires. Certainly, Remington's 521T bolt action 22 is another favorite that should do well in years to come. Then there's another series of Remington rimfires that's coming into its own rather quickly— the Nylon stocked series of rifles introduced in 1962: The Model 10 single shot bolt action (10,670 produced); the Model 11 bolt action repeater (22,423 made); the Model 12 bolt action, tube-fed repeater (27,551 made) and Nylon 76 lever action rimfire (26,947 made).

The world of rimfire collecting is blossoming like never before, and bargains can still be found. In the past, most rimfires have filled a less than high-ticket niche on retail shelves; hence, dealers, buyers and sellers didn't pay as much attention to rimfires as they should have. This is where the alert rimfire collector came into his own. Can you still get lucky? You bet. I know of two shooters who recently got *very* lucky.

In one case a neighbor of one of those fellows refused to "take a penny less than $40" for a *mint* 62 Winchester pump. The other "lucky" fellow got an unfired 52 Sporter for under $200 from a seller who didn't "hold much truck in bolt action 22s." Now it's your turn.

●

Schroeder Finds the Schrader

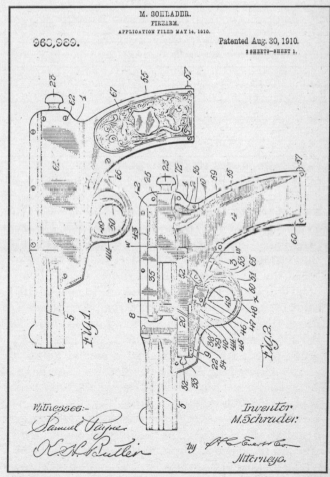

The first Schrader pistol to turn up in collector's hands, in 32 caliber but with a chamber too short for 32 ACP. It's probably chambered for the uncommon 7.65mm Roth Sauer cartridge, though the ejection port is too short for even that stubby round if the projectile is still in it! Note the elaborate grip carving, reproduced precisely in the patent drawings.

by JOSEPH J. SCHROEDER

SEVERAL YEARS AGO I was passing the Service Armament tables at the Ohio Gun Collectors' show when Val Forgett stopped me. "You've a weakness for screwy auto pistols, Joe," he said, "and I've got one you ought to own!" With that he handed me an all-brass 32 caliber pocket automatic that was unlike anything I'd ever seen . . . or had I?

"What is it?" I asked. "I don't know," Val replied, "but it's supposed to be some sort of a patent model and was once in a flood." I noticed the trigger was badly corroded, and some small parts seemed to be missing.

"What do you want for it?" I asked. Val quoted a figure which, though not unreasonable, was more than I wanted to put into an anonymous dead-end gun with no pedigree. Still, as I looked it over something was nagging at the back of my mind. I had seen something very similar in the past, but where . . . ? Perhaps my patent file?

I noted the intertwined initials "MS" and the word "McKeesport" carefully carved into one of the hard rubber grips, thanked Val for thinking of me, and went on my way.

About a week later I was reviewing my notes from the show when I remembered Val's "whatziz." I pulled open the patent file drawer and started in at "A." When I got to "S" I hit paydirt, letting out a yell that brought my family running to see if I'd dropped a broomhandle Mauser on my foot and permanently crippled myself.

"Look," I yelled, "I've found a Schrader pistol . . . Our name (almost) . . . Once in a lifetime find?...Hot Dog!" My wife murmured something soothing and

Patent drawing for the 32 Schrader. Note the unique loading system, with the magazine inserted through a "trap door" in the gun's backstrap, and the details of the grip carving.

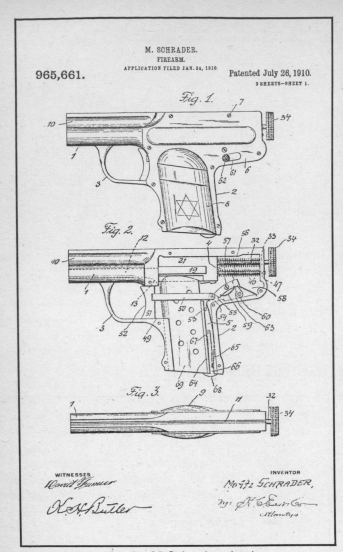

Patent drawing for the 25 Schrader pistol.

25 Schrader pistol. The Star of David and two diagonal bars are carved into the wooden grip, just as shown in the patent drawing. It's chambered for the 25 ACP cartridge.

Right-hand side view of the 25 and 32 Schrader pistols together, showing their abnormally small ejection ports. The 25 will eject a fired case, but not a loaded cartridge. The stress crack at the rear of the frame indicates the gun was actually fired and is not just a model.

backed out of the room apprehensively. The kids shook their heads and went back to the TV set. I picked up the phone, called Val, and 5 minutes later the Schrader was mine. I owned a "namesake" pistol!

Moritz Schrader of McKeesport, Pennsylvania, received the patent for my pistol on August 30, 1910. There's no doubt that my gun is the patent model, as the pattern in the well-worn, hand-carved hard rubber grips appears in the patent drawings.

My patent file also revealed a second automatic pistol patented by Moritz Schrader, for a smaller and somewhat more conventional design that must have been a 25. This patent, issued July 26, 1910, also revealed an interesting piece of personal information about Moritz Schrader. Between the time he filed for the patent on the 25, January 24, 1910, and the May 14, 1910, application date for his 32, Moritz Schrader became a citizen of the United States. In the earlier application he had described himself as "a subject of the Czar of Russia . . ." though both applications gave McKeesport as his residence.

Using this meager information, photographs of my gun, and copies of the patent drawings, I wrote up a short article which appeared in *Auto Mag,* the journal of the National Automatic Pistol Collectors Association. I'd tried telephone information for Schrader in the McKeesport area, but to no avail. A NAPCA member who lives not far from McKeesport, Jim Shaffer, was intrigued enough by my writeup to go out sleuthing. Not much later I heard from Jim. He'd found the last surviving member of the Schrader family, who now spelled his name Shrader, explaining why I hadn't found him. He was Moritz Schrader's nephew, and he had the 25!

At the time it wasn't for sale, but Jim was able to borrow it and bring it to an Ohio show for me to look at. Nickel plated, it was in much better condition than my 32, and, like that gun, was absolutely faithful to the patent drawings. Even the wooden grips bearing the star of David were shown in the patent. I expressed my enthusiasm for it to Jim, and told him if Mr. Shrader should ever decide to let the gun go I'd like to own it.

A year or so passed, and then I heard from Jim. Mr. Shrader's wife had passed away, and now that he was alone and along in years he was worried about what would happen to the pistol. Rather than take a chance that it would be destroyed or fall into the hands of someone who might misuse it, better to pass it along to someone who appreciated it . . . .me!

The arrangements were completed, and soon I had the second Schrader pistol. With it came a real bonus, an old fashioned photo postcard showing Moritz

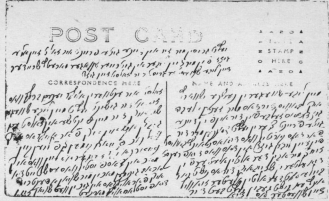

Moritz Schrader's postcard to his sister-in-law, telling her (in Yiddish) that he was working on a fourth pistol.

Schrader sitting at a table studying a pistol. It was my 32. The back of the card contained a message in a language I didn't recognize, but which I was eventually able to have identified as Yiddish. A friend was able to get it translated for me, and though it's addressed to Moritz Schrader's sister-in-law and is mostly news of the family it does state, "We are now making a fourth pistol and I hope that the patent will soon be on the market."

I later received a nice letter from Mr. Shrader, stating that his uncle had been a first-class gunsmith and later an officer in the Russian army before emigrating to the United States in the early 1900s. After his arrival, Moritz Schrader worked for a while as a machinist for the National Tube Company, then opened his own gunshop in McKeesport. He apparently patented several other inventions as well as the two pistols I now own.

A chance encounter at a gun show and a nagging half-memory. A bit of research that scores, followed up by more successful detective work. Add a large dose of luck, and what began with an incomplete, unidentified gun at a gun show ends up as a well-documented mini-collection. Now Moritz mentioned making a fourth pistol in his postcard so somewhere there must be at least one more Schrader . . . . ●

The designer, Moritz Schrader, with the 32 Schrader pistol.

Detail of the pistol in the photo above, showing that it is the 32 Schrader with the sideplate removed and action exposed.

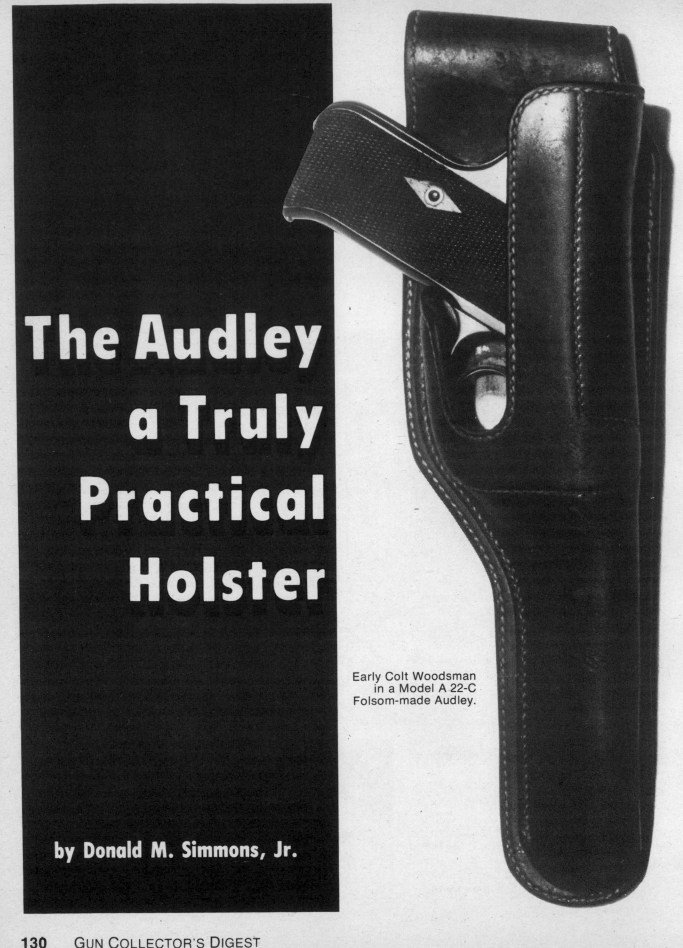

The Audley a Truly Practical Holster

by Donald M. Simmons, Jr.

Early Colt Woodsman
in a Model A 22-C
Folsom-made Audley.

OVER THE YEARS at gun shows, you may have noticed a certain type of collector who ignores most of what is on the exhibitor's table and is found poring over a carton of old leather. At one time, we holster fanciers were in the cheapest form of hobby one could find; used holsters were a dollar or two at the most, often being sold for a quarter or even given away. Most of us leatherphiles were after German holsters of the Nazi period and even though most of us were basically gun collectors, we liked to have a holster to go with each handgun.

Today, the holster lover is no longer a cheapskate or else he is no longer collecting. Most German holsters with military acceptance marks are in the $25+ range with some bringing as high as $100. Forced away from German military holsters, some of us moved first to German police leather and from there to just any police holsters.

The police of any country have generally been a poor relation to that country's military, so very naturally the original handgun holsters for the police were used military holsters. However, the police in many ways had requirements which were very different from those of the military. For example, under combat conditions, a soldier may draw his sidearm just on a hunch. Not so a policeman. The soldier must have a holster which is impervious to rain or snow which means, practically, it must have a flap. The policeman doesn't need or want this protection. Since a policeman today spends a great deal of time sitting down, his holster should have a pivot for his convenience, during motor patrol for example. One thing that a policeman must have is a handgun which is immediately accessible to himself, but can't be accessible to others. This last criterion spells out the Audley holster.

The first holster patent by Francis H. Audley of New York City, is one for an improvement in shoulder holsters, filed with the United States Patent Office on July 5, 1910. This patent covered an extremely complicated shoulder holster which could also be attached to a pair of suspenders. I have never seen such a holster to date and I doubt if it got beyond the design stage. Mr. Audley's next invention had to do with locking the trigger guard of a handgun into its holster, with the gun readily released by the user's trigger finger during the act of drawing the arm. He applied for a patent on that idea April 20, 1912, and renewed his application on March 16, 1914, finally receiving a U.S. Patent on October 13, 1914—patent number 1,113,530. We are indebted to Mr. Joseph Wotka of the National Automatic Pistol Collectors Association (NAPCA) for this patent research and other data on the Audley holster.

To market his invention, Mr. Audley seems to have contacted the H. & D. Folsom Arms Company at 314

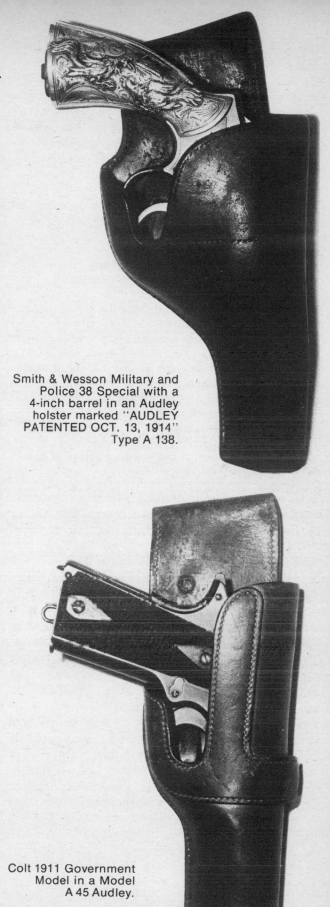

Smith & Wesson Military and Police 38 Special with a 4-inch barrel in an Audley holster marked "AUDLEY PATENTED OCT. 13, 1914" Type A 138.

Colt 1911 Government Model in a Model A 45 Audley.

Broadway in New York City, sometime in late 1919 or early 1920. Folsom was a gun supply house which made holsters as well as the Crescent shotgun. They also were a supplier of police equipment, so Audley's patent holster got good exposure to the gendarmerie. Audley and Folsom got together and Folsom became Audley's manufacturer. The product made by Folsom was a high quality holster line. The Folsom-Audley holster was well made and well fitted and was one of the most expensive holsters in its day.

To describe the Audley holster, let us take the entire copy from a catalog of Von Lengerke & Antoine of Chicago, Illinois, circa 1929:

Audley Patent Holsters
The Only Positive Lock Holster
Made

The revolver or pistol slides into the holster with perfect ease and is automatically and securely locked which prevents its jarring out of holster under any circumstances, yet is instantly released by the slight touch of the finger. These holsters are made for all standard automatic pistols and revolvers. The style, fit, material and workmanship put these holsters in a class by themselves. They have been adopted by most Police departments and military organizations of the leading cities of the United States.

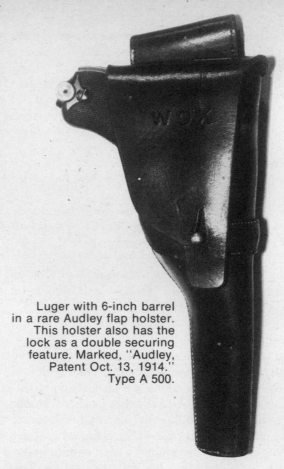

Luger with 6-inch barrel in a rare Audley flap holster. This holster also has the lock as a double securing feature. Marked, "Audley, Patent Oct. 13, 1914." Type A 500.

While these words may sound a little high flowing to our overworked ears they are really true. The Audley was the best holster of its day, and may still be one of the best.

The principle of operation of an Audley holster is very simple, but in order to maintain this simplicity much thought and extra work had to be added during its manufacture. A flat spring-operated brass locking lug is found in the area of the trigger guard notch of the holster. This lug automatically, on the insertion of the firearm, locks on the forward edge of the trigger guard. In order to reduce and control the motion of the lug, there is a bent guard at the lower end of the lug. Both the lug's spring and the guard are riveted to the holster's rear wall and covered by an extra piece of leather, except where the lug and guard protrude through it. Because of the required cut-away "U" at the trigger guard, the front leather is weakened in this area. To overcome this weakness, another formed steel plate is added to the holster. This plate is neatly held in place by stitching between the two pieces of leather that form the front wall of the holster. The plate gives great rigidity to the holster in the area of the trigger guard "U"notch. As can be appreciated, a great deal of extra work and material went into making an Audley holster. Each that I have seen also had an added piece of leather at the bottom, so that foreign matter couldn't enter the barrel of the gun.

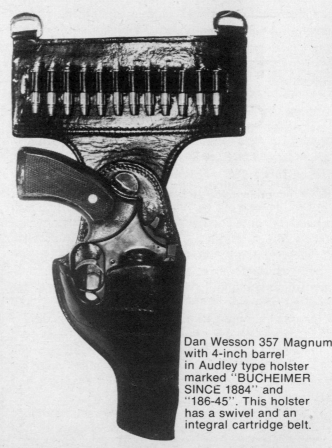

Dan Wesson 357 Magnum with 4-inch barrel in Audley type holster marked "BUCHEIMER SINCE 1884" and "186-45". This holster has a swivel and an integral cartridge belt.

Smith & Wesson Model 1917 45 ACP caliber in an unmarked Audley type holster. Type A 145.

In drawing from the holster, the handgun is removed by the wearer by simply grabbing the fully exposed butt. The user's index finger drops into the trigger guard, automatically depressing the holster's locking lug, and the gun can then be withdrawn. The speed of draw can be equal to that obtained with a simple open holster, yet someone unfamiliar with Audley's locking system and trying to remove the gun from someone else's holster will be completely foiled in the attempt. It is this benefit that made the Audley holster so popular with the police—no snap equipped strap or loop to fumble with—just a normal draw, but yet secure from all tampering by others.

The Line

In the Audley holster's heyday, when made by Folsom, the line consisted of the following different holsters. The "A" in the model number was for Audley. From a 1924-25 Folsom catalog:

Model A 132 was made for S&W hand ejector 32 cal.; Colt Pocket Positive 32 cal., Police Positive & Police Positive Special 32 cal. and 38 cal.; and other small frame revolvers.

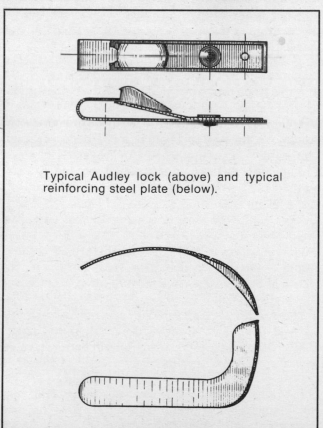

Typical Audley lock (above) and typical reinforcing steel plate (below).

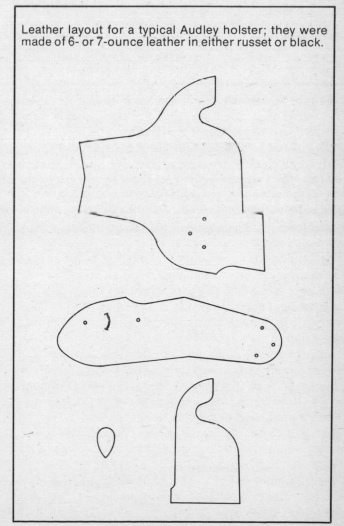

Leather layout for a typical Audley holster; they were made of 6- or 7-ounce leather in either russet or black.

Page from Edward K. Tryon Co. of Philadelphia Catalogue of 1927 showing most of the Audley holster line of that time.

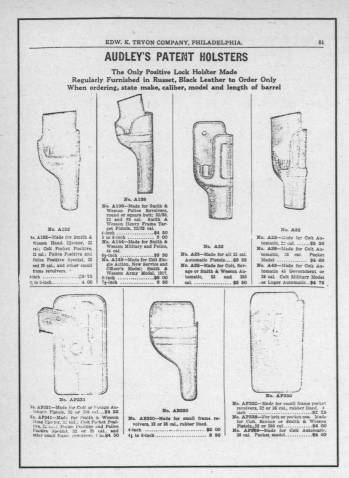

AUDLEY'S PATENT HOLSTERS

The Only Positive Lock Holster Made
Regularly Furnished in Russet, Black Leather to Order Only
When ordering, state make, caliber, model and length of barrel

No. A132
No. A132—Made for Smith & Wesson Hand Ejector, 32 cal.; Colt Pocket Positive, 32 cal.; Police Positive and Police Positive Special, 32 and 38 cal., and other small frame revolvers.
4-inch $3 75
4½ to 6-inch 4 00

No. A138
No. A138—Made for Smith & Wesson Police Revolvers, round or square butt; 32/20, 32 and 38 cal. Smith & Wesson Heavy Frame Target Pistols, 22/32 cal.
4-inch $4 50
5 to 6-inch 5 00
No. A144—Made for Smith & Wesson Military and Police, 44 cal.
6½-inch $5 50
No. A145—Made for Colt Single Action, New Service and Officer's Model; Smith & Wesson Army Model, 1917.
5-inch $6 00
7½-inch 6 50

No. A32
No. A25—Made for all 25 cal. Automatic Pistols....$3 25
No. A32—Made for Colt, Savage or Smith & Wesson Automatic, 32 and 380 cal....................$3 50

No. A22
No. A22—Made for Colt Automatic, 22 cal. $5 50
No. A38—Made for Colt Automatic, 38 cal. Pocket Model $4 60
No. A45—Made for Colt Automatic 45 Government or 38 cal. Colt Military Model or Luger Automatic..$4 75

No. AP331
No. AP331—Made for Colt or Savage Automatic Pistols, 32 or 380 cal.....$4 25
No. AP341—Made for Smith & Wesson Hand Ejector, 32 cal.; Colt Pocket Positive, 32 cal.; Police Positive and Police Positive Special, 32 or 38 cal., and other small frame revolvers, 4 in..$4 50

No. AB350
No. AB350—Made for small frame revolvers, 32 or 38 cal., rubber lined.
4-inch $2 00
4½ to 6-inch 2 50

No. AP332
No. AP332—Made for small frame pocket revolvers, 32 or 38 cal., rubber lined. 4 inch $2 25
No. AP338—For belt or pocket use. Made for Colt, Savage or Smith & Wesson Pistols, 32 or 380 cal............$4 00
No. AP339—Made for Colt Automatic, 38 cal. Pocket model............$4 00

Model A 138 was made for S&W Police Revolvers, round or square butt, 32-20 32, 38 cal.; S&W Heavy Frame Target Pistol 22/32 cal.

Model A 144 was made for S&W Military & Police 44 cal.

Model A 145 was made for Colt Single Action, New Service, and Officer's Model; S&W Army Model 1917.

Model A 25 was made for all 25 cal. Automatic Pistols.

Model A 32 was made for Colt, Savage or S&W Automatic 32 and 380 cal. pistols.

Model A 22 was made for Colt Automatic 22 cal. (Woodsman).

Model A 38 was made for Colt Automatic 38 Pocket Model.

Model A 45 was made for Colt 45 Government or 38 Colt Military Model or Luger Automatic.

Model A 500 was also made for the Colt Automatic 45 cal. Government but had a flap in addition to Audley's lock.

Model A 502 was like the A 500 except it had, instead of a belt loop, the U.S. Military bronze metal loop attachment for a military web belt.

Model AP 331 was made as a back pocket holster for Colt, S&W or Savage Automatic Pistols, 32 or 380 cal.

Model AP 341 was made for S&W Hand Ejector, 32 cal.; Colt Pocket Positive, 32 cal.; Police Positive and Police Positive Special, 32 or 38 cal.; and other small frame revolvers.

Model AB 350 was a variation of the usual Audley locking system which locked on a shoulder for small frame revolvers, 32 or 38 cal.

Model AP 332 was like AB 350 except a back pocket Model.

Model AP 338 and AP 339 was also a back pocket holster for small and medium automatics.

The prices for these holsters ranged from $2 for the Model AB 350 up to $7.50 for the A 502. If a left-handed Audley holster was desired, there was an extra 10 percent charge for this variation. Just to show that an Audley was expensive in its day, the standard Folsom made holsters ranged from a low of 30¢ for a 25 cal. open belt holster to $4.25 for a U.S. Army 45 automatic holster with swivel and bronze loop for web belt attachment.

There is one other very important quality feature that had to be built in to every Audley holster. Because of the close fitting requirements of this system, each holster had to be very accurately formed for just that model of handgun. Therefore, when ordering, it was necessary to give not only the holster catalog model number but also to specify the type of gun and its barrel length, if it was a revolver.

Who Sold Audley Holsters?

Audley holsters were sold by the most prestigious sporting stores of the day. The 1925-1926 catalog of Von Lengerke & Detmold of New York carried the Audley as did P. Von Frantzius of Chicago in their 1927 catalog. The supply house of Edward K. Tryon of Philadelphia devoted an entire page to Audley's holsters in 1927. Von Lengerke & Antoine in both 1928 and 1929 had the Audley line as did Hudson Sporting Goods Co. of New York in their catalog of 1930. The great Abercrombie & Fitch of New York did not have Audley holsters in 1928, but by their 1937 catalog, Audleys are prominently displayed. Strangely, the House of Stoeger does not seem to have ever carried the Audley holster.

The Audley locking holster was a great idea and enjoyed popularity for two decades, from 1920 to 1940. With today's interest in quick draw and combat shooting, the Audley may have lost a little of its appeal. However, anyone who has taken an all-day horse ride, wearing a sidearm, will testify it is very comforting to know that during a gallop his sidearm is secure in an Audley holster.   ●

Sixty Years of Rivalry:

the story of British and German Air Pistols, 1920-80

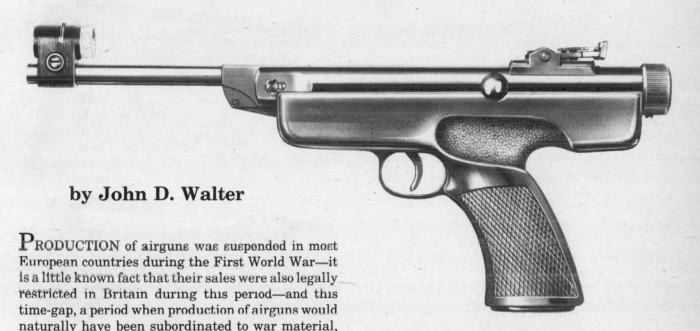

by John D. Walter

PRODUCTION of airguns was suspended in most European countries during the First World War—it is a little known fact that their sales were also legally restricted in Britain during this period—and this time-gap, a period when production of airguns would naturally have been subordinated to war material, provides a convenient place to begin this discussion.

Only two countries can lay claim to any notable airgun design expertise prior to 1914: Britain and Germany. Most of the pistols produced by the latter had been confined to the cheaper types—low-power pressed or cast-metal designs (a style that was to remain in vogue for some decades) made by Mayer & Grammelspacher and others, and shortened derivatives of barrel-cocking long arms. None of these cheap pistols, however, made an appreciable contribution to airgun history. It was not until after the war that air pistols began to attract significant attention.

BRITAIN, 1918-39

The story of the British industry prior to 1900 differed little from that of Germany, though several inventors soon tried to devise a better, more powerful air pistol. The best known of these men was Lincoln Jeffries, who produced a highly advanced and distinctive fixed-barrel spring-air gun with the air cylinder in the grip—where the piston was cocked by a downward swinging backstrap lever. This gun, the *Bisley*, marketed in small numbers in 1912-13, was the subject of British Patents 10,250 of 1910 and 9,684 of 1911. Jeffries also developed the rather better known *Lincoln* pistol in the same era (British Patent 1,405 of 1911) but series production apparently did not commence until the early 1920s, when an improved ver-

Pictured above—The Webley Premier Mk 2 (top) and the Diana Model 6. (Photos courtesy of Webley & Scott Ltd. and Mayer & Grammelspacher.)

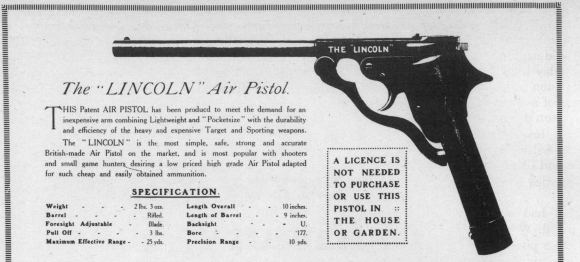

The "LINCOLN" Air Pistol.

THIS Patent AIR PISTOL has been produced to meet the demand for an inexpensive arm combining Lightweight and "Pocketsize" with the durability and efficiency of the heavy and expensive Target and Sporting weapons.

The "LINCOLN" is the most simple, safe, strong and accurate British-made Air Pistol on the market, and is most popular with shooters and small game hunters desiring a low priced high grade Air Pistol adapted for such cheap and easily obtained ammunition.

SPECIFICATION.

Weight - - - -	2 lbs. 3 ozs.	Length Overall - - - 10 inches.
Barrel - - - -	Rifled.	Length of Barrel - - 9 inches.
Foresight Adjustable -	Blade.	Backsight - - - U.
Pull Off - - - -	3 lbs.	Bore - - - - ·177.
Maximum Effective Range -	25 yds.	Precision Range - - 10 yds.

A LICENCE IS NOT NEEDED TO PURCHASE OR USE THIS PISTOL IN :: THE HOUSE OR GARDEN.

The Lincoln pistol, from a leaflet of the early 1920s.

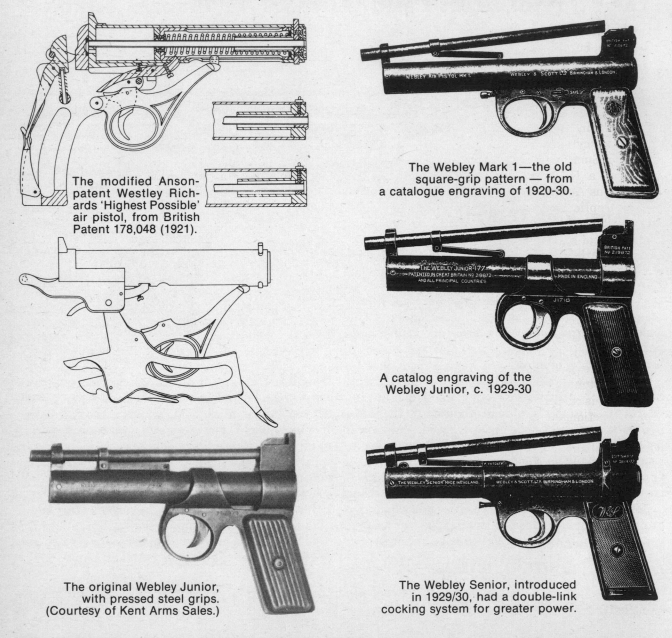

The modified Anson-patent Westley Richards 'Highest Possible' air pistol, from British Patent 178,048 (1921).

The Webley Mark 1—the old square-grip pattern — from a catalogue engraving of 1920-30.

A catalog engraving of the Webley Junior, c. 1929-30

The original Webley Junior, with pressed steel grips. (Courtesy of Kent Arms Sales.)

The Webley Senior, introduced in 1929/30, had a double-link cocking system for greater power.

sion was registered (patent 181,277) in 1921.

The Lincoln is easily recognized by its unique lines resembling a grease gun, as many rival manufacturers could not have been slow to point out! Similar to the Bisley insofar as its butt-mounted air cylinder and piston assembly was concerned, it cocked by means of a downward-tipping barrel which pushed the piston down the grip through an intermediate cocking lever cum trigger-guard. The Lincoln is widely believed to have inspired Fritz Walther's *LP52* and *LP53,* described later in this article—the similarities are really too remarkable to be coincidental.

There had been other attempts to devise a better air pistol. William Whiting, better known for his cartridge pistols and revolvers, designed and patented an air pistol for Webley & Scott in 1910 (patent 4,213/1910), and George Norman of BSA patented another in the following year (12,692/1911 and 5,283/1912). There is no evidence that anything other than a toolroom model of the Norman/BSA pistol was ever made, but it remains the *only* BSA air handgun to be developed prior to the appearance of the *Scorpion* in the early 1970s.

The curious Westley Richards *Highest Possible* pistol was designed by Edwin Anson and patented (24,837/07) in 1907. This carried its barrel above the massive air cylinder, and cocked by breaking the grip forwards. Small numbers of these guns—perhaps as many as a thousand—were made by Westley Richards as Anson (though usually described in his patent applications as a 'gunmaker') obviously lacked facilities large enough to undertake series production of his pistol. An entry in *Arms & Explosives* in 1915 records that Westley Richards had exhausted all its stocks of the Highest Possible and no large-scale manufacture recommenced after the end of the First World War.

Anson patented an improvement to the basic design in 1921 (British Patent 178,048, sought on 17 December) with a barrel running through the air cylinder, a revised concentric mainspring and a new annular piston unit. However, only a single example of this gun is currently known to exist and it is clear that production was highly restricted; by the 1920s, the Highest Possible was something of an anachronism—complicated, possessing some design weaknesses, difficult to make and a poor rival for some of its more efficient contemporaries.

The British airgun industry revived considerably after 1920, largely helped by the restrictive provisions of the 1920 Firearms Act, which left airguns unscathed; more money, therefore, was expended on research and development. BSA remained committed to the production of Jeffries-pattern air rifles, Norman's 1911 vintage patent being shelved, but Webley & Scott soon gained a notable and important lead by exploiting patents granted to its employees Douglas Johnstone and John Fearn. The first of these was sought on 19 February, 1924 and resulted in the Webley & Scott *Mark 1* air pistol. This gun was protected by the basic patent, 219,872 of 1924, together with additional grants for the safety arrangements (229,851 of 1924) and the piston washer system (231,270 of 1924). The Webley, with its highly distinctive lifting-barrel cocking system, pivoted at the front of the air cylinder, is said to have made its first public appearance at the Empire Exhibition at Wembley in 1924.

It was later joined by an essentially similar *Mark 2* (incorporating an improved bronze piston ring seal patented by 252,651, sought in May, 1926), the simpler *Junior* and then a collection of slightly modified versions that has lasted until the present day. There is no doubt that the Johnstone/Fearn system is one of the most elegant and compact units ever designed, particularly as it permits a very long barrel in relation to overall length—unlike the types in which the barrel acts as an axial extension of the air cylinder.

Webley Production			
Type	Introduced/ Discontinued	Serial Numbers	Major Changes
Mark 1	1024/1064[1]	1 60,000 pre-1939[2]	1925 (no. 1,000 approx.) sliding barrel catch added; 1927/8? (10,000), trigger adjusting screw; 1929/30 (37,500), front of air chamber made removable; 1937 (1936?), grip raked above gun number 50000.
Mark 2	1925/1930	Numbered in the Mark 1 sequence; between 24000 and 40000.	As above, prior to 1930.
Senior	1929-30/1964[1]	S1-S18250 pre-1939[2]	1931 (at about S1500), trigger/sear mechanism changed; 1934, modified cocking linkage to prevent "tumble-over" (S3850); 1937 (S7000) grip angled and barrel shortened.
Junior	1929-30/1973	J1-J31000 pre-1939[2]	None of any significance.
Premier Junior	1964/1973	—[2]	PTFE piston washer added in 1967. Increasing use of sintered metal parts in the early 1970s.
Mk 2	1973/78[3]	—[2]	
Premier Mk 2	1973/78[3]	—[2]	

Notes: [1]Designs merged to provide Premier. [2]Most postwar guns bear only batch numbers. [3]New parts — and new guns, of course — were still being sold in the 1980s.

There were many other British designs, some successful and some short lived. Lincoln Jeffries continued to market the powerful (if a little unorthodox)

Right—The Webley double-link cocking system, designed by Douglas Johnstone and patented in 1929 (326, 703).

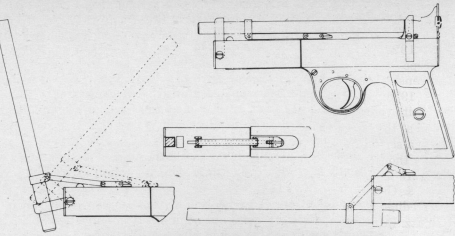

Below—The Lincoln Jeffries Scout, from the instruction pamphlet.

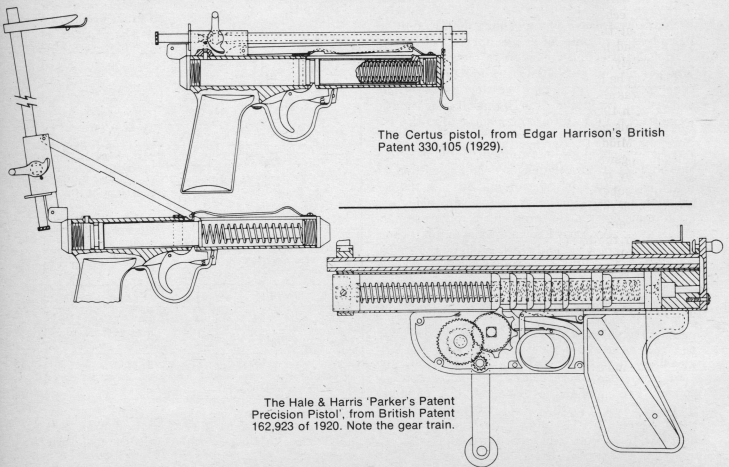

The Certus pistol, from Edgar Harrison's British Patent 330,105 (1929).

The Hale & Harris 'Parker's Patent Precision Pistol', from British Patent 162,923 of 1920. Note the gear train.

Lincoln butt-cylinder pistol, and also produced large quantities of a much simpler push-in-barrel-cocking pocket pistol christened the *Scout*. This appeared in about 1922. It also served as the basis for a prototype—the only known example—of the Jeffries design enshrined in British Patent 254,640, sought in March, 1926, to protect a very distinctive fixed-barrel pistol with a top-mounted cocking lever. The lever, pivoted at the muzzle, was locked in the closed position by a screw-threaded bolt at the rear.

Many thousands of cheap pressed and cast-metal guns were imported into Britain—such as the early Mayer & Grammelspacher *Dianas* and the *Dolla Mk 2* credited, though by no means with certainty, to Anschütz. But this did not prevent various indigenous designers continuing the quest for the 'ideal' air pistol. A typically ambitious and rather eccentric solution was *Parker's Patent Precision Pistol*, whose unique crank-handle, attached to a massive housing ahead of the trigger guard, cocked the piston through a gear-train. This curious pistol was patented (162,923, sought on 10 May, 1920) by Alfred Hale and Ernest Harris of A.G. Parker & Co. Ltd, Bisley Works, Whittall Street, Birmingham. This company changed its name to Parker-Hale in 1936.

Only a few hundred pistols were made in 1921-30; they were complicated and expensive compared with the contemporary Webley Mark 1. It must be noted here that W.H.B. Smith's *Gas, Air & Spring Guns of the World*, echoed by the more recent *Airgun Digest*, claims that the Hale & Harris patent was never granted and infers that no guns were made. This, quite clearly, is erroneous—several surviving guns are still to be found in Britain.

There was also the *Certus* pistol, patented by Edgar Harrison in 1929 (330,105, sought on 9 May); Harrison gave his address as 'The Small Arms Factory, Feltham, Middlesex' and was a partner in the well known Cogswell & Harrison gunsmithing establishment by whom the Certus was made. Though bearing a superficial resemblance to the Johnstone/Fearn Webleys, the Certus is a rising-barrel design of quite different execution. Its barrel is pivoted at the rear rather than the front and the piston systems differ greatly. The Certus also has an auto-opening loading port and cocks on the closing stroke of the barrel/cocking lever stroke.

Among other notable designers was Frank Clarke, who had designed the *Titan* in 1917. The first Titan patent (110,999) was sought in January, 1917, when Clarke was working from Whittall Street in Birmingham, and his original prototype has survived. It is distinguished by an unusual cocking system that consists of a pivoting rod normally kept down the backstrap. This can be lifted and rotated, then pushed in on the piston until the latter is caught by the sear—a system that obviously incorporates no me-

chanical advantage and thus will only develop low power. The block through which the rod runs can be rotated sideways to give access to the breech.

Clarke patented a modified or perfected version of the Titan, incorporating refinements such as an automatic safety preventing piston release until the backstrap rod was replaced in its correct position. Several differing versions of the Titan were made to this particular patent (208,341 of 1922) in the 1922-5 era. One survivor, for instance, has a 9.5-inch barrel, while others show detail differences in their frame designs. They are believed to have been made by Accles & Shelvoke Ltd. in the Talford Engineering Works in Aston, on the outskirts of Birmingham. Accles & Shelvoke also made the later side-lever-cocking *Warrior*, patented by Clarke (who had moved to Lower Loveday Street in Birmingham) and Edwin Anson, designer of the Westley Richards Highest Possible.

The Warrior was the subject of British Patent 351,268, sought in July, 1930, and also of US patent application 538,057; small quantities, perhaps less than 5,000, were made in 1932-8. It was being advertised by Stephen Laszlo, founder of the Hy-Score organization, in some 1934-vintage issues of *The American Rifleman* for $15. Unlike most modern sidelever action pistols, the Warrior cocks from the right side, a disadvantage for the average right-handed marksman who must change hands to cock it.

Frank Clarke was also involved in the design of a curious pistol seemingly based on the Lincoln, in which the piston in the butt cylinder was cocked by a spigot riding in a helical channel . . . the first and possibly only time such an idea has been considered. Interestingly, Clarke's associates in this venture (British Patent 231,557 sought in December 1923/January 1924) were none other than Webley's designers Johnstone & Fearn. The reasons for this link have yet to be properly explained.

There were other ventures in Britain that came to nothing at all. These included the Hill & Williams pistol of 1923 (British Patent 425,555), cocked by an underlever, but it and these others never progressed beyond the drawing board or prototype stage.

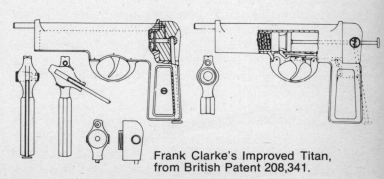

Frank Clarke's Improved Titan, from British Patent 208,341.

GERMANY, 1922-39

The German airgun industry took some time to re-establish itself in the 1920s, largely because of the postwar political dislocation and the weakness of the Mark. One major manufacturer, Friedrich Langenhan (FLZ) of Zella St Blasii, left the scene in the 1920s never to return with any force; another, Oscar Will, sold the Venuswaffenwerk in Zella-Mehlis to Wilhelm Foss; and Mayer & Grammelspacher, founded in 1890 and one of the premier German airgun makers prior to 1918, initially marketed its *Dianas* with little vigor.

However, several new companies provided fresh impetus in the mid 1920s. They included C.G. Haenel Waffen- und Fahrradfabrik, a well-known firearms manufacturer founded in Suhl in 1840, whose first airguns—despite persistent claims to the contrary—date from 1925. Smaller companies also saw airguns as a potentially lucrative market, including Immanuel Meffert of Suhl, maker of the *Hubertus* push-in barrel pistol from c.1927 onward, and the fledgling J.G. Anschütz company of Zella-Mehlis.

The German products present a very mixed bag. Mayer & Grammelspacher at first showed little inclination to experiment, and its wares were usually solid and unspectacular. Until the early 1930s, its major pistol line was apparently represented by a rather primitive low powered stamped-metal design dating from c.1923/4. These guns are normally identifiable by the company trademark—a huntress discarding her bow and arrows in favor of an air rifle—struck into the frame above the ribbed 'grip' portion. The word *Diana* usually appears as well.

However, Mayer & Grammelspacher then produced the well-known *Diana Model 2,* a cheap but solidly-made push-in-barrel spring air pistol that is still in production. It was followed by the *Diana Model 5*, the subject of German patent 574,329, granted in the name of Mayer & Grammelspacher, with effect from December, 1931. An unaccepted patent sought in Britain in December, 1932, records the designers as Erwin & Rudolf Mayer.

Though not especially sophisticated, the Model 5 offered good performance, solid construction, good accuracy and appreciable power. Some original prewar guns will still develop velocities in excess of 400fs in 0.177in caliber—the only one of such power available prior to the 1950s. The Model 5 remained in production, with hardly any mechanical changes, until the improved *Model 5G* appeared in 1978/9.

Venuswaffenwerk (sometimes known as VWW, after its trademark) was spurred on by its new owner, Wilhelm Foss, and produced the interesting Tell pistols—beginning with the diminutive *Tell II* or 'Baby Tell' in the early 1930s. This pocket pistol was only some 5.5 inches long and cocked by means of a backstrap lever. It was followed by the larger and more sophisticated *Tell III,* patented by Foss in Britain in July, 1937 (patent number 483,899). This featured a combination barrel and top-lever cocking system in which downward movement of the barrel pulled the entire piston and sear assembly forward, completing the cycle on the return stroke. The movement of the sear—disconnected from the trigger for much of the cocking cycle—provided a simple automatic safety feature. The rarely seen Tell III is a very elegant design owing much of its excellent balance to the Parabellum (Luger) pistol; regrettably, only a few were made before the outbreak of the Second World War stopped production.

Haenel's contributions to airgun design were largely due to Hugo Schmeisser, an extremely talented firearms designer whose patents ranged from improvements in manufacturing processes to the design of assault rifles and submachine-guns. The company, as has already been noted, did not make airguns prior to 1925, but then rapidly established a reputation for mass production of some surprisingly sophisticated items.

Haenel's airguns were distributed in Britain by Modern Arms Company ('Marco') and in the USA by Von Lengerke & Antoine and later by Stoeger. Five differing Haenel pistols are known. The magazine fed *Model 50* and the similar single-shot *Model 51* were push-in barrel cockers dating from the late 1920s, the former being fitted with a magazine for 50 ball shot. Neither is commonly seen. The *Models 26, 27* and *28* are more interesting. Schmeisser was granted a German patent (480,270) for the basic action of these guns, which was also protected by British patent 277,265 sought in May 1927.

The cocking mechanism consists of a backwards-pivoting grip unit which, once released by the Parabellum-style transverse-locking bolt ahead of the trigger guard, pushes the piston back by way of a short intermediate link. The Model 26 has a lightweight alloy frame/grip unit (some have been found with what are assumed to be replacement wood grips), while the Models 27 and 28 are much more robust gunmetal products. The barrels of all three types pivot downwards for loading and a magazine version of the Model 28, known as the *Model 28R*, was also made. This is believed to have been patented in Germany in 1930-1 (588,629), which would mean that the 28R post-dates the standard Model 28 by some 3 years. The patented tube magazine contains 20 slugs (0.177in) or 15 (0.22in). Only a few thousand of the elegant, well balanced but essentially low-powered Haenels were made prior to 1939.

Another of the Zella-Mehlis companies to become a force on the airgun scene was Moritz & Gerstenberger (EmGe), whose three pistols—*Herkules, Krone* and *Zenit*—achieved widespread distribution

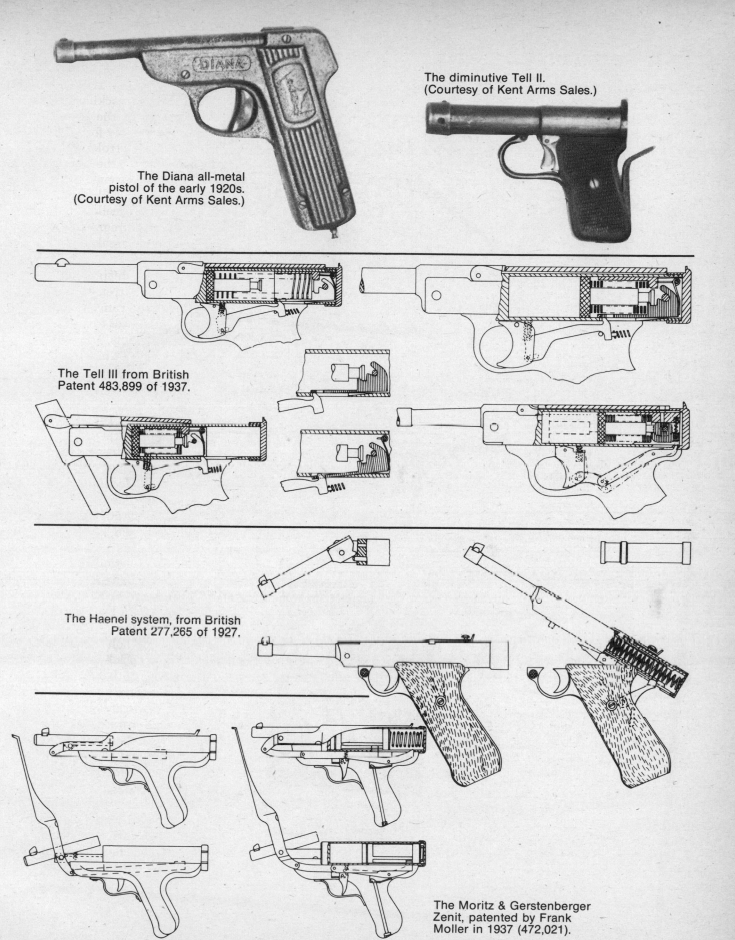

The Diana all-metal
pistol of the early 1920s.
(Courtesy of Kent Arms Sales.)

The diminutive Tell II.
(Courtesy of Kent Arms Sales.)

The Tell III from British
Patent 483,899 of 1937.

The Haenel system, from British
Patent 277,265 of 1927.

The Moritz & Gerstenberger
Zenit, patented by Frank
Moller in 1937 (472,021).

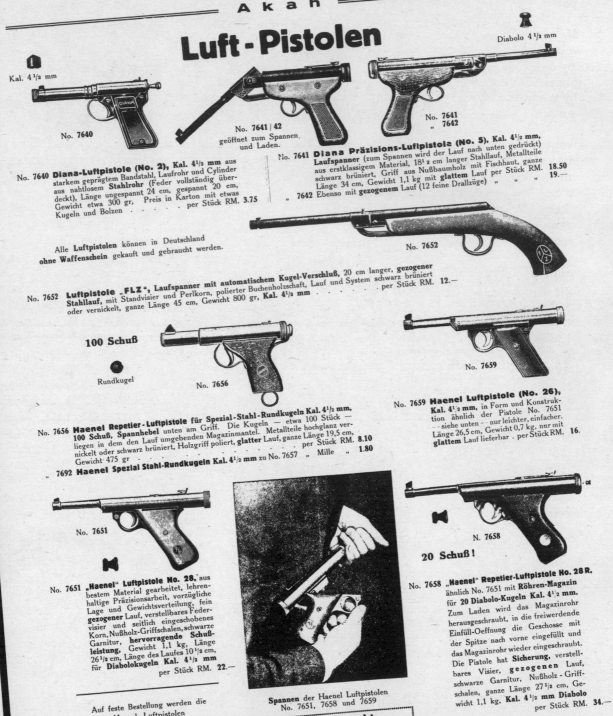

Akah
Luft-Pistolen

Kal. 4 1/2 mm

Diabolo 4 1/2 mm

No. 7640

No. 7641 / 42 geöffnet zum Spannen und Laden

No. 7641 7642

No. 7652

100 Schuß

Rundkugel

No. 7656

No. 7659

No. 7651

No. 7658

20 Schuß !

N. 7658

No. 7640 Diana-Luftpistole (No. 2), Kal. 4 1/2 mm aus starkem geprägtem Bandstahl, Laufrohr und Cylinder aus nahtlosem **Stahlrohr** (Feder vollständig überdeckt), Länge ungespannt 24 cm, gespannt 20 cm, Gewicht etwa 300 gr, Preis in Karton mit etwas Kugeln und Bolzen . . . . per Stück RM. 3.75

Alle **Luftpistolen** können in Deutschland **ohne Waffenschein** gekauft und gebraucht werden.

No. 7641 Diana Präzisions-Luftpistole (No. 5), Kal. 4 1/2 mm, Laufspanner (zum Spannen wird der Lauf nach unten gedrückt) aus erstklassigem Material, 18 1/2 cm langer Stahllauf, Metallteile schwarz brüniert, Griff aus Nußbaumholz mit Fischhaut, ganze Länge 34 cm, Gewicht 1,1 kg mit **glattem Lauf** per Stück RM. 18.50
„ **7642** Ebenso mit **gezogenem Lauf** (12 feine Drallzüge) „ „ „ 19.—

No. 7652 Luftpistole „FLZ", Laufspanner mit automatischem Kugel-Verschluß, 20 cm langer, gezogener Stahllauf, mit Standvisier und Perlkorn, polierter Buchenholzschaft, Lauf und System schwarz brüniert oder vernickelt, ganze Länge 45 cm, Gewicht 800 gr, **Kal. 4 1/2 mm** . . . . . per Stück RM. 12.—

No. 7656 Haenel Repetier-Luftpistole für Spezial-Stahl-Rundkugeln Kal. 4 1/2 mm, 100 Schuß, Spannhebel unten am Griff. Die Kugeln — etwa 100 Stück — liegen in dem den Lauf umgebenden Magazinmantel. Metallteile hochglanz vernickelt oder schwarz brüniert, Holzgriff poliert, **glatter Lauf,** ganze Länge 19,5 cm, Gewicht 475 gr . . . . per Stück RM. 8.10
„ **7692 Haenel Spezial Stahl-Rundkugeln Kal. 4 1/2 mm** zu No. 7657 „ Mille „ 1.80

No. 7659 Haenel Luftpistole (No. 26), Kal. 4 1/2 mm, in Form und Konstruktion ähnlich der Pistole No. 7651 — siehe unten — nur leichter, einfacher. Länge 26,5 cm, Gewicht 0,7 kg, nur mit **glattem Lauf** lieferbar · per Stück RM. 16.

No. 7651 „Haenel" Luftpistole No. 28, aus bestem Material gearbeitet, lehrenhaltige Präzisionsarbeit, vorzügliche Lage und Gewichtsverteilung, fein **gezogener Lauf,** verstellbares Federvisier und seitlich eingeschobenes Korn, Nußholz-Griffschalen, schwarze Garnitur, **hervorragende Schußleistung,** Gewicht 1,1 kg, Länge 26 1/2 cm, Länge des Laufes 10 1/2 cm, für **Diabolokugeln Kal. 4 1/2 mm**
per Stück RM. 22.—

Auf feste Bestellung werden die Haenel - Luftpistolen No. 7651 und 7658 auch für **Kal. 5,5 mm** (= engl. —.22) für Export geliefert.

Spannen der Haenel Luftpistolen No. 7651, 7658 und 7659

Sonder-Prospekt auf Wunsch zu Diensten!

No. 7658 „Haenel" Repetier-Luftpistole Ho. 28 R. ähnlich No. 7651 mit **Röhren-Magazin** für 20 Diabolo-Kugeln Kal. 4 1/2 mm. Zum Laden wird das Magazinrohr herausgeschraubt, in die freiwerdende Einfüll-Oeffnung die Geschosse mit der Spitze nach vorne eingefüllt und das Magazinrohr wieder eingeschraubt. Die Pistole hat **Sicherung,** verstellbares Visier, **gezogenen** Lauf, schwarze Garnitur, Nußholz - Griffschalen, ganze Länge 27 1/2 cm, Gewicht 1,1 kg, **Kal. 4 1/2 mm Diabolo** per Stück RM. 34.—

Page from an early 1930s AKAH catalog, showing the rare FLZ as well as early Diana and Haenel models.

in the late 1930s. The Herkules, which seems to date from about 1933/4, was a conventional barrel-cocking design, but the Zenit was a much more interesting top-lever cocker patented by Franz Moller in 1937 (British patent 472,021). The Zenit was revived after the war in Britain, where thousands were made as the *Milbro G4* by Millard Brothers Ltd. of Motherwell. Smaller quantities were also made in Sweden by Stiga AB of Tranås. The EmGe Krone was simply a repeating version of the Zenit, distinguished by a small pan magazine mounted above the breech—an idea revived by Walther in the early 1950s.

The advent of the Second World War again spelled an immediate end to airgun production in most of the belligerent nations, even though companies like Webley & Scott continued limited advertising programs to keep their products in the public eye. The postwar scene was altogether different when the time came to recommence production. While British industry had been largely put to the manufacture of war material, most of the German companies, though surprisingly less affected during the early days of hostilities, had been virtually destroyed at their close. Some had simply disappeared, swallowed up by the Soviet advance across Eastern Germany, while the principal designers of others had been imprisoned, interned or forced to flee elsewhere.

GERMANY, 1947-70

Germany was a conquered country and the Allied occupation authorities were understandably reluctant to permit the production of firearms; similar views initially applied to airguns, but soon some interested parties obtained permission to recommence work. Development was to proceed along unique lines.

Haenel and the Venuswaffenwerk had ceased production (though the former was later resurrected by the nationalized GDR firearms industry), while Moritz & Gerstenberger had also temporarily disappeared—to recommence production as Gerstenberger & Eberwein in Gussenstadt in the mid 1950s. Mayer & Grammelspacher's production machinery had been seized by the Allies and finally sold to Millard Brothers, who subsequently installed it in a new factory in the Scottish steel town of Motherwell and began production of German-style Diana airguns in 1949. Milbro also recommenced production of the EmGe Zenit, though there is no evidence in this case that the original equipment had been acquired.

The disappearance of several well-known names was counterbalanced by the efforts of other companies—mostly former firearms manufacturers—to join what promised to be a lucrative market. This was particularly true as airgun shooting had rapidly

The Walther LP53 factory cased with auxiliary sight blades.

been established as a bona-fide sport in countless shooting clubs and Bierkeller. In addition, few profits were likely in the extremely restricted firearms industry.

Among the important newcomers was Carl Walther Sportwaffenfabrik, formerly of Zella-Mehlis, which was finally re-established in Ulm/Donau in 1951 to make a new air rifle designed by Fritz Walther. This was soon followed by the highly advanced *LP52* spring air pistol, based on the old British Lincoln and patented in Germany in April, 1952 (DBP 940,692). The essentially similar *LP53* was to become the finest gun marketed prior to the appearance of the Feinwerkbau *LP65*, as Walther's perfected pistols, beginning with the *LP2* of 1964, were single stroke pneumatics rather than spring-air designs.

The story of Walther, a company that never bothered with cheaper guns, contrasts markedly with the rise of J.G. Anschütz GmbH, once also of Zella-Mehlis and now also of Ulm/Donau. Anschütz's postwar commitment to airguns, in addition to some very high class target and sporting rifles, makes it difficult to assess its role prior to 1945. It is clear, at least during the early 1930s, that Anschütz was primarily a retailer/distributor of airguns bought (judging by a contemporary 'abridge catalogue') from Mayer & Grammelspacher, Haenel and others. However, the 1937 *WUM* catalog includes the push-in barrel *JGA* pistol alongside the Hubertus, the Haenel and the *Dolla Mk 2*, a cheap design also credited to Anschütz—on, perhaps, rather doubtful grounds.

Production of the JGA recommenced in the early 1950s, as some were then being sold in Britain by Frank Dyke & Co. Ltd of London and in the USA by Stoeger. Though Anschütz has devoted a considerable amount of research into the development of advanced spring air rifles, including a recoilless target gun, there is no evidence that any pistols were considered other than an interesting 'push through' barrel-cocking gun protected by German registered design 1,855,666 of 26, July, 1962.

The affairs of Mayer & Grammelspacher are rather more interesting. Production of airguns recommenced in September, 1950, when the *Diana Model 16* rifle, a prewar design, was put back into production on a newly made production line. The *Diana Model 2* push-in-barrel pistol reappeared in January, 1955, and a slight revision of the 1931-vintage *Diana Model 5* target pistol in February, 1958. The latter had wooden thumbrest-style grips and a fully adjustable backsight. It rapidly regained much of its predecessor's popularity and was joined in April, 1960, by the unique *Diana Model 6*—the world's first truly recoilless spring-air pistol, incorporating the contra-piston system patented some years earlier by Kurt Giss (British Patent 803,028, sought in March, 1956).

The first examples of the Model 6 had one-piece synthetic grip/frame units, which were also produced for the more conventional Model 5. Both guns were conventional-looking barrel cockers, though the Model 6 actually featured *two* pistons. These were driven by a single spring assembly in opposite directions. The principal recognition feature is the transverse 'cap' that lies approximately halfway along the Model 6 air cylinder, but is absent from the simpler Model 5. Both remained in production—with occasional revisions to sights and machining of some minor parts—until replaced by the modified *Models 5G* and *6G* in the late 1970s. The revised guns display a new cast-alloy frame with separate plastic grips raked to give better handling qualities.

The top of the Mayer & Grammelspacher range is the *Diana Model 10,* a version of the Giss contra-piston gun that is a masterpiece of complexity, and, perhaps, the only spring-air pistol currently capable of challenging the all-conquering Feinwerkbau. The *Diana Model 6M* is the standard Model 6G fitted with the Model 10-type rotary barrel sleeve.

Among other manufacturers who entered the postwar production of airguns was Albert Föhrenbach GmbH of Hannover-Wennigsen (not Bennigsen, as Smith records), a relatively short-lived company founded in 1947 to recondition conveyor-belt-making machinery. Föhrenbach made 'Falke' (Falcon) brand airguns including the good-quality *Falke Model 33* underlever-action pistol, which featured a built-in automatic safety and a separate downward-tipping barrel. Production of the Model 33 was confined to 1953-8, as production of all the Föhrenbach guns ceased by 1959 and liquidation of the company occurred in October, 1961.

A few guns were also made by Friedrich Wilh. Heym GmbH & Co. KG, founded in Suhl in 1865 but re-established in Münnerstadt (in northern Bavaria) in the late 1940s. Only about 4,000 assorted rifles and 1,500 push-in barrel air pistols were made in 1949-52. The Heym *Model 103* exhibits better than average quality but is still fundamentally a very simple design.

Tens of thousands of rather rudimentary spring-air pistols were marketed in the 1948-67 period by Voere, Schwarwälder Jagd- und Sportwaffenfabrik Voetter & Co. (otherwise known as Koma-Werk, 1947-55), operating from Furtwangen/Schwarzwald until 1958 and thereafter from Vöhrenbach. The *LDP3,* advertised as a boy's model, had a push-in barrel while the *LDP4* was a barrel-cocker rarely seen outside Germany.

Large numbers of a solitary pistol design, the *Model 20* or *S20*, have been made since c.1952/3 by Bayerische Sportwaffenfabrik Hans Schütt OHG (BSF) of Erlangen in Bavaria. Many bear the 'Wischo' brandname of Wilsker & Co. of Erlangen, an export and distribution agency associated with BSF. A minor modification of the basic design, the *BSF Model 20 Match*, is made for target shooting. The BSFs represent a powerful but rather traditional design of barrel-cocker, strongly made, well finished but not especially sophisticated. Their manufacturer was founded in 1935 to make airguns, but there is no evidence that much production was undertaken prior to 1939.

The products of Hermann Weihrauch KG, originally of Zella-Mehlis in Thuringia (trademark: HWZ), did not include airguns prior to 1939, though designs had been produced in 1935-7. However, after a postwar move to Mellrichstadt (mark: HWM) in Bavaria, air rifle production began in 1950. Weihrauch was exclusively a long arm maker until the introduction of the *HW70* Barrel-cocking pistol in the early 1970s, a moderately sophisticated design incorporating some unusual low-cost manufacturing techniques.

The products of Fritz Barthelmes Sportwaffenfabrik KG, founded in 1954 by the inventor of the Walther P38 pistol, also display advanced low-cost fabricating techniques. There are four *FB Record* pistols, the *LP1, LP2, LP68* and *LP77*, the first of which was patented in 1967 (DBP 1,250,763). All display high-class stamped and cast-alloy construction, methods that allow a tiny workforce of 20 to make over 40,000 guns per annum in the Oggenhausen Kreis Brenz factory. The LP1 and LP2 are relatively simple, the former being a very cheap smoothbore, but the large LP68 and LP77 are worthy of special mention.

Gerstenberger & Eberwein of Gussenstadt, successor to the EmGe name of the prewar Moritz & Gerstenberger, has made two barrel-cocking target-type pistols known as the *EmGe LP3A* and the *EmGe*

Below—The push-in barrel Heym Model 103, from a contemporary leaflet. (Courtesy of Friedrich Wilh. Heym GmbH & Co. KG.)

The current Diana Model 2. (Courtesy of Mayer & Grammelspacher.)

The Barthelmes FB Record Pistols —LP 1, 2, 68 and 77. (Courtesy of Fritz Barthelmes Sportwaffenfabrik KG.)

A cutaway view of the Feinwerkbau LP65. (Courtesy of Feinwerkbau Westinger & Altenburger GmbH.)

LP100. Both have fully adjustable sights, and the newer LP100 displays a synthetic grip/frame unit greatly resembling the Weihrauch *HW70*. Another smaller company, Herbert Schmidt of Ostheim von der Rhön, markets the push-in barrel *HS9A* and the sidelever action *HS71*, a low-cost repeater designed for ball ammunition.

Apart from rarely seen pistols such as the *Eusta LP 100* and *LP210*, lifting barrel cockers made by Alpina-Werk and distributed by Hans Wrage & Co. GmbH of Hamburg in 1968-76, only the Feinwerkbau remains to be considered.

There can be no doubt that the *Feinwerkbau LP65* is the world's best spring-air pistol, holder of all the world records and the victor in countless national, international and Olympic championships. Made by Feinwerkbau Westinger & Altenburger GmbH, founded by ex-Mauser-Werke employees in Oberndorf am Neckar in 1949, the first pistols appeared on the market in 1966-7. They incorporate a sledge-type recoilless system patented by Ernst Altenberger, Karl Westinger and Edwin Wöhrstein (DBP 1,140,489 sought in February, 1961). Unlike the British Warrior of the 1930s, discussed earlier, the Feinwerkbau cocking lever lies on the left side of the frame and can be operated by a right-handed marksman with minimal disturbance. The modified *LP80* appeared at the end of the 1970s with a new trigger system, improved barrel weights and other minor improvements.

BRITAIN, 1945-80

The history of the postwar airgun industry is a complete contrast to what happened in Germany, which is undoubtedly due to the very different ways in which the air pistol has been viewed. The Germans saw it as capable of the very highest development; the British, largely as a means of inexpensive entertainment. The sophistication of the products varied accordingly.

In 1945 the British industry found itself in the doldrums, even though limited advertising had been undertaken during the war. Postwar production was almost entirely confined to the Birmingham area, as Webley naturally continued to market variations on the Johnstone/Fearn theme, The *Junior, Mark 1* and *Senior* pistols continued in production until the Senior and Mark 1 were finally superseded in 1964 by the *Premier*—displaying features taken from both its predecessors—and a *Junior Mark 2* appeared in 1973. Few further developments, apart from minor changes in components and the substitution of alloy for gunmetal in some parts, were made until the Premier was finally replaced by the *Hurricane* in 1977. The *Typhoon* of 1979 is similar, but with a smaller 'junior' grip and a weaker mainspring, while the *Tempest*

(also dating from 1979) is simply a modernized version of the traditional compact guns. All three have safety catches on the left side of the frame above the grip.

The Webley has proved much more successful and durable than its contemporary rivals, many of which appeared in the heady postwar days, full of promise and sure to dominate the markets—or so their designers believed. Edwin Anson & Co., an old-established firm, was liquidated in 1945, whereupon stocks of partly complete *Star* pistols (a prewar design of uncertain chronology that may have originated in the 1920s) were acquired by Curry & Keen. The latter, with no assembly shop, passed the parts to A. & A. Brown & Sons, who then completed a few Stars—said to be no more than forty—before turning to the *Abas Major*.

About two thousand of these were made—in blue, nickel or crackle-black finish—to the designs of three members of the Brown family, whose patent (British 604,411) was sought in 1945. Despite Smith's disparaging comments, the Abas Major is an elegant, powerful design. The barrel runs axially through the air cylinder and annular piston assembly, which is cocked by the specially strengthened combined under-lever and trigger guard, the lower end of which contains a pellet sizer. The Abas Major has a separate loading port and a special ratchet-type safety system. Several minor variations of the basic design are known: the earliest guns, for example, had a two-piece sear and a small cocking lever lock-catch. The former was replaced by a one-piece unit and the latter discarded altogether.

The Abas Major was contemporary with another Birmingham product, the Accles & Shelvoke-made *Acvoke*. This manufacturer had enjoyed some prewar success with Clarke's *Titan* and *Warrior*, but the patent specification protecting the Acvoke (British Patent 619,108 sought in 1946) credits it to John Arrowsmith. The pistol is another concentric barrel/mainspring design, cocked by a combination of a downward-hinged backstrap lever and a break-forward action. Despite its rather off-putting appearance, the Acvoke is very strongly made, well finished and a competent performer. Like the Abas Major, it has a built-in pellet sizer—a device that is currently being hailed as a 'new' invention!

Production of the Acvoke began about 1948 and ceased in the mid-1950s, after a number of minor variations had been made; the design of the catch retaining the backstrap lever, for instance, changed from time to time. About 20,000 are said to have been made, though the serial numbers may have begun at 10000 or 10001 and the actual quantity may only have been *ten* thousand.

Other postwar British designs have included the *Thunderbolt Junior,* a modification of the prewar

Above—The Webley Junior Mk 2. (Courtesy of Webley & Scott Ltd.) Right—The Acvoke. (Courtesy of Kent Arms Sales.)

The Milbro SP50. (Courtesy of Millard Brothers Ltd.)

German *Tell II* patented in Britain in 1947 (number 623,869) on behalf of William Walker and Frank Clarke (Lead Products) Ltd. Exploitation of the design, however, was left to Produsit Ltd. of Precision Works, Lombard Street, Birmingham, who made about 8,000 pistols in the early 1950s. The *Gat* was introduced in 1938, discontinued and finally put back into production in 1946/7—a simple push-in barrel pistol usually made of nickel plated or black-finish cast alloy. It is capable of firing darts, corks, pellets and a number of other projectiles, and is made in Walton-on-Thames, Surrey, by T. J. Harrington & Co. Ltd. There is also an unidentified gun called the *Limit*, listed by Smith as German but clearly stamped 'Made in England' and sometimes thought to be a Harrington product. It is, however, more likely to have emanated from Millard Bros., being a version of the old-style Diana Model 2.

Millard Brothers Ltd. ('Milbro') began production of airguns in 1949, on machinery formerly owned by Mayer & Grammelspacher. The first pistol was a British version of the push-in barrel Diana Model 2, followed by a derivative of the prewar EmGe Zenit known as the *Milbro G4* or *G4/1* (the suffix being the caliber, No. 1 Bore or 0.177 inch). After several changes of sights and a few other modifications, the G4 was discontinued in 1976/7.

Milbro also made large numbers of a unique 'air pistol' deriving its power from a large rubber bulb inset in the front of the grip. When squeezed, the bulb generated enough pressure to propel No. 7 shot—diameter 2.4mm or 0.095 inch—for a short distance at low velocity. The result was known as the *Milbro*

Cub, made under license from its French inventor, Réné Boulet, who had applied for British Patent 614,470 in 1945. Milbro has gone on to make a modified version of the Diana Model 2, the *Milbro G2/5* dating from 1965, and the modernized *G3/1* or *SP50* dating from 1972. Both are simple push-in barrel cockers. The *Milbro G5 Cougar* is a large barrel-cocking pistol of unusual but fairly conventional design. However, its interesting features include a sliding skeletal shoulder stock, a synthetic telescope sight bracket and a satin finish synthetic fore-end—unusual on an air pistol.

Lastly, we come to the powerful barrel cocking *BSA Scorpion,* a heavy pistol developed in the early 1970s. Its hammer-fired trigger unit was patented by Roger Wackrow, Robert Cranston and Harold Jones in 1972 (British Patent 1,423,153), but the gun was not placed in volume production until 1977 after some teething troubles, which included (in its 0.22 inch form), exceeding the British legal power limit of 6fp.

Acknowledgements

This article could not have been written without the help of my good friend Dennis Commins, until recently compiler of the 'Airgun Scene' column in the British magazine *Guns Review*. His work included an exhaustive survey of the airgun patents filed in Britain in the 1849-1949 period, and it is with his permission that many of the drawings are reproduced here. I feel I must also thank Dr. J.S.E. Gilbart and Mark Newcomer for the pieces of their scholarship I may have unwittingly borrowed, and also the many companies who supplied material and illustrations. I hope they will accept a 'blanket' thank-you, otherwise the article would have doubled its size . . !

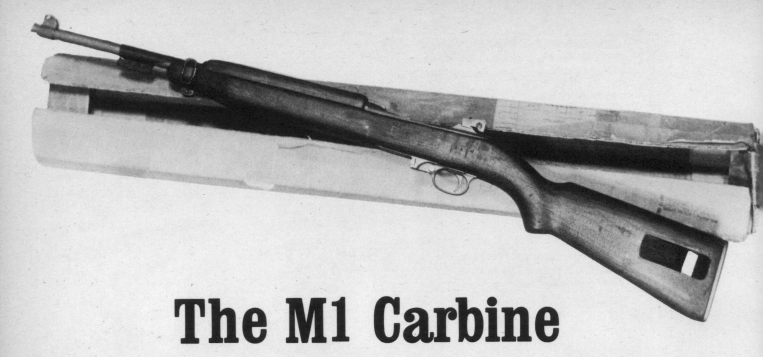

The M1 Carbine
G.I.'s Friend and Collector's Prize

by Gerald R. Reagle, Jr.

The arrival of a long, skinny carton on a Railway Express truck back in 1963 or 1964 signaled a new field for collectors interested in military arms. Thousands upon thousands of the handy little 30 caliber M1 carbines that had served GIs so well during World War II and Korea were being sold, for very nominal sums, by the Director of Civilian Marksmanship to members of the National Rifle Association. Through the efforts of the DCM, NRA and concerned legislators, the arm that had been so popular with its wartime users was at last made available to civilian shooters and collectors.

At first glance one M1 Carbine certainly looks just like any other, and even for some advanced collectors that's the way they'd like to keep it. However, with its many variations an M1 collection can become almost as extensive as one of Lugers or single action Colts. Having had ten prime contractors, countless modifications, and hundreds of parts sub-contractors, assembling even the basic M1 variations can be a real challenge.

The M1 has an interesting history. It was designed to replace the 1911 Colt 45 automatic pistol as the arm of rear echelon troops. Prior to our entry into World War II our military took careful note of the tactics and equipment of the German Wehrmacht as it "Blitzkrieged" its way through Europe. What they decided was that some type of weapon between a pistol and the full-sized Garand rifle was badly needed for other than front line troops. The Ordnance Department requested proposals for such an arm, and several firms responded. After testing and evaluation, the design submitted by Winchester was accepted. A production contract was let just before the U.S. got involved in the war.

The demand for carbines far exceeded the capabilities of Winchester, whose facilities were already fully occupied with military production, so the Ordnance Department went to various non-gun manufacturers to produce the M1 carbine. Of the ten they found, only one, Irwin-Pederson, failed to perform to their satisfaction, and that company's production was taken over by Saginaw Steering and Gear. The successful manufacturers did such a good job for the Army that their production actually exceeded the demand during the first half of 1943, so for a few months in late 1943 and early 1944 Carbine production was slowed or possibly stopped. The same thing happened again in late 1944.

The accompanying list gives the prime contractors for the M1 Carbine—it's worth noting, with a touch of American pride, that with the exception of Winches-

Very early World War II vintage M1 Carbine, with flip type rear sight and early barrel band without bayonet lug, as made by National Postal Meter.

An early Inland-made M1A1 Paratrooper Carbine, still with the original flip sight.

The early M1A1 with the stock folded. Note the oil bottle mounted in the stock frame.

A standard arsenal reworked Carbine of Korean War vintage, originally made by Underwood. The oil bottle doubles to retain the sling in the butt.

ter none of the companies that made the M1 went into its production with any previous gun manufacturing experience! That they all (with the one exception noted previously) succeeded so well has to be a tribute to America's manufacturing know-how.

Company	Percent of Total Production
Inland Mfg. Div. of G.M.C.	43.0%
Winchester	13.5
Underwood-Elliot-Fisher	8.9
Saginaw Steering and Gear	8.5
National Postal Meter	6.8
Quality Hardware Mfg. Co.	5.9
IBM Corp.	5.7
Standard Products Co.	4.0
Rock-Ola Mfg. Corp.	3.7
Irwin-Pedersen Arms Co.	0.1

Total production from all contractors was 6,221,220 carbines.

From those figures it's obvious that examples from some makers are going to be a lot harder to find than others. For collection purposes it's always wise to look for the best possible condition, and the Carbine collector should stick strictly to nice, original condition guns from the largest volume makers in the table. Cheap "beaters" are rarely a bargain, and may be hard to dispose of as "shooters" when an opportunity to upgrade comes along. As for the scarcer makes, let your heart be your guide. Though 4 percent of 6 million is still almost a quarter-million guns, some of those near the bottom of the list don't seem to turn up very often.

The principal maker of an M1 Carbine will have marked his name on the rear of the receiver, just behind the rear sight. For early models that still have the original two-position "flip" rear sight, this poses no problem. However, the later type micrometer adjust peep sight extends back far enough to cover the maker's name on most of the Carbines you'll find today, and it literally takes a bright light, magnifying glass and some wild contortions to make out the name.

The barrel on an M1 is also usually marked by the manufacturer. For instance, an Inland Carbine will usually have a barrel marked **INLAND MFG.** and a date code such as **11-43** just behind the front sight. Most Wincester barrels are marked simply **W**. A barrel marked **ROCK-OLA** won't have to be on a Rock-Ola Carbine, as they supplied a number of barrels to Quality Hardware. Buffalo Arms barrels may be found on any make of Carbine, as barrels were all that Buffalo made and almost all Carbine manufacturers used them at one time or another. (Note: Be

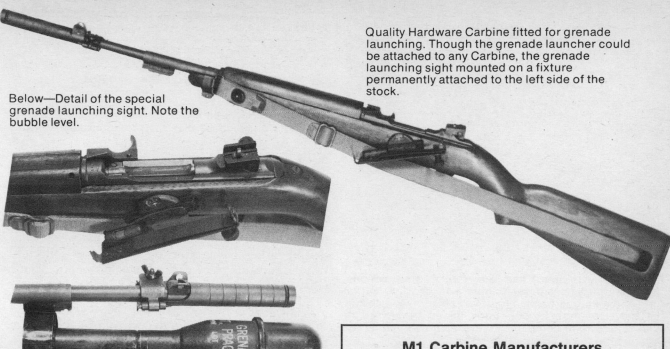

Quality Hardware Carbine fitted for grenade launching. Though the grenade launcher could be attached to any Carbine, the grenade launching sight mounted on a fixture permanently attached to the left side of the stock.

Below—Detail of the special grenade launching sight. Note the bubble level.

Closeup of the grenade launcher, which clamps over the muzzle of the gun and is fastened with a thumb screw. Grenades were launched with a special blank cartridge, and range was determined by the position of a spring set in one of the grooves around the launcher. This determined how far the launcher could extend into the base of the grenade, which in turn established how much ''boost'' it received before leaving the muzzle.

wary of Carbines with barrels marked **SA** (Springfield Armory) as a number of these barrels were sold as unfinished scrap after the war and later installed—sometimes improperly—in madeup Carbines.)

A large number of makers were involved in parts contracts for the Carbines. As you become more experienced in Carbine collecting the marks of these makers will start to sort themselves out. Many, of course, are simply the first initial of the maker's name, such as **W** for Winchester or **U** for Underwood.

Collecting the various models is just as important as collecting makers. One of the more striking variations is the M1A1, which had a folding stock for use by paratroopers and was made only by Inland. Another very interesting variation is the M2, an M1 with a special sear group with a selector switch permitting full-auto as well as semi-auto fire. This makes it a machine gun, of course, and thus puts it under the strict control of the Bureau of Alcohol, Tobacco and Firearms. Though legal M2 ownership is possible in most states, the gun must be legally registered and its transfer (sale) requires a $200 transfer tax along with a fair amount of red tape. For that reason most collectors stay away from them, but if you are interested in an M2 the best bet is probably to

M1 Carbine Manufacturers

Receiver/barrel marking	Company name and location
IBM CORP.	International Business Machines Corp., Poughkeepsie, New York
INLAND DIV.	Inland Manufacturing Division of General Motors Corp., Dayton, Ohio
IRWIN-PEDERSEN	Irwin Pedersen Arms Co., Grand Rapids, Michigan
NATIONAL POSTAL METER	National Postal Meter Co., Rochester, New York
QUALITY H.M.C.	Quality Hardware and Machine Co., Chicago, Illinois
ROCK-OLA	Rock-Ola Manufacturing Corp., Chicago, Illinois
SAGINAW S.G.	Saginaw Steering & Gear Division of General Motors Corp., Saginaw, Michigan
STD. PROD.	Standard Products Co., Port Clinton, Ohio
UNDERWOOD	Underwood-Elliot-Fisher Co., Hartford, Connecticut
WINCHESTER	Winchester Repeating Arms Co., New Haven, Connecticut

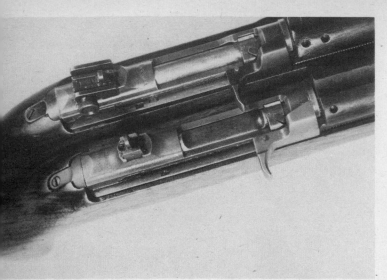

Above—Early (bottom) and late (top) Carbine actions. Note the differences in rear sights, bolts (early is flat on top), and handguards (late has two sets of rivet holes for the barrel clamp). Below—Early milled trigger guard housing (bottom) compared to the later stamped, housing.

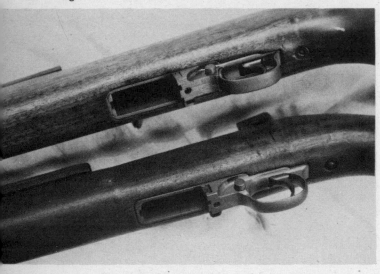

Early (top) vs. late barrel band.

discuss it with a friendly licensed machine gun dealer.

The M3 is an M1 modified to mount the M2 infrared sniperscope, in itself one of the most interesting of the Carbine accessories. Finding an M3 complete with sniperscope would be a real treat, but don't expect to buy it cheap! There were also a number of Carbines of various makes modified for experimental purposes. Some were equipped with telescopic sights, micro-groove barrels, and so on. There were even a few "presentation" Carbines made up especially for company officers or other dignitaries. The list is almost endless, and it's important to the collector that he be able to distinguish between such legitimate collector's items and Carbines that were modified by either shooters or less scrupulous collectors to take advantage of the unknowledgeable. That's where experience and education come in.

Along with his first example, the novice Carbine collector should invest in everything in the way of books and literature about the arm that he can. He should then use that first Carbine as a study guide, taking it apart and checking it part by part with the information in both collector publications and GI manuals. That's the only way to begin learning what's needed to buy intelligently at gun shows or gun shops.

Chances are, when you do come across a promising Carbine at a show there'll be some self-styled Carbine "expert" nearby to tell you, "The only good ones are Winchesters," or some similar pearl of wisdom. First of all, even if it were true (which it isn't) that should not keep you from the other makes, since you're buying for a collection. In fact, every M1 Carbine made had to pass a set of rigorous inspections and tests administered by government inspectors. Every Carbine that passed those tests was a good one! You'll find differences in finish, of course, and the fit of various parts varied not only between makes but even from time to time in a given maker's production.

When you see a Carbine you're interested in buying, ask the owner if he'll let you field strip it. If you look like you know what you're doing (and you should, if you did your homework), many owners will give their OK. If they won't, beware. One problem you're sure to encounter some time is a damaged piston housing, and without stripping the gun it's impossible to detect.

Another thing to avoid is rewelds. Many M1s were cut up and sold for scrap, and some enterprising dealers bought up the scrap and were able to reweld the torched receivers well enough to make them into functioning actions. Though a properly done reweld is probably a safe shooter, to a collector it isn't much better than scrap metal and not worth investing in. Last year at the gun show a young fellow walked by with a really nice looking Carbine. My heart leaping with excitement, I asked him, "Is it for sale?" "No," he responded with a big grin. "I just bought it!" He offered it to me for examination.

I pulled back the bolt and saw the bad news . . . it was a reweld! At least whoever had done it had marked it, but in any case the poor guy who'd just bought it sure lost his smile when I pointed out the welds. Had he been better informed and more careful, he would never have bought it.

Along with the rewelds—though generally of a much better quality—are the various commercial copies of the M1. Many are essentially exact copies of the military M1, and some were even assembled with surplus military components, but to a collector they simply aren't the real thing. Buy one for shooting, if you wish, but don't waste your collecting dollars on them. A copy is still a copy!

Carbine accessories offer a very appropriate sideline for the M1 collector. The basic items such as cleaning rod kits, bolt disassembly tools, gas piston wrenches, grenade launchers and flash hiders belong in any Carbine collection. Carbine magazines and magazine pouches provide almost a collecting sideline in themselves—at a very nominal cost. The two Carbine bayonets, the M3 fighting knife (early) and M4 bayonet (late) are also certainly appropriate additions. Unfortunately, thanks to the increasing popularity of knife collecting, a decent Carbine bayonet is getting to be expensive.

Carbine collecting is a fascinating field and a challenging one, and it's up to each individual to decide what direction he wants his collection to go. Some collect certain makers, while others look for production variations and still others for accessories. Despite the ever increasing interest in the Carbine as a collectable, there are still a lot of questions that have not yet been answered about this fine arm. Join us, and perhaps you'll be the one who helps fill in some of those information gaps!

(*Author's note:* A group of Carbine collecting enthusiasts have formed a Carbine collector's club in order to better facilitate the exchange of information on these fascinating arms. For details on the organization contact the author through the publisher.) •

Bibliography

Gibson, Robert. *The Guide to Collecting the M1 Carbine*. Greeley, Colorado: J-B Publications, 1976.

Ruth, L. Larry. *M1 Carbine: Design, Development and Production*. Cornville, Arizona: Desert Publications, 1979.

FM 23-7, AFM 50-4, Department of the Army Field Manual, Department of the Air Force Manual, Carbine .30 M1, M1A1, M2, and M3, October 19, 1953.

Above—Basic Carbine accessories: cleaning rod in case at the top, trigger spring tool at left, gas piston wrench at center, and bolt disassembly tool at the right. The grenade launcher carrying case is at the bottom.

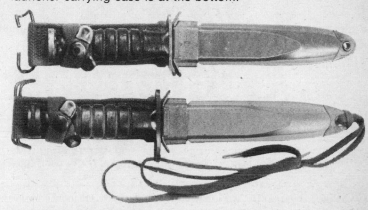

M3 fighting knife (top) and M4 bayonet (bottom).

Above—Bandolier and web belt carriers for Carbine ammunition.

G.I. scabbard for the M1 Carbine, used principally for carrying the arm in a Jeep.

WILLIAM
Gunmaker to the Trade

WILLIAM TRANTER is best known to gun collectors as the manufacturer of a variety of percussion revolvers embodying several types of complicated and ingenious trigger mechanisms which led eventually to a truly double-action design. In collector's eyes his fame lies only just below the better-known firms of Webley and Adams, both of whom have had books written about them in fairly recent years. An examination of historical evidence indicates that both Tranter's activities and his influence upon firearms manufacture in England have been sadly underrated, and that he was in fact one of the leading manufacturers amongst the titans of the Birmingham gun trade, who in themselves—with close rivalry from Liège—led the world during most of the 19th Century.

Quiet Beginnings

William Tranter (1816-1890) was born at Oldbury, near Birmingham, and his education was largely paid for by his uncle William Tranter. If he served an apprenticeship (and his subsequent knowledge of the technology connected with firearms manufacture and design suggests that he did), it would have commenced about 1830 and terminated towards the end of that decade—of clear evidence there is none. But, we do know that by 1839 he was in a position, both financially and otherwise, to purchase the business of Robert Dugard, a gunmaker at 29½ Whittall Street, Birmingham. The few examples of Dugard's work which we have examined, indicate that he was not above the ordinary commercial gunmaker then operating in Birmingham, and it may well have been with him that Tranter served his apprenticeship.

Tranter remained at this address for only a few years, and there is little evidence of his activities during this period; however, in 1844 he abandoned independent operation and joined the old-established gunmaking firm of the Hollis brothers, and in 1846 this arrangement became a formal partnership under the name of Hollis Brothers & Company, at 11 Weaman Row.

Throughout their long history, the various firms operated by the Hollis family have concentrated upon the manufacture of a wide variety of longarms and handguns for military and export markets. At various periods they were contractors to the British Board of Ordnance and to the East India Company. Their products were not of the highest quality, but were always sturdily and cleanly made. They were responsible for a number of minor innovations in the design of military firearms in the 1850s, but at the time William Tranter was associated with them their activity was not marked by any startling advances. However, there can be little doubt that Tranter learned a great deal about the mass-production of firearms, factory techniques and wholesale marketing methods from the functioning of the highly successful Hollis establishment which was, and remained into the 20th Century, one of the largest of the Birmingham "gun factories."

In March 1849 the 3-year term of the partnership expired and Tranter must have felt himself able to cope with the problems of independent operation, since he established himself in premises at 13, St. Mary's Row, in the heart of the gunmaking district of Birmingham; his former co-partners continued at their Weaman Street address as Hollis & Sheath.

TRANTER

by **DOUGLAS A. NIE**
and **DE WITT BAILEY**

On October 13, 1849, Tranter obtained coverage under the Registered Designs Act, No. 2054, for a lever safety catch for pistol locks and a pepperbox mechanism on which this device was applied. We have not yet found any examples of this design.

Tranter's earliest production—and here we speak of the years 1839-44 and 1849-52 without differentiating—was extremely small and apparently very ordinary. One of two plain percussion shotguns have been reported signed W. Tranter, but without further address, and obviously intended for the cheap end of the market, whether in England or abroad. Smith & Swanson in their *Antique Pistol Book* published in 1948, show two examples of typical "transition revolvers," one of which is stamped **Tranter's Patent** while the other is described in the caption as being a Tranter revolver. Both are self-cocking bar-hammer revolvers with the nipples mounted at right angles to the axis of the bore. The unmarked example has a flash-guard as part of the casing or frame; neither is fitted with a loading rod. Given that they closely resemble the typical pepperbox of the time, it is not impossible that these revolvers were manufactured for Tranter in the Hollis factory.

All of the foregoing items were in America at the time they were described, and the writers are most anxious to locate the Smith & Swanson examples and any other Tranter-marked firearms from this early period.

The Model 1851 Adams Revolver

The first significant production of William Tranter was a group of percussion revolvers produced for Robert Adams of London under Adams' Patent No.

13,527 of 24 February, 1851. Although these revolvers were made by other Birmingham manufacturers such as Hollis & Sheath (Tranter's old firm) and Joseph Brazier of Wolverhampton, Tranter undoubtedly had the lion's share of their production. He produced frames and complete revolvers for Adams, and made other complete revolvers with his own double-trigger mechanism incorporated, about 12,000 in all.

Tranter's first production of revolvers *for* Robert Adams commenced late in 1851. These will bear externally an Adams serial number with or without an R-suffix. But the distinguishing feature appears *internally*, being the letters **WT** stamped on one side of the hammer slot in the frame, and a number on the other. When reporting information on any Tranter revolver of this type it is essential to include both numbers, as either on its own has little meaning, e.g.:

Internal Number	External Right-frame Number
WT 6507	10,155 R

The mechanism for which William Tranter is best remembered formed the subject of his first British Patent, No. 212 of 28 January, 1853. At this time Tranter was engaged in manufacturing revolvers and revolver frames for Robert Adams, so it is hardly surprising that he applied his double-trigger mechanism first to the Adams revolver. These differ from the standard Model 1851 Adams only in having the variant trigger mechanism (Figure 1).

The hand production methods used in the British gun trade create a great many minor variations—and

Fig. 1
Upper: Adams' Model 1851 self-cocking percussion revolver.

Lower: Tranter's Double-Trigger self-cocking percussion revolver, built on the Model 1851 Adams frame. The stud at the bottom front of frame is for a separate loading lever; note also the Y-shaped safety spring.

some not so minor—for which there are no explicit explanations, and literally dozens of plausible theories. This situation is nowhere more common than in the production of percussion revolvers, and regrettably Tranter does not escape the general confusion, even though his system appears to have been somewhat less complicated than most. There are, nevertheless, numerous departures from any generalization, and these will be dealt with in detail in our forthcoming book—it must suffice in this general survey to indicate that general descriptive statements must not be interpreted as being without exceptions!

Having expressed the above *caveat* it can now be said that these double-trigger Adams revolvers will bear three different numbers, each of which possesses an importance in relation to the others. The first of these will be a serial number in the 20,000 range with a Y-suffix, being the block group assigned by Adams to Tranter for revolver frames to be sold by Tranter for Tranter's benefit. This appears, as with other Adams serial numbers, on the right-hand side of the frame. The second number is the *internal* WT and number as described above. The third number is on the blade of the trigger, stamped within a small oval marking of **W. Tranter's Patent No.** This number represents the number of Tranter-patent triggers made, and does not, so far as we know at the time of writing, bear a direct correlation to the Adams serial number, although we may ultimately find that it does bear a relation to the internal WT number. It is therefore essential to report all three numbers when describing a Tranter double-trigger revolver made on the Adams Model 1851 frame. It should be noted that a few ordinary self-cocking Adams revolvers have been found with 20,000 Y numbers, and, in like vein, some Tranter double-trigger revolvers have been

noted with Adams R-suffix frame numbers. Furthermore, some Tranters without a number suffix-letter may not have a patent number within the markings on the trigger.

Tranter's Percussion Production

Although Tranter could not avoid paying royalties on the Adams solid frame (a feature quite as confining to revolver development as the Smith & Wesson bored-through cylinder in America) before 1865, he designed a larger and stronger frame of his own which went into production in 1856. The current system of "models" used to designate the various patterns and variations of Tranter's percussion revolvers is entirely inadequate and frequently incorrect. It does not account for several patterns which, although of extremely limited production, were nonetheless clearly part of the general production series, and it attributes a chronology to the appearance of various patterns which is not supported by a detailed study of either documentary evidence or a large sampling of the revolvers themselves.

It is quite clear from this latter examination that several Tranter percussion revolver models were marketed concurrently for several years at a time, and that various features (loading rods, sights, safety catches) could be had on more than one "model" at the request of the customer or at the whim of the people setting up the revolvers who might have been faced with a shortage of one part or another. Hand fabrication of rough-forged parts and hand-finishing produced many minor differences in the shape and location of various components which have too often been assigned a significance entirely inconsistent with their origins and the whole method of production. For these reasons, until an even larger sampling of existing revolvers can be made and carefully analyzed, we will refrain from making any but the most general references to the various patterns of Tranter percussion revolvers.

Within this deliberately large frame of reference it may be noted that there were at least four distinctive patterns of the Double-Trigger revolver *not* including the several types made on the Adams frame. Of these the earliest appeared in 1853, but the serious production of the D/T Tranter was not achieved until 1854. The final basic variety of D/T revolvers appeared early in 1858, and continued in production for several years thereafter, although eventually largely supplanted by the double-action design.

The multiplicity of items covered in each of Tranter's many firearms patents makes the study of those features which actually went into production much more difficult. An excellent example of this occurs with his Patent No. 1913 of 16 August, 1856, which includes no less than seven different revolver-lock mechanisms, amongst which are the two remaining types which formed the basis for the models which achieved large-scale production in the coming years: the Single-Trigger revolver, and the "Treble-Action" model.

There were at least two distinct variations of the Single-Trigger revolver which need clarifying within the overall picture, and the Treble-Action pattern is quite incorrectly known as the "Export Model." This is a misnomer, since a large number were offered for sale by a wide selection of British retailers, and very few have been located with foreign retailer's names engraved thereon. It is true that several of this design have been found with American retailer's names, whereas earlier models are extremely rare with such markings, but this would appear to be a question of marketing practice rather than any absence of the earlier models or prevalence of the Treble-Action abroad. Both types were advertised in America before the outbreak of the Civil War created an artificial demand for all types of firearms; and there were a number of Continental copies of both pirated and licensed origins made before 1861.

The system of manufacture, although involving the use of a considerable number of machines, was all based upon hand labor and hand-operated machines with a myriad of specially designed and hand-made jigs, formers and dies. For this reason various features could be combined if the customer were willing to pay. An example of this is a number of metallic cartridge revolvers of standard Tranter pattern for the 1870s made with the conventional 1853 double-trigger mechanism. On the other hand it is extremely important to remember, whenever attempting to assess the origins of some special feature, or the overall design of some unusual specimen, that *Tranter was a wholesale manufacturer only, and did not sell retail*. Therefore a large number of minor modifications which may be found on his products, although of excellent finish and workmanship, will have originated in gunsmith's workshops at the order of a purchaser from a retail outlet, and not in Tranter's workshops. We have amassed a good deal of documentary evidence concerned with the capacity and nature of Tranter's manufactories which indicates that although he was ahead of the majority of his contemporaries in the extent to which he utilized machinery, he still used it in what can only be considered as a "traditional" framework, and that the modern concept of factory mass-production was as alien to him in practice as it may have been familiar to him in theory. That he possessed the knowledge and the machinery to manufacture completely interchangeable parts we know to be a fact—as regards military gunlocks—but that he made use of this facility in any other area of his very considerable manufacturing complex is, at the moment, completely unsubstantiated.

The Years of Expansion

William Tranter became a member of the "Birmingham Small Arms Trade" association of gunmakers in 1854, not long after its establishment as an administrative organ to coordinate and in some degree control the activities of the leading Birmingham contractors for military gun work for the Board of Ordnance and its successor, the War Office. Just what Tranter's actual contributions to the production of Pattern 1853 Enfield parts were is not yet entirely clear. In March, 1854, he had testified that he had tendered for contracts but had not completed them as he did not like the arrangement. He did furnish components for the Pattern 1853, and he may have set up complete arms, but not many in either case. He did produce Pattern 1853 arms and components for the commercial trade, and numbers of these rifles have been found with **W. Tranter** stamped inside the locks and on the underside of barrels. All of these bear non-Government **TOWER** marks externally, with Birmingham commercial proofmarks, and lack the crucial letters **V.R.** beneath the Crown, even when the crown alone may be present.

Tranter was an active purchaser of land throughout his career, and it is clear that much of his income derived from rents and leases of his properties. In 1854 he had acquired premises with shops, sheds and steam machinery at 50 Loveday Street, which he retained at least until 1860. In 1864 he bought the land at Aston Cross upon which he began slowly to build a new factory in 1866. This plant obviously suffered the vicissitudes of the general if shortlived slump in the Birmingham gun trade in the mid-1860s, but was nearing completion in 1867. Henceforth this new factory formed the backbone of his operations, although he retained the St. Mary's Row

Fig. 2.
The fully developed Tranter Double-Trigger revolver, shown with an interchangeable "split-cylinder" patented by Tranter in 1865 for metallic centerfire cartridges. Inset: Tranter's Triple-Action percussion revolver: note the hammer spur.

property until 1875. He also acquired the shops and premises at 1, 2, and 3 Lower Loveday Street which were occupied by the several firms with which Francis Augustus Braendlin was associated; and there is strong evidence that Tranter was the manufacturing element behind these operations. By the late 1860s William Tranter possessed one of the most extensive and modern gunmaking operations in Birmingham, and there is no question but that, if external developments had favored the Birmingham trade generally, Tranter would have been one of the main gainers. The fact that Birmingham lost its preeminence in the coming years was due largely to the fact that other entrepreneurs did not have the foresight and ability to adapt which Tranter had displayed.

With his new factory and modern facilities Tranter should have been an obvious producer for the British government, but during those years the British government was turning increasingly towards a self-contained arms manufacturing system based upon the Royal Small Arms Factory at Enfield, to the exclusion of private industry as far as was possible. The Birmingham Small Arms Company (1861) and the London Small Arms Company (1866) were the only two private firms to whom the government had any large-scale recourse in times of need, and Tranter, although he attracted some government work, failed to secure the large contracts for conversion and re-equipping which might have made his name a household word.

Perhaps the most frustrating factor in studying Tranter's career is the growing conviction that he deliberately operated on a low-profile basis, and that aside from his own patented products which achieve greatest production and popularity during the earlier percussion years, the image of the faceless, anonymous gunmaker who made up the bulk of the Birmingham and Liège trades suited not only his activities, but his temperament, best. He worked first and foremost for the gun trade itself, making parts, and arms in the white, and doing various forms of roughwork which was completed and finished by other gun makers. What advertising of Tranter products that does appear in the contemporary press usually occurs under the names of retailers and mention of Tranter's own activities are extremely rare. There is none of the familiar "puff" so typical in Victorian advertising, merely short factual reports of some aspect of Tranter's operations which generally suggest that he is doing well. Between 1862 and 1884 he took out 12 patents relating to firearms, each with a variety of devices claimed, and there is now no question but that he was instrumental in developing the revolver which became, in 1880, the Mark I British service revolver.

Cartridge Handgun Production

Tranter was one of the first English gunmakers to introduce a line of rimfire metallic cartridge revolvers. His Patent No. 1862 of 27 July, 1863, covered, as usual, a variety of mechanisms, although the revolvers themselves exhibit very few important variations. The first of the series were pocket revolvers with a stud or sheath trigger, single action, and offered in 230 and 320 calibers with seven-chambered cylinders (Figure 4). The second arm in this early Tranter cartridge series was the Model 1863 Army revolver, a double action 442 rimfire whose design

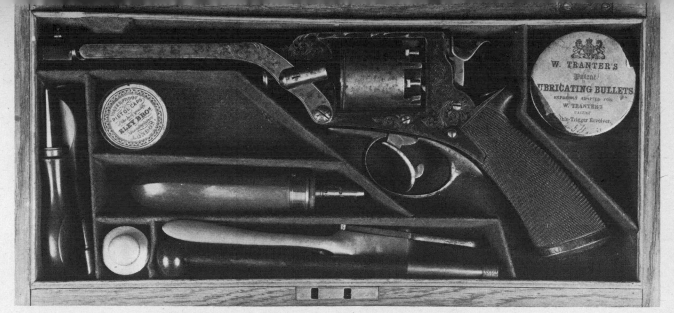

Fig. 3.
Tranter's Double Action percussion revolver, first marketed early in 1858. The case is not the standard Tranter design.

was widely copied in Birmingham and Liège for the remainder of the 1860s (Figure 5).

The second series is perhaps more familiar to collectors, and formed the basis of Tranter's production until the closure of the firm. These revolvers (Figure 6) are generally termed collectively as "Bulldogs" because of their short stubby design relative to their calibers, but as can be seen from the illustrations, long-barreled versions were available. There are a great many structural variations found in this series which cannot be dealt with here in the space allowed. There are four different patterns of cylinder, chiefly distinguished by the design of the cylinder-stops and whether or not the front edge of the cylinder is knurled. Five different designs of loading gate are found, as well as five patterns of extractor rods.

All of this series are double-action, and they were offered in 230, 297, 320 and 380 rimfire and in 320, 380, 450 and 500 centerfire, with five or six-chambered cylinders. A wide variety of finishes was available, from completely plain to fully engraved and nickel-plated. They were frequently supplied as cased outfits with compartments for cartridges and a cleaning rod. All of these revolvers are marked with a

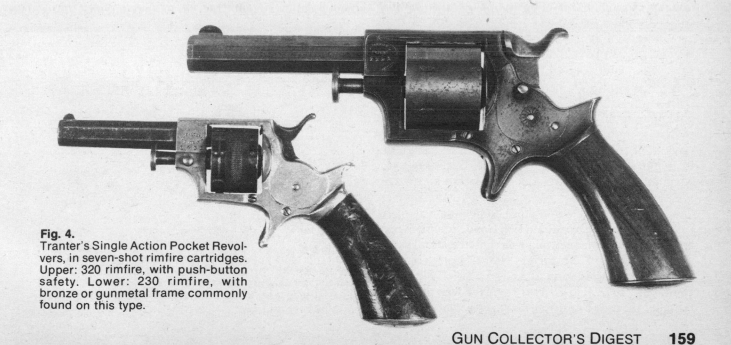

Fig. 4.
Tranter's Single Action Pocket Revolvers, in seven-shot rimfire cartridges. Upper: 320 rimfire, with push-button safety. Lower: 230 rimfire, with bronze or gunmetal frame commonly found on this type.

Fig. 5.
The Tranter Model 1863 Army Revolver in 442 rimfire. This is a double-action revolver, and is new production, not a conversion, or using converted parts.

small oval stamp on the left side at the breech of the barrel which reads **W. TRANTER'S PATENT** with the serial number below. Retailer's markings, engraved or etched, will appear on the top strap or on the top barrel flat of the octagonal barrels.

Contemporary with the above series of revolvers, Tranter produced a variety of tip-down barreled single-shot pistols and rook rifles (Figure 7) covered by his Patent No. 1889 of 20 July, 1865, and 2113 of 17 August, 1866. These were offered primarily in 320 and 380 rimfire, although calibers as large as 430 in both rim- and centerfire are known. As with the revolvers, there were two basic forms, one with a stud or sheath trigger, and the other with conventional trigger and guard bow; the latter usually combined with a side-lever opening mechanism.

Although not as popular in England as in America, the conversion of percussion revolvers to metallic cartridge was carried on to some extent, and Tranter's patent of 20 July, 1865, included a method for converting revolvers which is found on some of his products, usually cased with a spare percussion cylinder (Figure 2).

In 1877, when the British Army was trying to decide upon some improvement in the handguns issued to their mounted troops (percussion single-shot models of the 1850s were still standard issue), one idea put forward was for a double-barreled pistol. Tranter submitted such a design with a single trigger, but it fell flat.

In 1878 Tranter came close to getting one of his revolvers adopted by the British Government, even to the extent that an example was sealed as the Tranter revolver, Mark I. However, the projected contract was never fulfilled, and although a small number of the Model 1878 Rod-Ejector revolver was purchased for colonial use (Figure 8), its service was considered

as unofficial. Some of this pattern also found its way into the hands of the Royal Navy, but again the numbers and exact status of this issue remain uncertain.

Tranter's final effort in the military revolver field came in 1879-80 when the government was considering various types of break-open revolver designs incorporating automatic ejection of the spent cartridges. Tranter's design, covered in his Patent No. 3171 of 14 July, 1879, was the Model 1879 Self-Extracting Army Revolver (Figure 9). It failed to be adopted primarily because by this time the government had decided to manufacture its own design of revolver at Enfield. This was a conglomerate design owing origins to Warnant, Owen Jones, Tranter and several others, and did not prove successful or popular in service. By the time the government had learned its lesson and decided to return to the products of private enterprise, the Tranter firm was no longer in business. The Model 1879 was marketed commercially in both conventional blue and with a nickel-plated finish. It was chambered either for the 450 Boxer Government cartridge, or for the 450/455 which would accept either cartridge.

Fig. 6.
Tranter double action cartridge revolvers of the type usually known as "bulldogs" from their short, chunky appearance. There are many structural variations within this general type and a wide variety of calibers, and barrel lengths.

Fig. 7.
Tranter's Tip-Down Single Shot series, the mechanism being essentially the same for both pistol and rook rifle.

Despite the fact that Tranter had a large factory equipped with machinery for producing interchangeable-part firearms, there is no evidence that any of this was ever employed in the production of his cartridge revolvers and single-shot pistols and rook rifles, nor for his two Army revolvers of the late 1870s. All appear to have been fabricated by the traditional hand-work methods, and to the best of our experience none of the parts can be considered as interchangeable.

Military Production

This aspect of Tranter's career remains shrouded in uncertainty, despite the fact that we know he produced a wide variety of military pattern longarms and some pistols. How many of each type he produced, exactly when some of them were produced, and the full extent of the range of different types remains largely unknown. We hope through the reports of collectors to be able to expand our knowledge in what was unquestionably one of the most important areas of William Tranter's activities.

Tranter stated in March, 1854, that he had already dabbled in military contracts for the Board of Ordnance, but did not complete them. In the same year he became one of 19 gunmaking firms to join the Birmingham Small Arms Trade and thus receive a proportion of all military work put out to the gun trade by the British government. During the last half of the 1850s we have knowledge of a Pattern 1856, 10-Inch Rifled Pistol set up by Tranter. This is dated 1858 on the lock and bears the stamp **W. TRANTER** on the left side of the stock between the two lockscrews—the usual location for the markings of the contractor who set up (assembled) the complete arm. The inside of the lockplate is also stamped **W.T.** A number of **TOWER** marked Pattern 1853 Enfield Rifle Muskets have been noted with **Wm TRANTER** stamped on the underside of the barrel and **W. TRANTER** inside the lockplate (Figure 10). In addition, some Volunteer rifles and carbines based on the Enfield series have been found with similar markings.

Despite the fact that he advertised himself as a manufacturer of "Gunlocks to interchange by machinery" from 1863 to 1865, and that some of this work was displayed at the International Exhibition

Fig. 8.
Upper: the Model 1878 (or Rod Ejector) Revolver, caliber 450 centerfire, as bought by the British Government and almost adopted by them.
Lower: the 577 revolver, some of which are marked "W.T" beneath the grips and "Tranter's Patent" and "Braendlin's Improvement" on the cylinder plate.

Fig. 10.
A commercial Pattern 1853 Enfield rifle lock bearing the W. Tranter mark stamped round the mainspring boss.

Fig. 9.
Tranter Model 1879 Self-Extractor double action revolver: the last of Tranter's revolver designs.

of 1862, we have yet to locate locks of this description, and to strip them and see whether they fulfill the requirements of interchangeability.

We know that he was involved, during 1862, with the manufacture of Enfield pattern rifles (and perhaps short rifles and carbines as well) for the Spanish government, many of which bear the merchant's name Glukman stamped on the butt, but to what extent remains uncertain.

Although the evidence is purely inferential at this time, it seems highly probable that he participated in the manufacture of components or complete weapons of the Enfield patterns for export to North America during the War Between the States.

In 1864 the B.S.A.T. contracted to supply the Ottoman Government with 50,000 Enfield Short Rifles. Of this number 20,000 were to be supplied by the Birmingham Small Arms Company (of which Tranter had been a founding director, and of which he remained a shareholder after it became a public company), and the remainder were to be completed by the trade. The entire contract ran into difficulties and had to be partially fulfilled by the government making a loan from its stores, and whether Tranter, as a member of the Birmingham Small Arms Trade, ever actually supplied any rifles is not known. Both government and trade examples of this contract are known, but we have been unable to strip and examine them.

In 1866 a total of 1,082 rifles were exported to Brazil, and Tranter definitely manufactured a proportion of these: a Pattern 1860 Enfield Short Rifle marked **TOWER 1866** and bearing the cypher of Pedro II. of Brazil on the lockplate bears **W.T.** stamped in the stock to the rear of the trigger guard, on the bayonet bar, and is twice stamped **W. Tranter** inside the lockplate.

At this period the new factory at 31 Lichfield Road, Aston Cross, was nearing completion, and it was expected to have a capacity for producing 1,000 rifles per week. Even before it was completed, Tranter had 60 men hard at work on a contract for Model 1866 Chassepot Needle Rifles for the French government. The terms of this contract were apparently not attractive and only one other contractor is believed to have participated.

Chassepot rifles were manufactured for the French at this period through the agency of Cahen-Lyon who worked Chassepot's patents for him (he was debarred from so doing as being a member of the French civil service). Cahen-Lyon let contracts in Birmingham, Vienna, Liège, Italy and Spain. Rifles made under these contracts will have serial numbers with U or V prefixes (sometimes suffixes). We have not yet located a Chassepot rifle with any markings which might suggest Tranter origins, but any such markings would almost certainly be internal, on the underside of the receiver or barrel, or both. Tranter was certainly the first or second gunmaker in England to undertake manufacture of the Chassepot, and his late nephew Walter Tranter informed Doug Nie that his uncle "was very busy during the Franco-Prussian War making Chassepot and Snider rifles." This latter activity would have been quite separate from the original production in 1867 previously referred to, but no Tranter-marked Chassepots from the later group have yet come to light.

During 1869-1871 the Birmingham Small Arms Trade undertook the manufacture of Krnka and Berdan II rifles for the Russian government, and examples of both these types which have been stripped and examined show machine manufacture and an extremely high degree of finish. Although bearing no marks whatever aside from tiny **BSAT** and inspec-

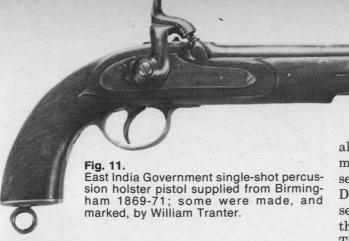

Fig. 11.
East India Government single-shot percussion holster pistol supplied from Birmingham 1869-71; some were made, and marked, by William Tranter.

tor's stamps, some of this work was almost undoubtedly done at Tranter's factory.

Another early product of the Tranter factory at Aston Cross was a group of 500 Braendlin-Albini rifles for the government of South Australia. These were ordered through their agent who placed the order with Henry Holland of 98 New Bond Street, who in turn passed the work to Francis Augustus Braendlin (the major patentee who had taken a lease on the premises at 1, 2, and 3 Lower Loveday Street from William Tranter). Several of these South Australian rifles have been minutely examined and in addition to the Braendlin trademark of crossed pennants stamped on breechblock and stock, the locks, barrels, hammers, sight-bases and bayonets are all stamped **W.T.** Some of these marks are surmounted by a small crown in imitation of government inspection marks, a common commercial practice at the time.

Tranter's connection with F. A. Braendlin was extensive and basic. Many Galand & Sommerville revolvers made by the firm of Braendlin Armoury Company Ltd., have been examined and some bear internal W.T. markings. Martini-Henry rifles of early design with Braendlin marks also bear the W.T. mark on various components. Tranter's own 577 revolver is known with the Braendlin crossed pennants and **Braendlin's Improvement.**

It seems likely that Tranter furnished the majority of the items retailed by the Braendlin firms, either in the white, as components, or as complete arms. He also probably supplied a part if not all of an order for Braendlin-Albini rifles to the Portuguese Navy.

During 1869-1871 Tranter also fulfilled a proportion of the East India government's order for 8-inch Smooth Bore Pistols (Figure 11). Several of these have been examined with Tranter's name stamped as the setter-up, and with the W.T. stamp under the barrel. Tranter was also supplying, during the earlier years of the 1860s, some of the smooth bore Enfield-pattern arms made for the use of native troops in India.

After 1870 the Snider rifle became one of the major weapons available for general commercial sale at a very low price, and large quantities were kept in stock by the English gun trade for sale to all comers. They also gradually replaced the earlier muzzle-loading arms for troops raised locally and serving throughout the far-flung British Empire. During the first half of the 1870s Tranter received several large batches of stocks for machining from the War Office—one in 1874 amounting to 5,000. These were returned into Government Store. Both Portugal and Japan purchased Snider rifles during these years, and Tranter, in his capacity as member of the Birmingham Small Arms Trade, may have supplied a proportion of them. But the rough stocking work mentioned above is the only direct contact between government and Tranter that we have thus far located during the 1870s, aside from the revolvers purchased in 1878.

Sporting Production and Abortive Projects, 1865-1885

During the last 20 years of its operation, the Tranter firm produced a number of miscellaneous rifles and shotguns, some of them based upon Tranter's patents, and developed a number of weapons for submission to various government committees, none of which got beyond the experimental stage.

Tranter's Patents No. 2113 of 17 August, 1866, and 2228 of 1 August, 1867, contain projects for breech-loading bolt action rifles. One such, a needle-rifle, is known to exist. Tranter also submitted bolt action rifles to the War Office trials of 1867-68, but they were rejected as being made unserviceable when sand was thrown over the breech. It seems likely that Tranter was also cooperating with Braendlin in the latter's efforts during these trials. Patent No. 2509 of 23 September, 1871, covered a Martini-type dropping-block action which Tranter manufactured and sold commercially as a rook rifle. Several examples have been noted in widely differing grades of finish, caliber and barrel length (Figure 12). A final attempt at getting a bolt action rifle into government hands was made by Tranter after his retirement from the gun business. His patent of 28 February, 1887, No. 3049 covered a bolt action magazine rifle, but it literally did not get past the front office of the War Office, even though Tranter seems to have delivered the sample rifle in person. He received a polite, but firm, rejection.

Tranter made two attempts to "break into" the shotgun market, one in 1866 and the other in 1882. Patent No. 2113 of 17 August, 1866, included a drop-down barrel action which was produced in very small quantities as a 12 gauge shotgun, but Tranter obvi-

Fig. 12.
Tranter's 1871 Patent Martini-type sporting rifle. Many have a lever safety on the right. Note the one-piece guard and lever, with the spring-catch at the tip of the lever.

Fig. 13.
Tranter's 1882 Patent double barreled shotgun. The box form housing in front of the trigger guard is characteristic. These "Carlton" model shotguns were all marketed by Watson Brothers, and do not, so far as we know, bear Tranter's name on them.

ously had more important fish to fry and did not push the project. At this date all breech-loading shotguns were very much the victim of poor and inconsistent ammunition, and until the introduction of the choke-bore could not compete seriously with the muzzle-loading shotgun, their noisy but numerically small advocates notwithstanding. The second attempt was more successful, but ill-timed. These guns, covered by Tranter's Patent No. 1881 of 19 April, 1882, were marketed entirely through the London firm of Watson Brothers under the trade name of the "Carlton" model (Figure 13). They were sold between 1883 and 1885 in 10 and 12 bores, with a variety of barrel lengths and styles, and in several grades of finish, the most costly of which was priced at £17.10.

Tranter's last ill-fated project concerned a machine gun upon which he apparently lavished a good deal of time and effort in developing. It flits in and out of government reports during the early 1880s, and the late Walter Tranter spoke of it as occupying much of his uncle's last years in business, and of its having a public trial in Birmingham (of which we have as yet found only partial evidence).

As early as the 1850s Tranter had submitted the drawings for a solid and a shrapnel-type of artillery shell to the Board of Ordnance, but it was not taken up. The range of Tranter's interests within the gun-making field may thus be seen to have been about as wide as they could possibly have been, covering virtually every aspect current during his period of operation, and some in advance of it.

By 1885 William Tranter was 69 years old. The prolonged economic depression and specific decline in the British gun trade had obviously taken their toll of his business, yet his other financial interests left him with no necessity to push on in the gun business, and he decided to retire. The Lichfield Road factory was leased to George Kynoch, who created the "Kynoch Gun Factory."

The Kynoch Gun Factory sold off a considerable number of Tranter revolvers, many of them marked rather crudely **KYNOCH GUN FACTORY** and without Tranter's Patent markings. Others have the usual Tranter marks. Many of them appear to have been assembled from parts left at the factory. The other chief productions of this firm during its short life were a series of revolvers covered by the patent of the firm's manager, Henry Schlund, and Chassepot and Gras rifles converted also on designs patented by Schlund. These, like the Schlund revolvers, are stamped on the receiver, **KYNOCH GUN FACTORY** and despite American-style cartridge markings, are chambered for the 11mm Model 1871 Mauser cartridge and are believed to have been sold to the Imperial Chinese Government.

The factory, still owned by William Tranter, passed into the hands of another even less successful firm, The Aston Arms Co. Ltd., in 1890. Once again, a small number of Tranter revolvers are known with this mark, but Aston Arms does not appear to have produced any new arms, and may have concerned itself solely with ammunition manufacture.

William Tranter died at his home in Birmingham in 1890. His effects and properties were auctioned off during the next few years, and show him to have been a man of considerable wealth for his time and station in life.

We hope that in presenting this general historical survey of William Tranter and his products, to receive the cooperation and assistant of collectors who own or know of Tranter-marked firearms, or firearms which may possibly be of Tranter manufacture. It is, obviously, in this latter category, covering such a vast number of possibilities, that we stand mainly in need of additional information. ●

Editor's Note: The authors of this article have been preparing for the future publication of a book on Tranter, and are still seeking information on some of that maker's more elusive arms. Copies of their detailed survey forms may be obtained from DBI Books for a stamped, self-addressed envelope.

The arsenal building at Springfield Armory, Springfield Massachusetts. Now the home of the world famous Springfield Armory Museum collection of firearms.
Springfield Armory Museum Photo.

COLLECTING THE SPRING-FIELD MODEL 1903 RIFLE

by LT. COL. BILL BROPHY U.S.A.R. (Ret.)

A FREQUENTLY overlooked military collecting field is that of the United States Model 1903 ('03) rifle. The number of variations, scarcity of some, and the historical significance of this family of arms, makes collecting them a challenging and rewarding experience.

Still within the means of the average working man, many fine examples can be found in acceptable collectors' condition and will, in time, increase in value.

The usual tendency is to want to charge into a new field without learning the variations or fully understanding condition and scarcity. Each would-be '03 collector is advised to read the fine references now available and to look forward to new works to be published soon. The more we learn of this fascinating '03 field, the more diligent our efforts will be to find worthwhile and valuable pieces.

There is no end to the many variations of the '03—therefore, the purpose of this work is to cover only some of the basic Springfield Armory *models* and some of the variations within the model. No attempt will be made to discuss Rock Island, Remington, or Smith-Corona '03s, line throwing guns, dummy '03s, sectionalized '03s, pressure and accuracy gauges, air service rifles, sniping rifles, '03s used by foreign countries, and other limited purpose '03s.

The new collector should be alert to the fact that a great number of the Model 1903 rifles were rebuilt and repaired by ordnance shops and depots. Also, parts and pieces in surplus channels have been as-sembled into hybrid rifles that have only "parts" value. There are many reliable, honest and helpful dealers and traders in the gun collecting game. Be sure of yours, to prevent expending time and money on an unwise acquisition that will not enhance your collection.

Along with the rifles themselves, '03 ancillary items such as tools, slings, cartridge belts, ammunition boxes, bandoleers, bayonets, special sights (including 'scopes), gauges and manuals also provide a worthwhile sideline. They not only enhance the collector's knowledge and heighten the educational value and interest in his display, but may well become an area which can, for a relatively small investment, become a collecting interest in its own right.

On the following pages are pictured and described some of the many Springfield variations I've encountered in my collecting of the '03. Among them are both the more common variations and a few that are almost unknown. Look them over carefully . . . that '03 you find at the next gun show or on the rack at the local gun show could just be a sleeper!

Rifle, U.S., Cal. 30, Model 1903, w/rod Bayonet

The rarest of the '03s for the collector to add to his collection is the original model that has an under-the-barrel rod bayonet.

There are two reasons for this rarity: first was the

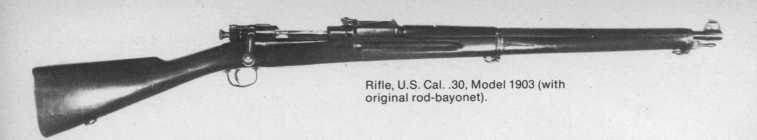

Rifle, U.S. Cal. .30, Model 1903 (with original rod-bayonet).

elimination of the original rod bayonet and the return to the knife bayonet system of its predecessor, the Krag rifle Model of 1898, and, second, the change from the Model of 1903 cartridge to the Model 1906 cartridge. Both of these changes required introduction of different manufacturing operations and the modification of existing rifles that were already in the field. As a result, very few of the early production rod-bayonet rifles have survived in their original form.

The rear sight of the first '03 is much like the Model 1902 rear sight of the Krag rifle, except that it is mounted on a band just forward of the receiver. The bolt body is polished bright and the bolt handle is the original heat-treat dark color. The extractors are a bright purplish-blue color. The lower band is a solid ring and not split like later variations. The hand guard is smooth on top, and extends almost out to the front sight. The stacking swivel, upper band, bayonet catch, and front sight are all different from any later models. All parts other than the bolt are highly polished and blued, except the receivers which are a grey case-hardened color. All '03s stocks are oil finished.

Two different types of safety are found. The early type is like the Mauser Model 1898 safety. The later variation has a spring detent that requires a special tool to remove it from the bolt sleeve.

The original '03 was caliber 30-03. This cartridge had a longer neck than that of the 1906 cartridge and will not chamber in a 30-06 rifle. However, the reverse is possible.

The first alteration of the rod bayonet '03 was the change from the rod bayonet to the Model 1905 bayonet. When this was done, a new rear sight (Model 1905) was also installed.

This change in the type of bayonet was the result of an order by President Teddy Roosevelt, dated January, 1904, to stop '03 rifle production. It appears that the president was not in favor of the limited-use rod bayonet and felt that the knife bayonet should be reconsidered. After a board of officers reviewed the subject of bayonets and tested a number of prototypes, the 1905 bayonet was wisely adopted and put into production.

The change to the 1905 bayonet and the 1905 rear sight required a new hand guard, new upper band with stacking swivel, new front sight, complete new rear sight (with 2,400-yard graduated leaf), and alteration of the long stock by shortening, reshaping, and plugging the front end.

Model 1903 rifles with only the modifications of 1905 are very rare, possibly as rare as the original rod-bayonet '03s.

The second alteration of the rod bayonet '03 (most frequently done at the same time and in conjunction with the first alteration) is the 1906 modification—to caliber 30-06. This change required removal and modification of the original barrel by shortening it, re-threading it, moving the 1905 rear sight forward (or installing the 1905 sight, if the sight change had not already been done) and re-cutting the chamber for the 30-06 cartridge.

Original Springfield Armory rod bayonet Model 1903 rifles were in the serial number range of 1 to just over 90,000. The barrels did not have a date stamped to the rear of the front sight.

Rod-bayonet rifles modified for the 1905 bayonet and sight are thus below serial number 90,000 and have shortened, reshaped and plugged stocks. The hand guards are new, and have the sight-protecting hump at the rear end.

Newly manufactured Model '03 rifles with the 1905 modifications were produced from April, 1905, to about November, 1906. These rifles do not have the altered rod bayonet stocks and the barrels are dated.

An easy way to establish if an '03 barrel is the early long length (prior to 30-06) is to place a narrow flexible steel tape in the bore and measure from the face of the closed bolt to the muzzle end of the barrel. It should be at least 24.2 inches, if unmodified.

Pristine examples of the three variations of the original rod bayonet '03 can hardly be expected to be found, but examples of each in any condition should be added to an '03 collection, even if only representative of the type.

Rifle, U.S., Cal. 30, Model 1903 (with modifications of 1905 and 1906)

The standard service Model 1903 rifle produced from 1906 to 1927, had numerous subtle changes made in the design, configuration, finish or heat treatment of parts. Some of the generally accepted variations and some identifying features are:

1. Stock without reinforcing bolt and with a straight edge to the top of the right side of the wood along the receiver ring: Produced from 1906 to about 1908. Caliber 30-06. Small windage knob on sight. Hand guard has smooth hump without clearance cut or spring clips. Straight bolt handle. Casehardened receiver. Smooth buttplate and trigger. Metal parts polished and blued. Serial range above 250,000.

2. Stock with one reinforcing bolt: From about 1908 to about 1910. Same as first variation except stock bolt added to the rear of the magazine to reinforce the stock and prevent splitting. Serial range above 250,000.

3. Stock with sloping right side at receiver ring: From 1910 to World War I production. Same as second variation except sight windage knob slightly larger, buttplate and trigger checkered. Some of those sold to NRA members have **NRA** and ordnance shell and flame markings stamped just to the rear of the front guard screw. Serial range above 380,000.

4. Stock with two reinforcing bolts (World War I production): In the interest of economy and speed of production during the war, some parts of the old configuration were manufactured. For example: the buttplate and trigger were manufactured without serrations. Also, some old parts that were on hand in ordnance inventory were used, even if they did not conform to the latest changes.

All '03s manufactured until very late in World War I were blued. The Parkerizing plant at the Armory was not installed until the war was just about over. In fact, it appears that few of the Parkerized '03s got overseas before the war ended in November 1918.

Both thick and thin triggers were used. The thin ones are all smooth. Both smooth and serrated thick profile triggers were used. Likewise, smooth and checkered buttplates were used until the supply of checkered ones was exhausted. During this period the bolt handle shape was changed. Originally straight, the second type has the knob bent to the rear. Most World War I-produced rifles have since been repaired or rebuilt and few have survived in excellent, unmodified condition. This variation is

difficult to find today. Serial range above 630,000.

5. Parkerized, having straight stock and finger grooves: Manufactured from the end of 1918 until manufacture of complete '03 rifles ended in 1927. The workmanship and finish of parts was restored to pre-war quality. The handguard had a new shape to the swell. Instead of being grooved and concave, it was grooved and slightly convex up to the lower band. All metal parts were Parkerized. Serial range over 1,200,000.

After 1927 only special target, sporting or National Match rifles were manufactured. The Springfield Armory '03 was to be replaced by a semi-automatic rifle—the M1.

6. Receiver marked Mark I: Over 100,000 of the '03s manufactured at Springfield Armory were designed for use with the "Automatic Bolt Model 1918" (Pederson Device). Receivers of these special-purpose rifles are marked **MARK I.** There is an ejection port cut into the left side of the receiver. A special trigger, sear, cut-off, cut-off spindle and shaped stock are original to the Mark I rifle. The special trigger and sear were necessary to trip the sear of the device; the special cut-off and spindle locked the device into the receiver, and the stock was relieved along the left edge below the ejection point.

Mark I rifles were produced in 1919 and 1920. None saw actual combat in War I, but most were issued during War II and eventually were processed through rebuild. Many were not originally Parkerized. Original excellent condition Mark I rifles are scarce. Most have had the original parts removed and during field and ordnance repairs were refinished. A must for every '03 collector. Serial range above 1,000,000.

7. Pistol grip stock: In 1929, upon adoption of the type "C" pistol grip stock, the designation, when the new pistol grip stock was installed, was changed to M1903A1.

An original Model 1903A1 rifle is exceptionally difficult to identify. Identical to the regular straight stocked '03, there are no other identifying features to pin down when and why the pistol grip stock was installed. Fortunately, some individual sales records exist that do identify that at the time the rifle was sold, it had the new pistol grip stock and was, in fact,

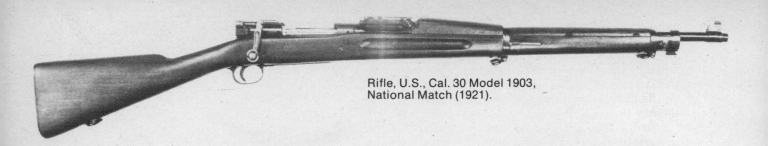

Rifle, U.S., Cal. 30 Model 1903,
National Match (1921).

an '03A1. Additional reasons few M1903A1 rifles exist are that most "C" stocks manufactured at the Armory were used in assembly of the Model 1929 National Match rifles and because straight grip stocks were to remain in service until the supply of them was exhausted. Very few "C" stocks were ever shipped to the field to be used for repairs, and only limited numbers of them reached the rebuild program at the Armory. The supply of excess war production straight stocks was more than adequate to take care of the slowed-down rebuild program.

National Match Rifles

The first Model 1903 National match rifle was the Model of 1921. To insure accuracy in its description, and to show the care and finesse exercised by Springfield Armory in producing this arm, a September, 1921 Armory description of the work done is quoted here:

Rifle, U.S. Cal. .30, Model 1903, National Match (1921):
The 1921 National match Rifle is the United States Rifle, Model 1903, especially manufactured from steel billet to completed rifle according to very close dimensions that have been found by careful test and experience to give the best results, both for accuracy and ease of manipulation. The barrels are machined from special heat-treated steel known as Springfield Armory Class "A", and have stood tests at chamber pressure of 125,000 pounds per square inch. Barrels of this stock have been frequently fired 10,000 rounds before losing their accuracy. The barrel is rifled with double scrape cutters to insure a smooth uniform groove and to avoid pockets and ratchets. The rifling is uniform, right hand, one turn in ten inches. The minimum diameter of bore is .3000 inch, maximum .3005 inch. Minimum diameter of groove is .3080 inch, maximum .3085 inch. The variation in diameter of bore and groove in each individual rifle must not exceed one ten-thousandth of an inch.

The chamber and bullet seat entrance are as near minimum as possible to insure the bullet starting true in the bore. Care has been exercised in the manufacture of barrels to reduce the amount of straightening to a minimum. The receiver is machined from special double heat treated Class "C" steel, and the bolt runways and cam surfaces polished to insure a smooth working bolt. Special care has been taken in assembly of barrel and receiver to see that the well hole of the receiver is in line with the bore.

The bolt is specially double heat-treated of Class "C" steel, is polished and the cam surfaces burnished by hand, with head space held to a minimum dimensions. The firing pin is minimum to prevent punctures and pulling of primers with any type of ammunition. The main spring is carefully gauged and tested to pull from 16½ to 19 pounds after compression for 36 hours. The stocks are made from selected walnut and machined with special care so that the barrel and receiver will bed properly. The upper and lower bands are loose enough to be put on by hand so as to prevent undue strain and allow the proper vibration of the barrel. The stock after machining is soaked four times in linseed oil and dried from two to four hours. The rear sight is assembled with great care to eliminate lost motion, looseness and back lash. All rifles are fitted with drift slides having .06" aperture. One size smaller and one size larger are available for each rifle. The front sight is specially machined on top so as to be square and true with the sides. The trigger has a grooved finger-piece to prevent slipping. The sear nose is slightly shortened and carefully stoned by experts to insure release. The sear notch is carefully ground.

The trigger pull is adjusted from 3½ to 4½ pounds and must be smooth without creep. The butt plate is checked for the purpose of insuring a firm seat at the shoulder when firing.

Inspection and Test: The assembled rifle is given a rigid inspection by the most expert inspectors of the Armory. One proof charge developing 75,000 pounds pressure per square inch is fired and in addition 25 rounds of service ammunition are fired to settle the action in the stock and test the action for smoothness of operation.

The bolt lift is controlled by the careful gauging of parts and stoning cam surfaces, so that the pull-up of the bolt does not exceed 15 pounds.

The rifle is targeted for accuracy by expert riflemen at 200 yards, muzzle and elbow rests are used. Sights are first adjusted by firing at an inverted T (1) target measuring 4 inches horizontally and vertically. The front sight must not be offset more than .015". Aim is taken at the bottom of the inverted T (1) with just a line of white. With sights properly adjusted to zero, 5 rounds are fired. If all five shots are in the vertical strip and do not measure more than 8 inches vertically the rifle is accepted, provided it does not show a tendency to walk. The rifles are inspected again after firing, the bore cleaned in the usual way and metal parts coated with cosmic. The rifles are then packed in arm chests. With each rifle is the target made with the rifle and a card giving the interior dimensions of bore and groove for each inch of the barrel.

Some pre-1929 National Match '03s will be encountered with either headless or headed cocking pieces. Both left and right-hand safeties will also be found with either type cocking knob. These features, and other parts, could be special ordered, therefore are valid differences found extant today and do not detract from the value of the rifle.

All National Match Rifles were star-gauged, and the star mark should be present at the 6 o'clock position on the crown of the muzzle.

Unfortunately for the collector, during one short period of time the NM '03s that were used at the National Matches were returned to the Armory and were refurbished. The refurbishment consisted of replacing NM parts with service parts. In 1929 and 1930 these rifles were sold through the DCM for $35.48.

Also, from 1924 through 1928, the Model 1921 National Match rifle could be purchased with the full length Model 1922 pistol grip stock—like Sporter-type and Style T rifle stocks—except with full military wood, for $40-45.

This type stock could also be purchased as a separate stock and then be fitted by the purchaser to any '03. This also adds to the confusion of the National Match Rifle collector and creates another rare variation to find.

Thousands of the early, straight stock, National Match rifles were manufactured between 1921 and 1928. To obtain full value, the collector should only invest in one that is correct, unmodified and in excellent condition.

Rifle, U.S., Cal. .30, Model 1903A1, National Match (1929):

The 1929 National Match rifle (pistol grip stock) had the same care in construction and selection of parts as the earlier straight stock National Match model of 1921. The major difference was in the stock. The new '03A1 model had an excellently shaped pistol grip and the forearm was without finger grooves. It was designated the "C" stock.

The headless cocking piece was discontinued in this model. (To insure deflection, away from the eye, of any gases from a ruptured cartridge case or

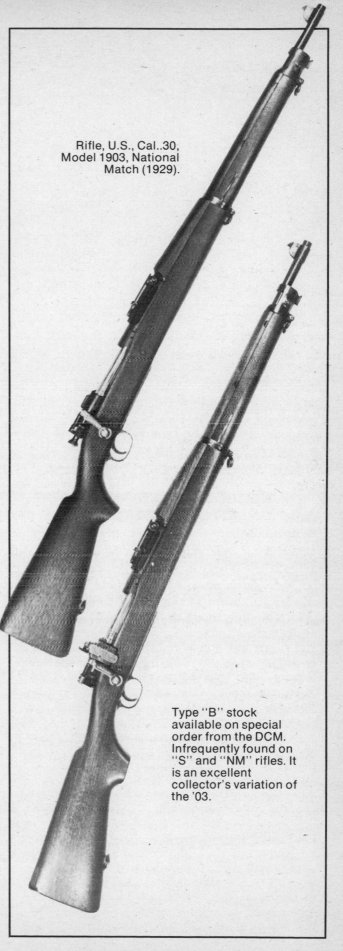

Rifle, U.S., Cal..30, Model 1903, National Match (1929).

Type "B" stock available on special order from the DCM. Infrequently found on "S" and "NM" rifles. It is an excellent collector's variation of the '03.

Rifle, U.S., Cal. 30, Model 1922,
w/heavy match barrel.

punctured primer, the National Match rules required that a knob-type cocking piece be used.)

A total of over 24,000 National Match rifles were assembled at Springfield Armory. Of this number, over 10,000 were the Model 1903A1 National Match rifle. Perfect pieces can still be located in military rifle collecting channels. Only an unmodified and good condition one should be considered worthy of collecting.

Note: The collector should recognize that NM stocks ('03A1), polished bolts, and NM barrels could be purchased through the DCM. Quite a few "home-brewed" NM rifles were put together by shooters who were not able to afford the rather expensive Armory models. Interesting, and frequently the source for "correct" parts, the buyer should beware of any "sales pitch" that may be offered as authoritative. Let the rifle speak for itself!

Model 1922 Target Rifle
(Caliber 30-06)

When describing some of the '03 variations and models, it is accurate and fair to call them rare. But, after rare what comes next? It could easily be the Model 1922 caliber 30 heavy barrel target rifle.

Available only in 1922, the 1922 DCM sales list described it as follows:

Rifle, U.S., cal. .30, Model 1922 star-gauged with heavy match grade 24-inch barrel, Lyman No. 48 receiver sight, pistol grip stock and blocks for A5 telescope, including postage $71.34.

The stock has a pistol grip and finger grooves and is like the Model 1922 cal. 22 stock except two stock bolts have been added. The buttplate is also like the one used with the cal. 22 stock and is commonly referred to as the Model 1922 or NRA-type buttplate.

The receiver and parts of this rifle are of National Match quality. The receiver, drilled and tapped for the Lyman No. 48 sight, is not drilled and tapped on top of the front ring for a telescope block. Both telescope blocks are mounted on top of the barrel a distance of 7.2 inches between centers.

The 24-inch heavy barrel is unique to this model and is unusual by having the front sight fixed dovetail integral with the barrel. The front sight is the same as for the issue '03.

The barrel band is like the Style T band and is fabricated by alteration of the lower band of the Model 1917 rifle.

Designed with long range (800- to 1,000-yard), and International (300-meter) rifle competition in mind, the Model 1922 was short-lived because of the shooters' desire for the advantages offered by a longer sight radius, more weight forward and better accuracy of the longer 28-and 30-inch barrels of the International and Style T rifles.

So seldom encountered that only a few of the most serious collectors own an unaltered example of this rifle, it is speculated—in the absence of accurate production records—that fewer than 80 of these rifles were manufactured. It is a true "gem" among the '03s.

Sporting Type Rifle
(NRA Sporter)

Most frequently called the NRA Sporter, the official designation of the sporter is: "Rifle, U.S. cal. .30, Model 1903, *sporting type,* star-gauged, fitted with Lyman No. 48 receiver sight."

To fill the demand for a quality bolt action sporting rifle, this desirable collector's '03 was first announced in 1924. The 1925 DCM sales list priced it at $49.50.

Rifle, U.S., Cal. .30, Model 1903,
sporting type (NRA Sporter) with
Winchester A5 telescope.

It was available only by purchase. The last year of availability was 1932 when it was priced at $42.50.

The action of this rifle is hand fitted. The bolt and extractor are polished, to provide smooth operation, and the serial number is etched on the bolt body. The barrels are star-gauged. The muzzle has a mark stamped on the crown to indicate successful passage of the star-gauging test. Issue-type front sight and Lyman No. 48 receiver sights were standard.

The sporter stock is the Model 1922 caliber 22 rifle stock without finger grooves and with two stock reinforcing bolts added. The barrel band is specially manufactured to fit the shape of the barrel and stock.

The barrels are nicely polished and do not have the rough turning marks typical of the service barrel when the Model 1905 rear sight band is removed. The contour and shape of the sporting-type barrel is very much like the caliber 22 barrel. It is marked to the rear of the front sight with **S.A.,** the Ordnance bomb and flame and the manufacturing date of the barrel. During a short period of time the Sporter could be special-ordered drilled and tapped for telescope blocks.

None of these rifles were Parkerized. All had a quality blued finish that was equal to any commercial finish on the market. The wood was finished by hand and treated with linseed oil.

Sporting-type barrels and the Model 1922 sporter-type stock, as well as polished bolts and all other National Match parts, were available for purchase from the Ordnance Department through the Director of Civilian Marksmanship.

Unfortunately for the uninformed collector of the '03, the availability through the DCM of stocks, barrels and parts and pieces of many of the '03 models resulted in hybrid rifles of mismatched parts that were intended by the original owner to be a working rifle and quite adequate for his original purpose. However, close inspection will usually reveal a flaw in the quality of finish or matching of parts, or signs of amateur gunsmithing, and establish that the rifle is not "right."

During 1926 the Armory manufactured 589 of the Sporter-type rifles with a slightly different shape to the pistol grip, which was like the M1922 M1 caliber 22 issue rifle stock. The new stock was not liked and quickly dropped in favor of the original Model 1922 sporter stock.

A total of approximately 5,538 of the NRA Sporting type '03s were manufactured. It was discontinued, only because the Ordnance Department was being criticized for competing with commercial enterprises in the sporting rifle industry. Yet, until that industry introduced similar rifles, the Springfield Armory Sporter was the finest American-made bolt-action rifle available to the sportsman.

After the sporting-type rifle was discontinued from

American Ordnance Assn. trophy awarded to the winner of the President's Rifle Match held during the National Matches at Camp Perry, Ohio.

Secretary of Navy's Trophy Rifle awarded to the top Naval Academy marksman.

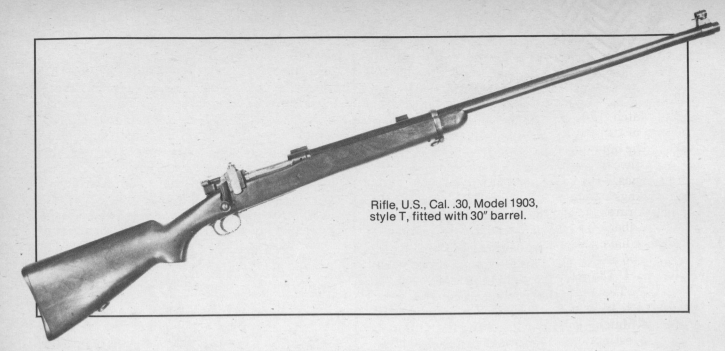

Rifle, U.S., Cal. .30, Model 1903,
style T, fitted with 30″ barrel.

production, some few were specially assembled to be used as trophy rifles.

Illustrated here are both the Secretary of Navy's Trophy Rifle and the American Ordnance Association President's Match Winner Rifle. It should be noted that both have stocks selected for fancy grain and that they are crudely checkered. (This must have been done by a hobbyist working at the Armory). Appropriately engraved silver plates are nicely fit into the stocks.

The rarest of rare, as fewer than five of each are known to have been awarded.

Style "T"

The official Ordnance description of this very special target rifle was as follows:

U.S. Rifle, cal. .30, Model 1903, Style T, 26, 28 or 30-inch heavy service barrel, fitted with Model 1922 pistol grip stock, Winchester hooded front sight, Lyman No. 48 rear sight, Springfield action, weight about 14 pounds.

The Style T was introduced in 1929 by the Director of Civilian Marksmanship for sale to National Rifle Association clubs, teams, and individuals, and for Ordnance issue to Service teams competing at the National matches. It sold for $85. In 1933 it was dropped from the DCM sales list.

The upper band for this rifle was fabricated by modification of a Model 1917 Enfield lower band. The special front sight band was manufactured by the Armory by modifying a Browning Automatic Rifle front sight band. The Model 1922 stock was the same as the similar stock for the caliber 22 rifle, except it has two stock reinforcing bolts, the barrel channel is enlarged to accept the large-diameter target barrel, and it does not have finger grooves.

The receiver, bolt, and trigger guard are the same as used in the National Match Rifle.

The bolt is polished and the receiver and barrel are drilled and tapped for telescope blocks 7.2 inches apart, center-to-center. The receiver is drilled and tapped for the Lyman 48 receiver sight.

Illustrated here is a typical Style T, 30-inch barrel rifle. It has a headless cocking piece and a left-hand safety. Perfectly correct examples of this rifle also exist that have the conventional '03 cocking piece and a left- or right-hand safety. These features, or the various parts, could be ordered through the DCM.

This rifle was not allowed to be used in service rifle competitions. It was, however, allowed and preferred for use in the 1,000-yard events held during the National Championships. The coveted Wimbledon Cup 1,000-yard individual "any rifle match" and the Herrick Trophy team match were two such events in which it excelled.

On occasion, competitive shooters used the Style T rifle as the foundation for an International-type rifle by adding set triggers, hook buttplate and a palm rest. They are still valuable collector's pieces, but should be examined carefully to avoid the purchase of a put-together rifle "professed" to be a Style T. It should also be recognized that Style T barrels, stocks and receivers could be purchased individually through the DCM. Examples of standard service receivers with Style T barrels and home-made target stocks have been observed. Although most are well-done, they are not original armory-produced Style T rifles. The true style T rifle has an armory-manufactured barrel. Except for a few special International rifles, Winchester and Remington heavy target weight barrels were not used by Springfield Armory. Barrels of neither of these makers were used in the manufacture of the Style T.

All Style T barrels were star-gauged to insure the bore dimensions were within the standards established for target work. A star-gauge number is stamped on the bottom of the barrel. None have the star-gauge mark on the muzzle, as is found on National Match rifles.

Many of these rifles have had minor alterations, such as the butt stock shortened, shaping of the grip, or even checkering to the owner's desire. Unless a Style T has been really butchered, however, such minor things should not detract from the desirability of such a rare rifle.

The caliber of all Style T rifles was 30-06. However some have been rechambered by gunsmiths and at least two are known to have been rechambered to 300 H & H. The rifling is four groove, 1 turn in 10 inches. All T's were targeted at 200 meters and would average 2¾ inches or less, for 10-shot groups with National Match quality ammunition.

A rare (estimated that fewer than 150 were manufactured) and desirable '03 Springfield, the Style T is a "must" for the serious '03 collector.

International Rifles

As a result of post-World War I changes in equipment rules for Olympic, World and Pan-American competitions that allowed "any rifle with metallic sight" to be used—instead of the previous requirement that the rifle be the service rifle of the host country, or the service rifle of the competing country—the Ordnance Department, working with the DCM and recognized leading United States shooters, developed in the early 20s rifles suited to the accuracy and versatility demands of World-level rifle competition.

Most Olympic, World and Pan-American rifle matches were fired at 300 meters in the prone, kneeling and standing positions. Very special stocks, sights, buttplates, palm rests, triggers and ammunition were required to obtain results appropriate to the ability of the leading American shooters and also to be competitive among the world's best shooters.

It is impossible to here describe and illustrate all the various attempts by our Ordnance Department to produce various pieces of equipment acceptable to the shooters and that would perform better than that of any other country. Therefore, only the two basic and most widely-used models will be discussed.

International Rifle Model 1923: In 1923 about 50 of the first model of an International rifle were assembled at Springfield Armory. They had a special stock, adjustable fiber and steel hook buttplate, adjustable cork-ball palm rest, adjustable front sling swivel, heavy 26- to 30-inch barrel, Lyman No. 48 rear sight, special hooded aperture front sight and German-type set-trigger.

This is the only '03 International that had a barrel band. The band did not encircle the stock, but went around the barrel and the stock was then secured to it by means of a screw through the front swivel plate.

The front end of the stock has a blended shape to the barrel channel and is coarsely checkered at the pistol grip.

It was not uncommon for shooters to tailor their equipment to their own desires. Therefore, most International '03s have had one or more alterations.

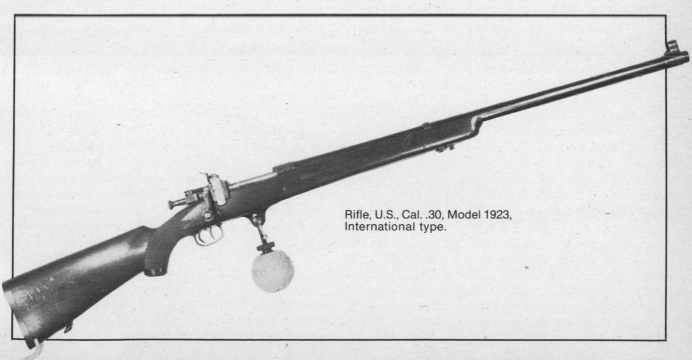

Rifle, U.S., Cal. .30, Model 1923,
International type.

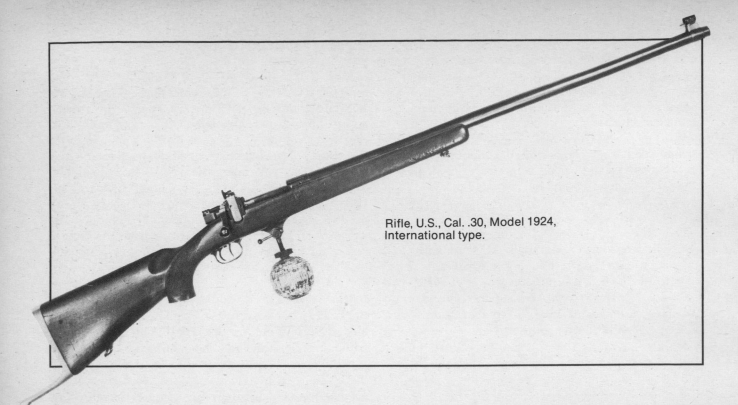

Rifle, U.S., Cal. .30, Model 1924,
International type.

The most frequent encountered are: butt stocks shortened, cork balls of the palm rest replaced or altered, front sights changed, rear sights peened to remove play, and grips and forends reshaped to individual desires. Some have seen considerable use and abuse. Most Internationals are worth restoration and preservation. Few have survived in any condition.

International Rifle Model 1924: The parts of the Model 1924 rifle were common to the previous rifle only in the receiver, rear sight, palm rest, and adjustable front sling swivel. The hook buttplate is of one-piece design and of aluminum. The set-trigger is of the Woody type and the 30-inch barrel is the same as used in the Style T rifle. The front sight was the Winchester aperture type, having interchangeable inserts.

Fewer than 60 of these very special Model 1924 rifles were assembled at Springfield. All are highly prized by the '03 and match rifle collector.

It should be noted that an even rarer variation of the Model 1924 International rifle is the one in caliber 22. Except for the Model 1922 receiver and the 22 bore, it is a dead ringer for the caliber 30 rifle. Only 12 of this model were fabricated at Springfield. ●

Rifle, U.S., Cal. .22, Model 1924,
International type.

Imperial Japan's Military Revolvers

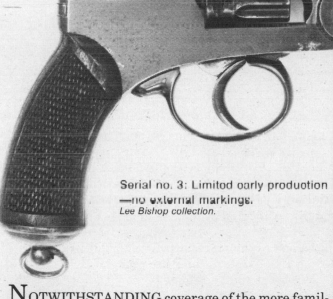

Serial no. 3: Limited early production —no external markings.
Lee Bishop collection.

THE SLIGHTED TYPE 26

Harry Derby

NOTWITHSTANDING coverage of the more familiar Type 14 over the years, very little published information relative to Japanese military handguns in general has been made available to collectors. Japan's first adopted native design—the Type 26 revolver—is no exception.

For some time now there has been a growing need to consolidate the many bits and pieces of knowledge accumulated by individual collectors, historians and

*Editor's Note: The information in this article and in Harry Derby's article on the Hino-Komoro pistol came from his forthcoming book, *The Hand Cannons of Imperial Japan*, which is scheduled for publication by the author.

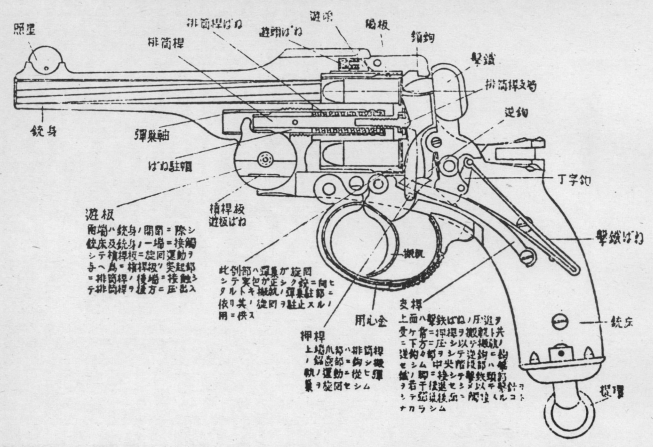

照星　排筒桿ばね　避頭ばね　避頭　閉板　鎖鈎

撃鐵　排筒桿支筍　逆鈎

銃身　彈巣軸　ばね駐帽

避板　楨桿板　楨桿板ばね

丁字鈎

撃鐵ばね

比例部ハ彈巣ガ旋回シテ實包ガ正シク銃ニ向ヒタルトキ撥瓜ハ彈巣駐部ニ依リ其ノ旋回ヲ駐止スルノ用ニ供ス

避板　兩端ハ銃身ノ開閉ニ際シ銃床及銃身ノ一端ニ接觸シテ楨桿板ハ旋回運動ヲ與ヘ爲ニ楨桿板ノ突起部ニ排筒桿ノ後端ニ接觸シテ排筒桿ヲ後方ニ壓出ス

撥瓜

用心金

支桿　上面ハ撃鐵ばねノ壓迫ヲ受ケ筒ニ楨根ヲ搬轉ト共ニ下方ニ壓シ以テ撥瓜ノ逆鈎ノ部ヲシテ逆鈎ニ掛セシム中央階段部ハ撃鐵ノ脚ニ接シテ撃鐵顯部ヲ若干後退セシメ以テ撃針シテ底板接瓜ニ觸接ルコトナカラシム

銃床

押桿　上端爪部ハ排筒桿ノ鋸齒部ニ鈎シ撥瓜ノ運動ニ從ヒ彈巣ヲ旋回セシム

搬瓜

Diagram drawing from original manual. *Courtesy Kokusai Publishing, Inc., Tokyo, Japan.*

authors concerning these and the many other unique "hand cannons" of Japan. When placed in perspective and compared to the vast quantities of material on pistols of other major powers, it becomes increasingly obvious just how little technical data and meaningful historical information has been previously assembled and presented to satisfy the rapidly increasing collector appetite. Reflecting on Japan's feudal past and the consequence of her modern conflicts, this, in itself, is not especially surprising. The passage of time, however, continues to erode the opportunity to capture much of this information. With these considerations in mind, a sense of urgency to begin the task follows—the Type 26 revolver comprises a small but important part of the story.

During the late 1870s, the Japanese Imperial Army and Navy adopted the 44 caliber Russian Model Smith & Wesson revolver. It remained as Japan's first and only officially adopted military sidearm until about 1887, when the decision to produce a domestically developed replacement revolver was made. The next year, the Tokyo Artillery Arsenal began conducting research and development activities. Six years later, in 1894, the final acceptable design was adopted.

The year 1893 previously has been accepted as the official adoption date, because the right side of the frame on most examples is stamped with Japanese characters *(kanji)* reading *Nijuoku, Nenshiki,* which translates "26 Year Type." (Since the beginning of the Meiji Era in 1868, the Japanese have used numerals, indicating the year of adoption, to identify military ordnance. During the reigns of Emperor Meiji [1868-1912] and Emperor Taisho [1912-1926], the year of the particular emperor's reign was assigned to the new weapon—e.g., 26th year of the Meiji Era, Western calendar year, 1893.)

While the final design was completed in 1893, the actual year of adoption was 1894 (Meiji 27). Notwithstanding, the revolver was designated the Type 26, and became Japan's first officially developed and adopted military pistol.

In view of the development period, it is not surprising to find that its top-break system is very similar to the old Smith & Wesson revolvers, while the lockwork and sideplate designs closely resemble the Austrian Rast & Gasser 9mm models introduced in the 1880s. Similarities to the old British MkI Webley in the Type 26's extraction and trigger action, are also present.

The Type 26 is a double-action-only revolver that requires a long trigger pull. This is only one of several

Example of standard production Type 26. Note issue lanyard.

Type 26 stripped for cleaning or repair.

shortcomings. A far more serious fault involves the design of the cylinder stop: It engages the cylinder notches only while the hammer is being cocked and in the rearward position. Once the trigger is released after firing, the cylinder is free to revolve, which could well result in an empty or already fired chamber rotating into position for the next shot, a potentially fatal event for the user in combat.

The 9mm, a thin-rimmed, centerfire cartridge with unjacketed hard-lead bullet, is strictly Japanese, and today, far rarer than the pistols themselves. Ballistically it also leaves a lot to be desired. Although the standard military cartridge is most often reported to have a muzzle velocity of 650 to 750 fps, recent tests conducted in Japan by Hiromasa Ikeda, of the Fukuoka Prefectural Police Crime Laboratory, using the 9.8-gram bullet, showed muzzle velocities of only 150 meters per second (492 fps).

Unbreeching the revolver for loading and unloading is accomplished by simply lifting the latch on top of the barrel and pivoting the barrel downward. This movement automatically activates the single extractor for all six chambers. Interestingly, the chambers have been recessed at the rear of the cylinder so that the cartridge heads are flush. This "improvement" was first incorporated into the 1871 Colt "House Pis-

Type 26 Revolver

Designation: Type 26 (1893).
Caliber: 9mm.
Action: Double only.
Overall Length: 231mm (0.00 in.).
Height: 130mm (5.12 in.)—excluding lanyard ring.
Weight: 2 pounds, 0 ounces.
Barrel Length: 121mm (4.76 in.).
Rifling: 4 lands, 4 grooves—right-hand direction of twist.
Cylinder Capacity: 6 cartridges.
Distribution: Imperial Army.
Manufacturer: Tokyo Artillery Arsenal (Tokyo Arsenal), Koishigawa, Tokyo.
Production Period: 1893-1935.
Quantity Produced: 59,200.
General Serial Range: 1-59200.
Known Serial Range: 1-59183.
Markings: Arsenal, type and serial.
Finish: Early, bright charcoal blue with heat treated hammer and trigger—late, all rust blue.
Grip Panels: Wood—checked and grooved beech (*Fagus* sp.).
Serialization: All major parts—assigned serial and assembly number.

Rare limited modified production, exhibiting revised features.

tol," but was discontinued a few years later—only to be reintroduced in America during the late 1940s with a great deal of fanfare. Apparently the Japanese appreciated this feature, which must have been present on one or more sample pistols reviewed as part of the Tokyo Artillery Arsenal's development program for the Type 26.

Perhaps the pistol's most outstanding feature is the ease with which the mechanism can be exposed for minor repair and cleaning without using tools. This is done by pulling the rear of the trigger guard downward (the checked area on the guard is provided to assist in this action), releasing it from an indentation in the frame and then pivoting it forward. In this position, the left sideplate can be released from the frame, permitting it to be swung outward and rearward, exposing the lockwork. Unfortunately, many T-26 examples have been mutilated in the finger recess area of the sideplate and frame because screwdrivers or other tools have been used to force open the sideplate before its release through the pivoting movement of the trigger guard. Once exposed, the left grip panel may be lifted out of its seat in the grip frame. The cylinder is removed from the barrel assembly by lifting the unbreeching latch, and while holding it up, unscrewing the cylinder in a counterclockwise direction.

The Type 26 has been constantly and undeservedly maligned for the shortcomings of its design and its poor ballistic performance, not to mention the potshots often taken at it for fit and finish. Those who do criticize it do not really appreciate its place in history. For a revolver developed in the 1880s, the Type 26 can hold its own, if judged by the standards of the times.

As far as workmanship is concerned, examples in original new condition (admittedly most difficult to find) display an exceptionally high standard of hand-fitting and finish excellence. The crystal blue (bright temper blued) hammer and other parts finished with this process are equal in quality to the finest of the era. Use of the charcoal (carbon deposit) bluing technique, long considered to be the most esthetically attractive, on all major metal surfaces further indicates the high manufacturing standards which military and arsenal designers placed on the new pistol. The charcoal process is the most costly and time-consuming bluing procedure used and requires an exceptionally high quality level of final metal preparation. Again, it would be unfair to judge the T-26 as inferior to most of its contemporaries.

Attempting to establish definitive production periods and quantities, along with other data of interest about Japanese pistols which are unmarked with manufacturing date information (as carried by the Type 14 and 94 pistols), is almost impossible. The reasons are that all information on military weapon development and production was never made public and most pertinent military records were destroyed during or immediately after the war. The only sources available are from positive evidence obtained from individuals involved, limited remaining Japanese records, U.S. Ordnance Reports, or from examples of the weapons themselves. This latter source, as is the case with many Japanese pistols, must be used to a greater extent for the Type 26. One must be thankful for the souvenir-loving American G.I. for the adequate sampling available for study today.

Development, adoption and manufacturing starting dates have been documented. To determine the quantity made, identify design modifications and establish when production was terminated, we must examine the available examples and the clues they offer. This can be best accomplished by first establishing significant feature variations and then arranging known examples into the following four categories:

Arsenal "rework"—serial no. 1 was refinished and externally marked during major refurbishing program.

1. **Limited early production—no external markings.**
2. **Standard production.**
3. **Limited modified final production.**
4. **Arsenal "rework."**

The most significant factors in determining the proper category of an example, and thus its collector value, are the characteristics of metal finish and grip panel design. Original manufacturing specifications called for the hammer, strut, hammer stirrup, hinge pin, hinge pin screw and all other screws except the two right grip panel screws to be heat blued (bright temper blue). The extractor, hand, rebound lever and mainspring were to be polished bright metal. All other metal parts were to receive a bright, charcoal blued finish similar to the type found on most imported revolvers of the period.

Grip panels were designated to be of beech wood (*Fagus* sp.), with a bordered, fine checked pattern. Formerly, most sources had identified the panels on all Type 26 revolvers as mahogany while, in fact, all Tokyo and Kokura arsenal produced T-26 and T-14 pistols used beech wood only.

These finish and feature characteristics will be found on all pistols of the original manufacturing run, including those examples which have no external markings. Any deviation presents the possibility that the pistol has been arsenal refinished or otherwise later altered by an owner or gunsmith.

During the standard production period, several minor modifications are apparent. These include variations in hammer shape, the somewhat enlarged grip frame and trigger guard contours which were introduced during mid-production, and the significant changes in die sizes used for marking the arsenal symbol, model identification and serial numbers on the external frame surface. The original very light and delicate stampings were replaced by a somewhat heavier style soon after the 10,000 serial range was reached, then by still larger and wider dies around the 30,000 range.

Several years after the original production run had ended and as part of a planned, concerted effort to refurbish all Type 26's that had been taken out of service for one reason or another, a limited quantity of revolvers was manufactured which exhibit pronounced feature and finish characteristic modifications. By serial no. 58971, and continuing through the highest serial number recorded to date, no. 59183, approximately 200 pistols were produced with all parts which had formerly received other bluing processes, now rust blued. Grip panels now had a horizontally grooved design (or serrated as they are referred to by most collectors). This replaced the original checked pattern. In addition, all but a few examples of the last 200 manufactured have a simplified, grooved (serrated) trigger guard pattern, identical to the design found on Japanese Type 10 35mm Army flare pistol guards.

In fact, all three revised features are very closely related, if not identical to the characteristics found on both the Type 10 (1921) signal and the Type 14 (1925) automatic pistols. It can therefore be assumed that these late production revolvers were manufactured sometime after 1921, and more probably after 1928 when the new Type 14 was in production and had virtually rendered the Type 26 obsolete.

It is just as logical to speculate that all or most of the arsenal "reworks" were also completed at about the same time. Further support for this can be found in the clues offered by inspection markings and arsenal history, and even more definitive dates established. Inspection markings approximately 2mm in size, signifying acceptance of parts and assembly, as well as final firing performance approval, are found stamped on the butt plate, on the frame under the left grip panels, in the extractor well, and on most other

Original delicate frame markings were replaced by heavier styles during later production.

Butt plates are profusely identified with assembly and performance acceptance markings.

parts designated by the original arsenal specifications. As might be expected, pistols from the limited final production show fewer marks than do examples from the earlier standard production series. Most importantly, all inspection marks appear to be those used by the Tokyo Arsenal, rather than the Kokura facility. It is apparent, however, that different dies were used for marking arsenal symbols, type identification and serial numbers during the limited final production and arsenal reworking, for the size and style differ from those of the standard production.

The Great Earthquake

At two minutes after noon on September 1, 1923, possibly the most destructive natural catastrophe in modern human history began. This was the start of the *Kanto Daishinsai,* or "Great Kanto Earthquake Disaster," which devastated Tokyo and took the lives of 144,000 people. It lasted only 15 seconds, but rated 8.3 on the Richter Scale. More relevant than its duration or intensity was the time of occurrence—just when lunch was being cooked over red-hot coals in millions of wooden houses with paper windows. Only an estimated 10,000 of the lives lost in the next 48 hours were attributed to falling debris or tidal waves. The rest perished from the resulting firestorms—storms that would be closely duplicated in 1945 by American B-29 bombers.

As a result of the extensive damage inflicted on the Tokyo Arsenal and surrounding area, plans were drawn up and officially announced on October 22, 1927, to disperse ordnance manufacturing throughout Japan. Kokura City was chosen as one of the new sites. The new Kokura Arsenal became officially functional on November 1, 1933, although it was not until March 31, 1935, that the transfer of small arms production from the Tokyo Arsenal was completed. During part of this time, primarily 1934, component parts for the Type 10 and Type 14 pistols were still made in the Tokyo Arsenal but sent to Kokura for assembly.

In view of the complicated transfer and the ultimate termination of all Type 14 production by the Kokura Arsenal in June of 1936, it is very unlikely that any Type 26 production or arsenal refurbishing took place in the newly established Kokura Arsenal. This seems to be supported by the inspection markings found on the revolvers.

Based upon the facts at hand, it would appear that the original standard production of the Type 26 ceased in 1923 as a result of the earthquake, and certainly no later than 1928 with commencement of Tokyo Type 14 production. It also seems probable that prior to the final transfer of small arms production to the new Kokura Arsenal in 1935, a decision was made to restore all revolvers which had been taken out of service due to damage or extensive use.

At the same time, in order to utilize existing tooling and parts inventories and close out T-26 production before the relocation, a small number of new revolvers was made in the Tokyo Arsenal.

These arsenal "reworks" and the limited late production were fabricated and finished under the prescribed ordnance procedures and the arsenal's capability at that time. Therefore, both groups of pistols exhibit the prevailing rust blue finishing process and the use of grooved grip panels.

Having established variations and other significant factors, Type 26 examples can now be categorized into four major groups, with relative values of rarity placed upon each:

1. **Limited early production—no external markings:** Eight examples, with no external arsenal, type or serial markings, in the 3-298 range, have thus far been reported. Thus, quite possibly up to 300 revolvers were made in late 1893 or early 1894 before the Type 26 received official adoption approval. As previously noted, although the design was completed in 1893, it was not adopted until 1894—which would perhaps explain the hesitancy in stamping the frames of any finished pistols before the substantiating acceptance year had been determined.

   To date, no conflicting serial numbered examples of externally marked and unmarked pistols have been reported, and only three examples with external markings (serial numbers 1, 13 and 28) under the 300 serial series are known. Interestingly, serial numbers 1 and 13 have been arsenal refinished, with new external markings obviously added at that time. Although the external markings on serial no. 28 appear to be of the early style, the pistol was definitely reblued sometime in its history. On the other hand, unmarked serial no. 297 appears to be the highest known example, passing the feature and finish tests. There are some questions about serial no. 298, regarding its finish and serialization.

   Based upon an estimated production figure of only 300 revolvers, this T-26 variant would be second in rarity only to the "final production" variant, and thus a highly valued collection addition. Prototypes would, of course, be rarer than either production model.

   The importance of applying the "finish" test to any example without external markings must not be minimized. Several revolvers are known which were thought to be rare variants, but, in fact, have been arsenal refinished—and should, as a result, be placed in the "rework" category. Early production pistols were so lightly stamped with the external markings that during arsenal reworking the markings could easily have been removed and not replaced.

   Several other examples are known with external arsenal symbol and *kanji* model identification, but without an external serial number stamped on the frame. These are special cases where external serial numbers were omitted either inadvertently or through official authorization. Little extra value can be given these examples, except perhaps by collectors who desire such variants.

2. **Standard production:** All examples in this category should have checked pattern grip panels, as well as the prescribed original finish characteristics. Examples will most likely be serialized from no. 300 to approximately no. 58900. The finish on reported serial no. 58907, with checked grip panels, has not been confirmed. However, serial no. 58543 has all the early original feature and finish characteristics, as does serial no. 58486, which is in "like-new" condition.

   "Mint" examples in this category are extremely rare because of the age and long service use of the pistols. A Type 26 in this condition should be considered a most desirable collection acquisition.

3. **Limited modified final production:** based upon the serial range established today from known examples, numbers 58971 to 59183, possibly less than 250 revolvers were originally made which have the final modifications and should be classified in this grouping. If this continues to hold true as new examples are reported, this variant is potentially the rarest of all Type 26 revolvers, except prototypes, and should command special collector attention.

4. **Arsenal "rework":** Any T-26 revolver, up to approximately serial no. 58900, that does not have the original bright charcoal blued finish with temper blued parts as prescribed, or has grip panels other than the standard early checked pattern style, most likely has received some refinishing attention, and should be placed in this category. Value is totally on condition, serial number uniqueness, or some other desirable feature—i.e. personal ownership, etc.

The serial chart presented covers all Type 26 revolvers observed or reported to the author. Of special interest are the internally-marked-only examples and the interspersement of the grooved style grip panels throughout the standard production range. Interestingly, only one example, serial no. 13053, has been reported with other than standard markings.

Standard issue cowhide holster with original cleaning rod and ammunition box.

Serialization

The original Tokyo Artillery Arsenal specifications required that the following components of the Type 26 be stamped with all digits of the revolver's assigned serial number and with the appropriate inspection marks:

- Frame
- Side plate
- Trigger guard
- Grip panels
- Barrel
- Latch
- Cylinder
- Extractor
- Extractor release
- Extractor cam
- Hammer
- Trigger
- Rebound lever
- Hand

From observing a number of examples, it is apparent that the original serialization specifications were amended in several ways almost immediately. Although initially only the full serial number was used on the prescribed parts, use of a sub-assembly number for the hammer and cylinder assemblies was introduced sometime after serial no. 2610 and before serial no. 5523. The sub-assembly number, a one or two-digit number, will usually be found stamped on the right grip frame, hammer, cylinder assembly and on the upper flat of the barrel at the hinge. This sub-assembly method continued throughout the entire standard production period. A very small single-digit number will also be found stamped on right grip frame, hammer and cylinder assembly. The same number will often be found on the left grip frame and several other parts. It is obviously part of the sub-assembly procedure though the purpose is unknown. In any case, it does not appear to be significant for our use.

By the 10,000 serial range, the procedure of serializing all the prescribed parts with the revolver's fully assigned number was also revised. During the 10,000 and into the early 20,000 range, all parts were now numbered using one, two or three-digit assembly numbers. This was in addition to the established sub-assembly number method, which was retained.

From the early 20,000 serial range (example no. 24303), and continuing through the 30,000 range, the procedure appears to have been modified to the use of the last two or three digits of the revolver's serial number. The use of three digits was far more prevalent.

The method of serialization was again changed when the 40,000 range was reached. From this point, until standard production ended, a separate assembly number of one, two or three digits was again assigned to the parts of each revolver. The sub-assembly procedure for hammer and cylinder, however, was also continued.

All examples of the "limited modified final production" examined use only the last two digits of the pistol's assigned serial number for parts identification. The separate hammer and cylinder sub-assembly procedure was discontinued during this period.

The key factor in determining which serialization method was used on a particular revolver are the numbers stamped on the left and right side of the grip frame beneath the grip panels. Exceptions will be found, but generally the described procedures will hold true, except for revolvers which have been arsenal "reworked." These examples are often found with a mixture of procedures, overstamping and unnumbered parts. For clarity and ready reference, the accompanying chart of select examples illustrates the various serialization methods used during the Type 26's production history.

For the collector, it is important to be aware of these various serialization methods, and thus be able to check the method applied to any revolver. Many times a revolver thought to be mismatched will, in fact, be a totally correct specimen. There are also instances where, through omission, a specified part for serialization would not be stamped.

Tenure of the Type 26 as Japan's principal sidearm was somewhat limited, although it remained in service as a substitute standard until the end of hostilities in 1945. Initially issued as a replacement for the 44 caliber Russian Smith & Wesson, it played its major role in the Sino-Japanese war of 1894-95, and the

Examples of type 26 Serialization Methods*

1 - 10,000 Serial Range

Revolver Serial Number	Grip Frame Code Numbers Left - Right		Parts Serial	Hammer Serials	Cylinder Assembly Serials		Barrel Hinge Serials Lower - Upper	
1	1	None	1	1	None	1	None	1	None
297	297	None	297	297	None	297	None	297	None
2610	2610	None	2610	2610	None	2610	None	2610	None
5523	5523	32	5523	5523	32	5523	32	5523	32
6726	6726	37	6726	6726	37	6726	37	6726	37
9270	9270	58	9270	9270	58	9270	58	9270	58
10,001 - 20,000 Serial Range								
10810	480	41	480	480	41	480	41	None	41
14974	734	85	734	734	85	734	85	734	None
16482	42	84	42	42	84	42	84	42	84
16944	4	33	4	4	33	4	33	4	33
20,001 - 40,000 Serial Range								
22541	341	96	341	341	96	341	96	341	96
23799	699	5	699	699	5	699	5	699	5
24303	303	71	303	303	71	303	71	303	71
31886	886	45	886	886	45	886	45	886	45
37062	62	69	62	62	69	62	69	62	69
40,001 - 58,900 Range								
40550	257	35	257	257	35	257	35	257	35
42553	974	73	974	974	73	974	73	974	73
51095	93	10	93	93	10	93	10	93	10
52598	1	19	1	1	19	1	19	1	19
57167	11	28	11	11	28	11	28	11	28
Final Modified Production Serial Range								
59085	85	None	85	85	None	85	None	85	None
59154	54	None	54	54	None	54	None	54	None
59159	59	None	59	59	None	59	None	59	None

*Standard production revolvers which have been arsenal reworked will often display variations to prescribed serialization procedures.

"Last-ditch" fabric holster.
Bill Ratcliffe Collection.

the most complete have been compiled by Hiromasa Ikeda, Chief, Physics Section, of the Scientific Crime Laboratory, Fukuoka Prefectural Police Headquarters, Japan, and are presented through his courtesy:

9mm Revolver Cartridge

Overall length: 30.5mm	(+0, −0.6)
Cartridge Weight: 13.2gm	(0.0)
Bullet diameter: 9.0mm	(+0.6, −0.0)
Bullet length: 16.0mm	(+0.2, −0.75)
Bullet weight: 9.8gm	(+0.1, −0.3)
Case length: 22.0mm	(+0.2, −0.3)
Case mouth (inside dia.): 9.0mm	(+0.0, −0.13)
Primer pocket diameter: 4.5mm	(+0.01, −0.05)
Rim diameter: 11.2mm	(+0.02, −0.24)
Rim thickness: 1.0mm	(+0.1, −0.24)
Primer diameter: 4.5mm	(+0.06, −0.02)
Primer height: 2.3mm	(+0.04, −0.02)
Powder (smokeless): 0.17gm	
Primer mixture: 0.007gm	
Propellant composition: Antimony trisulfide (4)	
Mercury fulminate (6)	
Potassium chlorate (6)	
Bullet composition: Pb. 94%—96%	
Sb. 4%— 6%	
Impurities—less than 2%	
Muzzle velocity: 150 m/s	
Maximum range: 1000m	
Maximum effective range: 100m	

Russo-Japanese War of 1904-05. Its importance was lessened with the introduction of the Nambu designed and developed automatic pistols in 1903. The official adoption and production of the Type 14 in 1925 quickly relegated the Type 26 to its final back-up status and near obsolescence.

As an example, a T-26 revolver was issued to a personal associate of this author, Dr. Tetsuo Aso, in November of 1937. He retained it until January of 1939. During this period, Dr. Aso completed his preparatory military training as a Japanese Army medical officer—certainly not a front line assignment.

For training purposes, Type 26 cutaway pistols were prepared. Although never mentioned in any previous publication, one example is known. These must therefore be classified as extremely rare.

9mm Revolver Cartridge

The Japanese 9mm cartridge was developed in conjunction with the 1893 Type 26 (Meiji 26) revolver, and used exclusively in this weapon. It has a straight brass case with very thin rim and no headstamp. The brass primer is of the two-hole Berdan type and, like all Japanese pistol cartridges, is not staked in place. Bullets are unjacketed solid ogival lead. It has been reported that rounds loaded prior to 1900 were charged with black powder. A smokeless propellant was employed after this date. Although published specifications vary greatly among sources,

The 9mm cartridges were packaged in 50-round tan cardboard boxes measuring 100x50x33mm. Construction and marking of the boxes varied slightly during production periods and among manufacturers. All are profusely identified. Major markings on the top include: manufacturer, weapon designation, package contents (expressed as "Loaded Ammunition" and the number of rounds) and powder data (i.e. manufacturer, year and month made and lot number). This latter data, which varies, is most often identified with red or green ink rather than black, especially on early dated boxes. Bottom markings also vary. Boxes packaged before 1939 usually lack any identification, though some will carry "Grade" data. Those packaged in the early 1940s are normally marked on the bottom with the weapon designation, powder data and package data. Because of the number of variations, it is always best to have the markings on each box individually translated.

Boxes identified with the symbols of the Tokyo Army Arsenal (four stacked cannon balls), 1st Tokyo Arsenal (a five pointed star with two inner circles) and the 2nd Tokyo Arsenal (ordnance bomb) have been observed thus far. Recorded package dates vary from Taisho 5.6 (June, 1916) to Showa 15.4 (April,

1940). According to U.S. Ordnance records, all pistol ammunition which was packaged in 50-round cardboard containers was shipped in metal lined wooden crates containing 66 boxes of cartridges (3,300 rounds).

All 9mm Japanese cartridges are scarce—far more so than the revolvers themselves—and only a few exercise (dummy) examples are known. These extremely rare cartridges have a cannelured lead projectile and a single knurled ring around the lower case body.

Holsters and Accessories

The standard Type 26 revolver holster is constructed of high quality cowhide leather, varying in color from very dark reddish brown to light tan. Several early black examples have been reported, but no pigskin or other leather material holsters are known.

A hard moulded clamshell closure flap is used for better pistol protection, while an ammunition pouch containing 18 cartridge loops has been installed on the front of the holster body. This pouch also has a protective closure flap. A leather pocket for the cleaning rod is also provided.

Closure flap hardware, and the oval shoulder strap rings, are made of various metals with a variety of finishes. Early holsters have all brass fittings, while later examples will be found with different combinations of brass, galvanized steel, blued and black lacquered steel, all on the same holster. A few holsters, manufactured in 1943, have been noted with all black lacquered hardware.

Most examples are stamped on the inside of the clamshell flap with the maker's identification symbol and arsenal inspection markings, as well as the year of manufacture. Tokyo Arsenal symbols will normally be found marked only on holsters of early manufacture which were distributed with the revolver while T-26 production continued. Replacement holsters manufactured by private civilian contractors are usually devoid of the arsenal symbol. As would be expected, minor construction variations will be found between holsters made by different manufacturers.

A large number of holsters in near new condition, dated in the late 1930s, have been observed. This is not surprising considering the long length of service and hard use experienced by many revolvers and their accessories, resulting in the need for holster replacement.

Type 26 holsters were originally issued with leather cowhide shoulder straps, 25mm in width, having a buckle and two leather "keepers" for length adjustment. Early straps were welted along both outer edges, while later straps were left plain. Strap hardware material and finish also varied greatly during production and among manufacturers.

Very early holsters, manufactured and issued in the late 1890s and early 1900s, were of a slightly different size and shape. They did not have a pocket for the cleaning rod although the cartridge pouch and loops were provided. These holsters are found in a variety of designs, all of which are extremely rare. Care should be taken not to confuse these early variants with the very similar French revolver holster. Most French holsters will be so marked, and do not have the 18 cartridge loops in their ammo pouches.

Three examples of a "last-ditch" fabric T-26 holster have been reported which are similar in material and construction to the more familiar Type 94 late-war design, although they have no shoulder strap hardware, cleaning rod or ammunition pouches. Six cloth cartridge loops, however, have been sewn onto the front of the holster body and are protected when the holster closure flap is secured.

Original Type 26 cleaning rods are extremely rare and a desirable collection accessory. They are approximately 177mm in length, and have a distinctive off-set oval loop at one end, with the oval closed by a weld. This feature greatly assists in identifying the original rods. All known examples are made of steel or nickeled steel—steel being far more prevalent. Nickeled rods are usually stamped on their shanks with a single inspection mark, while steel rods are seldom identified. Several steel examples have been observed which are crudely made and have a single examiner's mark stamped on the weld rather than on the shank. Material, length and oval configuration differ slightly between rods manufactured during different periods by various manufacturers. A brass variant has been mentioned in several publications, but never confirmed, and it is doubtful that one was ever officially adopted. On the other hand, a large variety of cleaning rods and other tools were used with the Type 26 revolver, and are found with their holsters. But, as with other Japanese pistols, only those rods which were officially approved and issued with the designated pistol and holster should be considered as original and correct.

A 7mm diameter braided cord lanyard, with stitched leather joiner and "keeper," was issued with the Type 26 revolver, although the more often encountered 6mm diameter size associated with the Type 14 was often used. Cord color varies from light tan to mid-brown while lengths from 26 to 38 inches have been observed. A comprehensive instruction manual was also made available with each revolver. Unfortunately, original specimens are extremely rare today.

Based upon its history and limited production, all variants of the Japanese Type 26 revolver and pertinent accessories should be considered as desirable additions to any collection. Although slighted in the past, hopefully, they will soon take their rightful place in the hierarchy of the firearms of the world. ●

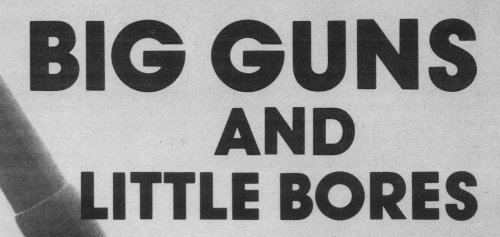

BIG GUNS AND LITTLE BORES

the story of U.S. Army artillery subcaliber devices

by **KONRAD F. SCHREIER, JR.**

A 75mm subcaliber mounted on a U.S. Army coastal defense gun, 16-inch Model 1919 as used in the 1920s and 1930s.

When the first breech-loading cannon came into service soon after the Civil War there was one unpalatable fact about them—they cost a lot more to fire than the old muzzleloaders did. Muzzle-loading cannon, even the best of the rifled variety, fired simple shot or shell which were relatively cheap and easy to make. The new breech-loading guns were precision machines, firing projectiles which were carefully and expensively produced, and the result was many times the cost per bang than with the best muzzle-loading cannon.

It also took extensive practice to make gun crews for the new breech-loading guns able to get the best from their weapons—this all provided a great incen-

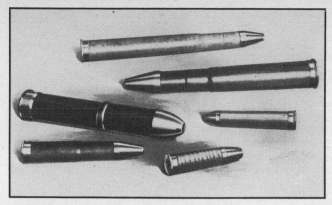

37mm to 3-inch drill cartridges pictured in the catalog of the American Ordinance Co., which represented the Hotchkiss Co. in America, about 1895.

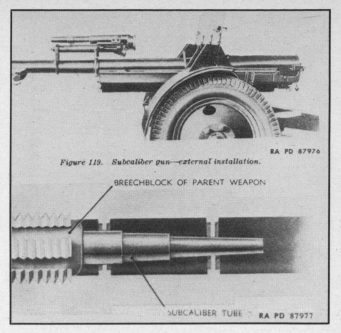

Figure 119. Subcaliber gun—external installation.

RA PD 87976

BREECHBLOCK OF PARENT WEAPON

SUBCALIBER TUBE   RA PD 87977

A 37mm Subcaliber Gun M1916 mounted on a U.S. Army 75mm Field Gun M1897A1—the French 75—as used in the 1930s.

tive for the invention of systems which would save on firing cost. The cost problem was particularly bad in the United States services, which traditionally had to live within restricted budgets in peacetime. Fortunately, an answer to the firing cost problem became readily available. The answer was "subcaliber devices and systems," which make use of a gun of a smaller (sub)caliber in conjunction with the large bore cannon for practice firing. These subcaliber units mount on the "parent weapon" in a manner which allows them to be aimed with the sighting system of the parent weapon. The range over which the subcaliber unit is fired is also proportionally reduced from that of the parent weapon, and scoring systems which relate the subcaliber fire to the actual performance of the parent weapon firing its regular ammunition are used.

Two Classifications

There are two basic classifications of subcaliber systems—depending on how they mount to the parent weapon. There is the externally mounted, usually a complete small caliber breech-loading gun which is mounted on top of the parent weapon's barrel. Most external subcaliber devices are cannon in their own right, such as the U.S. Army 37mm subcaliber gun M1916 mounted on guns from 75mm up to 240mm, plus the 75mm subcaliber gun M1919 which mounted on seacoast and railway guns of from 10- to 16-inch bores. Both were actually field guns, with special

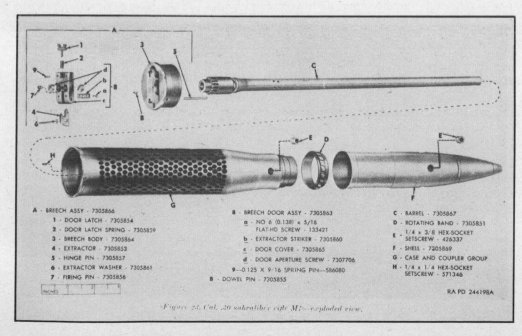

A - BREECH ASSY - 7305866
   1 - DOOR LATCH - 7305854
   2 - DOOR LATCH SPRING - 7305859
   3 - BREECH BODY - 7305864
   4 - EXTRACTOR - 7305853
   5 - HINGE PIN - 7305857
   6 - EXTRACTOR WASHER - 7305861
   7 - FIRING PIN - 7305856

B - BREECH DOOR ASSY - 7305863
   a - NO 6 (0.138) x 5/16
        FLAT-HD SCREW - 133421
   b - EXTRACTOR STRIKER - 7305860
   c - DOOR COVER - 7305865
   d - DOOR APERTURE SCREW - 7307706
   9 - 0.125 X 9/16 SPRING PIN - 586080
B - DOWEL PIN - 7305855

C - BARREL - 7305867
D - ROTATING BAND - 7305851
E - 1/4 x 3/8 HEX-SOCKET
      SETSCREW - 426337
F - SHELL - 7305869
G - CASE AND COUPLER GROUP
H - 1/4 x 1/4 HEX-SOCKET
      SETSCREW - 571346

RA PD 244198A

Figure 24. Cal. 30 subcaliber rifle M7—exploded view.

The Cal. 30 Subcaliber Rifle M7 drill cartridge for use in the post-World War II 75mm Recoiless Rifle, M20.

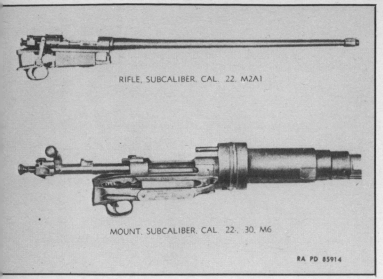

The Cal. 22 rimfire Subcaliber Rifle M2A1 shown in and out of its mount. Although it was still standard in the late 1940s, this subcaliber version was most used around 1940 as World War II began and it is very rarely encountered today.

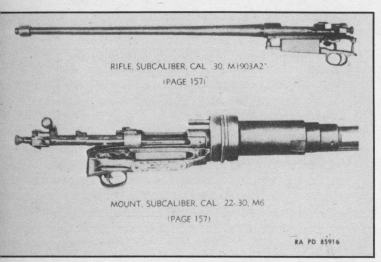

The Cal. 30 Subcaliber Rifle M1903A2. Much used in World War II, is a very scarce Springfield '03 variation today.

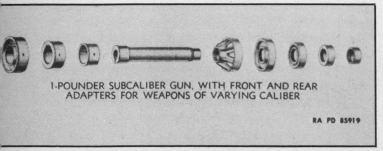

The 1-pounder Subcaliber Gun which the U.S. Army used in a variety of coast defense guns by means of the set of adapter rings shown. Although this device was used from about 1900 to mid-World War II it was never assigned a model number.

mounts adapting them for subcaliber use—they fired ammunition adapted to their special use.

The other basic classification of subcaliber system is a type which is fired through the bore of its parent weapon, and is thus called internally mounted. While a few of these fired ammunition of 37mm or even 75mm caliber, the vast majority of them used standard military rifle caliber ammunition. A few of them even fired the ubiquitous 22 rimfire cartridge. These internally mounted devices are encountered fairly often, and for the collector or student of military arms they can be most interesting.

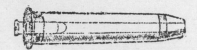

The Drill Cartridge

The oldest of all subcaliber devices is the internally mounted type usually called a *drill cartridge;* it was invented about the time metallic cartridge firing cannon came into use in the 1870s. (The U.S. Army first procured them with some breech-loading Hotchkiss cannon made in France at that time.) Drill cartridges consist of a metal or wood and metal body with the same outside shape as the parent weapon's regular ammunition. It has a chambered rifle-caliber barrel mounted concentrically within it, so the cannon's firing pin will strike the cartridge primer and fire the rifle caliber ammunition through the drill cartridge barrel and the parent weapon's bore, just as it fires its regular full-sized ammunition.

In the U.S. armed forces drill cartridges have been made and issued for cannon from 37mm "one pounders" up to guns of 75mm or 3-inch size (a few were made for even larger calibers). They have been made in 22 rimfire, 30 U.S. Army (Krag), 30-'06, and 45-70 rifle ammunition sizes, and a very few were even made up to fire 37mm subcaliber ammunition in cannon of 3-inch or larger size.

Drill cartridges have not been used much in the U.S. Armed Forces since World War II, with one exception. The reason for this is a good one: Subcaliber devices firing rifle caliber ammunition are only suitable for training in what is called "direct fire," in which the parent weapon is aimed directly at its target just as a rifleman aims his rifle at its target. Except for tank and anti-tank cannon, most modern artillery weapons seldom engage in direct fire, but normally operate at ranges that require "indirect fire." They shoot at an angle of elevation which gives the projectile a high trajectory to allow it to reach a target which cannot be seen from the gun. Obviously, hits from rifle caliber subcaliber devices fired in indirect fire would be impossible to locate and record. Indirect subcaliber fire can be, however, completely

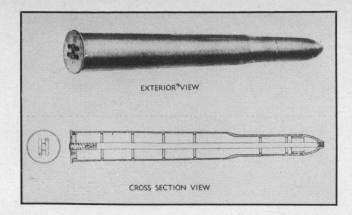

EXTERIOR VIEW

CROSS SECTION VIEW

Left—The subcaliber or drill cartridge used in U.S. Army 3-inch guns from the turn of the century until after World War II. These cartridges were originally made to fire regular 30 caliber Army-Krag ammunition, but in the 1920s they were all modified to fire a special Krag cartridge called the Cal. 30 Subcaliber Cartridge M1925, which had a special extra thick primer. This special cartridge had a spitzer (pointed) bullet and often confuses cartridge collectors when it turns up. Below—

This is a 75mm subcaliber gun which mounted in guns from 6 to 16 inches. The barrel and rings fit in the chamber of the parent gun, and the stem behind them is a special firing-lock for the 75mm ammunition which fits in the parent gun's breechblock. This device was 7 feet long and weighed hundreds of pounds.

practical if the subcaliber ammunition fires a projectile which bursts on impact so the hit may be seen and scored. Despite the potential savings which could be realized in subcaliber firing training, the system is out of fashion in the U.S. Armed Forces today except for use with some tank guns and recoiless rifles.

Some of the U.S. Armed Forces subcaliber drill cartridges are encountered fairly frequently today. From the post-World War II era we have those used in the recoiless rifles like the 57mm and 75mm, developed before "spotting rifles" were added to these weapons. (These spotting rifles are themselves actually highly refined subcaliber guns.) From the era before World War II there are a number of drill cartridges for use in guns up to 3-inch or 75mm bore. Probably the commonest of all drill cartridges is one which was used to fire a 22 rimfire in a 37mm tank or anti-tank gun from the World War II era. Some drill cartridges are made with special firing pin energy transfer devices, so the blow of the parent weapon's heavy firing pin would not pierce the primer of the subcaliber ammunition.

The Subcaliber Gun

Another type of internally mounted subcaliber device is known as the *subcaliber gun*—its use dates back to about 1890. Consisting of a barrel with large

75-MM SUBCALIBER MOUNT, M3, ON 16-IN. HOWITZER CARRIAGE, M1920

75-MM SUBCALIBER MOUNT, M4, ON 16-IN. BARBETTE CARRIAGE, M1919M1

75mm subcaliber gun mounts used on very heavy coast defense guns between World Wars I and II.

rings around it, it is designed to be locked in the chamber of the parent weapon and loaded with its special ammunition one round at a time. The subcaliber gun's barrel may be provided with several sets of different diameter adapter rings for different parent weapons as a "subcaliber gun kit." On cannon 155mm (6-inch) and larger in the U.S. Services which use "separate loading" ammunition with a projectile and bag of propellant, a special firing lock is used to fire the subcaliber gun. There were devices of this type to fire 30-06 caliber ammunition in guns around 75mm or 3-inch, 37mm for use in cannon from 3- to 8-inch bore, and 75mm for use in cannon from 8- to 16-inch bore. One of these subcaliber guns encountered fairly frequently consisted of a 30 caliber Browning water-cooled machine gun barrel with adapter discs fitting the U.S. Army World War II 75mm tank cannon.

Of all the subcaliber devices used in the U.S. Armed Forces the most interesting are those known as *subcaliber rifles*. These fire a regular or slightly modified infantry rifle held in some sort of adapter so that it is centered in the bore of the parent weapon. While the actual date of introduction of these into the U.S. Armed Forces is uncertain, the oldest known types adapt the 45-70 Trap-Door Springfield rifle to fire in the U.S. Army's 3.2-inch breech-loading Field

This 37mm subcaliber gun of the World War II era could be used with adapters for 75mm, 90mm, or 105mm guns.

sion, so it had to be removed. However, it never did stop the use of subcaliber devices, and more were developed.

The Krag Subcaliber Rifle

When the U.S. Army adopted the 30 caliber Krag in 1892, that cartridge soon became the basis for subsequent subcaliber rifles. The first of these was for the 3.2-inch Field Gun, Model of 1885, and was noth-

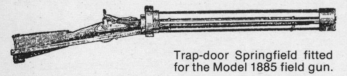

Trap-door Springfield fitted for the Model 1885 field gun.

Gun Model of 1885. These were advertised for sale in Bannerman's catalogs of the early 1920s as allowing practice with, "rifle cartridges (at) $1.75 per hundred rounds instead of expensive cannon shells costing over $3 each." That was back when a working man made about $5 a day, and a hundred bucks a week was a fortune. This old Trap-Door Springfield subcaliber rifle consisted of a frame which locked a complete rifle in the back of the 3.2-inch field gun's bore, with the action out in the open where it could be easily operated. It was usually fired at standard 100-yard rifle targets using the cannon's regular sights, and the hits were scored after compensating for range setting and sight parallax.

The accuracy of these subcaliber rifles, and all subcaliber devices for that matter, was more than adequate for training cannoneers. However, all those firing through the bore of their parent weapon had one minor drawback: Unless the bore of the parent weapon was carefully cleaned after subcaliber firing it would develop minor spots of corrosion caused by the combustion products of the subcaliber ammunition. While this wasn't a real problem in cannon bores, it looked awful and could spawn worse corro-

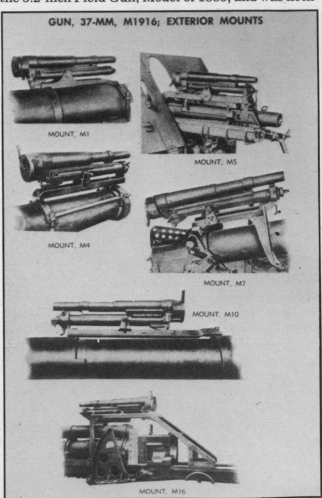

GUN, 37-MM, M1916; EXTERIOR MOUNTS

MOUNT, M1

MOUNT, M5

MOUNT, M4

MOUNT, M7

MOUNT, M10

MOUNT, M16

These subcaliber mounts for the 37mm Gun M1916 were used from the 1920s until after World War II. They fit on guns from 75mm up to 8-inch, and were primarily used on field guns.

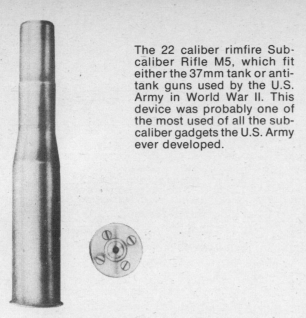

The 22 caliber rimfire Sub-caliber Rifle M5, which fit either the 37mm tank or anti-tank guns used by the U.S. Army in World War II. This device was probably one of the most used of all the sub-caliber gadgets the U.S. Army ever developed.

ing but a modification of the mount for the 45-70 Trap-Door Springfield in that cannon. There was a Krag subcaliber rifle for the 3-inch Coast Defense Gun adopted in 1898; both were not discarded until 1948. There were a number of variations in this sub-caliber rifle adapter, and all mounted the rifle barrel and action without stock or sights. Some used Krag actions lacking the machine cuts for the magazine, and modified for lanyard instead of trigger firing.

The Krag subcaliber rifle for the 3-inch Coast Defense Gun was the prototype for a whole series of these devices which used an adapter to lock the barreled action of an infantry rifle into the chamber and bore of a cannon. The rifle action was supported outside of the gun's breech so it could be manipulated. There was also a provision, usually an adjustable concentric disc on the infantry rifle's muzzle, to allow its point of aim to be coordinated with the sights of the parent weapon. These devices were usually fired at paper targets at ranges from 50 to 100 or so yards, depending on the space available around the gun position. Although these Krag subcaliber rifles for the 3-inch gun were in use until after the end of World War II, there are very few of them found today.

Krag subcaliber rifles were also developed for the U.S. Army 3-inch Field Gun, Model of 1902, and several other pre-World War I U.S. Army field guns. These Krag devices had short lives because the U.S. Army converted to the 30 caliber Springfield rifle, Model of 1903, as soon as it went into general use. At the time of World War I there were '03 Springfield subcaliber rifles for use in all U.S. 3-inch and 75mm cannon including U.S. Navy shipboard guns, and subcaliber firing training was at an all-time high in the U.S. Armed Forces.

After World War I, subcaliber artillery training was continued as a way of training gunners at posts which had limited firing ranges, and as a means of conserving the costly, short-lived and difficult to procure barrels of very large bore cannon. As far as field artillery training went there was so much ammunition left over from the war that, so long as suitable ranges could be located, much training was conducted with regular "service ammunition."

Training Gunners

Around 1930 the U.S. Army began to give serious consideration to how it could train tank and anti-

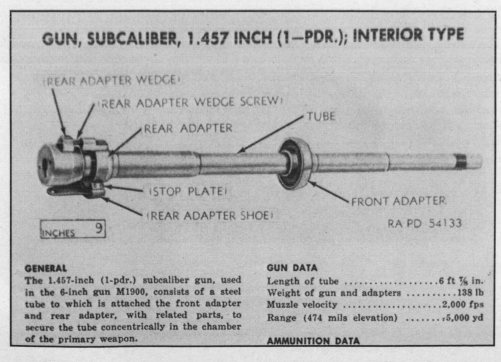

GUN, SUBCALIBER, 1.457 INCH (1—PDR.); INTERIOR TYPE

(REAR ADAPTER WEDGE)
(REAR ADAPTER WEDGE SCREW)
REAR ADAPTER
TUBE
(STOP PLATE)
(REAR ADAPTER SHOE)
FRONT ADAPTER
RA PD 54133
INCHES 9

This 1-pounder subcaliber gun of the 1930s was specially made for 6-inch coast defense guns, and was later used to a limited extent in other guns.

GENERAL
The 1.457-inch (1-pdr.) subcaliber gun, used in the 6-inch gun M1900, consists of a steel tube to which is attached the front adapter and rear adapter, with related parts, to secure the tube concentrically in the chamber of the primary weapon.

GUN DATA
Length of tube ....6 ft ⅞ in.
Weight of gun and adapters ....138 lb
Muzzle velocity ....2,000 fps
Range (474 mils elevation) ....5,000 yd

AMMUNITION DATA

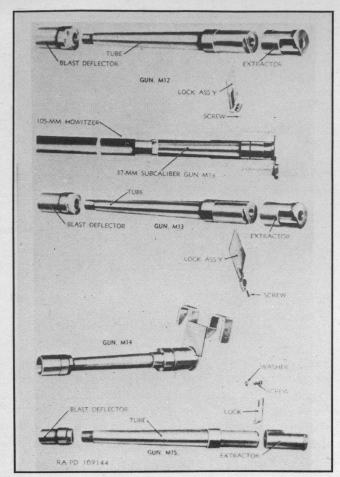

These 37mm subcaliber guns were made for use in guns from 75mm up to 105mm, in the World War II era. They all mount in the chambers of their parent guns.

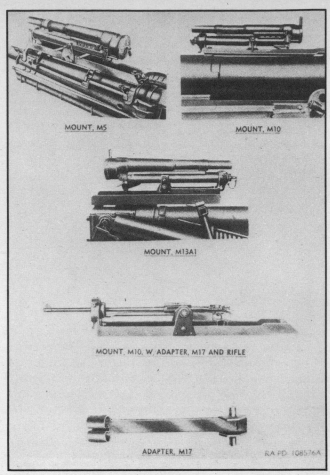

Above are three adapter subcaliber mounts for the 37mm Gun M1916 on 75mm, 155mm and 8-inch guns. Below is a special adapter mount allowing the 37mm gun to be replaced with a standard Cal. 30 Rifle M1903 with its stock removed. These World War II era devices all became obsolete around the end of or just after World War II.

tank gunners for the future. The Army planners knew they would be short of new equipment when the time came to teach these gunners, so they began considering subcaliber devices. They correctly determined that hitting a moving target, be it a tank or anything else, is basically a rifleman's skill, so they started intensive rifle marksmanship training. The system as it finally worked out was both practical and highly successful, and it gave birth to two practically unknown models of the '03 Springfield rifle.

These '03 Springfield subcaliber rifle models were developed in the 1930s, and they were extensively used for tank and anti-tank gunner training in World War II. They are the *Cal. 22 Subcaliber Rifle M2A1*, a variation of the 22 caliber M2 Springfield target rifle, and the *Cal. 30 Subcaliber Rifle M1903A2*, a model of the '03 Springfield service rifle. Although their receivers were not marked with the word "subcaliber," they were marked with the model designations **M2A1** and **M1903A2** respectively. Any receiver so marked began life as one of these Springfield subcaliber rifles. However, the markings

M-6 Subcaliber Mount which adapted the M2A1 or M1903A2 subcaliber rifle to the 37mm anti-tank gun.

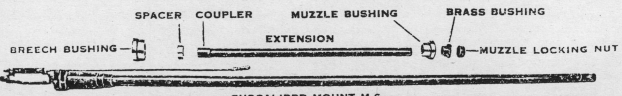

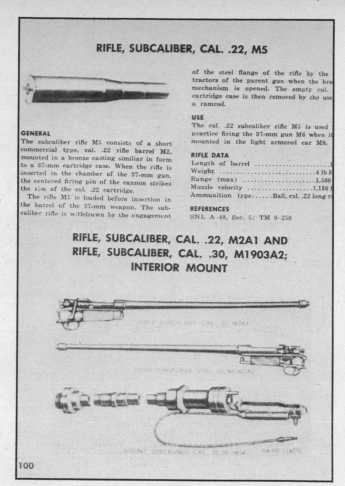

RIFLE, SUBCALIBER, CAL. .22, M5

GENERAL

The subcaliber rifle M5 consists of a short commercial type, cal. .22 rifle barrel M2, mounted in a bronze casting similiar in form to a 37-mm cartridge case. When the rifle is inserted in the chamber of the 37-mm gun, the centered firing pin of the cannon strikes the rim of the cal. .22 cartridge.

The rifle M5 is loaded before insertion in the barrel of the 37-mm weapon. The subcaliber rifle is withdrawn by the engagement of the steel flange of the rifle by the tractors of the parent gun when the breech mechanism is opened. The empty cal. cartridge case is then removed by the use a ramrod.

USE

The cal. .22 subcaliber rifle M5 is used practice firing the 37-mm gun M6 when it mounted in the light armored car M8.

RIFLE DATA

Length of barrel 1
Weight ....4 lb 8
Range (max) 1,500
Muzzle velocity ....1,130 f
Ammunition type......Ball, cal. .22 long ri

REFERENCES

SNL A-48, Sec. 5; TM 9-250

RIFLE, SUBCALIBER, CAL. .22, M2A1 AND
RIFLE, SUBCALIBER, CAL. .30, M1903A2;
INTERIOR MOUNT

Above—The 37mm tank and anti-tank gun 22 caliber rimfire Subcaliber Rifle M5, perhaps the most used subcaliber device of the World War II era. Below—The Subcaliber Rifle M2A1, Cal. 30 Subcaliber Rifle M1903A2 and the Subcaliber Mount M14 to be used with them.

on earlier Springfields used as subcaliber rifles are, at the very best, erratic and confusing. In any case, these last two Springfield subcaliber '03's had no stocks, and both had special bushings on their muzzles. Of the two, the 30 caliber was by far and away the more common model—the 22 rimfire was not much used. Today both are very seldom seen.

There were a series of adapters to fit interchangeably either the 22 caliber M2A1 or the 30 caliber M1903A2, and these were designated *Subcaliber Mounts, Cal. 22-30* with the *M6* version to fit the little 37mm anti-tank gun, the *M7* for the 37mm tank gun, and the *M14* for the 57mm anti-tank gun. While all of these models saw use, the most used were the M6 and M7 for the 37mm guns since introductory training could be done as well with a 37mm gun. Also, early in World War II the U.S. Army had an oversupply of 37mm anti-tank guns and light tanks mounting the 37mm gun. While these '03 Springfield subcaliber rifles were extensively utilized in World War II, their usefulness ended with the war.

Present Use

Since World War II not much subcaliber training has been done in the U.S. Armed Forces. There is still a special semi-automatic model of the 50 caliber Browning Machine gun, the *M2HB*, which mounts on the top of a tank cannon barrel and which is fired by the firing mechanism of the parent weapon, but its use is spotty. There were also a series of subcaliber drill cartridges for use in the older, and now obsolete, 57mm, 75mm and 105mm recoiless rifles. Practically all other subcaliber devices of older models were scrapped years ago, when their parent weapons were disposed of.

Perhaps the use of subcaliber devices will come back into the training scheme one day before long. They provide excellent systems for affording basic marksmanship training and practice to gunners, and particularly for firing at moving targets. The ammunition used costs an insignificant fraction of that fired in modern cannon, and the ranges required are relatively small—which is of considerable importance at a time when finding room is becoming ever more difficult. The standard range adopted for subcaliber training in the 1930s was 1,000 inches— 83 feet, 4 inches—and the targets were scaled for that distance. With a 30 caliber subcaliber adapter the range was usually 100 or 200 yards, and with a 37mm, 1,000 yards.

The economics of ammunition cost and range space not only led to the development of subcaliber devices and systems, but the training these schemes provided could be fun. There was a lot to be said for training in which miniature targets were used, and with which the noise and recoil of the parent weapon were practically eliminated. Unfortunately the actual subcaliber adapter equipment for such training is lost and gone forever, and so is the range material used with it. However, when surviving bits and pieces are found, they are important relics of a form of training which developed as good cannoneers as there ever were.

•

A 1,000-inch range unit.

Your Gun Collection as an

STURM RUGER advertises its M-77 rifle as "An Investment in the Future." In reality, every purchase of a firearm is an investment. The question is whether it is a good investment or a bad one. Most people buy guns for hunting, collecting, or target shooting. Can and should they be *investing* in these guns as well?

A few people, however, purchase guns purely as an investment. They are interested in guns as a commodity, offering low risk, high liquidity and high return. Isn't that what everyone should be interested in? Only the hunter and target shooter needs one more factor—good performance.

Risk means risk of capital, being careful to not buy an illegal weapon which could be confiscated, or altered weapons (fakes, counterfeits or reproductions), while paying a reasonable price. Maintenance includes storage costs, insurance, and fighting corrosion and leather or wood deterioration. Liquidity means being able to sell easily and quickly, and at a fair (not discounted) price.

Return speaks for itself. Only you can decide what you want (need) for a return on your investment, but you must remember how return is computed. For example, if you pay $100 for a gun and sell it three months later for $150, that is not a yield of 50 percent. On an annual basis, it was held for a quarter of a year so the gain is multiplied by four, yielding $200. Then divide the $200 profit by the $100 cost, for a 200 percent annual return on investment. In addition, of course, it's a short term capital sale for tax purposes.

Sub- and full-size machine guns would seem to be poor investments for most people. To own such a weapon requires a Federal Licensee for transfer, plus the payment of a Federal Transfer Tax of $200 payable to the I.R.S. by the buyer, which only serves to increase the cost of the gun. Some states totally prohibit machine gun ownership. The net result is that machine gun cost is high, and the ease of transferring ownership poor. This type of gun may be "fun" to own for a collector or shooter but it would be a poor investment for your family.

How will they sell it, and to whom? Will they even know the legal restrictions on its sale? One "slip-up" could land them in trouble with the law and, in addition, few people will be potential buyers!

Now contrast that investment with the purchase of a Brown Bess Tower Musket. Because this arm was made prior to 1898, there are no restrictions on its interstate sale, nor will there be a transfer tax. No state laws prohibit its purchase. Now, liquidity is greater. Most firearms manufactured after 1898 require a Federal license for interstate transfer. Some state laws delay delivery of modern firearms for days, and some states require that the owner be registered. Because most of these controls do not apply to antique guns, antiques are generally more liquid.

An investment can be in an object such as a gun which gives the owner pleasure or knowledge. Can one always rate an investment like this as good or bad? You may not be able to. When you die, however, your family or heirs will surely be able to judge whether your gun investments were good or bad!

If one wanted to collect guns as an investment, how would one start? Start with quality. It has been said that "expensive junk is still junk," and no one wants to own junk. That means a gun, to make a profit, must be salable to the next buyer. Which should be bought, a Colt 1860 Army in unaltered condition with 80 percent original finish, or the same model missing the wedge, with replaced grips and badly pitted. Even if you were to be *given* the latter, after properly restoring it you probably could not make the percent of profit you would by paying a fair price for the unaltered gun.

Using quality alone as a criterion is dangerous, and can limit your potential return. A finely cased, excellent condition, pinfire revolver has less chance for resale in the United States than a cased Smith & Wesson in only very good condition because there is much less interest in pinfires in this country. Of course, if pinfires interest you, a common model in excellent condition will be a better investment than a rare one in poor condition.

Investment/Legacy   by Rodney Washburn

Let's further consider popularity as an investing criterion. The more potential buyers there are, the better the chance for a good sale. This may be the most important decision. Are there more people collecting French army revolvers or Winchester rifles? Where you live may well determine your choice. If you collect in America, collect American made weapons—European weapons are not as popular here. Collect well known names like Smith & Wesson, Colt, Winchester, or Remington. Or collect arms from important periods such as wars; Civil War or Revolutionary War weapons are popular. Or just collect martially marked weapons. There are many possibilities.

There are instances when the criteria seem to be in conflict. For example, the Luger and Walther are well known names with many collectors. Are they then good investments? Yes and no. They sell well, but remember that a Federal license is needed to transfer them interstate because they are handguns manufactured after 1898. A Winchester 1866 does not have that limitation.

Premium guns—those that are engraved or cased, for example—pose a difficult decision. Special features add value if the engraving is factory or the casing is original and all the accouterments are still there. However, the price will be much higher so fewer people will be able to afford the gun upon resale—another liquidity problem.

Though the few remaining potential buyers can afford the weapon, if they do not need or want it, what then?

All of the above points should also be remembered when considering guns belonging to famous people. The price is higher because the gun becomes a one of a kind, just as is the case with prototypes or experimentals. Therefore, the potential buyers may be very limited both in interest and because of price. It should go without saying that such guns should be *thoroughly* documented. Jesse James and Billy the Kid would have had to buckle on a new gun every day to have owned all the guns attributed to them!

Again, the same holds true for any kind of rare variation. A Luger collector may desperately want one of the five Lugers made by George Luger in 45 caliber, but at a current estimated price of $50,000 to $150,000 for one, how many potential buyers are there? Only one is enough, but can *you* find him? More important, can your widow find him? Does he even exist in a tight economy?

Single digit serial number guns or those with unusual markings present the same problem. Can the resultant increase in their cost be justified at the time of sale, or does it price the piece out of the marketplace as an investment because it limits too greatly the number of potential buyers?

Engraved guns, cased guns, guns of famous owners, prototypes, experimentals, special markings (military units for example), low serial numbers, special calibers, presentations, limited production guns, all tend to go for premium prices, both to you and to a subsequent buyer. Though such arms are very desirable, prices tend to restrict the marketability of the weapon at the time of resale.

Collectors differ from investors in one important way. Collectors tend to be impulse buyers. When they need that one gun to complete a series or theme or collection, price is no object. They forget price *vs* value and can overpay. wthis, an investor can never do.

Finding and buying good guns is great fun. Owning them and showing them off may be even more fun, but fun is not the purpose of this discussion. An investor must sell his investment to "make" money, and whether hunter, collector, or investor, your guns must be sold some day. If you do not choose to sell them during your lifetime, someone else must do so after your death. Will they be able to? How many times have you or someone you know found a bargain buying guns from an estate at far less than their true value? How can you prevent your guns from suffering the same fate at the hands of the collectors and dealers who will appear at your death?

If your heirs are to keep the collection, your specific

wishes should be made known to them, either in a will or in an easily located memorandum, after you are gone. The question of who will inherit your guns is not necessarily as important as what they will do with them. Will your children have the same interest in your collection that you have? If they don't work on the collection and build it, will they at least be able to maintain it? Will they want to? Guns must be kept oiled and protected from theft. If they are kept locked up in a vault, will anyone look at them again? If the answer to these questions is no, a possible solution would be to suggest that your children and/or wife make a selection of a few of your guns that they would like to keep and would enjoy. The balance could then be sold.

You may also want to consider leaving your collection to a museum. This could have tax benefits. If you can find a museum that is interested, get it in writing that the museum agrees to accept the collection. However, even if they do, will they maintain it as your collection? More importantly, can or will they display it so others can enjoy it? Remember, if a museum inherits your collection, it's likely no future collector will ever have a chance to own what you do.

So now we are back to the problem of selling some or all of the collection after your death. A will simply directing that sale is not necessarily enough. When should they be sold, and for what prices? Should the executor sell them, or should your heirs sell them when they receive them later from the estate? The seller is responsible for the price, and obviously should know what he is doing when arranging such a sale.

Should the guns be priced and only sold if they bring those prices? What happens to those which do not sell? Does discounting these lead to finally "giving" the remainder away? Maybe the collection should be sold as a lot only. If the executor, widow or children cannot or should not set the prices, who should? A gun dealer who is brought in may be tempted to set prices low, so that he can buy them cheaply himself. If the collection has appreciable value, the new owners may need an expert appraisal. They should make sure that the person appraising them is a specialist in the type of guns in your collection, even if he must be brought in from a distance, at some expense. Should the dealer who agrees to price the collection be prohibited from buying from it?

Should estate guns be consigned to a dealer? If so, he will have to mark prices up to cover costs plus a reasonable profit. There will probably be some pieces left over under this system, too.

Many widows turn for help to gun collector firends of their late husband's. Not only is this a great imposition of time, but it is a great responsibility. They are obviously now "experts" by virtue of their being selected. A friend may be reluctant to ask for a fee for his time and knowledge, and yet he should certainly have one. Your widow should be advised to set a fee before she asks for help.

Back to setting values for your guns. To avoid the problems above, why not consider pricing them yourself. Make a list of every item that you own, described so that even your wife could not fail to identify it. Then price each item fairly. Update the list twice a year, or have it done for you if you cannot or will not do it yourself—many insurance policies require that the items be appraised by a professional, anyhow. Make sure the future owners know about this list, its purpose and where they can find it. You have now set the prices.

Still another method is to let the buyers set the prices at an auction. This could be a silent auction, where sealed bids are accepted up to a certain date for each separate item or for the entire collection. If it's to be a regular auction, should a local auctioneer hold it at your home? Or should your guns be auctioned by a local auction house? Probably *no* to both ideas.

Guns should be adequately cataloged and advertised in the proper periodicals and by direct mail to important collectors. Though there are many auction houses which can do this locally, there are only a few houses which specialize in gun auctions. A few top collections should demand an internationally known auction house. If your guns are sold at an unreserved auction, the items will be sold at any price that they bring. In a reserved auction, items may be removed from the bidding if the bids are considered too low.

Some of your guns may be purchased by individuals who live out of state. The seller will then have to deal with the problems of packing, mailing, insurance and obtaining copies of the purchaser's Federal licenses. A professional dealer or auction house can do all this and will, as part of the fee.

There's one more alternative solution, but not one likely to be palatable to most collectors. Should you hold your collection until your death? All that you own can be reduced to cash at its fair market value today. Should you, or do you wish to, dispose of your collection to those you wish at prices you set, now or later during your lifetime? Can you put the cash to better use while you are still alive? If you did sell now you would eliminate all the current problems of maintaining the condition of the collection, the fear of theft, and the fear of new government controls.

However, if you're reading this book you are probably a serious collector not interested in seeing your treasures dispersed. In that case, consider the preceding suggestions about the investment aspect of your collection, and give some thought to preparing the way for those who'll some day follow behind you. Then may you continue to enjoy that collection for many more years to come. ●

The Pistols of J.P. Sauer & Sohn

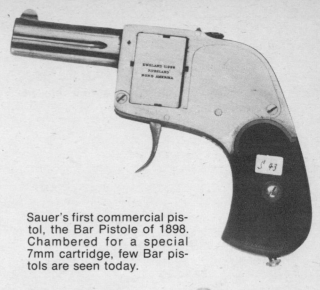

Sauer's first commercial pistol, the Bar Pistole of 1898. Chambered for a special 7mm cartridge, few Bar pistols are seen today.

by
Hans
Joachim
Tillig

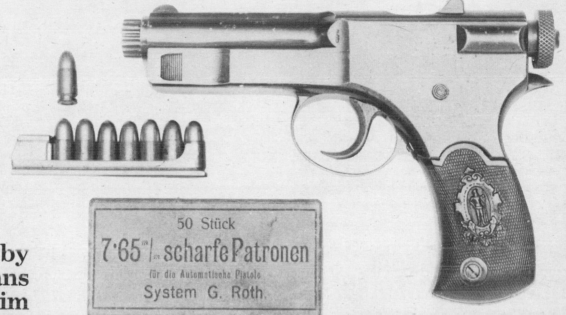

Sauer's first self-loading pistol, the Roth-Sauer of 1903. Note special short 7.65mm cartridge and charger.

THE ARMS company of J.P. Sauer & Sohn, founded in 1751, is surely the oldest sporting arms company in Germany. Though in early times Sauer must have produced some military arms, it is for the company's fine shotguns and other hunting arms that it has long been known throughout the world. Its first apparent excursion into handgun manufacture came in 1883, when Sauer was one of the contractors for the Reichsrevolver for the German army.

The first handgun Sauer made for commercial sale was the Bar Pistole. A unique design, the Bar Pistole was patented by Burkard Behr of Stuttgart in Switzerland March 4, 1898.

Though it resembles a revolver, the two-barreled Bar Pistole is more accurately called a "turn arm," with two chambers above and two below the "cylinder" axis. The action fires first one chamber and then the second, then the "cylinder" is turned 180 degrees to bring the two remaining loaded chambers to battery.

Sauer's introduction to the automatic pistol market was with the Roth-Sauer, a design of Karel Krnka (a Bohemian) that was patented in Vienna in 1903 by the noted ammunition manufacturer, Georg Roth. The Roth-Sauer was a smaller version of a Roth design that had been tested by the British government in 1900, and incorporates a long recoil locking system. In a long-recoil system the barrel and breech recoil together, then the barrel goes forward permitting the extractor to pull the fired cartridge from the

The Roth-Krnka pistol of 1900, made for British government tests of that year. The Roth-Sauer was developed from this experimental arm.

Very early example of Sauer's Model 1913. Note the complete patent date on the slide, and the small button release for the magazine safety located beneath the safety lever.

Right—Second version of the Model 1913, after the magazine safety had been deleted and a separate rear sight, which also doubled as the release for the takedown knob, had been added. Inset, left shows detail of rear sight/takedown catch.

chamber when it is ejected. The slide then goes forward, allowing the bolt to strip another loaded round from the magazine preparatory for a second shot.

Though the Roth-Sauer was of first quality it never became popular, both because its unique 7.65mm cartridge was not widely distributed and the arm itself was quite complicated. Production, which ran from 1904 to about 1908, totaled only about 3,000 pieces. Sauer did not become a success in the pistol field until 1913, when it introduced a completely new straight blowback design invented by Hans Zehner.

Produced in 7.65mm Browning (32 ACP), Sauer's new pistol was very well accepted because of its compact design and reliability. Accuracy was excellent due to the barrel being fixed to the frame, and mis-

fires were very rare due to its heavy striker.

Though Zehner's design bears a superficial resemblance to the 1907 Savage, the internal mechanism is much different. One unique feature was a lever inside the trigger, which when pushed up would latch the slide to the rear for cleaning or takedown. As with most designs, the 1913 Sauer went through a number of changes during production. The first 3,000 examples had no separate rear sight, but only a groove in the top of the knob at the rear of the slide. This model also had a unique magazine safety, which had its own release knob that had to be pressed after the magazine was inserted or else the trigger would still remain blocked. This "oversafe" feature was deleted after about 7,000 pistols were made. Further

Third version of the Model 1913, showing the modified safety.

First model of the Sauer 25 caliber pistol, introduced in 1919.

Second version of the 25, showing the safety modification. The slide catch inside the top of the trigger guard, which holds the slide back for cleaning or takedown, is clearly visible.

Final version of the original 25, with the new style safety which also doubles as a slide catch.

modifications of the 7.65mm pistol were also made in early production, chiefly concerning the safety and takedown.

In the turbulent days following World War I there was a great increase in demand for compact pocket pistols, particularly in 6.35mm (25 ACP). As did many other manufacturers, Sauer scaled down its 32 and introduced a 25 caliber version in 1919. Looking almost exactly like its bigger brother, the 25 was an immediate success. After the first 15,000 or so, the safety modifications added earlier to the 32 were made to the 25. Then, in 1926, the safety was further revised to provide capability to hold the slide open for cleaning. Serial numbers of this final version range from about 45000 to 65000, where production ended.

In 1920, shortly after the 25 caliber version of the 32 Sauer was introduced, the company brought out an entirely new and smaller 25 caliber pistol. Known simply as the "Kleiner Modell" in company literature and later as the "WTM" (*Westen Taschen Modell*, or "Vest Pocket Model"), the new arm was only 112mm long and featured an entirely new takedown system. Unfortunately for Sauer, it was introduced at the same time as Walther's even smaller Model 9 and thus did not do well on the market against the Walther offering. After only about 10,000 were produced, it was replaced in the Sauer line with an even smaller model, only 102mm long. Closely resembling the Model 9 except for its partially covered barrel, the Model 28 became Sauer's most successful 25 caliber pistol. A covered slide variation of the Model 28 was also made, but apparently in few numbers as examples are rarely found.

Production on the 32 caliber model also continued through the 1920s, with the slide holdopen capability added to the safety at about serial 166000. Then, in 1930, a updated version of the original 1913 pistol was introduced. An improved, broader, more "hand-filling" grip frame was added that not only made the pistol more comfortable to grasp and shoot, but also considerably improved its appearance. A magazine safety (of more conventional design) and cocking indicator were also added, and—as shown in the Modell 1930's patent drawings—a one-piece trigger bar was used. Serial numbers of this improved model started at 180000, leaving an apparent gap of 10,000 from the end of earlier production.

At almost the same time that the improved Model 1930 came on the market a further refinement, termed the *Behorden* ("Official") *Modell,* also appeared. Its special feature was a unique miniature trigger placed in the front edge of the regular trigger. Unless this tiny "grip safety" was pushed, the trigger was locked and the gun could not be fired. However, since it is almost impossible to pull the trigger without also pressing the "grip safety," it's hard to see what practical value this device really had. The cocking indicator was also replaced by a much more sensible loaded chamber indicator in the Behorden Modell.

Left—Sauer's first "Kleinen Modell" 25, introduced in 1920.

Above—Sauer's second "vest pocket" model, a redesign of the 1920 pistol directly competitive to Walther's Model 9.

Final version of the "Kleinen Modell," with the barrel entirely covered by the slide. Made in very small numbers.

Very late Model 1913, showing the combination safety lever/slide catch originally introduced on the 25 caliber pistol.

The trigger safety was apparently not too popular, and a number of later Behorden Modells are found without that feature.

But this model has a much better trigger action, because of a new two-piece trigger bar. The front part is an interrupter and the rear part is the sear. Except for the serial number, it is not possible to distinguish a Behorden Modell (without the safety trigger) from the earlier Modell 1930. Subsequent Behorden production seems to have had an inordinate number of other variations, as well. Both smooth and checkered sight ribs, fixed and adjustable front sights, and even a few examples made of duraluminum are to be found. At least one example in 22 and one in 9mm Browning short (380 ACP) calibers are also known.

Despite its many variations, the 1930 or Behorden Modell Sauers never achieved great success on the market. Unfortunately, again for Sauer, its new offering arrived at the same time as Walther's revolutionary double action PP and PPK.

Sauer's development engineers determined that they would not only meet Walther's challenge, but better it. By 1938 they'd succeeded, with a double action pocket pistol with an inside hammer. This feature answered one of the chief objections to the Walther design, whose external hammer let dust and dirt into its action and also was prone to catch in the pocket while being drawn. To provide manual cocking and uncocking of the hammer Sauer provided an ingenious manual cocking lever, a real milestone in

Left and right—Very early example of the Model 1930, clearly showing the hook of the safety that served as a slide latch. Some Model 1930s were purchased for official use in the Netherlands, and this example is marked "JOH.MUNTS-AMSTERDAM" on the slide.

"Behorden Modell" 1930 pistol. Note the tiny "grip safety" in the front of the trigger.

Below—Top view of two Model 1930 slides, showing differences in front sights and sight ribs.

Lightweight "Behorden Modell," with both frame and slide made of duraluminum and so marked.

Very early Modell 38, among the first several thousand that were made without safety lever and sold commercially.

Later Modell 38, as made for the German government with the slide-mounted safety lever.

One of the very few Modell 38s in 22 caliber.

pistol design. Since the pistol was "safe" with the hammer uncocked, the cocking/uncocking lever was considered by Sauer to be the only safety needed.

Sauer started production of its new pistol, the Modell 38, without any safety lever at serial 260001, but the authorities demanded a safety on an auto pistol so Sauer added this device at about serial 263000.

The Modell 38 startup at serial 260001 again left an appreciable serial gap between it and the 1930/Behorden Modell, which ended production at about serial 230000. Finish and fit of the early Modell 38 was of the highest, as would be expected from a company whose sporting arms were considered among the finest in the world. With World War II looming, however, relatively few examples reached the civi-

lian market. Starting with serial number 268469, Sauer Modell 38 production was taken for police and army use.

The Modell 38 was very popular in the German service, and before the war ended 250,000 of them were built for service use. As the war progressed fit and finish deteriorated, and a few late examples (above serial 465000) were made without a safety just as the early type had been.

Sauer remains today a respected name in firearms design and manufacture as it has been for over 200 years. Though pistols were never Sauer's major product, and despite the devastation of two World Wars, the company had produced about three-quarters of a million pistols—a remarkable number of which are still in use—when World War II ended.   •

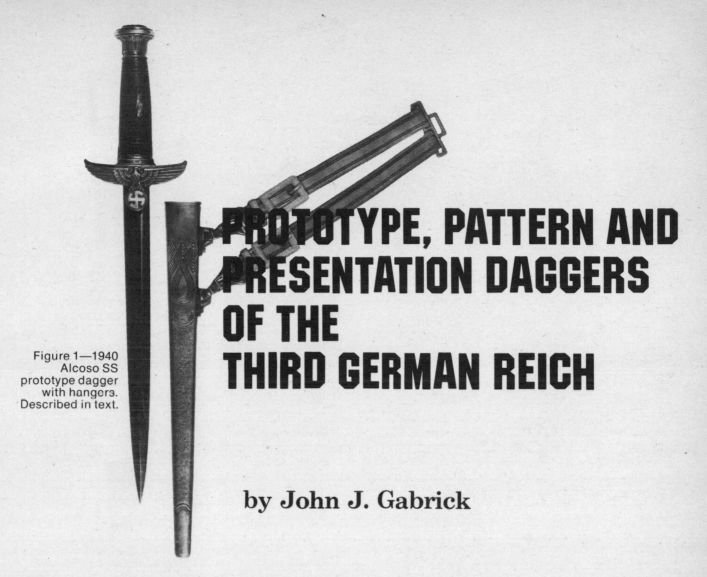

PROTOTYPE, PATTERN AND PRESENTATION DAGGERS OF THE THIRD GERMAN REICH

Figure 1—1940 Alcoso SS prototype dagger with hangers. Described in text.

by John J. Gabrick

Although a great deal has been published regarding the many blades of the Third Reich, relatively little has been written about the prototype or pattern one-of-a-kind pieces that were spawned during that period. Part of the reason for this lack of the written word relating to this type of dagger, is the dearth of information concerning these pieces. Consideration of prototypes or patterns was generally restricted to high-ranking factory officials, usually in concert with Nazi party or military leaders. The results of their discussions and the ensuing dagger designs were therefore not widely publicized, and surviving factory officials from the Nazi era have exhibited a remarkable unwillingness (or inability) to discuss any of the items which arose out of these meetings.

Many collector/researchers of the Third Reich period have been disappointed at receiving a very general reply (usually in German) from a factory in response to a question about a certain blade of their manufacture. I can only say that such an experience is akin to opening that long-awaited special gift on Christmas day and finding something other than what you wanted. Unfortunately, most of the people who were active in the German edged weapons factories during the Third Reich period are either deceased, retired or unapproachable. There seems to be an understandable unwillingness to show any strong connection with the Hitler years.

However, all is not as bleak as the above would indicate. Certain author/researchers have been quite successful in ferreting out information about some of these exotic daggers, and the information that they have provided has been of great value to other collectors and researchers. Probably the most successful of these has been Lt. Col. Atwood, who wrote the first authoritative work on Third Reich blades. Of no small importance to his work was the fact that a much larger number of the people active during those years were still available when Atwood did his research.

I wish I could say that this article will dispel all the lack of knowledge of these exotic daggers, but alas I

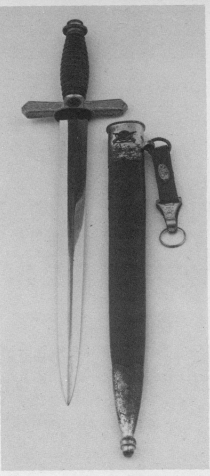

Figure 2—1933-34 Eickhorn navy prototype dagger. Described in text.

Figure 3—1935-36 Shooting Association prototype dagger with hanger. Described in text.

Figure 4—1933-34 Eickhorn Nazi Party prototype dagger. Described in text.

cannot. I can however, provide some interesting theories and photographs of unusually exciting pieces that it has been my pleasure to acquire over many years of collecting WWII German daggers. Webster defines prototype as: the original from which anything is formed; the first thing of its kind; a pattern; exemplar; archtype. In discussing some of the pieces in this article, I am not sure the word "prototype" really applies. I think you might agree as we proceed further.

SS Prototype

The first piece is probably the most exciting Nazi dagger find to be uncovered in recent years (Fig. 1). This is the SS Prototype dagger made by Alcoso. This piece was covered extensively in an earlier reference work, but it is of such significance no article on prototype Nazi daggers would be complete without it. The dagger was purchased from the nephew of the man who brought it back from the war, along with another SS dagger, a Himmler presentation dagger. As a child, the man I purchased the daggers from had played with both by throwing them at trees. Unfor-

tunately, this abuse had shattered the handle on the Himmler piece and knocked a rune from the handle of the prototype. Fortunately, when he realized he'd lost the rune from the handle of the prototype it was hastily put away, and remained safely in storage until about 3 years ago.

The dagger is rather large and would compare in size roughly to a Teno Sr. dagger. The handle is a dark brown celluloid and the fittings are cast from a heavy alloy and plated. Overall the piece has a very massive appearance, and it is rather heavy. I suspect that this piece was made about the same time that Krebs submitted its SS prototype for acceptance and both were rejected for the same reasons. (A rapidly deteriorating war situation and resultant shortages of basic materials.) There are some strong basic similarities in size and general shape between the Krebs and Alcoso prototypes; the Krebs prototype dagger has not been found to date.

Eickhorn Navy Prototype

A second noteworthy example is the Eickhorn Navy prototype of about 1933-1934 (Fig. 2). This

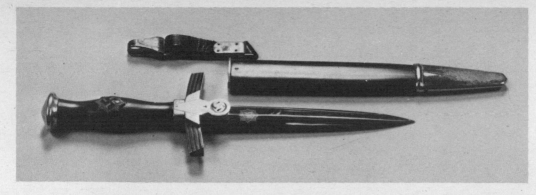

Figure 5 (left)—1938-40 RLB Subordinate's dagger, prototype, with hanger. Described in text.

Figure 6 (below)—E&F Horster 1934 Army prototype dagger. Described in text.

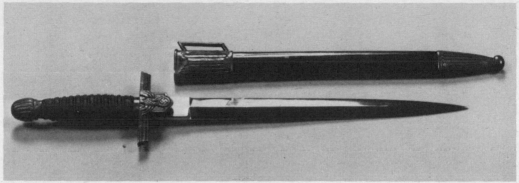

Figure 7 (right)—Eickhorn special presentation dagger, made for Baron Mannerheim following the pact between Germany and Finland. Notice the orientation of the Finnish swastika on the handguard, which stands flat, as opposed to the German swastika which stands on end.

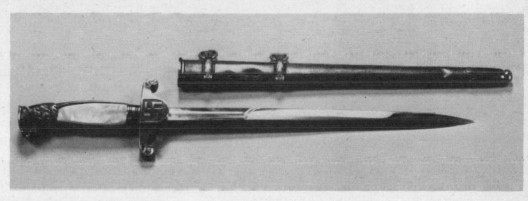

piece was made by the firm of Carl Eickhorn, the most prolific Third Reich blade manufacturer. Eickhorn made more prototype, one-of-a-kind, honor and special interest daggers than any other firm during that time period. This Eickhorn Navy dagger was purchased in Germany from a former employee of the Eickhorn firm who had apparently "liberated" the piece at some time during his employment there. Like the SS, it is a very massive piece, and quite possibly, the single most beautiful dagger of this period which I have seen. The reason that it was not accepted is quite apparent upon examining the dagger. It bears a strong resemblance to Imperial daggers of recent vintage and is absolutely devoid of the revered Nazi swastika. The pommel is a hand-worked Imperial crown sitting on a pillow with tassels hanging from all four corners. The handle is four-sided brass and is inlaid with real mother-of-pearl. The crossguard is two swans hand done and facing in opposite directions with a brass spacer. Each piece of

the handle is scored so that the dagger cannot be put together incorrectly. The blade bears the standard navy "fouled-anchor" etching on both sides. The scabbard is unique, bearing a Weimar eagle stamped into the front. Although the piece is extremely beautiful, the lack of a swastika doomed this design before it ever made the marketplace.

Shooting Association Dagger

The third described dagger (Fig. 3), shows the versatility and inherent frugality of the German people. It is a prototype of a Shooting Association dagger probably made around 1935 or 1936. The piece is largely made up of parts from the first model Luft dagger and the DLV/NSFK flier's knife. The blade is of the first model Luft type as is the handle. The handle differs only in that the leather wrap is dyed a green color. The pommel is of the NSFK type, but the crossguard is a totally unique and different piece with oak leaves engraved on the crossguard with a

center bearing a black enameled swastika as in the NSFK type. The scabbard is first Luft with an NSFK type hanger. All leather parts are dyed green. The top scabbard fitting bears a crossed rifle and bullseye badge which is soldered onto the scabbard fitting. Apparently, someone figured that if their design would be accepted, they would be ready to go into production almost immediately, having only to produce the crossguard from scratch. Apparently the people from the Shooting Association were less than impressed with the attempt and did not approve the dagger for production.

Nazi Party Prototype

Another Eickhorn piece, previously pictured in an earlier reference work, is the Nazi Party prototype dagger (Fig. 4). The handle and scabbard are covered with a brown leather, the handle having a gold-wire wrap. All the fittings are gold-plated aluminum. The time of manufacture is set around 1934 due to the hallmark used on the piece. Because of the gold and brown coloring, I would judge that the piece was intended for use by high-ranking party members. A letter to the Eickhorn factory in 1970 yielded only the admission that their firm had indeed produced this piece in about 1934 and no further information was available as their files had been destroyed. The letter was short, concise and completely without other useful information.

RLB Subordinate's Dagger

The next dagger is a very interesting variation of the 1938 RLB subordinate's dagger (Fig. 5). The blade was manufactured by Ernst Erich Witte, a very prominent maker of RLB blades. It differs from the standard dagger in size as well as general features. The blade is of a size more usually found on the NSFK dagger. The obverse of the blade is engraved with the

Figure 8 (above)—Eickhorn special presentation dagger, probably made for a high-ranking Rumanian official. Handle is of silver, peened over on the top and scribed with eagle feathers to match the handle. Period is 1941-1945.

Figure 9 (below)—Unattributed Nazi period dagger, probably made by a student at a trade school. Pommel bears a swastika as does top of scabbard. Slip-on hanger was lost from scabbard over years by veteran who brought it back.

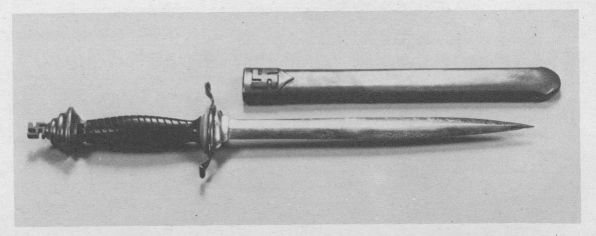

early-type RLB logo (RLB in sunburst over small swastika) and the reverse has a very deeply etched Witte hallmark. The crossguards are reminiscent of the leader crossguards, except they are much shorter and curved slightly downward. The swastika on the crossguard is of black enamel. The grip is a little smaller than usual, and is made of ebony. It bears the second style RLB logo. The pommel bears a resemblance to the officer's pommel except that it is smaller and much heavier. The entire piece is cast of a heavy metal and is much heavier than the regular 1938 RLB subordinate's dagger. Date of manufacture of this piece is probably around 1938-40.

Prototype Army Dagger

Finally, a dagger by E&F Horster, manufactured about 1934, which I feel is a prototype of the Army dagger (Fig. 6). I make this statement because of the style of manufacture and the type of materials used in its construction. The handle is wood, covered with sharkskin, all fittings are machined from brass and the scabbard is painted with black enamel. All this sounds very much like the construction of the Army swords of that period, and it is very likely that whoever designed the piece, did so by using the Army sword as a pattern. The estimated date of manufacture would be right about the time various companies would have been submitting designs for approval for the Army dagger, which was approved in 1935. The reasons why this piece was turned down are pretty obvious. Aside from the fact that it lacked pizzaz, it was just too heavy to carry for any length of time. A much more practical and aesthetically pleasing design was approved and subsequently put into production.

Aside from the pieces detailed within this article, my personal collection includes several other "prototype" or one-of-a-kind presentation pieces. There are also other pieces in the hands of other collectors which have been documented over the years. These include prototypes of Red Cross, NSKK, Army, Reichsmarshall and other pieces not, as yet, photographed or written about. In recent years, collectors have enjoyed a bonanza of exciting one-of-a-kind and prototype pieces which have "come out of the woodwork." There are still other pieces yet to be discovered as evidenced by the fact of the recent discovery of an Army/Field Marshall dagger which is currently in possession of a prominent midwestern collector. There are still some exciting finds to be made: daggers currently nestling in forgotten trunks or other hiding places in attics and garages just waiting for some lucky soul to discover them.

A small word of caution is in order at this point. There are always a few unscrupulous individuals who seek to profit from the sale of made-up spurious and fantasy-type pieces. The collector without a great deal of expertise in this type of blade should seek the counsel of someone a little more schooled in Nazi-era blades before parting with hard-earned dollars for something exotic which could turn out to be a clever fake. Fortunately the vast majority of collectors and dealers are scrupulously honest and willing to stand behind their merchandise, therefore cutting down on the chances of getting taken.

So, take heart all of you collectors out there; somewhere in an attic or a garage there's waiting a bladed treasure, as yet undiscovered, that will make even the most callous and worldly of us flush with excitement when you finally find it and proudly display it at a forthcoming show! •

AUTHOR'S NOTE: Thanks to Juergen Bauck of Winter Haven, Florida, for all photography except for Figure 1, taken by Tom Dunaway of Tallahassee. All daggers illustrated are from the author's collection.

Figure 10—1934 SMF Police Dress parade bayonet prototype. Handles are of cast aluminum and have a swastika cast into the obverse. All fittings on bayonet and scabbard are heavily chrome plated.

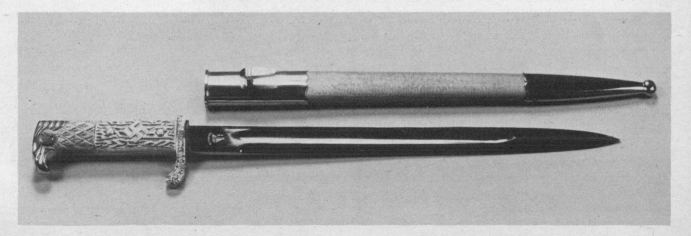

EUROPEAN REVOLVERS...

by Joseph J. Schroeder

IN THE PAST 3 YEARS I've been fortunate enough to make three gun collecting visits to Europe: the first trip as a guest exhibitor at Fred Datig's Swiss Lucern Waffenbourse in April, and the other two trips leading a small group of American collectors who wanted to see what gun collecting was like on the other side of the Atlantic. Although I found a number of European collectors who shared my passion for self-loading pistols, I couldn't help but notice an even larger number whose interest was in late 19th century and early 20th century cartridge revolvers.

After examining the collections and examples offered for sale at both the Lucern show and the week-later London Arms Fair, plus the displays at the various museums and Enfield Lock, I found a fascination with the variety and historical significance in these (to us) neglected arms that I'd never dreamed was there. For a collector whose idea of revolvers had been limited to top-breaks and side swingers, with a generous dose of the Single Action Army, it was a whole new world.

When I got back to the States I started looking for those odd-ball European revolvers, and I found them. I found big ones and little ones, complicated ones and simple ones, fancy ones and plain ones, and the nice thing about them was they were almost all at low prices. Few collectors on this side of the water seem to have any interest in them and many are for cartridges that can't be bought over here so they can't be sold as shooters. Thus, the collector or dealer who has one he wants to move has to practically give it away to sell it.

With a low priced market and my developing interest, the temptation has been too much. For over a year now I've been buying turn-of-the-century European revolvers when they were priced nicely, and—despite my advice elsewhere in this book—without a great deal of regard as to exactly what they were. As a result I've "collected" a fair number of European revolvers, with an investment that averages well under $100 each, despite a pretty close adherence to my "very good condition or better, or no purchase" policy.

The net result of this new interest is a small but still exciting collecting sideline that's turned out to be educational, as well. It's literally "a whole new field," and when returning home from a show with a couple of these new-found prizes I find I'm very impatient to get out the books to start digging and find out what I've got. It has been an education, too. I've learned things along the way about 19th century European politics that I'd never have dreamed of, and it's been fun, as well.

Though in those days Webley, Tranter and a few others kept the handgun market pretty well supplied in the British Isles, on the continent it was the Belgian gun industry that dominated the market. In my recent acquisitions five out of six are Belgian (as indicated by proof marks), though many of them bear subsequent dealer or government marks from all over the continent. Common origin doesn't mean common design, however: The offerings of the Belgian gunmakers come in all shapes, sizes, calibers, cylinder capacities, and—most interesting—design ideas.

The collector who is interested in plumbing this well of thus far neglected (domestically) handguns would find the going very hard indeed if it were not for some excellent research from across the Atlantic. Books by researchers such as Dowell, Taylorson, Lugs, Boothroyd, Hogg and Weeks contain almost all of the information you will need to identify and classify these 19th and early 20th century cartridge revolvers; Boothroyd's *The Handgun,* Dowell's *The Webley Story* (for Webleys), and all of Taylorson's revolver books are a must if you are at all serious about pursuing these interesting arms. The most valuable domestic coverage is provided by J. Howard Mathews' three volume set, *Firearms Identification,* and a surprising number of these old revolvers will be found in DBI Books' reprint of the 1911 ALFA catalog from Germany, *Arms of the World 1911.*

As will be evident from the accompanying photographs, the one thing that my new mini-collection can boast is variety. As my new acquisitions teach me more and more, I'm beginning to appreciate some of the more subtle differences and developments. It's a shame that these fascinating arms have been so neglected by the U.S. arms collecting fraternity. They deserve better. •

a fertile field for low-budget collecting

Right—A pair of "British Bulldogs," a very frequently found marking and style in late 19th Century European revolvers. A collector on a tight budget could make a career out of collecting British Bulldogs. Both of these examples are Belgian made.

Above—An early Webley, the "W-G" (for Webley-Greener) dated 1889 and marked 476 caliber. Webleys of this vintage are found with both bird's head and conventional gripframes, with either wood or hard rubber grips. Prices on all types of Webleys have been on the rise.

Left—A true sleeper, this large-frame Spanish-made revolver by Trocoala Aranzabal y Cia of Eibar is chambered for 455 Webley and bears British proofs. This establishes it as one of a small group of Spanish revolvers purchased by the British in 1910-17 to meet urgent wartime needs.

This well-traveled revolver was made in Belgium for the Danish Navy, where it was known as the Model 1891. Additional English proofing shows the gun also spent some time in England before ending up in the author's collection.

Continued on next page.

A small (7 inches overall) folding trigger revolver with most intriguing markings. On the right side of the frame is engraved a rope and anchor plus "Cart. 380," while a large crown over AE and the number 1410 is on the left. Undoubtedly a police or government issue gun, but whose? Proofing is Belgian.

Reichsrevolvers rarely come cheap, but these early German service arms may still well be bargains. The longer barreled Modell 1879 (above) is particularly sought after, with those made by Mauser bringing a premium. The shorter barrel Modell 1883 is more common, having been made for the German army by a variety of makers until the turn of the century. Commercial variations of the Modell 1883, some with double action lockwork, are sometimes seen.

One of Webley's most famous revolvers, The Royal Irish Constabulary model is a proper addition to any collection of 19th Century cartridge handguns. This is the very desirable first model of 1867, chambered for the 442 cartridge.

This German made double action revolver, though it closely resembles the Modell 1883 Reichsrevolver, is definitely a commercial product. Its only markings are double crown over U commercial German proofs, and the serial number is 5.

A very unusual pocket revolver, the proofs identify the lower revolver as Belgian. It's a right-hand-opening side-break action, chambered for 8mm Lebel and Marked "LE FORMIDABLE" on its barrel rib. It and its smaller folding trigger companion are both marked "Manufacture Francaise d'Armes & Cycles" on top of their frames, and both appear in the 1911 German ALFA catalogue.

This large frame 450 caliber British revolver is without any markings except British proofs. It looks like a Webley, but has Tranter type lockwork and a Tranter's Patent (1868) ejector rod.

This is one old revolver that won't come cheap. The Mauser "Zig-Zag" Modell 1878 was made in three calibers and only in small numbers. There is also a solid frame version that's even harder to find.

Swiss Model 1882 Service revolver in 7.5mm. 19th century Swiss military arms have never been popular in the United States, but in the last few years they seem to have become somewhat scarce.

Continued on next page.

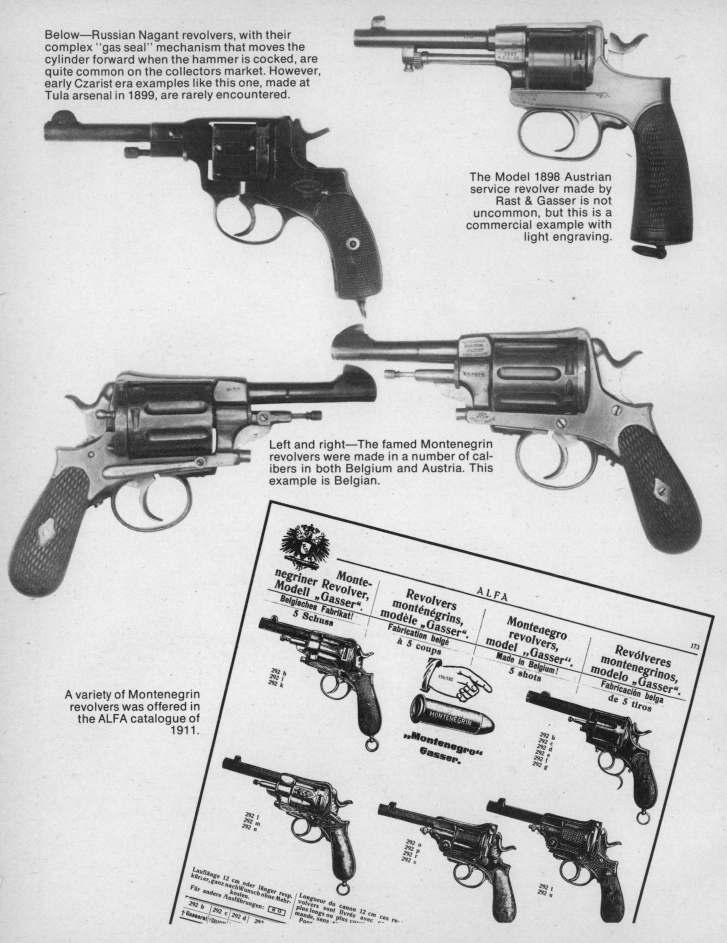

Below—Russian Nagant revolvers, with their complex ''gas seal'' mechanism that moves the cylinder forward when the hammer is cocked, are quite common on the collectors market. However, early Czarist era examples like this one, made at Tula arsenal in 1899, are rarely encountered.

The Model 1898 Austrian service revolver made by Rast & Gasser is not uncommon, but this is a commercial example with light engraving.

Left and right—The famed Montenegrin revolvers were made in a number of calibers in both Belgium and Austria. This example is Belgian.

A variety of Montenegrin revolvers was offered in the ALFA catalogue of 1911.

AUG. FRANCOTTE & C⁰

Revolver mod. 1301 A.

Constable acier.
Poignée noyer, noir ou trempé.
Cart. Lebel, suisse, Nagant ou 380 L.

Revolver mod. 600.

Lincoln cal. 320, 6.35.
Velo-dog.
Poignée fausse ébène,
noir.

Revolver mod. 4 M.

Lincoln Hammerless bossu.
Cartouches 6.35, 7.65, velo-dog,
bronzé noir, poignée fausse ébène.

Revolver mod. 301 N. W.

Imitation Smith et Wesson.

Poignée caoutchouc.

Nickelé ou bronzé.

Se fait en calibre 320,
380, 32 et 38.

Revolver mod. 70 B.

Canon acier, poignée ébène, trempé, bleui.

Cart. 6.35, 7.65, velo-dog
et Lebel.

Revolver mod. 50 H. A. S.
Poignée chêne quadrillé, trempé et
bleui. Se fait en 6.35, 7.65, velo-
dog et Lebel

Revolver mod. 50 H. P.
Puppy poignée ronde, canon
acier, poignée ébène qua-
drillé, avec ou sans sou-
garde. Bleui, incrusté ou
ornementé, trempé et bleui.

Revolver mod. 2763.

Modèle spécial, Hammer-
less démontable.
Jaspé et crosse ébène quadrillé.
Cartouches 6.35, Lebel et
velo-dog.

Above and below—Two pages from a Francotte
catalogue of the 1920s, showing many of the
same revolvers that were offered before the war.

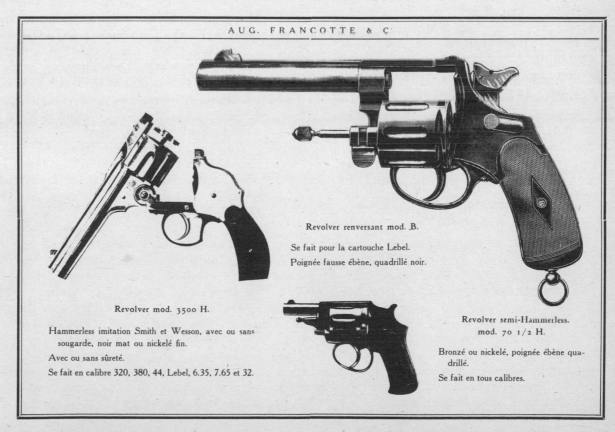

AUG. FRANCOTTE & C

Revolver mod. 3500 H.

Hammerless imitation Smith et Wesson, avec ou sans
sougarde, noir mat ou nickelé fin.

Avec ou sans sûreté.

Se fait en calibre 320, 380, 44, Lebel, 6.35, 7.65 et 32.

Revolver renversant mod. B.

Se fait pour la cartouche Lebel.

Poignée fausse ébène, quadrillé noir.

**Revolver semi-Hammerless.
mod. 70 1/2 H.**

Bronzé ou nickelé, poignée ébène quadrillé.

Se fait en tous calibres.

SOFTWARE vs HARDWARE
A Guide to Building a Gun Library

by Joseph J. Schroeder

"HARDWARE" is the gun, of course, and in this computer age "software" is the buzzword term for information that goes with it. Gun collecting software can come in many forms, almost all of them printed. The collector without software is a suspect collector—perhaps "gatherer" is a better term for him—because it's software that is the cement that holds a collection together and gives it meaning.

Some of the more valuable forms of gun collecting software include:

- Books
- Periodicals
- Factory Instruction Booklets
- Factory Catalogs and Flyers
- Distributor Catalogs and Flyers
- Military Instruction Manuals
- Military Test Reports
- Patents
- Manufacturer or Distributor Records
- Private Correspondence and Records

Any or all of these can provide information vital to a collector's effort to make his collection meaningful. The problem is to find such sources and properly utilize them. Here, arranged by category, are some directions you might take in assembling your gun software library.

Books

It should go without saying that you should own every book you can find that includes worthwhile information on your collecting specialty. If you are into Colts, Winchesters, Lugers, Walthers, Smith & Wessons or other popular fields this should not pose much of a problem (except to your pocketbook, and no matter how much you spend on useful literature it's bound to be a worthwhile collecting investment). However, whether yours is a well published or little appreciated specialty you're still faced with the problem of finding those needed books.

One way of keeping up with current releases is to read the reviews in gun periodicals. Some reviews are quite valuable as indicators of the quality of a book as well as its subject. A signed review is almost always better this way, as an unsigned review is more likely to be the publisher's release which, though it should be a good guide to the book's contents, is not likely to criticize it! Publisher's and bookseller's ads are another good place to watch for new releases as well as sales on older titles.

If your local bookstore or gun shop has a gun book section, plan to stop in and check it out every week or two. Some stores only order a few copies of a new title, and a new arrival could move right off the shelf before you ever saw it if you don't keep your eyes open. Shopping the book sellers has another distinct advantage, too. You can look through the new arrivals before laying your money out. The same advantage pertains to gun show book shopping, as well. Almost every gun show boasts at least one book dealer, and even though he may not have all his stock at any given show he likely will be happy to bring a title you want to see to the next show.

Watch book sales. Some very good gun books have been sold by book discount houses recently, often at prices a fraction of their original published price. Even the regular book stores have been getting into the discount business, with a "Bargain Table" of mixed titles for their customers to paw through.

Out-of-print books pose a special problem. There are a lot of very important gun books that simply aren't available from their publishers any more. However, there are very few that can't be found if the seeker is patient and willing to pay the price. Some dealers specialize in out-of-print books and, if they don't have what you want, will put you on their waiting list for the next copy that turns up. Gun shows are a great place to buy bargains in both out-of-print and current books. Some collectors sell books when their interests change or bookshelf space gets tight, often

A sampling of currently available arms periodicals.

at prices well below current market.

It pays to buy gun books even when they don't bear directly on your specialty. I'll readily admit that there are a lot of books in my gun library that I've never read, but I don't think there are any that I've never *used*. I buy *every* gun book with information about my specialty, early self-loading (automatic) pistols, but I also buy every gun book on any subject when I see it at a bargain price. It's surprising how often some of those bargain non-related books have yielded valuable information!

Periodicals

Periodicals are a sort of lifeblood to the collector. Through them he can tap the knowledge of a wide variety of fellow enthusiasts, without the long lead times that characterize book publication. They are also a rather painless way to broaden collecting horizons, by exposing him to the knowledge and experience of collectors with a wide range of interests. This same variety can be considered a drawback, of course, as no matter how broadly your collecting interest is shared, no publication is going to have something on it in every issue.

Which periodicals are best for you is something you'll have to decide for yourself. The thumbnail sketches found in the article on periodicals elsewhere in this book can provide some general guidance, of course, but the only proper way is to check out a number of issues and see if they include enough of what you're looking for to justify the subscription price. For a few magazines this is not too difficult, as they're widely available in newsstands. For the others you may be able to borrow some copies from friends, find them in a library or gun show (cheap!), or simply take the advice of fellow collectors.

It doesn't take long until storage of and access to periodicals becomes a problem. Many collectors make a card file of articles of interest, then store the magazines in chronological order where they can be ac-

cessed when needed. Others simply clip and file key articles and discard the magazine, but this approach is not recommended as other information you may need in the future will no longer be available. If magazine articles are to be filed, it is better to photocopy them and leave the magazines intact. Many magazines publish an index of each year's contents. A file of those indexes provides a quick and comprehensive reference to that publication's contents.

In addition to current periodicals you'll also be interested in older publications with useful articles. These are often available at shows very reasonably, or at used book shops.

Don't ignore the foreign gun publications. Some are truly outstanding, and all offer a perspective that can literally enrich the horizons of almost any collector. Those in foreign languages offer a special problem, of course, but for the collector with ability in another language these publications can be particularly rewarding.

Factory Instruction Booklets

In today's market these have truly become collectibles in their own right. Almost every firearm originally came with some sort of instruction booklet or sheet describing its operation and maintenance, but all too often these instructions were thrown away once the arm was mastered. As a result, most such literature is much rarer than the arm it accompanied.

In addition to its value as a collectible, a factory manual often contains related information that can prove extremely valuable to a collector. Since a manual should be available for the first commercial shipments of a new gun, the illustrations will often show a very early or even prototype example of that arm. Manuals will often refer to obscure other models or little-known special order features that might otherwise go unnoticed. Manuals can also help in dating a gun. They often bear a code marking, indicating the date and quantity published. The

Factory manuals come in all sizes and shapes.

manual for Mauser's famed Model 1896 Broomhandle, for example, contained a reference in its opening paragraph to the number of Mauser pistols then in service. That number was updated every time the manual was reprinted, thus providing clues as to the date of certain design changes.

Finding desirable old manuals can be very difficult. Though at almost every gun show there's at least one pile of old literature on someone's table, it's only luck when something in the pile belongs in your collection. Nevertheless, it is worth looking for. Like the old gold prospector, you may not find a nugget very often but when you do it's worth a celebration!

Gun shops are a possible source of such literature. Some years ago an old gun shop went out of business in Chicago, and stashed away in the dust of the basement were dozens of manuals for various German pistols of the 1920s and 30s . . . They were all in German, of course, so the proprietor had carefully removed them from the boxes when he'd imported the guns to sell to American buyers many decades ago!

Reprints are another source that's worth exploiting. In recent years a number of the more desirable and historically significant manuals have been reprinted, and though they may not provide the same collecting satisfaction as an original they do provide the same information and are a lot cheaper. Just one caution: don't let someone sell you a good reproduction as an original!

Factory Catalogs and Flyers

Much that's been said about factory manuals also pertains to this type of factory literature. It often turns up at gun shows, and a number of collectors even do a brisk business in it. As you begin to build a library of factory literature, you'll undoubtedly find other collectors who're doing the same thing. Make it a practice to make photocopies and do some swapping with them. The copies won't even be as elegant as reproductions are, but the information they contain will be worth every bit as much. Some sales literature is quite colorful, and can provide a nice decorative touch to a gun room or den when framed.

Distributor Catalogs and Flyers

Distributor literature rarely covers any given maker's guns in as much depth as factory literature, but offers another avenue of research that's very valuable in its own right. Since a distributor by definition handles the products of a number of makers, his literature provides a much more balanced overview of the gun—and gun accessory—market at any given time. For example, most manufacturers stop pushing a model shortly after production ends, but distributors will keep pushing that model until their stock is used up. This generally is a matter of at least several years, but it's not unusual to find some guns being offered for sale a decade or more after they were discontinued.

As with factory literature, some of the more interesting distributor catalogs are now being reproduced for the collector's market. Original or reproduction, these form a most valuable part of a gun collector's library.

Military Instruction Manuals

Military instruction manuals are often more devoted to tactics than to information of great value to the collector. Nevertheless, they are well worth having if only as an appropriate accessory for a military issue arm. Like the factory manual, a military manual will often provide insights into limited use special modifications of a given arm, and they are inevitably a good source of maintenance information and details of the appropriate issue accessories.

Military manuals are often available from dealers who specialize in military surplus—many of them at very low prices. Some of the rarer and more informative manuals, both domestic and foreign, have been reproduced for the collector's market. The quality of some of these reproductions is marginal at best (though some of the originals wouldn't win any graphic arts prizes, either), but if they are at least readable and reasonably priced, they shouldn't be passed up.

NOTE: Some reproductions were printed in very limited quantity, to take care of what was perceived as a small potential market. As a result they may be available for only a short time, after which the prices will climb—when and if they can be found at all. When a reproduction that fits in your collection turns up don't hesitate too long to buy it. If you do, you may well do without!

Military Test Reports

Every government at one time or another tests firearms. They may do so as a highly organized, well-publicized program leading to the adoption of a new issue arm, or simply as a means of keeping abreast of current arms developments. Such tests go into government records and eventually the archives, where they await discovery by the resolute researcher.

Many of these reports have been utilized by various authors in the past, with details of their contents or even excerpts from them appearing in various gun books and articles. Locating the original sources is often a task of considerable magnitude, though some such government reports may sometimes be found in the largest public libraries. Finding them is generally, however, a task for the advanced researcher.

Patents

Patents provide a very fruitful source of information on guns that is too often overlooked by the collector. A patent will include some details about the designer, pertinent dates of his invention, often references to related designs he's borrowed from, and even—as in the case of the Schrader pistols discussed elsewhere in these pages—the identification of an otherwise unknown arm. Copies of the patents themselves are easy to get if you have the right information. If you don't, they can be very difficult to locate.

The key to getting a copy of a U.S. patent is the patent number, and for a British patent the number and year it was issued. If you have the patent number a copy of the patent can be ordered from the U.S. Patent Office for a nominal fee. The problem lies with getting that number.

Some patented objects actually bear the patent number. In some cases instruction books or sales literature will list the patents that apply to that model. More often only the date of the patent is provided, but that is at least a starting point for your search. The public libraries in most major cities have patent indexes and/or patent files, as do the libraries of most technical schools. Using these facilities it's not a difficult task to locate a patent number and sometimes a copy of the patent itself, which can then be photocopied for study. Not too long ago it was not unusual to order a patent from the Patent Office and receive one of the original printed copies that was prepared at the time of issuance, even back into the late 19th century. Not any more. The supply of old originals seems to have dried up, and the Patent Office is supplying Xerox copies that vary from excellent to indifferent in quality. As with other non-original copies, however, the information is still there and very well worth having. Patents are a key part of the collector's software, well worth the effort to find.

Manufacturer And Distributor Records

All manufacturers and dealers maintain records. In earlier times it was simply a matter of good business, and more recently it has been a matter of government regulation. These records can be priceless sources for the collector. They can tell when (and often to whom) a given arm was shipped, and what if any special features it may have had.

Some manufacturers have an active program to support collectors in their search for historical information. Such a program costs them money, so it's not uncommon to pay some nominal fee for a search for information on a given gun. The resultant factory letter is a very good investment, however, increasing that gun's value both as a part of your collection and if you later decide to put it on the market.

Distributors pose more of a problem. In general they are not set up to allow access to their records, particularly those early enough to be of real interest to the collector/researcher. They are also likely to be sensitive to making such information available, on the grounds that it violates the privacy of their customers. Nonetheless, a low key approach by a researcher with known credentials may often succeed in opening up such records where others have failed. It can never hurt to try, but be well prepared before making your approach. Even the most public-spirited, collector-oriented distributor is not going to open his books for a fishing expedition.

Private Correspondence and Records

This is an area that both requires a lot of luck (to find really significant papers) and covers a lot of ground. Over the years a good deal of correspondence from key people in the gun business has surfaced and more is being generated all the time. The problem is locating it, and sometimes in recognizing it for what it is.

Any letter signed by George Luger or Samuel Colt is obviously of collector interest, no matter what the subject. Not every letter on DWM or Colt company stationery has such historical value, though some certainly do. Some such materials do turn up at gun shows on occasion and are well worth watching for. More often they are in private hands, and over a period of time their locations can be ferreted out.

Summing Up

It's hard to imagine a gun collector having too large a gun library. It's been said that knowledge is not so much *what* you know as it is knowing *where* to find what you need to know when you need to know it. To that I'd like to add the necessity for having that information conveniently at hand so you can find it *when* you need it.

Years ago, when I was still in college and just a neophyte collector, an old-school dealer/collector told me to buy a book every time I bought a gun if I ever intended becoming a serious collector. That was good advice then and even better advice today. Follow it! •

Collecting the ABCs... the Suicide Special from A to Z (almost)

by **FRANK M. SELLERS**

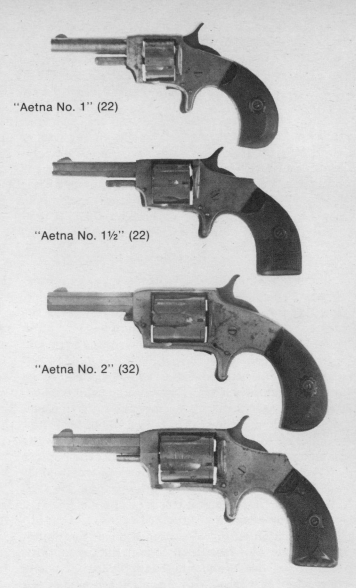

"Aetna No. 1" (22)

"Aetna No. 1½" (22)

"Aetna No. 2" (32)

Fig. 1. Just one name can form a mini-collection when you're dealing with stud-trigger revolvers. Harrington & Richardson's names for their Aetnas indicated both caliber ("1" for 22, "2" for 32) and the grip style.

ONE OF THE more neglected fields of antique gun collecting is that of the "Suicide Special," specifically those cheap (at the time they were made), single action, spur trigger revolvers so popular during the late 19th century. Coming on the market after Rollin White's patent (on bored-through cylinders) expired in 1869, these diminutive pocket revolvers were made by a myriad of manufacturers through the end of the century.

Aside from a scattering of articles in various magazines and two books, Donald Webster's *Suicide Specials* (1958) and W. Barlow Fors' *Collector's Handbook of U.S. Cartridge Revolvers, 1856-1899* (1973), there's been very little published on this fertile field.

Taken together, all of these efforts do little more than scratch the surface.

This article does not pretend to be the in-depth study of the subject, either. Such a study, involving hundreds of guns carrying almost as many different names, more than a hundred patents, dozens of manufacturers and almost as many distributors, is a suitable subject for a sizeable book. Instead, this article will outline the subject, including a list of names found on these guns and some brief descriptions of their major manufacturers.

As the title of the article implies, one way to collect suicide specials is by name, alphabetically. I've collected and photographed some whose names start

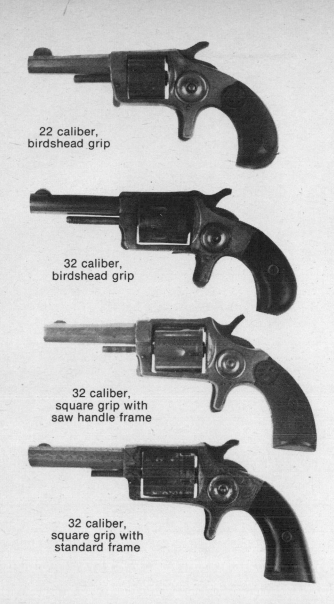

22 caliber,
birdshead grip

32 caliber,
birdshead grip

32 caliber,
square grip with
saw handle frame

32 caliber,
square grip with
standard frame

Fig. 2. Another group from one maker, the "Marquis of Lorne" by T.E. Ryan, shows variations in both size and grip style which are not distinguished by their designations.

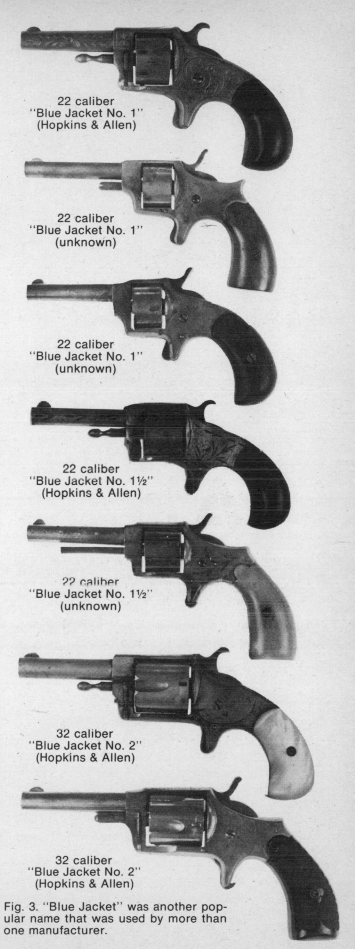

22 caliber
"Blue Jacket No. 1"
(Hopkins & Allen)

22 caliber
"Blue Jacket No. 1"
(unknown)

22 caliber
"Blue Jacket No. 1"
(unknown)

22 caliber
"Blue Jacket No. 1½"
(Hopkins & Allen)

22 caliber
"Blue Jacket No. 1½"
(unknown)

32 caliber
"Blue Jacket No. 2"
(Hopkins & Allen)

32 caliber
"Blue Jacket No. 2"
(Hopkins & Allen)

Fig. 3. "Blue Jacket" was another popular name that was used by more than one manufacturer.

with every letter of the alphabet except "Q," "Y," and "Z," and Fors' book holds out hope that some day I may find at least a "Q" or a "Y." Another challenge might be limiting one's efforts to guns whose name starts with a single letter of the alphabet. As the list that follows shows: "B," "C," "R," "S," would offer the greatest opportunity for that collection. Still another approach might be the seeking out of guns bearing the same name. I've located over 30 "Defenders," for example, and nearly as many "Blue Jackets," "Red Jackets" and "Robin Hoods." Or you might simply collect all the different guns made by a single manufacturer. The possibilities in the suicide special field are limited only by the imagination of the collector.

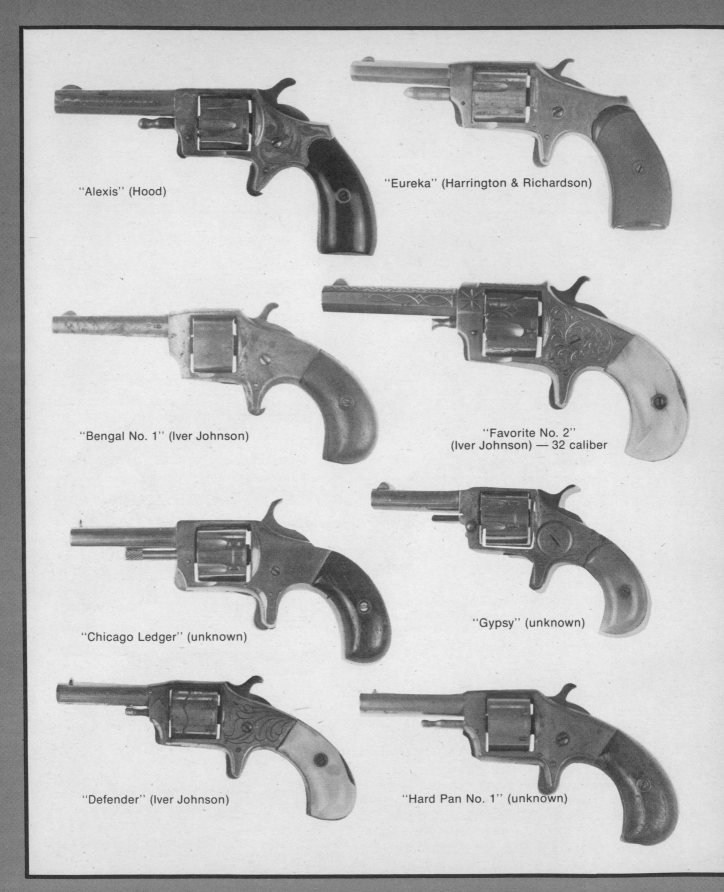

"Alexis" (Hood)

"Eureka" (Harrington & Richardson)

"Bengal No. 1" (Iver Johnson)

"Favorite No. 2"
(Iver Johnson) — 32 caliber

"Chicago Ledger" (unknown)

"Gypsy" (unknown)

"Defender" (Iver Johnson)

"Hard Pan No. 1" (unknown)

Fig. 4. Perhaps the greatest challenge for the collector of 19th century solid frame, stud-trigger revolvers is to assemble a complete alphabet of them. Here's what I've managed so far, all but two of them 22s. Can you help fill the blanks?

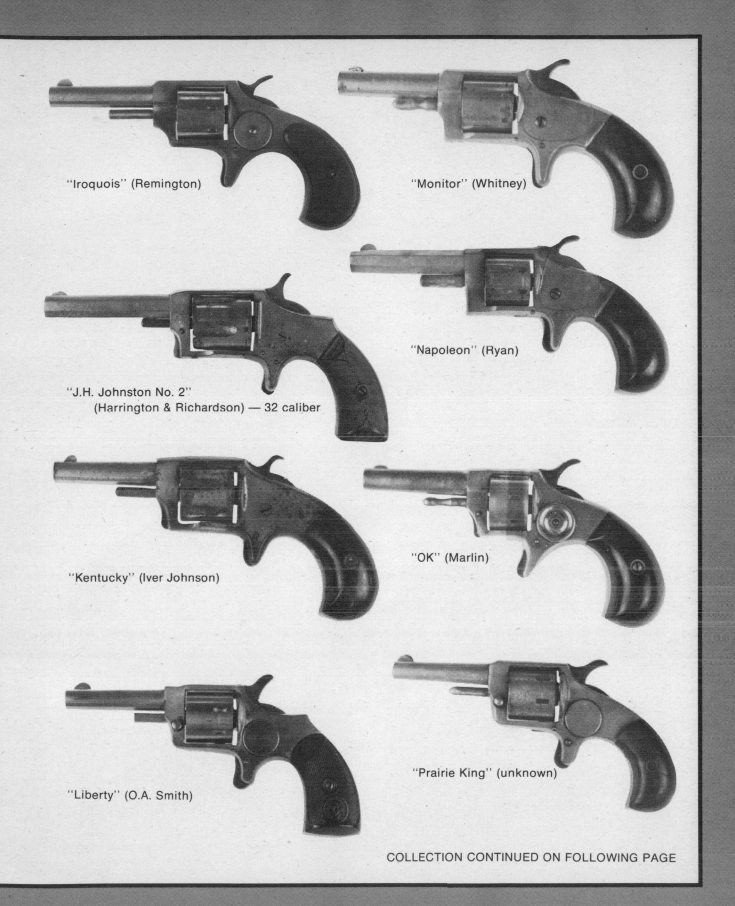

"Iroquois" (Remington)

"Monitor" (Whitney)

"J.H. Johnston No. 2" (Harrington & Richardson) — 32 caliber

"Napoleon" (Ryan)

"Kentucky" (Iver Johnson)

"OK" (Marlin)

"Liberty" (O.A. Smith)

"Prairie King" (unknown)

COLLECTION CONTINUED ON FOLLOWING PAGE

"Ranger" (Rupertus)

"Q": none located thus far

"Spy" (unknown)

"Victoria" (unknown)

"Trojan" (Hood)

"Whitney" (Whitney)

"Union NY" (Whitney)

"XL No. 1" (Hopkins & Allen)

"Y": none located thus far

"Z": none located thus far

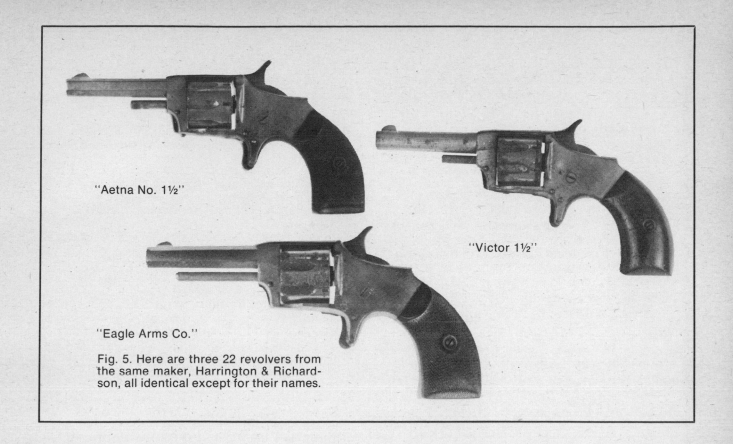

"Aetna No. 1½"

"Victor 1½"

"Eagle Arms Co."

Fig. 5. Here are three 22 revolvers from the same maker, Harrington & Richardson, all identical except for their names.

Most of the manufacturers who made suicide specials also made various other guns. Some made both rifles and pistols, though some made only handguns. The quality of manufacture varies greatly from maker to maker, In fact, among most collectors, the quality of the gun is often a prime criteria in deciding whether a particular example is or is not a "suicide special." Small revolvers by such makers as Colt and Remington are usually excluded, but those by Hopkins & Allen or James Reid—whose products were generally of equal quality but whose reputations were not—are invariably included in any roster of suicide special makers. Some makers names appear on some writers' lists but not on others.

To avoid such arbitrary distinctions, this article is going to be about a very specific group of guns and makers. The guns must have single action lockwork, a spur trigger, and a solid frame. Their makers are the companies that actually did manufacture them, though a few names that appeared in Webster's book (who have since been established *not* to have been manufacturers) are also included with appropriate notation in the accompanying listing to help clear the record.

Other manufacturers of the ubiquitous suicide special will undoubtedly be identified as time passes. At this time only about 60 percent of the suicide special revolvers have been properly identified as to maker.

Though most of the remainder should eventually be linked to one of the known makers, there are surely a few of the small arms companies that still need to be identified.

The list of gun names includes all of the names that I have been able to find on pistols meeting the earlier definition of "suicide special." A number have variants, and for the most part that is the addition of a number that indicated the caliber of the gun. These numbers are:

No. 1—22 caliber
No. 1½—30 caliber
No. 2—32 caliber
No. 3—38 caliber
No. 4—41 caliber

In some cases such numbers have an entirely different meaning, or perhaps no meaning at all. For example, the Kittemaug 3⅜ appears to be identical in every respect to both the Kittemaug and the Kittemaug 2, while several makers used 1½ to indicate a variation of 22 rather than 30 caliber.

Though this discussion has just scratched the surface of the very broad field that is the suicide special, it does offer some ideas as to how a collector might wish to pursue it. Collecting these cheap (in their day) and still mostly reasonably priced (comparatively) little handguns can challenge both the newcomer to collecting and the jaded old-timer as well.   ●

Suicide Special Makers

Bacon Manufacturing Co., Norwich, CT: Made a large variety of guns including suicide specials until bankruptcy in 1888. Most names continued by Crescent Firearms Co., who took over Bacon's assets.

Bliss & Goodyear, New Haven, Ct: Made *only* percussion revolvers, not in existence after 1865.

Chicago Arms Co., Chicago, IL: Trade name only. Did not make suicide specials.

Colt Patent Firearms Manuf. Co., Hartford, CT: High quality revolvers.

Continental Arms Co., Norwich, CT: Made only pepperboxes.

Crescent Firearms Co., Norwich, CT: Successor to Bacon Mfg. Co.

E. L. Dickinson, Springfield, MA: Made single shot pistols with his brother before starting manufacture of suicide specials.

Eagle Arms Co., New York City, NY: Made small size Plant front loading revolvers only, did not make suicide specials.

Ely & Wray, Springfield, MA: Made small numbers of suicide specials before selling out to Harrington & Richardson, who continued the same names.

Enterprise Gun Works, Pittsburgh, PA: Retailer only, did not manufacture suicide specials.

Ethan Allen, Worcester, MA: Complete line of guns.

Forehand & Wadsworth, Worcester, MA: Successors to Ethan Allen and makers of good quality guns in addition to the suicide specials, which were also above average in quality.

Great Western Gun Works, Pittsburgh, PA: Retailer only, did not manufacture suicide specials.

Harrington & Richardson, Worcester, MA: Made large numbers of suicide specials under many names.

Hood Firearms Co., Norwich, CT: The largest maker of suicide specials, using over 50 names.

Hopkins & Allen, Norwich, CT: Made rifles, shotguns, and other pistols besides suicide specials; best quality of any suicide specials.

Iver Johnson, Worcester, MA: Second only to Hood in numbers of suicide specials made. The quality was generally poor.

Lee Arms Co., Wilkes-Barre, PA: Made only suicide specials.

Mohawk Arms Co., Mohawk, NY: Does not exist, but is probably a confusion for Mohawk Mfg. Co., which was a trade name of Otis Smith.

New York Pistol Co., New York City, NY: Sales only, guns made by Bacon & Hood.

Norwich Arms Co., Norwich CT.: Made suicide specials.

Prescott Pistol Co., Hatfield, CT: Made double action revolvers and suicide specials.

E. Remington & Sons, Ilion, NY: Made quality spur trigger revolvers under Remington & Smoot patents.

Rome Revolver & Novelty Works, Rome, NY: Made (or retailed, it is not certain) suicide specials with several different names.

Rupertus Patent Pistol Manufacturing Co., Philadelphia, PA: Made rifles and pistols of many types besides the suicide specials.

Ryan Pistol Co., Norwich, CT: Made suicide specials of medium to poor quality.

Otis Smith, Rock Falls, CT: Made rifles, revolvers and tools in addition to suicide specials.

William Uhlinger, Philadelphia, PA: Made the Cone, Grant, Lower revolvers, which are not usually considered suicide specials.

United States Arms Co., New York City, NY: Retailer only.

Western Arms Co., New York & Chicago: Retailer only.

Eli Whitney, Whitneyville, CT: Made large quantities of rifles, shotguns, and other revolvers in addition to the suicide specials.

SUICIDE SPECIAL NAMES
WITH PRINCIPAL MAKER'S NAME
(When Known)*

A
A. A. CO.—Ryan
AETNA—H & R
ALASKA—Hood
ALERT—Hood
ALEXIA—Hood
ALEXIS—Hood
ALLEN 22—Forehand & Wadsworth
AMERICA—?
AMERICAN 38—Ely & Wray
AMERICAN EAGLE—?
AMERICAN BOY—?
ARISTOCRAT—?
AVENGER—Hopkins & Allen ?

*Question mark (?) indicates maker unknown or maker questionable

B
BACON—Bacon
BABY RUSSIAN—?
BANG UP—Ely & Wray
BANG UP—H & R
BEAUTY—?
BIG BONANZA—?
BENGAL—Iver Johnson
BISMARK—?
BLACK & OWEN—Hopkins & Allen
BLISS—F. D. Bliss
BLOODHOUND—Ely & Wray
BLUE JACKET—Hopkins & Allen
BLUE JACKET—Crescent
BLUE JACKET—Iver Johnson
BLUE LEADER—?
BLUE WHISTLER—?

BONANZA—Bacon
BOOM—Shattuck
BOYS CHOICE—Hood
BRUTUS—Hood
BUCKEYE—Hopkins & Allen
BUFFALO BILL—Iver Johnson
BUFFALO BILL—?
BULL DOG—Forehand & Wadsworth
BULLDOZER—Iver Johnson
BULLDOZER—Crescent
BULLDOZER—Forehand & Wadsworth
BULLS EYE—Otis Smith

C
CADET—Otis Smith
CAPT. JACK—Hopkins & Allen
CENTENNIAL—Hood

CHALLENGE—?
CHALLENGER—Iver Johnson
CHAMPION—Norwich
CHAMPION—Iver Johnson
CHEEVER & BURCHARD—Ryan
CHICAGO LEDGER—?
CHICHESTER—Hopkins & Allen
CHICHESTER—Hood
CHIEFTAIN—?
CLIPPER—?
COCK ROBIN—?
COMMERCIAL—Otis Smith
COLUMBIA—?
COLUMBIAN—?
COMET—? & Prescott
COMMANDER—Norwich
CONE—Uhlinger
CONQUEROR—Bacon
CONSTANT—?
CONTINENTAL—Hood
COWBOY—?
CREEDMORE—Chicago
CRESCENT—Crescent
CROWN—H & R
CZAR—Hood
CZAR—Hopkins & Allen

D
DAISY—Bacon
DASH—?
DEAD SHOT—Bacon
DEFENDER—Iver Johnson
DEFIANCE—Norwich
DESPATCH—Hopkins & Allen
DIAMOND—?
DICTATOR—Hopkins & Allen
DOMINION PISTOL CO.—?
DREADNOUGHT—Hopkins & Allen
DUCHESS—Hopkins & Allen
DUKE—Hopkins & Allen

E
EAGLE—Iver Johnson
EAGLE ARMS CO.—H & R
EAGLE CO.—Whitney
EARLHOOD—Dickinson
EARTHQUAKE—Dickinson
EASTERN ARMS CO.—?
ECLIPSE—Iver Johnson
ELECTOR—?
ELECTRIC—Forehand & Wadsworth
ELY & WRAY—Ely & Wray
EMPIRE—Rupertus
EMPRESS—?
ENCORE—Iver Johnson
ENTERPRISE—?
EUREKA—Iver Johnson
EUREKA—H & R
EXCELSIOR—Crescent
EXPRESS—Bacon

F
FAULTLESS—?
FAVORITE—Iver Johnson
FRONTIER—?
FITCH—Reid

G
GARRISON—?
GEM—Bacon
GOVERNOR—Bacon
GOVERNOR—Hopkins & Allen
GENERAL—Rupertus
GRANT—Uhlinger
GREAT WESTERN—H & R
GUARDIAN—Bacon
GUT BUSTER—?
GYPSY—Crescent

H
HALF BREED—?
HARD PAN—Hood
HARD PAN—Iver Johnson
HARRINGTON & RICHARDSON—H & R
HARTFORD ARMS CO.—?
HECLA—Iver Johnson
HECLA—Ryan
HINSDALE—Hopkins & Allen
HOLEY MFG. CO.—Reid
HOOD F. A. CO.—Hood
HOPKINS & ALLEN MFG. CO.—Hopkins & Allen
HORNET—Prescott

I
IMPERIAL—Lee
INTERNATIONAL—Hood

INVINCIBLE—Iver Johnson
IROQUOIS—Remington

J
JEWEL—Hood
J. H. JOHNSTON—H & R
JOKER—Marlin
J.S.T. & CO.—Iver Johnson

K
KENTUCKY—Iver Johnson
KING PIN—?
KITTEMAUG—?

L
LAKESIDE—?
LEADER—H & R
LIBERTY—Otis Smith
LION—Iver Johnson
LITTLE GIANT—Bacon
LITTLE JOHN—?
LITTLE JOKER—?
LITTLE PET—?
LITTLE SCOUT—?
LONE STAR—Otis Smith
LOWER—Uhlinger

M
MANHATTAN ARMS CO.—Iver Johnson
MARQUIS OF LORNE—Ryan
METROPOLITAN POLICE—Hopkins & Allen
MOHAWK—?
MOHAWK—Rome
MOHAWK MFG. CO.—Otis Smith
MOHEGAN—Otis Smith
MONARCH—Iver Johnson
MONARCH—Hopkins & Allen
MONITOR—Whitney
MOUNTAIN EAGLE—Hopkins & Allen
MY COMPANION—?

N
NAPOLEON—Ryan
NATIONAL—?
NERO—Rupertus
NEWPORT—?
NO. 3—Prescott
NONPARIEL—?
NON XL—?
NORTHFIELD KNIFE CO.—Rome
NORWICH ARMS CO.—Norwich
NORWICH FALLS—Norwich

O
ODD FELLOW—Otis Smith
OK—Marlin
OLD HICKORY—Hopkins & Allen
OLD HICKORY—?
OLIVER—Hopkins & Allen
ORIENT—?
OUR JAKE—Dickinson

P
PANTHER—Ely & Wray
PARAGON—Prescott
PAROLE—Bacon
PATHFINDER—?
PATRIOT—?
PEERLESS—Hood
PENETRATOR—?
PEORIA CHIEF—?
PET—?
PETREL—?
PHOENIX—Reid
PINAFORE—?
PIONEER—Forehand & Wadsworth
PLUG UGLY—?
POINTER—?
PRAIRIE KING—Bacon
PRAIRIE KING—?
PREMIER—Ryan
PREMIUM—?
PRINCESS—Hood
PROTECTOR—?
PROTECTOR ARMS CO.—Rupertus

R
RANGER—Rupertus
RANGER—Hopkins & Allen
RANGER—Dickinson
RATTLER—?
RED CLOUD—Ryan
RED HOT—Iver Johnson
RED JACKET—Lee
REID—Reid
RELIABLE—?

RELIABLE—Bacon
RELIANCE—?
RETRIEVER—Ryan
RIKER—Rupertus
RIP RAP—Bacon
ROBIN HOOD—Hood
ROB ROY—?
ROME REVOLVER & NOVELTY WORKS—
    ROME Revolver & Novelty Works
ROVER—?
ROYAL—Lee
ROYAL—Otis Smith
RUSSIAN MODEL—Forehand & Wadsworth
RYAN'S NEW MODEL—Ryan

S
SAFEGUARD—?
SCOTT—Hopkins & Allen
SCOTT ARM CO.—?
SCOUT—?
SECRET SERVICE—?
SENATOR—?
SENTINAL—?
SHATTUCK—Shattuck
SITTING BULL—?
SMITH'S NEW MODEL—Otis Smith
SMITH'S PATENT—Otis Smith
SMOKER—Iver Johnson
SMOKY CITY—H & R
SOUTHRON—Iver Johnson
SPORT—Ryan
SPORTSMAN—?
SPRINGFIELD ARMS CO.—Springfield Arms Co.
SPY—?
STAR—Prescott
STAR LEADER—?
STERLING—?
STERLING—Dickinson
STRIKER—?
SUCCESS—?
SWAMP ANGEL—Forehand & Wadsworth

T
T & R—?
T & R—Hood
T & H—Hopkins & Allen
TERRIER—Rupertus
TERROR—Forehand & Wadsworth
TIGER—Ely & Wray
TIGER—Iver Johnson
TOLEDO FIREARMS CO.—Hopkins & Allen
TOLEDO FIREARMS CO.—Dickinson
TORONTO BELLE—?
TOWER'S SAFETY POLICE—Hopkins & Allen
TRAMPS TERROR—Western Gun Works
TRAMPS TERROR—Iver Johnson
TROJAN—Hood
TRUE BLUE—?
TYCOON—Iver Johnson

U
U.M.C. ARMS CO.—?
UNION, NY—Whitney
UNION JACK—Hood
UNIQUE—Shattuck
U.S. ARMS CO., NY—Bacon
U.S. ARMS CO., NY—Hood
U.S. PISTOL CO.—Hood
U.S. PISTOL CO.—Crescent

V
VEILED PROPHETS—?
VENUS—?
VETERAN—?
VETO—?
VICTOR—H & R
VICTORIA—Hood

W
WASP—?
WESSON & HARRINGTON—Wesson & Harrington
WHISTLER—Hood
WHITE JACKETR—?
WHITE STAR—H & R
WHITNEYVILLE ARMORY—Whitneyville Armory
WIDE AWAKE—Hood & Forehand & Wadsworth
WILLIAMS—?
Wm. TELL—Lee
WINFIELD ARMS CO.—Crescent

X
XL—Hopkins & Allen

Mauser Kleinkaliber-Büchsen

by Bill Beacom

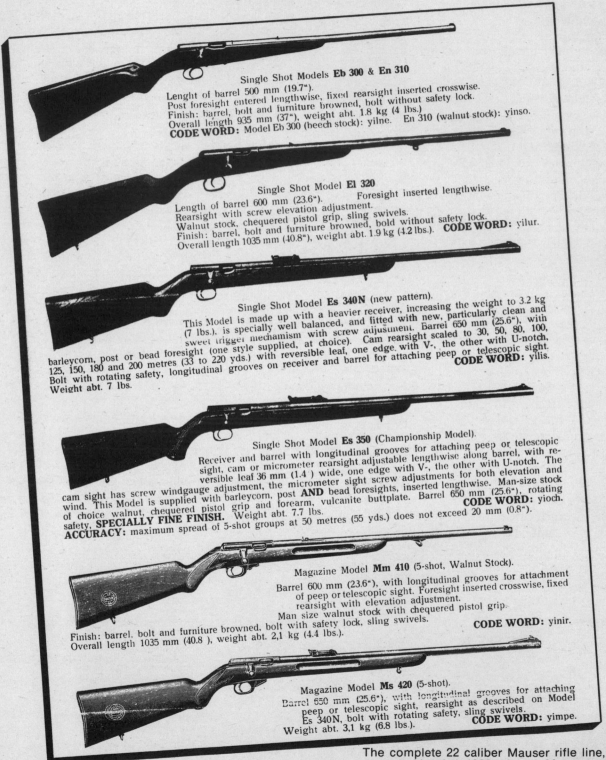

Single Shot Models Eb 300 & En 310

Lenght of barrel 500 mm (19.7"). Post foresight entered lengthwise, fixed rearsight inserted crosswise. Finish: barrel, bolt and furniture browned, bolt without safety lock. Overall length 935 mm (37"), weight abt. 1.8 kg (4 lbs.). **CODE WORD:** Model Eb 300 (beech stock): yilne. En 310 (walnut stock): yinso.

Single Shot Model El 320

Length of barrel 600 mm (23.6"). Foresight inserted lengthwise. Rearsight with screw elevation adjustment. Walnut stock, chequered pistol grip, sling swivels. Finish: barrel, bolt and furniture browned, bold without safety lock. **CODE WORD:** yilur. Overall length 1035 mm (40.8"), weight abt. 1.9 kg (4.2 lbs.).

Single Shot Model Es 340N (new pattern).

This Model is made up with a heavier receiver, increasing the weight to 3.2 kg (7 lbs.), is specially well balanced, and fitted with new, particularly clean and sweet trigger mechanism with screw adjustment. Barrel 650 mm (25.6"), with barleycorn, post or bead foresight (one style supplied, at choice). Cam rearsight scaled to 30, 50, 80, 100, 125, 150, 180 and 200 metres (33 to 220 yds.) with reversible leaf, one edge with V-, the other with U-notch, Bolt with rotating safety, longitudinal grooves on receiver and barrel for attaching peep or telescopic sight. Weight abt. 7 lbs. **CODE WORD:** yilis.

Single Shot Model Es 350 (Championship Model).

Receiver and barrel with longitudinal grooves for attaching peep or telescopic sight, cam or micrometer rearsight adjustable lengthwise along barrel, with reversible leaf 36 mm (1.4") wide, one edge with V-, the other with U-notch. The cam sight has screw windgauge adjustment, the micrometer sight screw adjustments for both elevation and wind. This Model is supplied with barleycorn, post **AND** bead foresights, inserted lengthwise. Man-size stock of choice walnut, chequered pistol grip and forearm, vulcanite buttplate. Barrel 650 mm (25.6"), rotating safety, **SPECIALLY FINE FINISH.** Weight abt. 7.7 lbs. **CODE WORD:** yioch. **ACCURACY:** maximum spread of 5-shot groups at 50 metres (55 yds.) does not exceed 20 mm (0.8").

Magazine Model Mm 410 (5-shot, Walnut Stock).

Barrel 600 mm (23.6"), with longitudinal grooves for attachment of peep or telescopic sight. Foresight inserted crosswise, fixed rearsight with elevation adjustment. Man size walnut stock with chequered pistol grip. Finish: barrel, bolt and furniture browned, bolt with safety lock, sling swivels. **CODE WORD:** yinir. Overall length 1035 mm (40.8"), weight abt. 2,1 kg (4.4 lbs.).

Magazine Model Ms 420 (5-shot).

Barrel 650 mm (25.6"), with longitudinal grooves for attaching peep or telescopic sight, rearsight as described on Model Es 340N, bolt with rotating safety, sling swivels. **CODE WORD:** yimpe. Weight abt. 3,1 kg (6.8 lbs.).

The complete 22 caliber Mauser rifle line, as it appeared in a late 1920s vintage Mauser catalog.

A History of Mauser's 22 Rifles

THE 22 caliber rifle did not find much favor in Germany prior to the First World War. Those that were made were either for export or their use was limited to boys' clubs and/or by the not-too-popular poachers. Rifles using this cartridge were generally small, and with any of several silencers available at this time could be used quite effectively without undue disturbance. The exception to this general indifference to the 22 was a number of riflemen who defied the major shooting clubs and fired 22 caliber in international style competition. A fine pre-war Schuetzen or falling block in 22 rimfire will be found now and then to verify this.

Following a dismal showing in the Olympic small bore matches in Stockholm in 1912, the Germans returned home vowing it would be different in 1916. World War I intervened. The defeat they suffered affected both the economy and sporting programs. By the early twenties, however, they remembered their poor showing in the last international competition and the decision by the Olympic Committee to make small bore shooting a permanent part of Olympic competition. National pride prompted several German arms companies to produce target quality 22s.

Mauser's research and development on 22 rifles had started before World War I. Like other German arms manufacturers, it took them a few years after the war ended to recover, but when they did, Mauser already had access to markets in several countries where their centerfire hunting rifles had long enjoyed a near monopoly. Introduction of a Mauser small bore rifle, a logical step, was made about 1921. These did not become available in any large number, however, until about 1925.

Mauser's initial effort included five basic models; three single shots, the En 310, El 320, and Es 340; and two repeaters, the Mm 410 and Ms 420. (The "E" in a model designation is for "Einzel" or single shot; "M" is for "Mehr" or more shot). The En 310 and the El 320

were small boys' rifles, and because of their high cost compared to competitive rifles of the period, they were never popular, even in Germany. The Es 340 and Ms 420 could be found at most target matches in Germany, and along with the Mm 410, enjoyed world-wide popularity. All of these models can be found widely advertised in various foreign arms catalogs of the period, including Stoeger, from 1925 to 1940 in the U.S.; Humbers, in France; Cymot, in South Africa; Tahir Arms, Bombay; Charles Heyer, Nairobi, and even several from South American arms dealers.

None of the Mauser line of rifles was ever cheap. In the U.S., the Ms 420 sold for $47.50 in 1925 and $50 in 1930. Their use was therefore confined to the more affluent. Their high cost and the general world economy during the late twenties and thirties explains why they were never found in large numbers. However, this situation changed briefly 10 or 15 years ago, when a large number of those originally sold to safari outfitters in India and Africa during the pre-WW II years were bought by U.S. surplus arms dealers and found their way here.

In 1930, not to be outdone by other German arms companies such as Walther, Erma, Simson, and Geco who were cashing in on the ever-increasing small bore market, Mauser improved their 22 action and introduced a new series. They dropped the old En 310 and El 320; but kept the Es 340, Mm 410 and Ms 420. However, the action was made heavier, trigger improved, safety changed and the receiver grooved to accept a diopter sight or tip-off scope. The Model Es 340 N ("N" for "Neues" or "New") could be bought with plain stock and steel buttplate or deluxe checkered pistol grip stock with grooved fore-end and horn buttplate. The new repeater models were the Mm 410 and the Ms 420 N which, with the exception of being a repeater, was identical to the deluxe Es 340 N.

The Es 350 match rifle, the one everyone had been

Mauser Es 340 N standard
target rifle, made in the mid
1930s.

Above—A group of Mauser 22s. From top, Model Es 340 B, Model Es 340 B DeLuxe, Model Ms 420, and a custom sporter built on an Es 340 B action with a Mannlicher-style stock and claw mounted Hensoldt scope.

Right—Another group of Mauser 22s, showing (from top) two Es 340 Bs, an Ms 350 B, and an Mm 410 B.

waiting for, was also introduced at this time. This rifle was guaranteed to shoot ¾-inch groups or better at 50 meters as it came from the factory. It was quality from buttplate to front sight. The rear sight was mounted on a long dovetail groove that reached from the back of the receiver to about 9 inches up the barrel. This allowed sight adjustment for astigmatism correction and a longer sighting radius. A diopter was optional. The stock was select walnut, blue was what you would expect on the finest shotgun, and fit and finish were superb.

Needless to say, this new rifle was soon well represented in all the local, state and national matches in Germany and won more than its share of medals. The fact that it was priced at $60 in the U.S. when the Winchester 52 was only $44.50, and the 52 would outshoot it, did not help its popularity in this country. The few that were sold here were probably bought out of respect for German craftsmanship, or to form a pair with a Mauser centerfire.

In 1934, in answer to a number of their centerfire customers' request for a military style rimfire and to mounting pressure for a 22 training rifle from a government whose entire army was using 98 type bolt rifles, Mauser Werke introduced the Deutches Sport

Modell 1934 B. Its action duplicated the functioning of the centerfire Mauser bolt rifles perfectly by placing the bolt off-center in the receiver, thus allowing the firing pin a center position in the bolt, as in the Mauser 98. The DSM thus fired a rimfire cartridge perfectly without the necessity of boring the barrel off center at the breech. Takedown and cleaning were also identical to the military K98.

It was made to order for military training, and at one time or another was manufactured for this purpose by just about every small rifle factory in Germany. The DSM was used for training of youth groups, militia, and women's groups as well as by servicemen. The fact that almost all Nazi party groups used these is attested to by the number found marked with unit markings of just about every political or paramilitary organization in Germany.

The DSM action was the basis for the 1934B series of sporters. The B series, as we shall call it, consisted of three single shots, two models of the Es 340 B with features in the plain and deluxe versions as before, and the Es 350 B. The Es 350 B had a new diopter peep sight available which mounted on the receiver, an optional tang peep sight and a wider fore-end. There were also three repeaters. The Mm 410 B and

Diopter

für Original Mauser-Klein-kaliberbüchsen

No. 7532

Above and below—Accessory sights for Mauser's 22 rifles, as offered in the 1937 AKAH catalog.

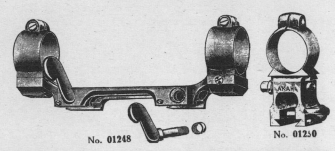

No. 01248   No. 01250

Nazi party marking burned into the buttstock of a Mauser-made DMS 34, showing that this particular rifle was owned by the NSDAP (*National Sozialistische Deutsche Arbeiter Partei*) in the province of Hochland.

Mauser-made DSM 34 training rifle. Note military configuration and furniture.

Ms 240 B answered the need for a companion rifle to the centerfire. The Ms 350 B, a sister to the Es 350 B, provided a five-shot repeater for the target shooter. The sights for the Es 350 B would fit any of the above rifles. These models were to be the last sporting 22 caliber rifles introduced before the war. All of the B series, except the Mm 410 B, were used by target shooters in Germany.

In the American market, even with all the above refinements, Mauser still could not compete with the Winchester 52 series. The 52, which perhaps never looked quite as good as the Mauser, was cheaper and would outshoot it in American-style competition. Keep in mind, however, target shooting in Germany was different than we know it today. All competitive shooting was done with military objectives in mind. No equipment was allowed that would be impractical in the field. For example: rifles too heavy to carry on the march, equipped with 3-oz. triggers, palm rests, hooked butts, etc., were *verboten*. These were used in international competition but not in domestic shoots.

All 22 Mauser rifles made from 1921 to 1940 were available with factory mounted scopes, utilizing either tip-off or claw mounts depending on model and year of manufacture. In addition, the 1934 B actions were sold separately to custom rifle makers. Guns, therefore, will be found with just about every imaginable stock style, scope mounting and sighting arrangement. However, the factory-made Mauser rifle will always have **Mauser** stamped on the buttplate as well as on the receiver top. The Mauser cartouche will generally be stamped on the right side of the butt stock as well, unless the stock has been refinished. **MAUSER WERKE A.G. OBERNDORF A. N.** will be found on the left side of the receiver near the top edge of the stock.

This summary, as most summaries in a specialized field leaves as much unsaid as said. New information becomes available from collectors and other sources every day. The basis for the information I have compiled comes directly from Mauser and others' catalogs and brochures and my own personal collection of more than 60 Mauser 22s and is, to the best of my knowledge, accurate.

The small bore Mauser rifles are mighty fine shooters as well as fascinating collectors' items. Here's wishing you luck in your quest for Mauser small bore rifles. You will find both a little bit of history and a mighty fine rifle when you find one! ●

Periodicals for the Collector

by Joseph J. Schroeder

As is pointed out in another article in this book, "software"—written documentation—is almost as important to the serious collector as is the hardware, the guns themselves. Without proper documentation the guns are simply pieces of machinery, interesting as mechanisms and, if you're of a mind and the ammunition is available, to shoot. History, designer, relationship to other arms past or present, are all mysteries to the collector whose collection consists *only* of guns.

Periodical publications are one of the most valuable sources of information for the collector. They attract inputs from authors in many related fields and with many sources of information, and can even provide a clearing house where arguments about the most trivial (to others) details can be fought over endlessly.

Every collector, whatever his specialty, should subscribe to at least some of the magazines and newspapers described below. No matter what your specialty, there will be at least one or two that will touch on it frequently enough to make your investment in a subscription quite worthwhile.

We've tried to make this listing the most comprehensive that has ever been published, and in so doing have included some publications that might not ordinarily be considered "collector oriented." However, along with the listing of name, mailing address and subscription rates there's also included a thumbnail description of the publication and its value to the arms collector.

We hope you enjoy this tabulation and find it both useful and reasonably accurate. There may well be some errors, particularly in the foreign publications which are not easy to come by. The editor would appreciate any comments or corrections from the readers.

American Blade
It may seem peculiar to begin a listing of gun collectors' publications with a knife magazine, but many gun buffs are also knife enthusiasts and *American Blade* comes first alphabetically. Very well done with

good illustrations, *American Blade* is directed toward collectors of knives of all vintages.
Bi-monthly: $10/year (U.S.); $16 (foreign)
112 Lee Parkway Dr., Suite 104, Chattanooga, TN 37421

American Firearms Industry
A trade publication as the title implies, *American Firearms Industry* sometimes has features of interest to the collector of current arms.
Monthly: $15/year
National Association of Federally Licensed Firearms Dealers
7001 North Clark St., Chicago, IL 60626

The American Handgunner
Though more directed toward the shooter than collec-

tor, the *American Handgunner* never-the-less sometimes has very worthwhile articles for the collector.
Bi-monthly: $9.95/year, $17.95/2 years, $24.95/3 years
591 Camino de la Reina, Suite 200, San Diego, CA 92108

American Rifleman
Membership publication of the National Rifle Association, to which every serious gun buff should belong. Almost every issue of the *Rifleman* has at least one worthwhile collecting article, though all phases of guns and shooting are covered. A must, if only to support your right to keep and bear arms!
Monthly: $15/year, $40/3 years, $60/5 years
National Rifle Association of America
1600 Rhode Island Ave., Washington, D.C. 20036

AMI
French Language. *Ami* stands for "Armes-Militaria-Informations-Tir" and this well-done monthly covers all those areas very well indeed. Includes current arms, collectors guns, cartridges, knives and various accouterments and even uniforms and military vehicles. Well illustrated, with much color.
Monthly: $4 (U.S.) per issue cover price; write for current subscription rates
Action Press SA
Avenue Louise, 60, 1050 Bruxelles, Belgium

Antiquarmes
French language. Covers both modern and antique arms, well illustrated.
Monthly: write for subscription rates
d'Agence Idees
B.P. 24 - Viroflay, RC B 741354 Versailles, France

Pattern 1842 Pistol (lancers)

Antique Arms & Militaria
A good deal of coverage of uniforms and blades, but more than enough on antique firearms to be worthwhile to the gun collector. Interesting perspective on the problems of gun collecting in the United Kingdom.
Monthly: $18/year
59, Ilford Lane, Ilford, Sussex, England

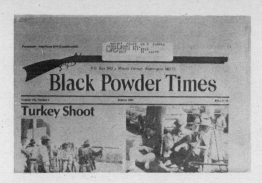

Black Powder Times
Newspaper format, directed primarily at the muzzleloader shooting fraternity. However, frequent good articles on muzzle-loading collectibles.
Monthly: $15/year
P.O. Box 842, Mount Vernon, WA 98273

Deutsches Waffen Journal
German language. One of the world's top gun periodicals. *DWJ* covers all phases of shooting, hunting and collecting. Every large format (9x11½") issue includes at least two well-researched historical articles. The excellent illustrations make *DWJ* worthwhile even if you don't read German. Highly recommended.
Monthly: about $30/year
Postfach 10 03 40, D-7170 Schwabisch Hall, West Germany

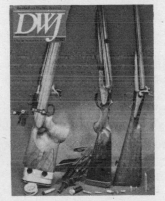

Diana ARMI
Italian language. Covers all phases of shooting and gun sports, but almost every issue has one or two good articles on collector firearms.
Monthly: Write for current subscription rates.
Editoriale Olimpia S.p.A.
Viale Milton, 7, 50.129 Florence, Italy

Gazette des armes
French language. Entirely collector oriented, with arms coverage from ancient times through recent production.
Monthly: write for current rates.
27, rue de Louvre, 75002 Paris, France

Gun Journal

New early in 1981, *Gun Journal* is still (at mid year) looking for a direction. It has some good writers on its staff, but so far has a curious mix of shooting, hunting, test reports and collectors features. Illustrations (thus far) tend to be muddy.
Bi-Monthly: $7.50/year
Charlton Publications
Charlton Building, Derby, CT 06418

The Gun Report

Now in its 27th year, *Gun Report* continues to provide excellent variety for the antique gun and cartridge collector. Very good show coverage and calendar. Highly recommended.
Monthly: $20/year, $37/2 years, $55/3 years; $25/year overseas
P.O. Box 111, Aledo, IL 61231

Gun Week

A weekly newspaper for gun enthusiasts, *Gun Week* is a must for every gun owner who's concerned about the anti-gun movement and his future right to own guns. As a bonus, frequent articles of value to the collector. Excellent gun show calendar. A must!
Weekly: $12/year, $16/year overseas
Hawkeye Publishing, Inc.
P.O. Box 411, Station C, Buffalo, NY 14209

Gun World

Though a general interest gun magazine, *Gun World* boasts a well-done "Collector News" column by Charles Karwan in each issue. Some feature articles on collector arms, as well.
Monthly: $12/year, $23/2 years (U.S.); $17/year elsewhere
Gallant Publishing Co.
P.O. Box HH, Capistrano Beach, CA 92624

The Gunrunner

Published in Canada, the *Gunrunner* consists principally of ads but, unlike *Shotgun News,* does include some editorial material that is often collector oriented. Frustrating to the collector to see some guns that are not available here at "bargain" prices.
Monthly: $9/year, $15/2 years
Kexco Publishing Co., Ltd.
P.O. Box 565, Lethbridge, Alberta, T1J 3Z4, Canada

Guns

Though general in scope, almost every issue of *Guns* has at least one worthwhile collector article. Several worthwhile regular columns, too.
Monthly: $14.95/year
Publishers' Development Corp.,
591 Camino de la Reina, Suite 200, San Diego, CA 92108

Guns & Ammo

Another general coverage gun magazine, *Guns & Ammo* provides coverage of collector arms as well as shooting and hunting.
Monthly: $11.94/year, $19.94/2 years (U.S.); $17.94/year elsewhere
Petersen Publishing Co.
8490 Sunset Blvd., Los Angeles, CA 90069

Guns & Combat

Another brand new and as yet hard to categorize book, *Guns & Combat* does seem to cover what its title implies along with some historical and collector-oriented material. Paper quality is poor, along with many of the illustrations, and all advertis-

ing is for products (mostly books) available from its publisher.

Bimonthly: $2.50/issue, apparently newstand only
S.J. Publications, Inc.
2470 Lemoine Ave., Ft. Lee, NJ 07624

Guns Review

Though it covers the hunting and shooting sports as well, *Guns Review* has at least one worthwhile article on collector arms in every issue. Regular coverage of cartridge and bayonet collecting. Highly recommended.

Monthly: U.S., $20.45/year (surface), $34/year (air);
    Canada, $23.50/year (surface), $38.70/year (air)
Ravenhill Publishing Co., Standard House, Bonhill
    St., London EC2A 4DA, England

Handgunner

Though directed more toward shooters and "general interest" gun buffs than are the other British arms periodicals, *Handgunner* has frequently carried worthwhile collector-oriented articles during its first year. It also offers a different perspective on English gun ownership than its companions, and American readers will find some familiar names (for example Jan Stevenson, Editor) on its title page.

Bimonthly: $20/year, surface; $30/year, air
7 Denton's Terrace, Wivenhoe, Colchester, Essex,
    England

Knife World

Strongly oriented toward commemorative and other current collector-quality blades, yet each issue includes worthwhile coverage of a variety of older knife collectibles.

Monthly: $8/year, $14/2 years, $20/3 years
Box 3395, Knoxville, TN 37917

Man

Though its title leads one to expect its pages would be adorned with voluptuous females wearing smiles and little else, *Man* is a genuine gun magazine, direct from South Africa. It's principally for the shooter, with both hunting and self-protection articles leading the way. Occasional collector articles, and an editorial slant from a part of the world North American gun buffs have little contact with.

Monthly: about $12.30 (plus postage)/year; write for
    precise rate.
SA Man (Pty) Ltd.
P.O. Box 11014, Vlaeberg 8018 South Africa

Man At Arms

Now in its third year, *Man At Arms* seems to be directed more at the upper echelon (financially) of arms collectors. It's very attractively done, with outstanding illustration, and early in 1981 took over *Arms Gazette's* subscription list when that publication unfortunately went out of business. Highly recommended.

Bi-monthly: $18/year; $32/2 years; add $5/year postage for overseas.
222 W. Exchange St., Providence, RI 02903

Reports From Washington

A newsletter devoted entirely to news of the anti-gun conflict and published by the National Rifle Association's Institute for Legislative Action, *Reports from Washington* is must reading for everyone who wishes to hold on to his guns. Highly recommended.

Bi-weekly: $6/year, $11/2 years (NRA members); $8/year, $15/2 years (non members)

NRA Institute for Legislative Action
1600 Rhode Island Ave., Washington, D.C. 20036

Rifle

Primarily for shooters, *Rifle* still has enough collector coverage to make it worthwhile for long gun collectors.

Bi-monthly: $13/year, $25/2 years; $16/year, $31/2 years outside U.S.A.

Wolfe Publishing Co.,
P.O. Box 3030, Prescott, AZ 86302

Shooting Industry

Directed at the arms trade, *Shooting Industry* is another entry from the publishers of *Guns* and the *American Handgunner*. Very good coverage of current developments.

Monthly: $25/year ($12.50/year to FFL holders)

591 Camino de la Reina, Suite 200, San Diego, CA 92108

Shooting Times

Primarily directed toward the shooter, *Shooting Times* still frequently has very good articles on collecting subjects.

Monthly: $11.95/year, $22/2 years; add $5/year outside U.S.A.

PJS Publications, Inc.,
News Plaza, P.O. Box 1790, Peoria, IL 61656

Shotgun News

Classified ads plus some display ads all devoted to guns and accessories, and over 200 pages of them in each recent issue, make *SGN* a must for any collector who's looking for anything or simply wants to know

current market prices. Hard on the eyes, but worth the effort. A must.

Semi-monthly: $9.50/year, $18/2 years; $65/year overseas

Box 669, Hastings, NE 68901

Soldier of Fortune

Though not a gun magazine per se, *Soldier of Fortune* devotes enough space to unusual current weapons to make it worthwhile for the collector of military firearms.

Monthly: $24/year (U.S.A.); $29/year elsewhere

Omega Group Ltd.,
5735 Arapahoe Ave., Boulder, CO 80303

Strelecka Revue

Czech language. General coverage gun magazine, with rather muddy illustrations but sometimes covers a real gem little or unknown this side of the iron curtain. Table of Contents is in English (as well as German, Russian and, of course, Czech).

Monthly: Write for current rates

113 66 Praha 1, Jungmannova 24, Czechoslovakia

TACARMI

Italian language. A well laid out, well illustrated magazine with a good deal of collector arms coverage.

Monthly: $37.20/year (U.S.A.)

Via Volta 60, 20090 Cusago (Milan), Italy

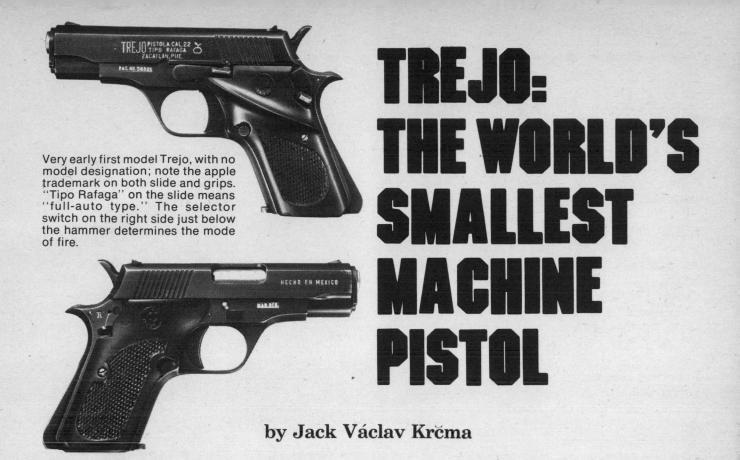

Very early first model Trejo, with no model designation; note the apple trademark on both slide and grips. "Tipo Rafaga" on the slide means "full-auto type." The selector switch on the right side just below the hammer determines the mode of fire.

TREJO: THE WORLD'S SMALLEST MACHINE PISTOL

by Jack Václav Krčma

A NUMBER of manufacturers in Spain, Germany and Russia have produced pistols capable of full automatic fire. These pistols are equipped with a rotating or sliding lever switch which enables the weapon to be fired either full or semi-automatic. A variation is found on the Heckler & Koch VP 70, with the selector on the shoulder stock. Due to high rates of fire of some of these pistols, they are equipped with slow down devices built into the mechanism.

Weapons which come to mind with the full auto capability are the Spanish Astra Models 901, 902, 903, 904 and Model F and the Star pistols Model A and Model MD. Germany produced the Mauser Model 1932 (M712 or *Schnellfeuer*) and Heckler & Koch's VP 70. Russia produced the Stechkin. These pistols were produced in a variety of calibers among which were: 7.63mm Mauser, 9mm Mauser, 9mm Bergmann Bayard (9mm Largo), 38 Super, 9mm Parabellum (Luger), 9mm Makarov and 45 ACP.

Only one maker has ever produced a pistol in caliber 22LR capable of selective fire. These were the Trejo pistols from Mexico.

Not far from Mexico City is the city of Zacatlán in the province of Puebla. Zacatlán is renowned for the excellent apples produced there and there is an annual Apple Fair to commemorate this fact. At #1 Gómez Farías was the home of Armas Trejo, S.A. (Dec. V.) "Primera Fábrica de Pistolas Tipo Ráfaga en México" (First Full-Auto Pistol Factory in Mexico). This factory was set up by Senor Gabriel Trejo and his sons probably in 1952. Due to the fame of Zacatlán apples, an apple was selected as the trademark for the new enterprise.

Trejo Pistol Production:

Altogether two models of 22 caliber pistols were produced—both models were made in both selective fire and semi-auto versions. (A centerfire semi-auto Trejo, in both 32 and 380 ACP, was also made.) All models were covered by a single Mexican patent, No. 50921.

Modelo 1:

The first model Trejo to be made was a small pistol of 48 parts which had no official model designation in its early versions; later production bore the designation **MODELO 1**. Its sharply angled grip immediately catches the eye. It is a blowback in design with a barrel bushing similar to the Colt 1911Al, and the barrel is pinned by the takedown latch. There is a thumb safety and a push-button magazine release, and the brown plastic grips bear a medallion with the Trejo insignia and apple trademark. There is an ingenious sear tripping mechanism located on the right rear upper side of the pistol, consisting of a three-part linkage and a piano wire spring, which enables the weapon to fire in full-auto.

When the selector switch is in the upper position "R", the pistol fires full-auto ("R stands for *Rafaga* which means full-auto in Spanish). When the switch

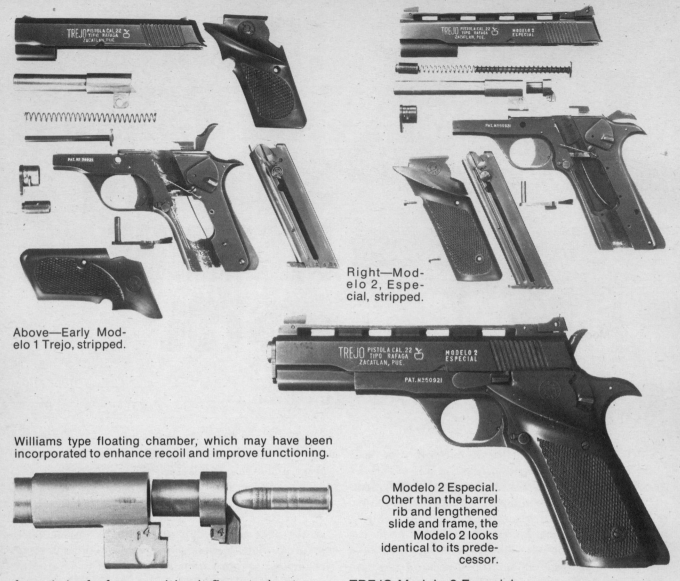

Above—Early Modelo 1 Trejo, stripped.

Right—Modelo 2, Especial, stripped.

Williams type floating chamber, which may have been incorporated to enhance recoil and improve functioning.

Modelo 2 Especial. Other than the barrel rib and lengthened slide and frame, the Modelo 2 looks identical to its predecessor.

lever is in the lower position it fires semi-auto.

There is no magazine disconnector in this pistol, and the pistol fires at an exceedingly high rate of fire due to its small caliber. It empties the contents of its 8-round magazine in one ripping roar.

I have fired more than 300 rounds of mixed ammunition from this pistol offhand without a single malfunction. Semi-auto, the pistol can be fired at three rounds per second rapid-fire. On full-auto the bullets scattered over a wide area. Later, a semi-auto version, designated the Modelo 1-A, was also made.

Technical data for the Modelo 1:
Caliber: 22LR
Over-all Length: 166mm
Barrel Length: 78.5mm
Magazine Capacity: 8 rounds
Mech. System: Blowback
Rifling: 6-R
Weight: 634 g (empty)
Height: 97mm
Thickness: (grips) 28.5 mm

TREJO Modelo 2 Especial:

This was the second production model, with a longer slide and longer grip than the Modelo 1. This large model consists of 46 parts and has a ventilated sight rib with micro adjustable sight. In the selective fire version it was produced in two variations with and without Williams type floating chamber. Apart from these features it is similar to the first model.

A semi-auto version, without floating chamber, was also made.

Technical Data for Modelo 2 Especial:
Caliber: 22LR
Over-all Length: 202mm
Barrel Length: 105mm
Magazine Capacity: 11 rounds
Mechanical System: Blowback
Rifling: 6-R
Weight: 834 g
Height: 127mm
Thickness: 31mm

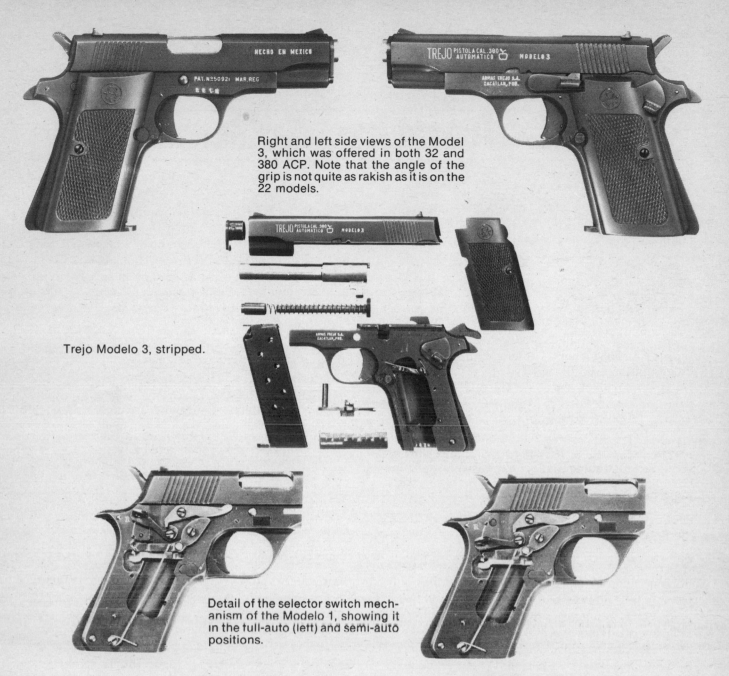

Right and left side views of the Model 3, which was offered in both 32 and 380 ACP. Note that the angle of the grip is not quite as rakish as it is on the 22 models.

Trejo Modelo 3, stripped.

Detail of the selector switch mechanism of the Modelo 1, showing it in the full-auto (left) and semi-auto positions.

TREJO Modelo 3:

This pistol is of blowback design and is capable of semi-automatic fire only. Consisting of 37 parts, it is equipped with a thumb safety and a magazine disconnector (when the chamber of the weapon is loaded and with the magazine removed, it cannot fire).

Technical Data for Modelo 3:
Caliber: 32 and 380 ACP
Over-all Length: 168.5 mm
Barrel Length: 99.5mm
Magazine Capacity: 7 rounds
Mechanical System: Blowback
Rifling: 6-R
Weight: 761 g
Height: 104mm
Thickness: 32mm

Conclusions

All Trejo pistols are well made and finished. I have seen the Modelo 3 advertised in the Swiss and German gun magazines, but was unable to find out how many pistols were manufactured. None seem to have marketed commercially in the United States or Canada. They are rarely seen in either country, even in the semi-auto versions.

I have fired and examined only eight pistols: On the first small model the highest serial number was 1751. Serial number 0764 was the highest Modelo 2, and 2212 the highest Modelo 3. According to information received from Capt. Toribio Cano Nieto of the Zacatlán Police, the factory was closed in 1971 by government order. Thus ended production of one of the most interesting 22 pistols ever made. •

Gun Collecting & Gun Law

Today's gun collector has to deal with gun laws on three levels, federal, state and local. In this discussion we're going to deal almost entirely with federal law because of the near impossibility of even trying to cover the laws of 50 states and thousands of communities. The Bureau of Alcohol, Tobacco and Firearms does, in a tightly packed book almost as large as this one. Its 235 pages of small type (in the 1980 edition) simply reproduces those laws that pertain to Federal license holders, without discussion or explanation, and it's slow reading!

However, to stay clear of the law you must know the gun laws of your state and community, plus those of the states and communities in which you attend gun shows. To do otherwise is foolish, because to break one of those laws, no matter how innocently, could cause you not only embarrassment and money but even the right to own those guns you enjoy so much!

Your friendly local gun dealer can help you avoid gun-generated tangles with the law. As a federal licensee he receives from the BATF a copy of *State Laws and Published Ordinances—Firearms* every year, and this is the book mentioned earlier that has the compilation of many of the nation's gun laws. Ask him to let you look at his copy, so you can review the laws of your state and community as well as those of the other places in which you do your collecting. Better yet, talk him into loaning it to you long enough to have the critical pages photocopied. One very important caution, however, The state and local gun laws included in the BATF book are for the most part only those that affect a federal license holder's dealing or collecting activities. Not included in that publication are state or local regulations about such things as transportation or the use (or misuse) of guns. To be on the safe side, check with your village hall or local police for other possible gun laws. Then, after you've got a thorough knowledge of all the state and local regulations that might affect you, it's time to start on the federal laws.

The Gun Control Act of 1968 imposed rather severe restrictions on the collector of modern firearms, though not without some benefits as well. The most severe of these restrictions is the ban on interstate transfer of guns by individuals, which means a visitor to an out-of-state gun show or gun shop cannot buy and bring home a "modern" rifle, pistol or shotgun. On the other hand, there are no federal restrictions on traffic in "antique" firearms. All is not lost for the modern gun collector, however. He does have some perfectly legal ways to get around those restrictions, which we'll get to a bit later. First, let's consider an important definition.

The Gun Control Act of 1968 defines an antique firearm as:

(A) any firearm (including any firearm with a matchlock, flintlock, percussion cap, or similar type of ignition system) manufactured in or before 1898; and

(B) any replica of any firearm described in subparagraph (A) if such replica—

(i) is not designed or redesigned for using rimfire or conventional centerfire fixed ammunition, or

(ii) uses rimfire or conventional centerfire fixed ammunition which is no longer manufactured in the United States and which is not readily available in the ordinary channels of commercial trade.

This means that a 38 caliber Smith & Wesson "Lemon Squeezer" made in 1898 is an antique, even though its ammunition is available everywhere and the identical gun manufactured a year later would be subject to all the federal restrictions. On the other hand, any double-barrel Remington derringer in 41 rimfire is an antique even though they were made up to 1935. It's a pre-1898 model, and the ammunition is not readily available.

Collectors whose interests lie only with guns that satisfy the GCA's definition of antique should have no problems with the Gun Control Act and Bureau of Alcohol, Tobacco and Firearms, the federal agency responsible for enforcing it. One word of caution, however: The GCA's definition of antique may not and generally does not agree with state and local definitions. As a result, the deal you make on that pre-1898 Lemon Squeezer or Remington derringer could be highly illegal in your state or community, even though it's perfectly legitimate under the federal law. Know *all* your gun laws!

To stay clear of federal gun law violations, *never* buy, sell or trade modern guns with any individual who is not a fellow resident of the state in which you live. It is illegal, and could cause you great problems, either immediately or even years later. Limiting your collecting activities only to your state of residence is not acceptable, either. If you're a serious collector you may very well have all the worthwhile guns (Lugers, SAAs, Winchester Model 70s . . . you fill in the blank) in your state cornered already. Don't despair. There are two legal ways in which you can expand your collecting horizons to include the other 49 states, or if appropriate, even to the whole world.

A federal collector's license is one alternative, and for some collectors it is by far the best answer. For the very active collector it's probably the only reasonable answer. We'll go into the pros and cons of the collector's license a bit further on. First, let's consider the approach taken by a number of today's collectors of modern firearms.

The Gun Control Act prohibits the interstate transfer of modern guns except between licensees. It does not prohibit an unlicensed individual from making a deposit on or even paying in full for a gun offered for sale in another state. It only forbids his taking possession of it. As a result you *can* buy a gun at an out-of-state gun show or shop, or through an ad, specifying that delivery will be made by the seller to a licensed dealer in your state of residence. You then have your local dealer send a copy of his license to the

seller, the seller ships the gun to your local dealer, and your new gun is now a giant step closer to being yours.

Many gun shops are happy to act as go-betweens for out-of-state purchases by their good customers. It creates good will for them and gets you into their place of business, where you're likely to be tempted into buying some of their merchandise. However, don't expect them to perform this service for free. They'll have to log your gun in and out, take care of the BATF's form 4473 and any local regulations before they'll hand that new jewel over to you.

Even though this procedure is a bit cumbersome, and it costs you a few dollars each time you use it, it's clean and it's proper and it keeps you out of trouble. If you're doing a lot of buying out of state, however, it can become a lot of extra bother and expense to you. Let's consider the alternative, a collector's license.

A collector's license costs $10 a year. With it you can buy and sell with other licensees and—with some restrictions—individuals, without regard for state lines. As a licensed collector you are restricted to trafficking in "Curios and Relics," a classification that includes any gun (or ammunition) made more than 50 years before this date. In addition, a vast number of guns (and ammunition) of later manufacture have also been classified as curios and relics. The latest list of these arms, just released by the BATF as

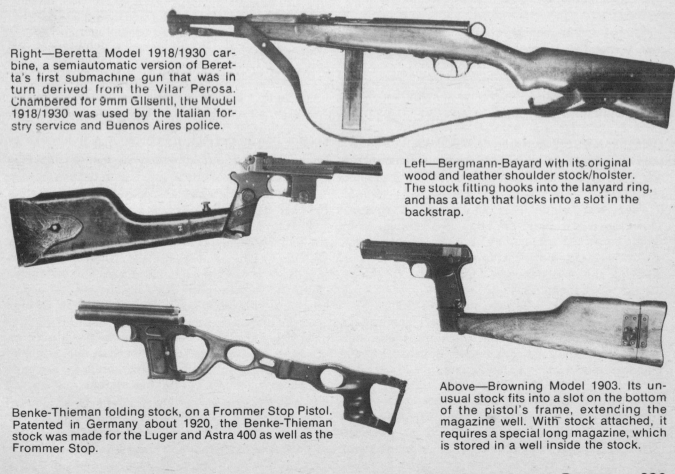

Right—Beretta Model 1918/1930 carbine, a semiautomatic version of Beretta's first submachine gun that was in turn derived from the Vilar Perosa. Chambered for 9mm Glisenti, the Model 1918/1930 was used by the Italian forstry service and Buenos Aires police.

Left—Bergmann-Bayard with its original wood and leather shoulder stock/holster. The stock fitting hooks into the lanyard ring, and has a latch that locks into a slot in the backstrap.

Benke-Thieman folding stock, on a Frommer Stop Pistol. Patented in Germany about 1920, the Benke-Thieman stock was made for the Luger and Astra 400 as well as the Frommer Stop.

Above—Browning Model 1903. Its unusual stock fits into a slot on the bottom of the pistol's frame, extending the magazine well. With stock attached, it requires a special long magazine, which is stored in a well inside the stock.

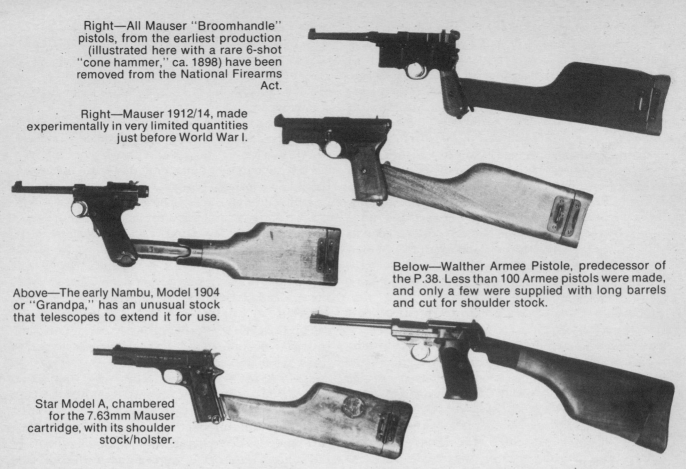

Right—All Mauser "Broomhandle" pistols, from the earliest production (illustrated here with a rare 6-shot "cone hammer," ca. 1898) have been removed from the National Firearms Act.

Right—Mauser 1912/14, made experimentally in very limited quantities just before World War I.

Above—The early Nambu, Model 1904 or "Grandpa," has an unusual stock that telescopes to extend it for use.

Below—Walther Armee Pistole, predecessor of the P.38. Less than 100 Armee pistols were made, and only a few were supplied with long barrels and cut for shoulder stock.

Star Model A, chambered for the 7.63mm Mauser cartridge, with its shoulder stock/holster.

this book was going to press, is included at the end of this article.

What, then, are the drawbacks of having a collector's license? The objection that seems to be raised most frequently is with regard to privacy. By accepting a federal license the individual agrees to keep a formal record of all of the post 1898 arms in his collection, and to make that record and the collection available for inspection by BATF representatives upon request. Many collectors feel that as long as they operate strictly within the law it is no one else's business what guns they have in their collections, and they are not willing to give up the degree of privacy that having a collector's license requires. This is obviously a matter of personal feeling—often strong personal feeling—but it's a consideration that should be thought out carefully before a decision is made as to whether or not to apply for a collector's license.

What benefit has the Gun Control Act of 1968 brought to the gun collector? The one clearcut gain the collector has made under the act is that it has made simple the legal ownership and transfer of a large number of arms whose ownership was formerly closely regulated. These include various short-barreled rifles, pistols with shoulder stocks, and certain other unusual arms that formerly came (like machine guns) under the controls of the National Firearms Act. A list of these arms, some of them illustrated here, appears at the end of this article.

The following pages are the Bureau of Alcohol, Tobacco and Firearms "Curios and Relics List for 1981." It is divided into four categories, and compared to previous lists, has seen a good deal of condensation. Note the explanation at the beginning of each grouping. The four categories are:

1. All rifles and pistols which have been specifically classified as "Curios and Relics." Important note: A "Curio and Relic" is *not* an antique, so its interstate transfer must always be through a federal license holder.

2. All cartridges that have received the "Curio and Relic" designation.

3. Weapons which, though they still come under the controls regularly associated with machine guns, may be bought and sold interstate by licensed collectors. Note that, unlike rifles and pistols, there are no "antique" machine guns. A machine gun made before 1898 must always be treated as a machine gun for transfer and possession.

4. Those arms that were previously classified with machine guns and short-barreled rifles but have now been removed from those controls. They are also classified as "Curios and Relics," so may be bought and sold interstate by licensed collectors.

Because group 4 has always been of special interest to the collecting fraternity, we are including pictures of a number of the guns in this fourth group. •

ATF Curios or Relics List for 1981

The following list contains those weapons and rounds of ammunition that ATF has determined to be curios or relics. The list is divided into four major subgroups, which are discussed in some detail in the preceding article. The subgroups in the following list are numbered from one to four to correspond with the subgroup number assigned to them in the article.

1 Firearms Classified as Curios or Relics Under 18 U.S.C. Chapter 44

The Bureau has determined that the following firearms are curios or relics as defined in 27 CFR 178.11 because they fall within one of the categories specified in the regulations.

Such determination merely classifies the firearms as curios or relics and thereby authorizes licensed collectors to acquire, hold or dispose of them as curios or relics subject to the provisions of 18 U.S.C. Chapter 44 and the regulations in 27 CFR Part 178. They are still "firearms" as defined in 18 U.S.C. 921(a)(3).

Armand Gevage .32ACP caliber semi-automatic pistols, as manufactured in Belgium prior to World War II.

Astra M 300 pistol, calibers 7.65mm and 9mm Kurz, marked with German Waffenamt acceptance stamp, 1939-1945.

Astra M 400 pistol, German Army Contract, caliber 9mm Bergmann-Bayard, Serial Number range 97351-98850.

Astra Model 400 semiautomatic pistol, second German Army Contract, caliber 9mm Bergmann-Bayard, in the serial number range 92851 through 97350.

Astra M 600 pistol, caliber 9mm Parabellum, marked with German Waffenamt acceptance stamp, 1939-1945.

Astra M 800 Condor Model, pistol, caliber 9mm Parabellum.

Baker Gun and Forging Company, all firearms manufactured from 1899 to to 1919.

Bannerman Model 1937, Springfield rifle, caliber 30-06.

Bayard Model 1923 semiautomatic pistol, caliber 7.65mm or .380, Belgian manufacture.

Beretta Model 1915 pistols, caliber 6.35mm, 7.65mm, and 9mm Glisenti.

Beretta Model 1915/1919 (1922) pistol (concealed hammer), caliber 7.65mm.

Beretta Model 1919 pistol (without grip safety), caliber 6.35 mm.

Beretta Model 1923 pistol, Caliber 9mm Glisenti.

Beretta Model 1931 pistol, bearing Italian Navy Crest consisting of the letters "RM" and an anchor on the grip medalion, caliber 7.65 mm.

Beretta Model 1932 pistol, having smooth wooden grips with "PB" medallion, caliber 9mm.

Beretta Model 1934 pistols, caliber 9mm post war variations bearing Italian Air Force eagle markings.

Beretta Model 1934 pistols, caliber 9mm, produced during 1945 or earlier and having serial numbers within the following ranges—500000 to 999999, F00001 to F120000, G0001 to G80000, 00001AA to 10000AA, or 00001BB to 10000BB. This classification does not include any post war variations dated sub-

sequent to 1945 or bearing post war Italian proof marks.

Beretta Model 1934 pistol, light weight model marked "Tipo Alleggerita" or "All" having transverse ribbed barrel, caliber 9mm.

Beretta Model 1935 pistol, Rumanian Contract, marked "P. Beretta—Cal. 9 Scurt—Mo. 1934—Brevet." on the slide, caliber 9mm.

Beretta Model 1935 pistol, Finnish Home Guard Contract, marked "SKY" on the slide, caliber 7.65mm.

Beretta Model 1935 pistols, caliber 7.65mm, produced during 1945 and earlier and having serial numbers below 620799.

Beretta M1951 pistol, Egyptian Contract, caliber 9mm Parabellum.

Beretta M1951 pistol, Israeli Contract, caliber 9mm Parabellum.

Bergmann-Bayard M1908 pistol, caliber 9mm Bergmann-Bayard.

Bernardelli Model 1956, experimental pistol, caliber 9mm Parabellum.

Bern Arsenal Experimental Gas Locked pistol, caliber 9mm Parabellum.

Bern Arsenal Experimental 16-shot pistol, caliber 9mm Parabellum.

FN Browning, Model 1902 (usually known as the Model 1903) semiautomatic pistol, caliber 9mm Browning long.

Browning Centennial Model High-Power Pistol, caliber 9mm Parabellum.

Browning Centennial Model 92 lever action rifle, caliber .44 Magnum.

Browning Superposed Centennial, consisting of a 20 gauge superposed shotgun, supplied with an extra set of .30-06 caliber superposed barrels.

Browning Hi-Power pistols, caliber 9mm having German Waffenamt inspector's marks.

Browning M1935 Hi-Power pistol, Canadian, Congolese, Indian and Nationalist Chinese Contracts, caliber 9mm Parabellum.

Browning "Baby" Model pistol, Russian Contract, caliber 6.35mm.

Browning M1910 and M1922 pistol, Contract pieces; M1910 Dutch Navy, M1922 Dutch or French Navy, and M1922 Yugoslavian Army calibers 7.65mm and 9mm Kurz.

Browning M1922 pistol, caliber 7.65 mm bearing German Navy acceptance stamps.

Browning M1922 pistol, caliber 9mm, bearing German Waffenamt acceptance stamp, 1939-1945.

Browning Model 1922 pistol, caliber 7.65mm, bearing German NSDAP or RFV markings.

Browning Model 1922 pistol, caliber 7.65mm or 9mm Kurz, marked with the Greek letters Epsilon Sigma denoting issue to the Greek Army.

Browning Model 1922 pistol, caliber 7.65mm or 9mm Kurz, marked "T.C. Subay" denoting issue to the Army of the Turkish Republic.

Browning Model 1922 pistol, caliber 7.65mm or 9mm Kurz, marked "C.P.I.M." denoting issue to the Belgian Political Police.

Browning Model 1922 pistol, caliber 7.65mm or 9mm Kurz, marked "S.P." and/or bearing the crest of the Kingdom Thailand.

Budischowsky, Model TP70, semiautomatic pistol, caliber .25 ACP, with custom serial number DB1.

Campo-Giro Model 1913 and 1913/16 pistol, caliber 9mm Largo.

Chinese Communist types 51 and 54 Tokarev pistols, caliber 7.62mm.

Chinese, Peoples Republic of China, copy of Japanese Type Sigiura Shiki semiautomatic pistol, caliber 7.65 mm.

Chylewski semiautomatic pistol manufactured by S.I.G. Switzerland, caliber 6.35mm (.25 ACP).

Clement pistol, Belgian manufacture, caliber 5mm Clement.

Colt Ace Service Model semiautomatic pistol, caliber .22, manufactured by Colt from 1935 to 1945, serial number range from SM1 to SM13803 including those marked "UNITED STATES PROPERTY" on the right side of the frame.

Colt Ace semiautomatic pistol, caliber .22, manufactured by Colt from 1931 to 1947, serial number range from 1 to 10935 including those marked "UNITED STATES PROPERTY" on the right side of the frame.

Colt Aircrewman revolver produced between 1951 and 1959, caliber .38 Special, marked "Property of U.S. Air Force" on back strap, having Air Force issue numbers of 1 thru 1189 and in the serial number range 1902LW thru 90470I W.

Colt Army Model double action revolver, any caliber, manufactured between 1899 and 1907.

Colt, First Model, Match Target Woodsman, caliber .22, semiautomatic pistol, manufactured from 1938 to 1944, serial numbers MT1 to MT15,000.

Colt, J frame, Officer's Model Match, .38 Special revolver manufactured from 1970 to 1972, identified by a J serial number prefix.

Colt Lightning Model double action revolver, any caliber manufactured between 1899 and 1909.

Colt Model 1900 semiautomatic pistol, caliber .38, in original configuration.

Colt Model 1902 semiautomatic pistol, sporting model, caliber .38, in original configuration.

Colt Model 1902 semiautomatic pistol, military model, caliber .38, in original configuration.

Colt Model 1903 Pocket (exposed hammer), semiautomatic pistol caliber .38 ACP.

Colt Model 1903 Pocket (hammerless), semiautomatic pistol, caliber .32.

Colt Model 1908, .25 ACP caliber, hammerless semiautomatic pistol having a grip safety, originally manufactured in Connecticut by Colt prior to 1956.

Colt Model 1908 Pocket (hammerless) semiautomatic pistol caliber .380.

Colt Model 1911 Commercial semiautomatic pistols, caliber .45 ACP, serial numbers C1 thru C130,000.

Colt Model 1911 pistol, English Contract, caliber .455.

Colt Model 1911-A1, commercial model, in caliber .45 and bearing Egyptian inscription meaning police, on the upper forward righthand side of the trigger guard and having serial numbers within the range of C186000 to C188000.

Colt Model 1911-A1, .45 caliber pistol, manufactured by Union Switch and Signal Company, prototype model, bearing serial number US & S Exp. 1 to US & S Exp. 100.

Colt Fourth Model Derringer, caliber .22 short rimfire, cased as a set of two pistols in a leather book titled "Colt Derringer, Limited Edition, by Colt," on the spine of the book and "A Limited Edition by Colt," on the cover.

Colt Government Model pistols in caliber .45 ACP, BB Series.

Colt Mk IV Series 70 semiautomatic pistols in all calibers, which were incorrectly marked at the factory with both Colt Government Model markings and Colt Commander markings.

Colt, Ned Buntline Commemorative, caliber .45. revolver.

Colt New Service revolvers as manufactured between 1898 and 1944, all variations, all calibers.

Colt Officers Model (1904-1930), .38 caliber revolver.

Colt Officers Model (1930-1949), .22 caliber revolver.

Colt Officers Model Match (1953-1969), .22 and .38 caliber revolvers.

Colt Officers Model Special (1949-1952), .22 and .38 caliber revolvers.

Colt Officers Model Target (1930-1949), .32 and .38 caliber revolvers.

Colt, single action Army (Bisley, Standard, and target variations), all original, manufactured from 1899 to 1946, serial number range from 182000 to 357869.

Colt, Abercrombie and Fitch, "Trailblazer," .45 New Frontier.

Colt, Alabama Sesquicentennial, .22.

Colt, Alamo, .22 and .45.

Colt, Abilene, .22 (Kansas City-Cow Town).

Colt, Appomattox Court House Centennial, .22 and .45.

Colt, Arizona Ranger Model Commemorative, .22 revolver.

Colt, Arizona Territorial Centennial, .22 and .45.

Colt, Arkansas Territory Sesquicentennial, .22.

Colt, Battle of Gettysburg Centennial, .22.

Colt, Belleau Wood, .45 Pistol, (World War I Series).

Colt, California Bicentennial, .22.

Colt, California Gold Rush, .22 and .45.

Colt, Camp Perry Single Shot, Target Pistols, .22 long rifle or .38 Special caliber.

Colt, Carolina Charter Tercentenary, .22 and .22/.45.

Colt, Chamizal Treaty, .22 and .45.

Colt, Chateau Thierry, .45 Pistol, (World War I Series).

Colt, Cherry's Sporting Goods 35th Anniversary, .22/.45.

Colt, Chisholm Trail, .22 (Kansas Series-Trails).

Colt, Civil War Centennial Single Shot, .22.

Colt, Coffeyville, .22 (Kansas Series-Cow Town).

Colt, Colorado Gold Rush, .22.

Colt, Colonel Samuel Colt, Sesquicentennial, .45.

Colt, Colt's 125th Anniversary, .45.

Colt, Columbus (Ohio) Sesquicentennial, .22.

Colt, H. Cook, "1 of 100," .22/.45.

Colt, Dakota Territory, .22.

Colt, Des Moines, Reconstruction of Old Fort, .22 and .45.

Colt, Dodge City, .22 (Kansas Series-Cow Town).

Colt, Wyatt Earp, Buntline Special, .45 (Lawman Series).

Colt, Wyatt Earp, .22 and .45 (Lawman Series).

Colt, European Theater, .45 Pistol (World War II Series).

Colt, Florida Territory Sesquicentennial, .22.

Colt, General Nathan Bedford Forrest, .22.

Colt, Fort Findlay (Ohio) Sesquicentennial, .22.

Colt, Fort Hays, .22 (Kansas Series-Forts).

Colt, Fort Larned, .22 (Kansas Series-Forts).

Colt, Fort McPherson (Nebraska) Centennial Derringer, .22.

Colt, Fort Scott, .22 (Kansas Series-Forts).

Colt, Fort Stephenson (Ohio) Sesquicentennial, .22.

Colt, Fort-Niner Miner, .22.

Colt, Pat Garrett, .22 and .45 (Lawman Series).

Colt, Genesco (Illinois) 125th Anniversary, Derringer, .22.

Colt, Golden Spike Centennial, .22.

Colt, Wild Bill Hickok, .22 and .45 (Lawman Series).

Colt, General Hood, Tennessee Campaign Centennial, .22.

Colt, Idaho Territorial Centennial, .22.

Colt, Indiana Sesquicentennial, .22.

Colt, Kansas Centennial, .22.

Colt, Maine Sesquicentennial, .22 and .45.

Colt, Bat Masterson, .22 and .45 (Lawman Series).

Colt, General George Meade, Pennsylvania Campaign, .22 and .45.

Colt, Meuse Argonne, .45 Pistol (World War I Series).

Colt, Montana Territory Centennial, .22 and .45.

Colt, Missouri Sesquicentennial, .22.

Colt, General John Hunt Morgan, Indiana Raid, .22.

Colt, Joaquin Murrieta, "1 of 100," .22/.45.

Colt, Nebraska Centennial, .22.

Colt, Nevada Centennial, .22 and .45.

Colt, Nevada Centennial "Battle Born," .22 and .45.

Colt, New Jersey Tercentenary, .22 and .45.

Colt, New Mexico Golden Anniversary, .22.

Colt, NRA Centennial, single action revolver, in calibers .357 Magnum and .45.

Colt, NRA Centennial, Gold Cup National Match pistol, in caliber .45.

Colt, Oklahoma Territory Diamond Jubilee, .22.

Colt, Oregon Trail, .22 (Kansas Series-Trails).

Colt, Pacific Theater, .45 Pistol (World War II Series).

Colt, Pawnee Trail, .22 (Kansas Series-Trails).

Colt, Peacemaker Commemorative, .22 and .45 revolver.

Colt, Pony Express, Russell, Majors and Waddell, Presentation Model .45.

Colt, Pony Express Centennial, .22.

Colt, Rock Island Arsenal Centennial Single Shot, .22.

Colt, St. Augustine Quadricentennial, .22.

Colt, St. Louis Bicentennial, .22 and .45.

Colt, Santa Fe Trail, .22 (Kansas Series-Trails).

Colt, Second (2nd) Marne, .45 Pistol (World War I Series).

Colt, Shawnee Trail, .22 (Kansas Series-Trails).

Colt, Sheriff's Model, .45.

Colt Single Action Army revolver, caliber .45, serial #85163A, Engraved and inlaid with a bust of President Abraham Lincoln.

Colt, Texas Ranger, .45.

Colt, "The Right to Keep and Bear Arms" commemorative, .22 caliber Peacemaker Buntline, single action revolver having a 7½-inch barrel with the inscription "The Right to Keep and Bear Arms" inscribed on the barrel and a serial number range of G0001RB thru G3000RB.

Colt, United States Bicentennial Commemorative, Python revolver, caliber .357.

Colt, United States Bicentennial Commemorative, single action army revolver, caliber .45.

Colt, West Virginia Centennial, .22 and .45.

Colt, Wichita, .22 (Kansas Series-Cow Town).

Colt, Woodsman, caliber .22, semiautomatic target pistol, manufactured from 1915 to 1943, serial number 1 to 157,000.

Colt, Wyoming Diamond Jubilee, .22.

Colt, 1873 Peacemaker Centennial 1973, single action revolver, 44/.40 or .45.

Czechoslovakian CZ50 pistol, caliber 7.65mm.

Czechoslovakian CZ52 pistol, caliber 7.62mm.

Czechoslovakian CZ27 pistol, caliber 7.65mm, with flanged barrel for silencer and bearing German Waffenamt acceptance stamp, 1939-1945.

Czechoslovakian CZ38 pistol, caliber 9mm Kurz, with or without German Waffenamt acceptance stamp.

Czechoslovakian Model 24 pistol, caliber 9mm Kurz, marked with German Navy acceptance stamps, Navy proof marks or issuance marks.

Czechoslovakian Model 27 pistol, caliber 7.65mm, marked with German Navy acceptance stamps, Navy proof marks or issuance marks.

Czechoslovakian Model 1927 pistol, caliber 7.65mm, bearing German Waffenamt acceptance markings.

Czechoslovakian Model 1952 and 1952/57, 7.62 x 45mm and 7.62 x 39mm caliber, semiautomatic rifles (Puska Vzor 52, 7.62 x 45mm, and Puska Vzor 52/57, 7.62 x 39mm).

Danish M1910/1921 Bayard, pistol, caliber 9mm Bergmann-Bayard.

Davis Warner Infallible, semiautomatic pistol, caliber .32.

Dreyse Military Model 1910 pistol, caliber 9mm.

Egyptian Hakim (Ljungman) 7.92mm semiautomatic rifle as manufactured in Egypt.

Esser-Barratt, English manufacture, slide action rifle, caliber .303.

French S.A.C.M. Model 1935A pistol, caliber 7.65 Long, marked with German Navy acceptance stamps, Navy proof marks or issuance marks.

French M1935 pistol, caliber 7.65 French Long, bearing German Waffenamt acceptance stamp for period of 1939-1945.

French Model 1949, caliber 7.5mm, semiautomatic rifle (Fusil Mle. 1949 (MAS) 7.5mm).

German P38 pistols, caliber 9mm Parabellum manufactured prior to 1947.

Gustloff semiautomatic pistol, in caliber 7.65mm, manufactured by Gustloff Werke, Suhl, Germany.

Hammond or Grant Hammond pistols, all models, variations or prototypes, made by Grant Hammond Corporation, New Haven, Connecticut.

Hammond/Hi-Standard semiautomatic pistols, in caliber .45.

Harrington and Richardson, Abilene Anniversary, .22 revolver.

Harrington and Richardson, Centennial Officer's Model Springfield rifle, .45-70 Govt.

Harrington and Richardson, Centennial Standard Model Springfield rifle, .45-70 Govt.

Harrington and Richardson, Self-loading semiautomatic pistol, caliber .32.

Hartford Arms and Equipment Company single shot target pistol, caliber .22LR.

Hartford Arms and Equipment Company repeating pistol, caliber .22LR.

Hartford Arms and Equipment Company Model 1928 pistol, caliber .22LR.

Hi-Standard experimental electric free pistol, caliber .22 long rifle.

Hi-Standard Model P38, semiautomatic pistol, caliber .38 special.

Hi-Standard experimental Model T-3 semiautomatic pistol, caliber 9mm Luger.

High-Standard Model C/S smoothbore .22 caliber shot semiautomatic pistols, bearing serial numbers 59279, 59473, 59478, or 59460.

Hi-Standard experimental ISU rapid fire semiautomatic pistol, caliber .22 short.

High Standard Model A pistol, caliber .22LR.

High Standard Model B pistol, caliber .22LR.

High Standard Model C pistol, caliber .22Short.

High Standard Model D pistol, caliber .22LR.

High Standard Model E pistol, caliber .22LR.

High Standard Model H-A pistol, caliber .22LR.

High Standard Model H-B pistol, first model, caliber .22LR.

High Standard Model H-B pistol, second model, caliber .22LR.

High Standard Model H-D pistol, caliber .22LR.

High Standard Model H-E pistol, caliber .22LR.

High Standard Model USA-HD pistol, caliber .22LR.

High Standard Model HD-Military pistol, caliber .22LR.

High Standard Model G-380 pistol, caliber .380.

High Standard Model G-B pistol, caliber .22LR.

High Standard Model G-D pistol, caliber .22LR.

High Standard Model G-E pistol, caliber .22LR.

High Standard Model G-O (First Model Olympic) pistol, caliber .22 Short.

High Standard Supermatic Trophy,

Model 107, .22 pistol Olympic Commemorative Model.

Hungarian Frommer Model 1937 pistol, caliber 7.65mm, marked with German Navy acceptance stamps, Navy proof marks or issuance marks.

Hungarian Model 1937 pistol, caliber 7.65mm, bearing German Waffenamt acceptance markings.

Italian Brixia M1906, pistol, caliber 9mm Glisenti.

Italian Glisenti M1910, pistol, caliber 9mm Glisenti.

Ithaca double barrel shotguns actually manufactured in New York by the Ithaca Gun Company, Ithaca, New York. All gauges and all models, having barrels at least 18 inches in length and an overall length of at least 26 inches, manufactured before 1950.

Ithaca Gun Company single barrel trap guns, break open all gauges, all models actually manufactured at Ithaca, New York, before 1950.

Ithaca, St. Louis Bicentennial, Model 49, .22 rifle.

Japanese Type I Hamada (1941) pistol, caliber 7.65mm.

Japanese Type II Hamada, pistol, caliber 7.65mm.

Japanese Type 14 (1925) pistol, caliber 8mm Nambu.

Japanese Type 94 (Model 1934), pistol, caliber 8mm Nambu (8 x 21mm cartridge), manufactured in Japan 1934-1945.

Japanese "Grandpa" Nambu, Model 1904, pistol, caliber 8mm Nambu.

Japanese "Baby" Nambu pistol, caliber 7mm Nambu.

Japanese Type Sigiura Shiki semiautomatic pistol, caliber 7.65mm and 6.35mm.

Jieffeco pistol, Belgian manufacture, caliber 7.65mm.

Jieffeco, semiautomatic pistol, in caliber .25 ACP, marked "Davis Warner Arms Corp., N.Y."

Kimball pistols, all models, all calibers.

Kolibri pistols, calibers 2.7mm and 3mm Kolibri.

L. C. Smith Shotguns manufactured by Hunter Arms Company and Marlin Firearms Company from 1899 to 1971.

Lahti L-35 pistol, Finnish manufacture, caliber 9mm Parabellum.

Luger, pistol, all models and variations manufactured prior to 1946.

Luger, Mauser commercal manufacture, semiautomatic pistol, 70 Jahre, Parabellum-Pistole, Keiserreich Russland, commemorative, caliber 9mm.

Luger, Mauser commercial manufacture, semiautomatic pistol, 75 Jahre, Parabellum-Pistole, 1900-1975, commemorative, caliber 7.65mm.

Luger, Mauser commercial manufacture, semiautomatic pistol, 75 Jahre, Parabellum-Pistole, Konigreich Bulgarien, commemorative, caliber 7.65mm.

MAB Model D pistol, caliber 7.65mm bearing German Navy acceptance stamp.

MAB Model D pistol, caliber 7.65mm bearing German Waffenamt acceptance stamp for the period 1939-1945.

MAB Model R pistol, caliber 9mm Parabellum.

Makarov pistol, Russian and East German, caliber 9mm Makarov.

Mannlicher pistol, M1900, M1901, M1903 and M1905, caliber 7.63mm Mannlicher.

Marlin 90th Anniversary, Model 39-A, .22 Rifle.

Marlin 90th Anniversary, Model 39-A, .22 Carbine.

Original military bolt action and semi-automatic rifles manufactured between 1899 and 1946.

Mauser, semiautomatic pistols manufactured prior to 1946, any caliber.

Menz Llllput, German manufacture, caliber 4.25mm.

Menz PBIII, in caliber 7.65mm, manufactured by August Menz, Suhl, Germany.

Menz PBIIIA, in caliber 7.65mm, manufactured by August Menz, Suhl, Germany.

Menz PBIV, in caliber 7.65mm, manufactured by August Menz, Suhl, Germany.

Menz PBIVa, in caliber 7.65mm, manufactured by August Menz, Suhl, Germany.

Menz Special, in caliber 7.65mm, manufactured by August Menz, Suhl, Germany.

Mexican Obregon, pistol, caliber .45 ACP.

Mugica Model 120, pistol, caliber 9mm Parabellum.

North Korean Type 1964, pistol, caliber 7.62mm Tokarev.

Norwegian M1914, pistol, caliber .45 ACP.

PAF "Junior" semiautomatic pistol, caliber .25, manufactured by the Pretoria Arms Factory Ltd. of South Africa.

PAF pistol, marked "BRF," caliber .25, manufactured by the Pretoria Arms Factory Ltd. of South Africa.

Phoenix (U.S.A.) pistol, caliber .25 ACP.

Polish FB "VIS," M1935 (Radom), pistol, caliber 9mm Parabellum, Original Republic of Poland model with an eagle crest and Polish inscription on left side of slide. Dated 1936, 1937, 1938, or 1939 and having small sized serial numbers in the range 1 through 50,000 without letter or number prefix or suffix.

Polish VB "VIS" Model 1935 (Radom) pistol, caliber 9mm Parabellum, bearing German military acceptance markings.

Reising .22 caliber, semiautomatic pistol.

Remington Canadian Territorial Centennial, Model 742, Rifle.

Remington, Model 51, semiautomatic pistol, calibers .32 ACP or .380 ACP.

Remington 150th Anniversary Model 1100SA semiautomatic shotgun, caliber 12 gauge.

Remington 150th Anniversary Model 870SA slide action shotgun, caliber 12 gauge.

Remington 150th Anniversary Model 742ADL semiautomatic rifle, caliber .30/06.

Remington 150th Anniversary Model 760ADL slide action rifle, caliber .30/06.

Remington 150th Anniversary Model 552A semiautomatic rifle, caliber .221r.

Remington 150th Anniversary Model 572A slide action rifle, caliber .221r.

Remington 150th Anniversary Model Nylon 66 semiautomatic rifle, caliber .221r.

Remington Montana Territorial Centennial, Model 600, Rifle.

Roth Steyr 1907, semiautomatic pistol, caliber 8mm.

Ruger Canadian Centennial, Matched No. 1 Rifle Sets, Special Deluxe.

Ruger Canadian Centennial, Matched No. 2 Rifle Sets.

Ruger Canadian Centennial, Matched No. 3 Rifle Sets.

Ruger Canadian Centennial, Model 10/22, Carbine.

Ruger, flattop, "Blackhawk" revolvers, calibers .44 Magnum and .357 Magnum, all barrel lengths, made from 1955 through 1962.

Ruger, flattop, single-six, .22 caliber revolvers with flat side loading gate, all barrel lengths, made from 1953 through 1956.

Sauer 38(h), pistol, caliber 7.65mm marked with Third Reich police acceptance stamps of Eagle C, F, K or L.

Sauer 38H pistol, caliber 7.65mm bearing German Waffenamt acceptance markings.

Savage Arms, semiautomatic pistols, caliber .45 ACP, all models.

Savage, Prototype pistols, caliber .25, .32 and .38 made between 1907 and 1927.

Savage, Model 1907 Pistols, caliber .32 and .380.

Savage, Model 1907 Pistols, caliber .45 military contract.

Savage, Model 1911 Pistol, caliber .45, Prototype.

Savage, Model 1915 Pistol, caliber .32 and .380.

Savage, Model 1917 Pistol, caliber .32 and .380.

Smith and Wesson, U.S. Border Patrol 50th Anniversary Commemorative, Model 66, stainless steel, caliber .357 Magnum, revolvers.

Smith & Wesson, Model .22/32 Hand Ejector (Bekeart Model), caliber .22 LR, serial numbers 138220 to 534636 (no letter).

Smith & Wesson, K-22 Hand Ejector, caliber .22 LR, serial numbers 632132 to 696952 (no letter).

Smith & Wesson, K-32 Hand Ejector (K-32 Masterpiece), caliber .32 S&W Long, serial numbers 653388 to 682207 (no letter).

Smith & Wesson, .38 Hand Ejector Military and Police, caliber .38, serial numbers 1 to 241703 (no letter).

Smith & Wesson, .357 Magnum Hand Ejector, caliber .357 Magnum, serial numbers 45768 to 60000 (no letter).

Smith & Wesson, .44 Hand Ejector, all calibers, serial numbers 1 to 62488 (no letter).

Smith & Wesson, .455 Mark II Hand Ejector, caliber .455.

Smith & Wesson Mercox Dart Gun, caliber .22 rimfire, blank.

Smith & Wesson, .22/32 Kit Gun, caliber .22 LR, serial numbers 525670 to 534636 (no letter).

Smith & Wesson, .32 Double Action Top Break, caliber .32 S&W, serial numbers 209302 and higher.

Smith & Wesson, .32 Safety Hammerless Top Break (New Departure), caliber .32 S&W, serial numbers 91401 and higher.

Smith & Wesson, .38 Double Action Top Break, caliber .38 S&W, serial numbers 382023 and higher.

Smith & Wesson, .38 Double Action Top Break Perfected Model, caliber .38 S&W.

Smith & Wesson, .38 Safety Hammerless Top Break (New Departure), caliber .38 S&W, serial number 119901 and higher.

Smith & Wesson, pistol, caliber .35, all variations.

Smith & Wesson, 2nd Model, single shot pistol, calibers .22 rimfire, .32 S & W and .38 S & W.

Smith & Wesson, 3rd Model, single shot pistol, caliber .22 rimfire, .32 S & W and .38 S & W.

Smith & Wesson, 1st Model, Ladysmith revolver, caliber .22 rimfire long.

Smith & Wesson, 2nd Model, Ladysmith revolver, caliber .22 rimfire long.

Smith & Wesson, 3rd Model, Ladysmith revolver, caliber .22 rimfire long.

Smith & Wesson Model 39-1 (52-A), pistol, caliber 9mm Parabellum.

Smith & Wesson Model 39, steel frame pistol, caliber 9mm Parabellum.

Smith & Wesson, pistol, caliber .32 ACP.

Smith & Wesson Model Straight Line, single shot pistol, caliber .22 rimfire long rifle.

Smith & Wesson, Model 16 (K-32 Masterpiece), caliber .32 S&W Long, "K" serial number series.

Smith & Wesson, .38/44 Outdoorsman & Heavy Duty, caliber .38, serial numbers 36500 to 62023 (no letter).

Smith & Wesson 150th Anniversary Texas Ranger Commemorative Model 19 revolver.

Smith and Wesson, Model 10 Victory Models, identified by the letter "V" prefix to the serial number, in the original .38 Special chambering, with U.S. Navy acceptance marks.

Smith & Wesson, U.S. Army Model of 1917, caliber .45, serial numbers 1 to 163476.

Standard Arms Co., rifle/shotgun combination, U.S., Model "Camp," slide action caliber .50.

Standard Arms Co., rifle Model G, slide action or gas operated, caliber unknown.

Standard Arms Co., rifle Model M, slide action caliber .25-.35, .30 Rem. and .35 Rem.

Star Model B semiautomatic pistol, caliber 9mm Parabellum, having German military acceptance marks and in the serial number range 21597 through 249687.

Steyr-Hahn M1912, pistol, caliber 9mm Steyr.

Steyr-Hahn M1912, pistol, caliber 9mm Parabellum marked with Third Reich police acceptance stamps of Eagle C, F, K or L.

Sosso pistols manufactured by Guilio Sosso, Turin, Italy, or Fabrica Nationale D'Armi, Brescea Italy, caliber 9mm.

Tauler Model military and police pistol.

Tokagypt 58, pistol, caliber 9mm Parabellum.

Unique Model 17 pistol, French manufacture, caliber 7.65mm bearing German Waffenamt acceptance stamp for period of 1939-1945.

Unique Kriegsmodell pistol, French manufacture, caliber 7.65mm, bearing German Waffenamt acceptance stamp for period 1939-1945.

U.S. Model 1911 semiautomatic pistol, military series, caliber .45, serial-number range from 1 to 629500, all original variations regardless of manufacture including: The North American Arms Company, Model 1911; the Springfield Armory, Model 1911 with NRA markings; the Remington Arms-UMC, Model 1911; and any Model 1911 cutaways.

U.S. pistols, Model 1911-A1, caliber .45, manufactured by the Singer Manufacturing Company in 1942, serial-number range from S800001 to S800500.

U.S. Model 1911-A1 semiautomatic pistol, caliber .45, manufactured by Remington Rand, bearing serial number prefix of ERRS.

U.S. Model 1911-A1 semiautomatic pistol, caliber .45, produced as original factory cutaways.

U.S. Rifle, caliber .30 MC-1952, equipped with telescopic sight mount MC, telescopic sight MC1, marked U.S.M.C. or kollmorgan.

Walther pistols, Manufactured at Zella-Mehlis prior to 1946, all models any caliber. *

Webley Model 1909, pistol, caliber 9mm Browning Long.

Webley and Scott, Model 1910 and 1913 high velocity pistols, caliber .38 ACP.

Webley and Scott, M1913, Navy or Commercial, self-loading pistol, caliber .455.

Webley-Fosbury, semiautomatic revolvers, all calibers, all models.

Winchester 1980 Alberta Diamond Jubilee Commemorative carbines, Model 94, in caliber .38/55.

Winchester Alaskan Purchase Centennial, Model 1894, carbine.

Winchester Antlered Game Commemorative, Model 94, carbine, caliber .30-30.

Winchester Apache Commemorative carbine, commemorative edition of Model 1894 Winchester with serial number prefix of AC.

Winchester Bicentennial 76, Model 94 carbine.

Winchester Buffalo Bill, Model 1894, carbine.

Winchester Buffalo Bill, Model 1894, Rifle.

Winchester Canadian 1967, Centennial Model 1894, carbine.

Winchester Canadian 1967, Centennial Model 1894, Rifle.

Winchester Centennial, Model 1866, carbine.

Winchester Centennial, Model 1866, Rifle.

Winchester Comanche Commemorative carbine, commemorative edition of Model 1894 Winchester with serial number prefix of CC.

Winchester Cowboy Commemorative, Model 94, carbine.

*Also includes postwar Model PP marked "Manhurin."

Winchester Golden Spike, Model 1894, carbine.

Winchester Illinois Sesquicentennial, Model 1894, carbine.

Winchester Klondike Gold Rush Commemorative Model 94, carbine.

Winchester Legendary Lawman Commemorative, Model 94, carbine, caliber .30-30.

Winchester Legendary Frontiersman Model 94 rifle, caliber .38-55.

Winchester "Limited Edition II" Model 94 rifle, caliber .30-30.

Winchester Little Big Horn Centennial, Model 94, carbine.

Winchester Lone Star Commemorative, Model 94, carbine.

Winchester Lone Star Commemorative, rifle, Model 94, .30-30.

Winchester "Ducks Unlimited" shotgun, Model 12, bearing serial numbers DU-001 through DU-800 (Commemorative).

Winchester "Matched Set of 1000," a cased pair consisting of a Winchester Model 94 rifle, caliber .30-30 and a Winchester Model 9422 rifle, caliber .22.

Winchester Model 52, rifle, bearing serial numbers 1 to 6,500.

Winchester Model 53, all original, manufactured from 1924 to 1947 with 16 inch or longer barrel, and 26 inch or longer overall length.

Winchester Model 54, rifle, speed lock variation, caliber .270.

Winchester Model 65, all original, manufactured from 1933 to 1947 with 16 inch or longer barrel and 26 inch or longer overall length.

Winchester Model 70 Ultra Match Target Special Grade rifle, caliber .308.

Winchester rifles, Model 70, .308, .270 Winchester, and 30-06 caliber, 19 inch barrel and Mannlicher type stock, made from 1968 to 1971.

Winchester Model 71, all original, manufactured from 1936 to 1958, with 16 inch or longer barrel and 26 inch or longer overall length.

Winchester Limited Edition, Model 94 carbine, caliber .30-30, serial numbers 77L1 through 77L1500.

Winchester Model 1873, all original, manufactured from 1899 to 1925, with 16 inch or longer barrel and 26 inch or longer overall length.

Winchester Model 1885 (single shot rifle), all original, manufactured from 1899 to 1920, with 16 inch or longer barrel, and 26 inch or longer overall length.

Winchester Model 1886, all original, manufactured from 1899 to 1935, with 16 inch or longer barrel and 26 inch or longer overall length.

Winchester Model 1892, all original, manufactured from 1899 to 1947, with 16 inch or longer barrel and 26 inch or longer overall length.

Winchester Model 1894 rifles and carbines manufactured prior to January 2, 1964, and having a serial number of less than 2,700,000, provided their barrel length is at least 16 inches and their overall length at least 26 inches.

Winchester Model 1895, all original manufactured from 1899 to 1938, with 16 inch or longer barrel and 26 inch or longer overall length.

Winchester Nebraska Centennial, Model 1894, carbine.

Winchester NRA Centennial rifle, Model 94, .30-30.

Winchester Model NRA Centennial, Model 94 carbine.

Winchester Mounted Police, Model 94, carbine.

Winchester Northwest Territories Centennial rifle.

Winchester rifle, Model 70, caliber .308 rifle, 19 inch barrel and Mannlicher type stock, made from 1968 to 1971.

Winchester Royal Canadian Mounted Police Centennial, Model 94 carbine.

Winchester 150th Anniversary Texas Ranger Commemorative, Model 1894, carbine.

Winchester Theodore Roosevelt, Model 1894, carbine.

Winchester Theodore Roosevelt, Model 1894, Rifle.

Winchester Wells Fargo and Company Commemorative, Model 94 carbines.

Winchester Wyoming Diamond Jubilee, Model 94 carbine.

Winchester Yellow Boy Indian, Model 94 carbine.

2 Ammunition Classified as Curios or Relics

The Bureau has determined the following ammunition to be curios or relics as defined in 27 CFR 178.11.

Such determination merely classifies the ammunition as curios or relics and thereby authorizes licensed collectors to acquire, hold or dispose of them as curios or relics, subject to the provisions of 18 U.S.C. Chapter 44 and the regulations in 27 CFR Part 178. They are still "ammunition" as defined in 18 U.S.C. 921(a)(17).

1. Foreign Military Rifle Cartridges
- 7.65mm Argentine Navy Match
- 7.92mm anti-tank cartridge for the Polish (Marosczek) anti-tank rifle described as a caliber 7.92mm, Gr 39 Granatbuchse.
- 7.92mm anti-tank cartridge for the German PzB 38, PzB 39, and Gr 39 anti-tank rifle.
- 8x52Rmm Siamese Mauser, manufactured in Japan, for the Government of Siam.
- 8x56Rmm Portuguese Kropachek, manufactured in Austria, for the Government of Portugal.
- 8 X 60mm Guedes M85 Portuguese
- 8 X 53mm Japanese Murata
- 9.5 X 60mm Turkish Mauser
- 10.15 X 61mm Jarman
- 10.15 X 63mm Serbian Mauser
- 10.75 X 58mm Russian Berdan
- 11 X 50mm Belgian Albini M67/72
- 11 X 53mm Belgian Comblain M71
- 11 X 60mm Japanese Murata
- 11.15 X 58mm (.43) Spanish Remington
- 11.15 X 58mm Austrian Werndl M77
- 11 X 59 French Gras
- 11.43 X 55mm Turkish
- 11.43 X 50mm (.43) Egyptian Remington
- 11.4 X 50mm Austrian Werndl M73
- 11.4 X 50mm Brazilian Comblain M74
- 11.5 X 57mm (.43) Spanish Reformado
- 11.7 X 51mm Danish Remington
- 11 X 52mm Netherlands Beaumont M71/78
- 11.3 X 50mm Beaumont M71
- 12.11 X 44mm Remington M67 (Norway & Sweden)

2. European Sporting Rifle Cartridges
- 6 X 29.5mm Stahl
- 6 X 57mm Mauser
- 6 X 58 Forester (Rimless and Rimmed)
- 6.5 X 27mm
- 6.5 X 53.5mm Daudeteau
- 6.5 X 48mm Sauer
- 7.7 X 60mm
- 8 X 48mm Sauer
- 8 X 51mm Mauser
- 8 X 42mm
- 8 X 71mm Peterlongo
- 8 X 75mm (Rimmed and Rimless)
- 8 X 58mm Sauer
- 9 X 70mm Mauser
- 9 X 71mm Peterlongo
- 9.1 X 40mm
- 9.3 X 53mm Swiss
- 9.3 X 53mm Collath
- 9.3 X 72mm Sauer
- 9.3 X 54mm Hebler
- 9.5 X 47mm
- 9.5 X 73mm Miller Greiss Magnum
- 10.25 X 69mm Hunter-Express
- 10.5 X 47mm
- 10.75 X 57mm
- 10.75 X 63mm Mauser
- 10.75 X 65mm Collath
- 10.8 X 47mm Martini

3. British Sporting Rifle Cartridges
- .255 Rook Rifle
- .375/.303 Axite
- .400/.360 Purdey Flanged
- .400/.360 Wesley Richards
- .360 No. 2 Nitro Express
- .369 Purdey Nitro Express
- .375 Rimless Wesley Richards Nitro
- .450 Nitro Express
- .450 No. 2 Nitro Express
- .450 Black Powder Express
- .450 Nitro for Black Powder Express
- .475 No. 2 Jeffery
- .476 Nitro Express
- .500 Black Powder Express
- .600 Nitro Express

4. Pistol and Revolver Cartridges
- 2.7mm Kolibri Auto
- 3mm Kolibri Auto
- 4.25mm Liliput Auto
- 5mm Clement Auto
- 5mm Bergmann
- 5.5 Velo Dog Short
- 6.5mm Bergmann (Without extractor groove)
- 6.5mm Bergmann, standard rimless
- 7mm Baby Nambu
- .30/7.65mm Borchardt
- 7.65mm Roth-Sauer
- .35 Smith & Wesson Auto
- .38 Long Colt
- 9.8 Auto Colt
- .44 Smith & Wesson (Martin Primer)
- .44 Colt-Remington (Martin Primer)
- 11mm German Service Revolver
- 11mm French Ordnance Revolver
- 11.75mm Montenegrin Revolver
- .450 Long Revolver
- .50 Remington (M71 Army)
- .577 Pistol

5. U.S. Rimfire Cartridges
- .22 Rimfire caliber cartridges with experimental aluminum or steel cartridge cases
- .25 Short
- .267 Rimfire caliber government experimental cartridge manufactured by Remington
- .30 Short
- .30 Long
- .32 Extra Short
- .32 Long Rifle
- .32 Extra Long
- .35 Allen
- .38 Extra Long
- .41 Long
- .44 Short
- .44 Long
- .44 Extra Long

.46 Short
.46 Long
.46 Extra Long
.50 Remington Navy
.50 Peabody Musket
.50-70 Government
.52-70 Sharps
.54 Ballard
.56-46 Spencer
.56-50 Spencer
.56-52 Spencer, Tapered
.56-52 Spencer, Bottleneck
.56-56 Spencer
.58 Joslyn Carbine
.58 Miller
.58 Gatling Gun
.58 Mont Storm (Also known as .61 Caliber)

6. U.S. Centerfire Rifle Cartridges
.22 Extra Long (Maynard)
.22-15-60 Stevens
.22 Newton (Wildcat)
.25-21 Stevens
.25-25 Stevens
.25-36 Marlin
.28 caliber centerfire experimental, manufactured at Frankford Arsenal
28-30-120 Stevens
.30-03 Government (Note: Also known as Springfield)
.30-06 Commemorative, commemorating 50 years of the .30-06 cartridge as the standard U.S. service cartridge (Headstamped USFA 1906-56)
.30-06 caliber cartridges manufactured by commercial manufacturers under government contract with headstamps indicating use for Palma Matches.
.30-30 Wesson
.30-40 Wesson
Winchester "Bicentennial 76," caliber .30-30 Super X
.308 Winchester, marked "Palma Match"
.32 Long Rifle
.32 Ballard Extra Long
.32-30 Remington
.32 Winchester Self Loading
.32-35 Stevens
.32-35 Maynard
.32-40 Remington

.32-40 Bullard
.32-30 Maynard 1882
.35 Winchester Self Loading
.35-40 Maynard
.38 Long
.38 Ballard Extra Long
.38-35 Stevens
.38-40 Remington-Hepburn
.38-45 Bullard
.38-45 Stevens
.38-50 Maynard
.38-50 Ballard
.38-50 Remington-Hepburn
.38-70 Winchester
.38-90 Winchester Express
.40 Martin Primed
.40-40 Maynard 1882
.40-50 Sharps (Straight)
.40-50 Sharps (Necked)
.40-60 Maynard 1882
.40-60 Marlin
.40-63 Ballard
.40-65 Ballard Everlasting
.40-70 Ballard
.40-70 Maynard
.40-70 Peabody "What Cheer"
.40-70 Winchester
.40-70 Sharps (Straight)
.40-70 Sharps (Necked)
.40-70 Remington
.40-75 Bullard
.40-85 Ballard
.40-90 Ballard
.40-90 Bullard
.40-90 Sharps (Necked)
.40-90 Sharps (Straight)
.40-90 Peabody "What Cheer"
.40-110 Winchester Express
.42 Martin Primer
.44 Henry
.44 Evans Short
.44 Evans Long
.44 Long C.F.
.44 Extra Long Ballard
.44 Wesson Extra Long
.44-40 Extra Long
.44-60 Peabody "Creedmoor"
.44-60 Winchester
.44-60 Sharps (Necked)
.44-70 Maynard
.44-75 Ballard Everlasting
.44-77 Sharps
.44-77 Remington

.44-85 Wesson
.44-90 Remington (Straight 2-6/10 inch case)
.44-90 Sharps (Necked)
.44-90 Remington (Straight)
.44-95 Peabody "What Cheer"
.44-100 Ballard
.44-100 Remington "Creedmoor" (Straight 2-6/10 inch case)
.44-100 Wesson
.45-50 Peabody (Sporting)
.45-70 Van Choate
.45-75 Sharps (Straight) Note: Identical to .45-70 Govt. Cartridge
.45-78-475 Wolcott
.45-80 Sharpshooter
.45-100 Ballard
.45-100 Sharps (Straight)
.45-100 Remington
.45-120 Sharps (Straight, 3¼ inch case)
.45-125 Winchester
.50 caliber experimental machine gun cartridge with aluminum cartridge case
.50-50 Maynard
.50 U.S. Carbine
.50 Government
.50 Remington
.50-70 Musket
.50-90 Sharps
.50-95 Winchester
.50-100 Sharps
.50-110 Sharps
.50-115 Bullard
.50-140 Sharps
.50-140 Winchester Express
.55-100 Maynard
.58 U.S. Musket (Berdan)
.58 Berdan Carbine
.60 Caliber experimental cartridge
.70-150 Winchester

7. Miscellaneous Cartridges
Duplex cartridges in all calibers with the exception of 7.62mm NATO
All cartridges intended for use in "squeeze bore" firearms e.g. Gerlach taper bore ammunition
Dardick cartridges (Trounds) in all calibers

3 National Firearms Act Weapons Classified as Curios or Relics Under 18 U.S.C. Chapter 44

The Bureau has determined that the following National Firearms Act weapons are curios or relics as defined in 27 CFR 178.11 because of their dates of manufacture.

These National Firearms Act weapons classified as curios or relics are still subject to all the controls under the National Firearms Act. However, licensed collectors may acquire hold or dispose of them as curios or relics subject to the provisions of 18 U.S.C. Chapter 44 and 27 CFR Part 178. They are still "firearms" as defined in the National Firearms Act and 18 U.S.C. 921(a)(3).

Alarm Pistol, serial number IRS-3591, caliber .22 rimfire, marked Patent Pending about 1883, which rings an alarm bell and also fires a cartridge when set to do so.

Astra Model 901 selective fire pistol, caliber 7.63mm (.30 Mauser).

Astra Model 902 selective fire pistol, caliber 7.63mm (.30 Mauser).

Astra Model 903 selective fire pistol, caliber 7.63mm (.30 Mauser).

Astra Model F selective fire pistol, caliber 9mm Bergmann.

Royal selective fire pistol caliber 7.63mm (.30 Mauser), copy of Mauser Model 1896 pistol.

Azul selective fire pistol, caliber 7.63mm (.30 Mauser), copy of Mauser Model 1896 pistol.

Austrian Swartzlose machinegun, Models 1905 and 1907/1912, caliber 8mm.

Belgian made, double barrel, caliber 9mm rimfire, shot pistol with external hammers and 7¾-inch barrels with the words "Foreign" stamped on the barrels.

Benet Mercie machine rifle, Model 1909 (French and American manufacture), caliber 8mm Lebel or .30.

Boys MK1, 0.55 inch anti-tank rifle.

Bren light machineguns, any model, any caliber, British Commonwealth manufacture.

British Lanchester (Lancaster) Mk 1 and Mk 1*, 9mm, submachineguns manufactured in England, during World War II.

British STEN submachineguns, Mk. I, Mk. II, Mk. III, Mk. IV, and Mk. V, caliber 9mm, original British Commonwealth Military issue only.

Browning Automatic Rifle (BAR), Models 1918 and modified Model 1918A2, manufactured by Colt, Marlin-Rockwell, and Winchester.

Cane Gun, cane with horn handle, silver tipped, wood covered steel, breech loading, smooth bore barrel, serial number IRS-5834, caliber .32 centerfire.

Cane Gun, English walking stick, bamboo covered steel rifled barrel and horn handle, serial number IRS-3589, caliber .38 centerfire.

Cane Gun, serial number IRS-3587, caliber .410 centerfire.

Chinese Type 24 (Maxim) machinegun, caliber 7.92mm, Chinese manufacture.

Chinese Type 26 light machinegun.

Colt machinegun, Model 1895, any caliber.

Colt machinegun, Model 1914, any caliber.

Colt, Model MG38 and MG38B, water-cooled machinegun, any caliber, manufactured by Colt.

Colt, Monitor Model machine rifle, caliber 30-06, commercial version of the BAR, 18 inch barrel, vertical pistol grip, Cutts compensator, manufactured by Colt.

Crescent Certified Shotgun, .410 gauge, with 12¼ inch barrel and pistol grip.

Czechoslovakian Model ZB 26 and ZB 30 light machinegun.

Danish Madsen machineguns, all models produced prior to 1946, all calibers.

Degtyarov-PTRD 1941, 14.5mm anti-tank rifle.

Enfield military bolt action rifle cut-a-ways, having barrels or less than 16 inches.

French Chatellerault model 1924/29 machineguns, caliber 7.5mm.

French C.S.R.G. (Chauchat) machinegun, Model 1915, caliber 8mm Lebel.

French C.S.R.G. (Chauchat) machinegun, Model 1918, caliber .30.

French, Model 37, 50mm (1.97 in.) mortar—also designated as a German, Model 203(f), 5cm (1.97 in.) mortar.

French Model 1934 M39 (Mle 34 K39) caliber 7.5 x 54mm, aircraft machinegun.

French St. Etienne machinegun, Model 1907, caliber 8mm Lebel.

Finnish Tampella (original), Model 1938, caliber 81mm mortars.

German anti-tank rifle, caliber 7.92 mm, Gr 39, Granatbuchse.

German assault rifles selective fire, produced during 1941 through 1945, in caliber 7.92mm Kurz (7.92 x 33mm).

German Bergmann model 1915 n/a air-cooled machinegun, caliber 7.92 mm.

German Bergmann model 1915 water-cooled machinegun, caliber 7.92mm.

German, Bergmann, MP-34, 9mm, machine pistol.

German, Bergmann, MP-35/I, 9mm, machine pistol.

German Dreyse model 1918 water-cooled machinegun, caliber 7.92 mm.

German, Erma (EMP), 9mm, machine pistol.

German Gast machinegun, caliber 7.9mm.

German, Erma (EMP), 9 mm. machine pistol, or MPE.

German 15cm Nebelwerfer, 41 (150-mm) Rocket Launcher.

German Parabellum machinegun, Models 1913, 1914 and LMG 14/17, caliber 7.9mm.

German Raketenpanzerbuchse 43 (8.8 cm, RPzB43), German Model 43, 88mm Rocket Launcher.

German Raketenpanzerbuchse 54 (8.8 cm, RPzB54), German Model 54, 88mm Rocket Launcher.

German, Schmaisser, MP-28/II, 9 mm, machine pistol.

German, Steyer-Solothurn, 9mm, machine pistol.

German submachinegun, Model MP 18-1, caliber 9mm Parabellum.

German MG 34 light machinegun, caliber 7.92mm.

German MP38 submachinegun, caliber 9mm Parabellum, manufactured by B. Geipel (Erma) prior to 1941.

German MP40 submachineguns, caliber 9mm, manufactured from 1940 through 1945 for the German military forces.

German MG 42 light machinegun, produced prior to 1946, caliber 7.92 mm.

German 8mm MG 81 and MG 81Z Aircraft Machineguns.

German 15/20mm MG 151 Aircraft Machineguns (all variations).

Harrington & Richardson (H & R), .410 gauge, "Handy Gun," with a 12¼ inch barrel.

High Standard USA Model HD, .22 lr caliber pistols, originally equipped with silencers for issue to the OSS and other military agencies, serial number range from 109110 through 153890.

Hotchkiss light machinegun, British Model 1909 Mark 1 and Mark 1*, caliber .303.

Hotchkiss Models 1897, 1900 and 1914 machineguns of French manufacture in all calibers.

Italian Breda Model 1930 machineguns, all calibers.

Italian Breda Model 1937 heavy machinegun, caliber 8mm.

Italian Fiat Revelli Model 1935 machinegun, caliber 8mm.

Italian Revelli Model 1914 machinegun, caliber 6.5mm.

Italian Villar Perosa submachinegun, Model 1915, 1916, and 1917, caliber 9mm Parabellum.

Ithaca "Auto and Burglar Guns," manufactured by Ithaca Gun Company from 1922 to 1933, all original guns.

Japanese experimental submachinegun "Bullpup" caliber 8mm Nambu.

Japanese (Model 1921 Browning Type), aircraft fixed machinegun, caliber 12.7mm.

Japanese, modified Bergmann (SIC), submachinegun, caliber 7.63mm, featuring bayonet mounting lug.

Japanese, Type 1 (1941), aircraft flexible machinegun, caliber 7.92mm, twin barrel type.

Japanese, Type 3 (1927), heavy machinegun, caliber 6.5mm.

Japanese, Type 10, 50mm Grenade Discharger (Knee Mortar) and variations thereof.

Japanese, Type 11 (1922) light machinegun, all variations caliber 6.5 mm.

Japanese, Type 38, (1905), machinegun (Hotchkiss) caliber 6.5mm.

Japanese, Type 89, 50mm Grenade Discharger (Knee Mortar) and variations thereof.

Japanese, Type 91 (1931), tank machinegun (modified Type 11), caliber 6.5mm.

Japanese, Type 92 (1932), heavy machinegun, Hotchkiss pattern, caliber 7.7mm.

Japanese, Type 92 (1932), light machinegun or aircraft machinegun, Lewis pattern, caliber 7.7mm.

Japanese, Type 92 (1932), tank machinegun, caliber 13.2mm.

Japanese Type 93 (1938), aircraft machinegun caliber 7.29mm.

Japanese, Type 96 (1936), light machinegun, caliber 6.5mm.

Japanese, Type 97 (1937), tank machinegun, caliber 7.7mm.

Japanese, Type 99 (1939), light machinegun, caliber 7.7mm.

Japanese, Type 99 (1939), Paratrooper model, light machinegun, caliber 7.7mm, featuring detachable butt stock and folding pistol grip.

Japanese, Type 100 (1940), aircraft flexible machinegun, caliber 7.92 mm, twin barrel type.

Japanese, Type 100, submachinegun, caliber 8mm Nambu, all variations.

Japanese 12.7 (13) mm Browning HO-103 Machineguns.

Japanese 20mm Browning Aircraft HO-5 Machineguns/Cannons.

Japanese 30mm Browning Aircraft HO-155 Type 1, Machineguns/Cannons.

Japanese 30mm Browning Aircraft HO-155 Type 2, Machineguns/Cannons.

Japanese 37mm Browning Aircraft HO-204 Machineguns/Cannons.

Japanese 40mm Caseless Aircraft Machineguns/Cannons.

Japanese 20mm Oerlikon Model 99, Machineguns/Cannons.

German 30mm MG 108 Aircraft Machineguns/Cannons.

German 13mm Rheinmetal-Borsig Model 131, Aircraft Machineguns (all variations).

Lahti Model 39, caliber 20mm anti-tank rifle.

Lewis Light machinegun (American or British manufacture), caliber .303 or .30.

Luger, Mauser commercial manufacture, semiautomatic pistol, 75 Jahre, Parabellum-Pistole, Mod. Karabiner, Commemorative, caliber 9-mm, accompanied by a carbine type shoulder stock.

M2 Browning .30 caliber machineguns (AN-M2), as manufactured by various U.S. Government contractors prior to and during World War II.

Marlin aircraft machinegun, Models 1917 and 1918, caliber .30.

Marlin tank machineguns, Model 1918, caliber .30.

Mauser manufactured Schnellfeuer selective fire pistols and all original prototypes, caliber 7.63mm Mauser.

Maxim machineguns of German manufacture, all models, all calibers.

Maxim machineguns produced by Maxim Nordenfeldt and Vickers Sons and Maxim from approximately 1885 through 1908, all calibers.

Maxim machineguns, Russian Model 1905, Russian manufacture having a brass water jacket in caliber 7.62 mm, Russian rimmed.

Pipe Pistol, serial number 420, caliber .22 rimfire (word "pipe" means smoking tobacco type).

Pipe Pistol, serial number IRS-3579, caliber 7mm centerfire, marked drgm Bucksom (word "pipe" means smoking tobacco type).

Russian Degtyarev machineguns, models DA, DP, DPM, DT, and RP46, caliber 7.62mm.

Russian Model 1910 (Maxim) machinegun, any caliber, Russian manufacture.

Russian 50mm Mortar Launcher.

Russian PPSH41, 7.62mm submachineguns and all copies and variations produced in the Communist Bloc countries prior to the mid 1950's.

Russian Model SG43 heavy machinegun, caliber 7.62mm, Russian manufacture.

Sedgley Glove Pistol, .38 centerfire, serial number IRS-3580, single shot, marked MK2S, manufactured by Sedgley, Philadelphia, for the U.S. Marines.

Simonov-PTRS 1941, 14.5mm anti-tank rifle.

Solothurn Model S18-100, S18-1000, and S18-1100, 20mm semiautomatic, anti-tank rifle.

Stevens, Offhand Number 35, .410 gauge shot pistols.

Stevens, Auto Shot Number 35, .410 gauge shot pistols.

Thompson semiautomatic carbine, Model 1927, caliber .45 ACP.

Thompson submachinegun including all models, prototypes, and variations manufactured by Warner & Swasey, Colt, BSA, and Auto-Ordnance prior to 1938. This does not include weapons manufactured by Savage Arms Company; Auto-Ordnance, Bridgeport, Connecticut; or Auto-Ordnance, West Hurley, New York. In addition, this classification does not include any Thompson submachinegun bearing a serial number higher than number 15,040.

Umbrella Gun, 6 shot pepper box revolver with dagger attachment extending from muzzle, combined with handle and umbrella, serial number 16, caliber .22 rimfire, with markings Brevette PT, manufactured by Marquis de Farbique, France.

United States, 3 inch Anti-tank Gun, Model M-5.

U.S. Browning machineguns (original), caliber .30, M1917 and M1917A1, manufactured by Colt's Pattern Firearms Company, New England Westinghouse Company, Remington Arms-Union Metallic Cartridge Company, Rock Island Arsenal, High Standard Company, Savage Arms Corporation, Buffalo Arms Corporation, Frigidaire, AC Spark Plug, Brown-Lipe-Chappin, Saginaw Steering Gear Division, and Kelsey Hayes Wheel Company.

U.S. Browning Model 1919A4 air-cooled machinegun, produced by various U.S. Government contractors prior to 1946, caliber .30.

U.S. Johnson Models 1941 and 1944 light machineguns, caliber .30.

U.S. Mortar (original), caliber 60 mm, M1 and M2, with mount M2.

U.S. Maxim machinegun, Model 1904, caliber .30.

U.S. Models 1915 and 1918 Vickers machineguns manufactured by Colt in calibers 30/06 or 11mm.

U.S. Model 1917 Marlin ground machinegun, caliber 30/06.

U.S. Model 1917 and 1917A1 water cooled machineguns manufactured by New England Westinghouse or Remington, caliber 30/06.

U.S. Model M1, caliber 2.36 inch Rocket Launcher (Bazooka) and variations thereof.

U.S., 3 inch Anti-tank Gun, Model M-5.

U.S. Model M6, 37mm gun, produced prior to 1946.

U.S. Model M9, caliber 2.36 inch Rocket Launcher (Bazooka) and variations thereof.

U.S. Model M18, caliber 2.36 inch Rocket Launcher (Bazooka) and variations thereof.

Vickers commercial water-cooled machinegun, any configuration, any caliber, British manufacture.

Winchester Model 92 Trapper carbines having barrel lengths of less than 16 inches (original Winchester manufacture only).

4 National Firearms Act Weapons Removed from the Act as Collector's Items and Classified as Curios or Relics Under 18 U.S.C. Chapter 44

The Bureau has determined that by reason of the date of their manufacture, value, design and other characteristics, the following firearms are primarily collector's items and are not likely to be used as weapons and, therefore, are excluded from the provisions of the National Firearms Act.

Further, The Bureau has determined that such firearms are also curios or relics as defined in 27 CFR 178.11. Thus, licensed collectors may acquire, hold or dispose of them as curios or relics subject to the provisions of 18 U.S.C. Chapter 44 and 27 CFR Part 178. They are still "firearms" as defined in 18 U.S.C. 921(a)(3).

Pre-war Belgian manufactured Hi-Power pistols, in caliber 9mm having tangent sights graduated to 500 meters, slotted for shoulder stock, having serial numbers of less than 47,000 without letter prefixes or suffixes and accompanied by original Belgian manufactured detachable wooden flat board type shoulder stocks.

Beretta Model 1918/1930 semiautomatic carbine, caliber 9mm, having a barrel length of 12.5 inches and a magazine capacity of 25 rounds.

Beretta Model 1923 semiautomatic pistol, in caliber 9mm Kurz (.380), accompanied by original Italian detachable leather and metal holster/shoulder stock.

Bergmann-Bayard Pistol, Model 1908, 9mm Bergmann-Bayard with shoulder stock and 4 inch barrel.

Bergmann self-loading pistol, Mars Model 1903, with accompanying shoulder stock.

Blue Jacket Revolver with Shoulder Stock (Veterinarians's Pistol) Serial Number IRS-3600 Caliber .22 Rimfire. Marked Blue Jacket Patented 3-28-1871, 10-1-1876 and 1877, made by W Vurflein, Philadelphia.

Browning Pistol, Model 1903, 9mm Browning Long, with shoulder stock and 5 inch barrel.

Canadian Inglis No. I, Chinese Contract, Hi-Power pistols, caliber 9mm Parabellum, having a tangent rear sight adjustable from 50 to 500 meters, slotted for shoulder stock, and having the letters CH in the serial number and accompanied by original Canadian manufactured detachable wooden holster/shoulder stock.

Clement Pistol Carbine, Caliber 9mm.

Chinese manufactured copies of the Mauser Model 1896 semi-automatic pistol, produced prior to 1945, any caliber, accompanied by original Chinese manufactured detachable wooden holster/shoulder stocks.

Colt cutaway demonstrator lightning rifle, and all other original cutaway demonstrator lightning rifles produced by Colt.

Colt Pistol, Model 1905, .45 rimless, with leather holster/shoulder stock and 5 inch barrel.

Colt Officers Model, .38 Special caliber, double action revolver, with 6 inch barrel and a detachable, experimental skeleton shoulder stock and holster combination.

Colt Single Action Army revolver, serial number 354096, caliber .44/40 having a smooth bored barrel and a barrel length of 7½ inches.

Colt Model Woodsman, .22 Long Rifle caliber, semiautomatic pistol with an experimental 10 inch barrel and an experimental wooden detachable shoulder stock.

Colt Model Woodsman, .22 Long Rifle caliber, semiautomatic pistols, manufactured between 1915 and 1943, together with the original leather detachable holster stocks, manufactured by the N&S Corporation, Ventura, California.

Czechoslovakian Model CZ24 semiautomatic pistol, in caliber 9mm Kurz (.380) accompanied by original Czechoslovakian detachable wooden holster/shoulder stock.

Fiala Model 1920 repeating pistol, caliber .22LR in all barrel lengths with accompanying detachable shoulder stock; original copies of the Fiala repeating pistol, marked Schall, Columbia or Botwinick Brothers, caliber .22LR, with accompanying original detachable shoulder stock.

Finnish Model L-35 Lahti Semiautomatic pistol, in caliber 9mm Parabellum, accompanied by original. Finnish detachable wooden holster/shoulder stock.

Frommer Model 1912, semiautomatic pistol with Benke-Thiemann folding shoulder stock.

German (WWI) antitank rifle (Pz Agew 1918), Model 1918, caliber 13.25mm.

German (Nazi) Belt Buckle Gun, .22 rimfire, marked "DRP Ausl Pat, Louis Marquis, W. Elberfeld."

German (Nazi) Belt Buckle Gun, 7.65mm, marked "D.R.P. Angem."

German Schiesshecher Grenade Launcher (G.Gr.Ger.), 27 mm, accompanied by a German Military Mauser 98 type rifle.

German VG1-5 (Volksgewehr) semiautomatic rifle, caliber 7.92mm Kurz, having a barrel length of 14.9 inches and an overall length of 34.8 inches.

Greener Cattle Killer (Original Model) No. B1201, .310 caliber.

Greener Cattle Killer (Pocket Pattern) No. B1203, .310 caliber.

Greener Safti Killer No. B1216, .22 caliber.

Greener Universal Safti Killer No. B1217, .310 caliber.

Hamilton Model 7, Rifle.

Hamilton Model 11, Rifle.

Hamilton Model 15, Rifle.

Hamilton Model 19, Rifle.

Hamilton Model 23, Rifle.

Hamilton Model 27 and 027, Rifle.

Hamilton Model 31, Rifle.

Hamilton Model 35, Rifle.

Hamilton Model 39, Rifle.

Hamilton Model 43, Rifle.

Heal Rifle No. 10, caliber .22.

High Standard Model C/S smoothbore .22 caliber shot semi-automatic pistols, bearing serial numbers 59279, 59473, 59478, 59460, or 59469.

High Standard Model S smoothbore .22 caliber shot semi-automatic pistols having slides marked: "HI-STANDARD MODEL "S" .22 L.R. SHOT ONLY," and bearing serial numbers 48142, 48143, 48144, 48145, 48146, 59474, 59496, 59458, or 59459.

"JGA" (J. G. Anchutz, Ulm, Germany), .22 Flobert single shot pistol.

Krupp Models 1902 and 1906 50mm Mountain Cannons as produced for the Siamese Government.

Luger, Artillery Model pistols having chamber dates of 1914 through 1918 plus the date 1920, having German Weimar Navy markings consisting of the letter M over an anchor and a German Navy property number accompanied by original Artillery Luger flat board stocks, bearing German Weimar Navy markings of the letter M over an anchor with or without Navy property numbers.

Luger, the 1920 Commercial Artillery Model, pistols as manufactured by DWM or Erfurt, having undated chambers, commercial proofmarks, and bearing the inscription Germany or Made in Germany on the receiver and accompanied by original, German manufactured, artillery type, detachable wooden shoulder stocks.

Luger DWM Pistol, Model 1900, 1902, or 1906, in 7.65 Luger or 9mm Parabellum caliber, having the American Eagle chamber crest, and barrel lengths of either 4 inches or 4¾ inches with original detachable Ideal shoulder stocks and Ideal frame grips.

Original Models 1904, 1906, 1908, 1914 and 1920 DWM Luger Naval pistols in 9mm Parabellum or 7.65 mm caliber, in both the Commercial and Naval military variations; in both altered and unaltered barrel lengths in the Model 1904 and in both altered and unaltered safety markings in the Model 1906; with original board-type detachable shoulder stocks bearing brass or iron discs, with or without markings, or, if without brass or iron discs, being of the Navy flat board-type. This exemption will apply only to the listed Naval Luger pistols if mated to the Naval Luger stock and will not apply if the Naval Luger pistol is mated to the Artillery stock. The Naval stock has an overall dimension of 12¾ inches, a rear width of 4⅝ inches, a front width of 1½ inches, a rear thickness of 9⁄16 inch, and a front thickness of 1³⁄16 inches.

Luger DWM Stoeger Model 1920 and 1923 semiautomatic pistols in 7.65 mm or 9mm Parabellum caliber, in barrel lengths of 8, 10, 12, and 12½ inches, having either American Eagle chamber crests and/or Stoeger frame and/or upper receiver marks, having either standard, Navy or artillery rear sights, having extractors marked either "Loaded" or "Geladen" and having frame safety markings of either "Gesichert" or "Safe," together with original commercial flat board stocks of the artillery type, which bear no serial numbers or military proof marks; may include a "Germany" marking.

Luger DWM Pistol-Carbine, Model 1920, 7.65mm or 9mm Parabellum caliber, with accompanying original commercial type shoulder stock, with or without forearm piece, having barrel lengths of 11¾ inches to less than 16 inches.

Luger, German Model 1914 Artillery Model pistol, manufactured by DWM or Erfurt, having chambers dated 1914 through 1918, bearing Imperial German military proofmarks and accompanied by original, German manufactured, artillery type, detachable wooden shoulder stocks.

Luger Pistol-Carbine, Model 1902,

7.65mm Luger with original commercial type shoulder stock and forearm and 11¾ inch barrel.

Luger pistols, Persian (Iranian) Artillery Model, as manufactured by Mauser prior to 1945, accompanied by the original artillery type, detachable wooden shoulder stock, bearing a serial number in Farsi characters stamped into the wood on the left side.

Luger semiautomatic pistol, certain variations with Benke-Thiemann folding shoulder stock.

Luger, Swiss Model 1906, semiautomatic pistol, Serial Number E772, with original attachable shoulder stock known as "Stock System Benke-Thiemann."

Manville, 18-shot-drum, 25mm, semiautomatic tear gas gun.

Marlin, Model 94 carbine, caliber .38-40 WCF, with 15 inch barrel, serial number 384186.

Marlin Model 1894 carbine, serial number 325609, .32/20, with original 15 inch barrel.

Marlin, Model 93 carbine, caliber .32-40 WCF, with 15 inch barrel, serial number 426311.

Mauser Model 1896 semiautomatic pistol accompanied by original German manufactured detachable wooden holster/shoulder stocks, all semiautomatic German manufactured variations produced prior to 1940, any caliber.

Mauser Model 1902, 6 and 10-shot magazine capacity, semi-automatic pistols in caliber 7.63 x 25mm (.30 Mauser), having the distinctive hammer safety, barrel lengths of either 3.9 or 5.5 inches, and accompanied by an original detachable wooden holster/shoulder stock.

Mauser Pistol, Model 1912/14, 9mm Mauser short or .45 ACP, with original detachable wooden holster/shoulder stock and 5 inch barrel.

One Pocket Creedmores and other original pocket rifles with extension shoulder stock, caliber .22, made by Samuel Watson Johnson (1838-1903).

Military type Nambu pistol, Model 1904, caliber 8mm Nambu (Riku Shiki Nambu Kenju) with an accompanying original detachable telescoping wooden holster/shoulder stock.

OSS Glove Pistol, caliber .38 S & W or .38 special.

OSS "Liberator" pistol, .45 ACP or 9mm.

British PIAT (Projector, Infantry, Anti-tank).

Remington Flare (Very) Pistol, Mark III, 10 gauge.

Royal, semiautomatic pistol, Caliber 7.63 x 25mm (.30 Mauser) having an integral 10 or 20 round magazine, 5½ inch, 6¼ inch, or 7⅛ inch barrel, and accompanied by an original Spanish manufactured detachable holster/stock.

Sedgley, Mark V, 10 gauge, signal pistol (Remain Title I).

The Shatuck "Unique" palm gun in .22 and .32 caliber rimfire.

Smith & Wesson Model 40 Light Rifle, caliber 9mm Parabellum.

Spanish Star Model A semiautomatic pistol in calibers 7.63 Mauser, 9mm Parabellum, 9mm Long, .38 ACP and .45 ACP, accompanied by original Spanish manufactured detachable wooden holster/shoulder stock.

Spanish manufactured copies of the Mauser Model 1896 semi-automatic pistol produced prior to 1946 in caliber 7.63mm or 9mm and having either integral or detachable magazines. Accompanied by original Spanish manufactured detachable wooden holster/shoulder stock.

Stevens Rifle, No. 20, with smooth bore barrel for .22 and .32 rimfire shot cartridges.

Stevens, Reliable Pocket Rifle, second issue, caliber .22 long rifle or .22 Stevens-Pope.

Stevens, New Model Pocket Rifle, first issue, caliber .22.

Stevens, New Model Pocket Rifle, second issue, caliber: .22 short, long or long rifle rimfire, .22 WRF, .32 long centerfire.

Stevens, New Model Pocket Rifle No. 40, caliber: .22 long rifle, .22 WRF, .22 Stevens-Pope, and .32 long centerfire.

Stevens, Hunter's Pet No. 34 Pocket Rifle, caliber .22 short rimfire to .44-40 WCF.

Stevens, Vernier Hunter's Pet No. 344/2 Pocket Rifle, caliber .22 short to 44-40 WCF.

Stevens, Vernier New Model Pocket Rifle No. 401/2, caliber .22 long rifle, .22 WRF, .22 Stevens-Pope, .32 long centerfire.

Stevens, 1898 New Model Pocket Shotgun, in calibers .38-40 and .44-40.

Stevens Number 39, New Model Pocket Shotgun, in calibers .38-40 and .44-40.

Steyr Hahn Model 1911/12 semiautomatic pistol, caliber 9mm Steyr or 9mm Parabellum having a 5 inch barrel and accompanied by an original European detachable holsterstock.

Swedish Model P-40 Lahti semiautomatic pistol, in caliber 9mm Parabellum, accompanied by original Swedish detachable wooden holster/shoulder stock.

The Taylor "Fur Getter" manufactured by the F.C. Taylor Fur Company, St. Louis, Missouri, .22 caliber rimfire.

U.S. Mark II, 10 gauge signal pistols.

Walther Pistol, Model 1937 "Armee Pistols," 9mm Parabellum, with original detachable shoulder stock and 4.9 inch barrel.

Webley & Scott Pistol, Mark I, No. 2, .455 caliber, with original detachable shoulder stock.

Winchester, Model 36 shotgun, 9mm rimfire.

Winchester, Model 1873, carbine, serial number 127884 and 380061, caliber .44 W.C.F. with original 15-inch barrel.

Winchester, Model 1873, carbine, serial number 382027 caliber 32 W.C.F. with original 15-inch barrel.

Winchester, Model 1873, carbine, serial number 695081B, 32 W.C.F. caliber, with a barrel length of 14 inches.

Winchester, carbine, Model 1873, serial number 486139, caliber .44 W.C.F. with original 15-inch barrel.

Winchester, Model 1873, carbine, serial number 514709, caliber .38 W.C.F. with original 14-inch barrel.

Winchester, Model 1873, carbine, serial number 92842A, caliber .44 W.C.F. with original 15-inch barrel.

Winchester, Model 92 carbine, serial number 998419, caliber .44-40, with original 15 inch barrel.

Winchester, Model 94 carbine caliber .30-30 WCF, with original 15 inch barrel, serial numbers 273691 and 758406.

Winchester, Model 1892 carbine, serial number 288562 and 848873, caliber .38-40, with original 14 inch barrel.

Winchester, Model 1892 carbine, serial number 848873, caliber .38-40, with original 14 inch barrel.

Winchester, Model 1892 carbine, serial number 999398, caliber .44 WCF, with 14 inch barrel.

Winchester, Model 1894 carbine, serial number 360587, caliber .30 WCF, with 15 inch barrel.

Winchester carbine, Model 1892, serial number 51976, caliber .44 W.C.F., with original 15-inch barrel.

Winchester, Model 1894 carbine, serial number 464604, caliber .30 WCF, with 15 inch barrel.

Winchester, Model 1894 carbine, serial number 662192 and 883055, caliber .30 WCF, with 15 inch barrel.

Winchester, Model 1894 carbine, serial number 938370, caliber .38 WCF, with 15 inch barrel.

Winchester, Model 1892 carbine, serial number 804878, caliber .38 WCF, with 15 inch barrel.

Winchester, Model 1892 carbine, serial number 981212, caliber .44 WCF, with 14 inch barrel.

Winchester, Model 1892, carbine, serial number 158145, 659700 or 988160, caliber .44 WCF, with 15 inch barrel.

Winchester, Model 1894 carbine, serial number 868769, caliber .30 WCF, with 15 inch barrel.

Winchester, Model 1894 carbine, serial number 1072755, caliber .30 WCF with 15 inch barrel.

Winchester Model 1885 single shot rifle, serial number 104783, caliber .25/35, having a 15-inch number 3 round barrel, shotgun butt, plain pistol grip, and Winchester Express sight.

The following firearms were removed from the National Firearms Act as collector's items and classified as curios or relics under 18 U.S.C. Chapter 44. However, since they are antiques as defined in Chapter 44, they should not have been classified as curios or relics. Since they are no longer NFA weapons and are antiques under Chapter 44, they are not subject to GCA provisions.

Belgian Cane Gun, 41 caliber rimfire.

Bergmann Model 1897, caliber 7.65 mm (7.8mm) pistol with accompanying shoulder stock.

Borchardt Model 1893, caliber 7.63 mm pistol with accompanying shoulder stock.

Chicago palm pistol, caliber .32 rimfire extra short.

Frank Wesson Bicycle Rifle with accompanying shoulder stock.

Gaulois palm squeezer, 8mm short.

"Little All Right" palm pistol, .22 caliber rimfire patented by Edward Boardman and Andrew Peavey, January 18, 1876.

Mannlicher Pistol-Carbine, Model 1896, 7.63mm Mannlicher, with rifle type shoulder stock and forearm and 11¾ inch barrel.

Merveilleux squeezer pistol, 6mm and 8mm short.

Peavey, A.J., Knife Gun, .22 short rimfire.

Protector palm gun, .32 rimfire extra short, patented by Jacques Turbiaux, Patent No. 732644.

Quackenbrush Bicycle Rifle with telescopic wire stock, .22 caliber.

Remington Cane Gun, Model 1, .22 rimfire.

Remington Cane Gun, Model 2, .32 rimfire.

Stevens, Old Model Pocket Rifle, caliber .22 short or long rimfire.

Stevens, Reliable Pocket Rifle, first issue, caliber .22 short, long or long rifle.

Stevens, New Model Pocket Rifle, first issue, in caliber .32 short or long rimfire.

Stevens, New Model Pocket Rifle, second issue, in caliber .25 Stevens or .32 long rimfire.

Stevens, New Model Pocket Rifle No. 40, in caliber .25 Stevens or .32 long rimfire.

Stevens, Vernier, New Model Pocket Rifle, caliber .22 short, .22 long rifle, .22 WRF, .32 long rimfire.

Stevens, Vernier New Model Pocket Rifle No. 40½, in caliber .25 Stevens or .32 long rimfire.

Tribuzio "Squeezer" invented by Catello Tribuzio of Turin, Italy, caliber 8mm short.

Winchester, Model 1873 carbine, serial number 380061, caliber .44 WCF, with 15 inch barrel.

Winchester, Model 1885, carbine, serial number 83304, caliber .44 W.C.F., with original 15 inch barrel.

Winchester, Model 1892 carbine, serial number 43844, caliber .38 WCF, with 15 inch barrel.

Winchester, Model 1892 carbine, serial number 158145, caliber .44 WCF, with 15 inch barrel.

Any pistol or revolver, manufactured in or before 1898, originally designed to accept a shoulder stock, and accompanied by an original shoulder stock.

PLEASE NOTE:

It is requested that persons having any of these exempted firearms registered with the Bureau of Alcohol, Tobacco and Firearms notify our NFA Branch at the following address so that the National Firearms Registration and Transfer Record can be annotated to show that the particular firearms no longer require registration.

NFA Branch
Bureau of Alcohol, Tobacco & Firearms
1200 Pennsylvania Avenue
Washington, D.C. 20226